ABOUT PREVIOUS BOOKS IN THE SERIES

"One of the best books on programming I have come across."
— *Philip Rezk, Ridgefield, CT*

"I like the easy-to-follow progression from basic to complex topics with thorough explanation of each topic."
— *Michael Mills, Boca Raton, FL*

"Gave me everything I needed to know. . . ."
— *Steve Dehues, Killeen, TX*

"It is wonderful that you can use the hands-on approach to learning."
— *Neil Laporte, Gatineau, Quebec*

"An easy-to-understand programming book with many helpful hints."
— *Ronald White, Newtown, PA*

"I liked the author's exceptional, readable writing style."
— *Jason Lee, Canada*

"I liked the author's experience and the fact that it's an IDG book . . . I knew right away I was buying a great book!"
— *Paul Joseph Walker, Greenville, RI*

"Simple, comprehensive . . . everybody can understand . . ."
— *Ural Gunaydin, Australia*

"Brilliant approach to teaching."
— *Paul Dugas, Richford, VT*

"[This book] explains stuff in a few paragraphs that others couldn't do in a whole book."
— *Robert Doucet, Toronto, Ontario*

ABOUT TOM SWAN, SERIES EDITOR

"Everything that's done by Tom Swan is satisfaction guaranteed."
— *Albert Lee, Indonesia*

"Tom's writing style makes even dense programming issues crystal clear."
— *Brett Salter, President, The Periscope Company*

"Tom Swan makes learning C simple and easy."
— *Brian Mayfield, Silverdale, CT*

"What I like most about this book: 'It's by Tom Swan.'"
— *David Peng, La Jolla, CA*

Learn
Visual Basic® 4
Today!

by Michelle Moore and Judi N. Fernandez

A Division of IDG Books Worldwide, Inc.
Foster City, CA • Chicago, IL • Indianapolis, IN • Braintree, MA • Southlake, TX

Learn Visual Basic® 4 Today!

Published by

IDG Books Worldwide, Inc.
An International Data Group Company
919 E. Hillsdale Blvd.
Suite 400
Foster City, CA 94404

Library of Congress Catalog Card No.: 95-81951

ISBN: 1-56884-317-8

Printed in the United States of America

10 9 8 7 6 5 4 3 2 1

1B/RU/QW/ZW/FC

Distributed in the United States by IDG Books Worldwide, Inc.

Distributed by Macmillan Canada for Canada; by Computer and Technical Books for the Caribbean Basin; by Contemporanea de Ediciones for Venezuela; by Distribuidora Cuspide for Argentina; by CITEC for Brazil; by Ediciones ZETA S.C.R. Ltda. for Peru; by Editorial Limusa SA for Mexico; by Transworld Publishers Limited in the United Kingdom and Europe; by Al-Maiman Publishers & Distributors for Saudi Arabia; by Simron Pty. Ltd. for South Africa; by IDG Communications (HK) Ltd. for Hong Kong; by Toppan Company Ltd. for Japan; by Addison Wesley Publishing Company for Korea; by Longman Singapore Publishers Ltd. for Singapore, Malaysia, Thailand, and Indonesia; by Unalis Corporation for Taiwan; by WS Computer Publishing Company, Inc. for the Philippines; by WoodsLane Pty. Ltd. for Australia; by WoodsLane Enterprises Ltd. for New Zealand.

For general information on IDG Books Worldwide's books in the U.S., please call our Consumer Customer Service department at 800-762-2974. For reseller information, including discounts and premium sales, please call our Reseller Customer Service department at 800-434-3422.

For information on where to purchase IDG Books Worldwide's books outside the U.S., contact IDG Books Worldwide at 415-655-3021 or fax 415-655-3295.

For information on translations, contact Marc Jeffrey Mikulich, Director, Foreign & Subsidiary Rights, at IDG Books Worldwide, 415-655-3018 or fax 415-655-3295.

For sales inquiries and special prices for bulk quantities, write to the address above or call IDG Books Worldwide at 415-655-3200.

For information on using IDG Books Worldwide's books in the classroom, or ordering examination copies, contact the Education Office at 800-434-2086 or fax 817-251-8174.

For authorization to photocopy items for corporate, personal, or educational use, please contact Copyright Clearance Center, 222 Rosewood Drive, Danvers, MA 01923, or fax 508-750-4470.

  is a trademark under exclusive license to IDG Books Worldwide, Inc., from International Data Group, Inc.

Welcome to the world of IDG Books Worldwide.

IDG Books Worldwide, Inc. is a subsidiary of International Data Group, the world's largest publisher of computer-related information and the leading global provider of information services on information technology. IDG was founded more than 25 years ago and now employs more than 7,500 people worldwide. IDG publishes more than 235 computer publications in 67 countries (see listing below). More than fifty million people read one or more IDG publications each month.

Launched in 1990, IDG Books Worldwide is today the #1 publisher of best-selling computer books in the United States. We are proud to have received 3 awards from the Computer Press Association in recognition of editorial excellence, and our best-selling ...For Dummies™ series has more than 18 million copies in print with translations in 24 languages. IDG Books, through a recent joint venture with IDG's Hi-Tech Beijing, became the first U.S. publisher to publish a computer book in the People's Republic of China. In record time, IDG Books has become the first choice for millions of readers around the world who want to learn how to better manage their businesses.

Our mission is simple: Every IDG book is designed to bring extra value and skill-building instructions to the reader. Our books are written by experts who understand and care about our readers. The knowledge base of our editorial staff comes from years of experience in publishing, education, and journalism — experience which we use to produce books for the '90s. In short, we care about books, so we attract the best people. We devote special attention to details such as audience, interior design, use of icons, and illustrations. And because we use an efficient process of authoring, editing, and desktop publishing our books electronically, we can spend more time ensuring superior content and spend less time on the technicalities of making books.

You can count on our commitment to deliver high-quality books at competitive prices on topics consumers want to read about. At IDG, we value quality, and we have been delivering quality for more than 25 years. You'll find no better book on a subject than an IDG book.

John J. Kilcullen

John Kilcullen
President and CEO
IDG Books Worldwide, Inc.

FROM THE PUBLISHER

Learn Visual Basic 4 Today! is part of the *Learn Today!* book series, brought to you by Programmers Press. The designers of the *Learn Today!* series understand that there are numerous obstacles to learning how to program. So we worked with one of the industry's finest authors, Tom Swan, to develop a learning method for you, the beginner programmer. *Learn Today!* is the result of extensive research and testing on the part of Tom Swan and IDG Books Worldwide.

The formula for the book is simple: Learn by doing. It's been proven that a hands-on approach not only speeds learning, but also helps you to remember what you learn. When you can perform an action and see the results, you'll remember what you did and why you did it.

Professional programmers often say that reading about programming is nice, but writing code is better. The fact is it's fundamental to your success. That's why each book includes a disk with software. This software is not casual filler; it is strategically linked to the content and topic of a book so you can begin programming immediately.

We believe that the author has the experience to teach programming as well as the skill to present complex topics to beginner programmers. We know that you will benefit from the informal, hands-on approach. When you finish this book, you will not only understand how a program works, but you'll have written several programs, and you'll be prepared to move onto the next programming level. So, turn the page and begin learning today!

Chris Williams
Publisher, IDG Books

CREDITS

Publisher
Chris Williams

Publishing Director
John Osborn

Senior Acquisitions Manager
Amy Pedersen

Managing Editor
Kim Field

Editorial Director
Anne Marie Walker

Project Editor
Jim Markham

Manuscript Editor
Deb Kaufmann

Technical Editor
Blake Ragsdell

Production Director
Andrew Walker

Supervisor of Page Layout
Craig A. Harrison

Project Coordinator
Phyllis Beaty

Production Staff
Diann Abbott
Ronnie Bucci
Laura Carpenter
Renée Dunn
Ritchie Durden
Dusty Parsons
Christopher Pimentel

Proofreader
Carol Burbo

Indexer
Elizabeth Cunningham

Cover Design
Tobi Designs

This book is dedicated to our loving husbands, Carlos Alston and Paul Knudsen.

ABOUT THE AUTHORS

Michelle Moore has developed software for many large corporations over the last eight years. She is a principal of VMT, Inc.

Judi N. Fernandez has over 30 years of experience in designing and developing training courses on computer topics and in developing documentation for computer systems. She has written more than 40 trade books on computer topics, including BASIC, COBOL, several assembler languages, DOS, and Windows. Ms. Fernandez claims to be the world's first teenage computer nerd, having learned IBM 650 machine-language programming in 1957 at the age of 16; so far, no one has been able to refute her claim.

ACKNOWLEDGMENTS

We would like to acknowledge Tom Swan, creator of the *Learn Today!* series. We would also like to thank Amy Pedersen of IDG Books and David Fugate and Matt Wagner of Waterside Productions for bringing us onto this project.

We can't thank project editor Jim Markham enough for his first rate supervision. We would also like to thank Deb Kaufmann, manuscript editor, and technical sleuth Blake Ragsdell. These three as well as others went over this work with a fine-tooth comb and came up with many valuable suggestions.

(The publisher would like to give special thanks to Patrick McGovern, who made this book possible.)

Contents at a Glance

Contents

Part V: Adding Help to Your Program 397

Part VI: Advanced Topics 425

Introduction

Visual Basic 4.0 was designed to make it easy to develop Windows applications. And it is *relatively* easy, once you know what you're doing. (Relative to, say, Visual C++.) But even experienced programmers, when faced with Visual Basic 4.0 for the first time, scratch their heads and wonder, "What am I supposed to do here?" Most beginning programmers are completely lost.

WHO'S THIS BOOK FOR?

This book is aimed at people with a limited background in or who have never used Visual Basic before—whether you are experienced with other languages or a newcomer to programming. It quickly gets you up and running; you create a complete, but simple, program in Chapter 1. Then you systematically add to you skills until you have mastered the basics of Visual Basic 4.0. In the last part, we even take on some advanced topics for those who want to get beyond the basics.

What Is Visual Basic 4?

What features are you going to find in Visual Basic 4.0? Well, first of all, you'll find a programming system geared toward windows, menus, dialog boxes, and all the controls that go with them (CheckBoxes, CommandButtons, and so on). If you install the 16-bit version, you'll be able to write programs for 16-bit operating systems such as Windows 3.3. If you install the 32-bit version, you can still write the 16-bit programs, but you'll also be able to write programs for 32-bit systems — Windows NT and Windows 95.

The 32-bit version of Visual Basic 4.0 comes in three editions:

▶ The Standard edition provides the basics plus a few bells and whistles.

▶ The Professional edition includes additional custom controls, such as a Slider and ProgressBar control, Crystal Reports for extracting reports from ODBC compliant databases, and CD-ROM documentation in the form of Visual Basic Books Online.

▶ The Enterprise edition gives you the ability to build client/server applications with features such as Remote Automation and Remote Data Control.

Assumptions

This book assumes that you have installed the 32-bit version of Visual Basic 4.0, and are running it under Windows 95. All the figures are taken from that setup. If you're running the 32-bit version under Windows NT, you'll find only minor differences from what you see here, and all the features and examples will be much the same. But if you're running the 16-bit version under, say, Windows 3.11, some of the features and examples will not work on your system. We'll warn you about features that don't work in the 16-bit version when necessary.

THE SCRATCHPAD APPLICATION

The best way to learn is by doing, and if you follow this book from start to finish, you'll develop many small programs that help you gain mastery over the features being discussed. We also have included one larger application, called ScratchPad, that acts as a running example throughout the book. By the time you have finished ScratchPad, you'll have an application that you might actually find useful. Feel free to use it, tailor it to your needs, and share it with your friends and colleagues.

ScratchPad simply lets you keep notes, lists, and the like. Figure 1 shows what the finished version looks like. If you keep it open on your desktop, you can use it as a scratch pad all day long, adding and deleting items as need be, saving and printing the page whenever you wish. In a 32-bit system, you can use all the features of rich text: fonts, color, font enhancements such as bold and italics, paragraph alignment such as centering, tabs, and so on. In addition, you can use OLE features to insert graphics and other objects, such as sound clips, on the page. Not only that but you can access a database of phone numbers and quickly look up a number that you need without loading a cumbersome database program.

In the process of creating ScratchPad, you'll learn how to create a menu bar and toolbar, use a Rich TextBox, use the Windows common dialogs for Open, Save As, Print, Font, and Color, create a Help system, access databases and OLE objects, and many other techniques.

ScratchPad Code

Even though you're supposed to develop ScratchPad yourself as you work your way through the book, we have included a disk containing all the code for the application. You can load the ScratchPad project from drive A to see what our code looks like.

Step-By-Step Exercises

As we said earlier, you learn by doing, so we have built into this book frequent exercises, which you should follow step by step as you read. Don't skip them— they're the most important part of the text. They make sure that you under-stand the current topic and know how to use it in your programs. A Step-By-Step exercise looks like the following one, and all you have to do is follow each numbered step.

1. Follow the directions in each step carefully. The results that you should see in your screen are often included in the step. Most of the time, the exercise will work perfectly. But if you make a typing error or accidentally skip a step, you'll probably get the wrong results.

2. If things don't work the way they're supposed to, try to figure out what went wrong and go back and fix it.

3. If you can't figure what went wrong, start the exercise over from Step 1. It's important that you complete each exercise correctly, not only because that's the best way to learn, but also because subsequent exercises often depend on the preceding ones.

TYPOGRAPHICAL CONVENTIONS

We use the following typographical conventions and icons throughout this book:

Futura Font   In exercises, Futura font indicates text that you should type, keys that you should press, or things that you should click. For example, "click the *Cancel* button" means that you should locate and click the button labeled "Cancel."

Italics   Indicates generic items that should be replaced with a specific item. For example, the date *mm-dd-yy* should be replaced by 10-15-97 for October 15th, 1997.

[Square brackets]   In statement syntax, square brackets indicated optional items. For example, in the following syntax, the word Sub is required but the word Private is optional:

[Private] Sub

As you read the text, look for Notes, Tips, and Alerts. Pay special heed to Tips and Alerts, as they can save you time and money.

This is a Note, some interesting information related to the current topic—something like a footnote or an aside.

This is a Tip, some information that will save you time, money, or hassle.

This is an Alert, which advises you of a pitfall which could cost you time and/or money, or which could cause you to lose data.

You're probably anxious to create that first program, so turn the page and have fun!

The Basics

Where else to begin but at the beginning—by writing a short, simple, but complete program. From there, we'll take you behind the scenes, so to speak, and show you how Visual Basic works and—one of the most important things you'll learn in this book—how to get help.

CHAPTER OBJECTIVES

In this chapter, we're going to dig right in and create a simple Windows program. We'll stick with tradition and begin with a program that simply displays the message *Hello, World!* But since this is *Visual* Basic, we're going to add some pizzazz to the usual message.

We're starting this way for three reasons:

▶ You'll see that writing Windows programs needn't be intimidating.

▶ You'll get a feel for how the Visual Basic environment works.

▶ You'll see all the elements that go together to create a Windows application. The rest of this book elaborates on the elementary concepts that you learn in this chapter.

By the time you have finished this chapter, you'll have a pretty good handle on how a Visual Basic program is created.

Creating Your First
Windows Program

1

We know that you're anxious to get going, so start up the Visual Basic program. You'll see that it opens five windows on your screen, as shown in Figure 1-1. We'll discuss these windows in more detail in Chapter 3. For now we'll just describe enough for you to create your Hello World program.

Just as a reminder, if you're not running the 32-bit version of Visual Basic 4.0 under Windows 95, your screens will look different from the ones reproduced in this book. Also, if someone has changed your Visual Basic options, you might see different tools, the form might not have grid dots, and so on. Since we can't hope to show, or even predict, all the possible variations that might appear, we'll show the most common setup for a new Visual Basic user. Hopefully, the common features in your setup and the one shown here should be obvious, and you won't be too distracted by any differences.

TIP

Because these windows are independent of each other, you can see the other things on your desktop between them. You might want to close or minimize any other windows to reduce clutter and confusion.

3

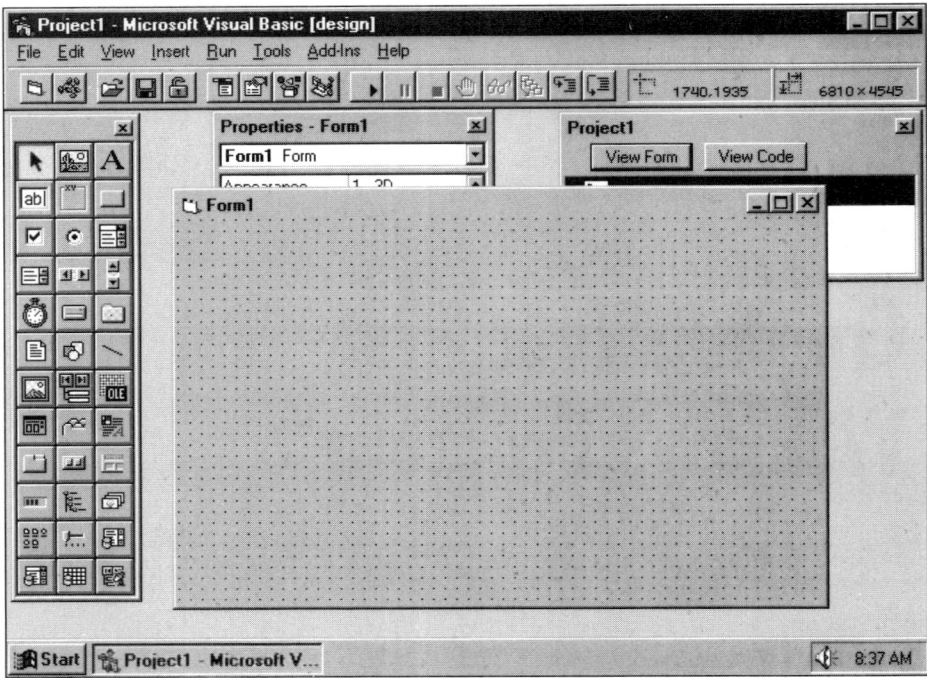

Figure 1-1: You work with five independent windows in Visual Basic.

CREATING A FORM

In Visual Basic, windows and dialog boxes are called *forms*. When you start a new project — which you have just done — Visual Basic gives you a blank form captioned *Form1*. This will be your application's primary window when your new program is ready to go. We'll use Form1 to display the Hello World message.

Drawing Controls on a Form

Everything you put on a form — a check box, a picture, text, or some other object — is called a *control*. You start developing your new application by putting controls on the main form. To do so, simply select them from the *toolbox* and draw them on the form. The toolbox is the tall skinny window shown in Figure 1-2.

Figure 1-2: You draw a control on your form by selecting one of these tools.

To put the Hello World message on the form, you need to draw a Label control, which lets you put text (that is, a label) on the form. Let's do that now.

1. Move the mouse pointer to the toolbox and pause over any tool. (Don't click yet.) A note pops up showing the name of the tool. This note is called a *ToolTip*, and it helps you identify the contents of your toolbox.

2. Keep moving the mouse pointer around until you find the Label tool, shown here:

3. Double-click the Label tool. A control captioned *Label1* should appear in the middle of your form, as shown in Figure 1-3.

Once you draw a control on a form, you'll see that it has eight black squares on its border. These squares are called *handles* and are used to resize the object. Experiment with resizing the Label control by dragging each handle. When you're ready, follow the steps below to make the Label box as large as possible, so that your Hello World message will fill your screen.

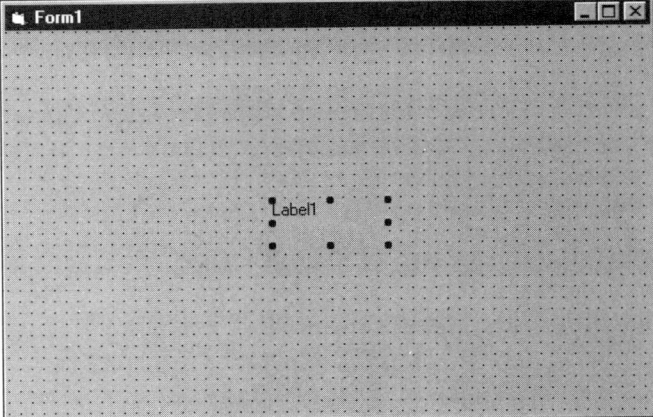

Figure 1-3: When you double-click a tool, Visual Basic draws the control in the center of your form.

1. Click Form1's Maximize icon to make it as large as possible.

2. Resize the Label control to fill the maximized form.

3. Click Form1's Restore icon to return it to its normal size. Now you can see just the upper left corner of the label, because it's still the size of the maximized form.

Setting Properties

Our next task is to make the label say *Hello, World!* To do that, you have to change its properties. Every form and every control has attributes called *properties* that determine its appearance, its behavior, and even its name. When you drag a control to a new location, you change its Top and Left properties, which describe where its top and left sides are. When you resized the Label control just now, you changed its Height and Width properties as well as Top and Left.

To create the Hello World message, you need to change several more properties. You change them by using the Properties window, shown in Figure 1-4. At the top of the window is a drop-down list box that shows the name of the current control or form. Right now, it should say *Label1 Label*, meaning that the object's name is Label1 and its type is Label.

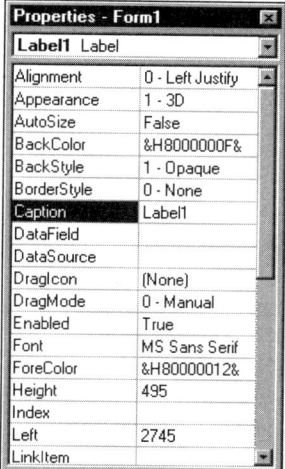

Properties - Form1	
Label1 Label	
Alignment	0 - Left Justify
Appearance	1 - 3D
AutoSize	False
BackColor	&H8000000F&
BackStyle	1 - Opaque
BorderStyle	0 - None
Caption	Label1
DataField	
DataSource	
DragIcon	(None)
DragMode	0 - Manual
Enabled	True
Font	MS Sans Serif
ForeColor	&H80000012&
Height	495
Index	
Left	2745
LinkItem	

Figure 1-4: The Properties window displays the properties of the currently selected object.

TIP If you can't see the entire Properties window, click it to bring it to the top.

If instead the Properties window says *Form1 Form*, click the Label control on your form to select it. When you select a control, two things happen. First, it gains handles to show that it is selected. And second, the Properties window automatically switches to show it.

Now let's create that Hello World message.

1. Make sure the Properties window shows the properties for Label1.

2. In the list of properties, click *Caption*. The word *Caption* highlights to show that the property is selected.

3. Replace the current caption (*Label1*) with *Hello, World!*. You'll see the new caption appear on your form as you type it. At this point, your form should look like Figure 1-5.

4. Now click the *Font* property. Notice that three dots appear in the value area. You know what three dots means in Windows — a dialog box is coming.

5. Click the three dots to open the Font dialog box.

6. Select any font that appeals to you and select a very large size. (In our version, we chose Times New Roman and set the size to 150 points.) Then choose *OK* to close the dialog box.

Size is a ComboBox. If the size you want isn't in the list, just type it in the TextBox above the list.

7. To set the color for the font, click *ForeColor*. A drop-down arrow appears in the value area.

8. Click the arrow to drop down the color palette and choose medium blue.

9. For the background color, select the *BackColor* property and choose light yellow.

10. Select the *Alignment* property and choose *Center*.

Figure 1-5: After you change the caption of the Label control, your form looks like this.

And that's all there is to it, your message is ready. Maximize the form to see it. If you don't like the way it looks, go ahead and try other fonts, sizes, and colors until you get what you want. Figure 1-6 shows what our message looks like at this point.

We'll come back a little later and add some graphics to this message. But for now let's set the properties for the form itself. The title bar should say *My Hello World Program*. And we want to maximize the form automatically when the program is run.

Figure 1-6: After setting the properties, the Hello Worlc message looks like this on the maximized form. (The background color is pale yellow, and the text is medium blue.)

1. In the Properties window, drop down the list at the top and choose *Form1 Form*. The window displays the properties for the form.

2. Change the *Caption* property to *My Hello World Program*. You'll see the change immediately in the title bar of the form.

3. Change *WindowState* to *2 - Maximized*. This determines the initial state of the window when the program is run.

And that's it. The first version of your program is ready to go! It's that easy.

CHECKING IT OUT

Wouldn't you like to see your first Windows program work? Let's do it.

1. Press *F5* to make Visual Basic run your program. Visual Basic hides the toolbox and the Properties window. A new window appears, called Debug, but it is quickly covered by your maximized form.

2. Experiment with the Minimize and Maximize icons. They work just like they do anywhere in Windows. You don't have to do anything special in your programs to make these icons work. (You'll learn later how to disable them when you don't want people to use them.)

3. Now end the program just like you end any program. If you're using Windows 95, click the Close icon. Otherwise, double-click the Control-menu icon at the left end of the title bar. When you end the program, the Visual Basic development environment returns.

From now on, feel free to test your program whenever you want. You don't have to wait for us to tell you to check it out. We tend to press F5 after each step , to make sure that each new feature works before adding the next one.

SAVING YOUR PROJECT

Now that you've got the initial version of your program working and have paused to catch your breath and think about what's next, this is an opportune moment to save your work on disk for the first time. Let's do that now.

1. Choose *File | Save Project* or click the Save Project icon shown here to open the dialog box shown in Figure 1-7.

2. Notice that this is the Save *File* As dialog. In order to save your entire project, you must save each form as a separate file. Right now, Visual Basic is asking for a file name for the form. Just type *Hello* and click *Save*; Visual Basic will add the extension *.frm* when it creates the new file.

3. After you have saved all the forms in the project, the Save Project As dialog box appears so that you can assign a name to the project itself. Again, type *Hello* and Visual Basic will add the default extension *.vbp*.

Notice that the caption in Visual Basic's title bar (the one at the top of the screen) has changed to include the project name you just created. Now that the project and the form have file names, it's easy to save them again. Just click the

Save Project icon, and the latest version replaces the former version on disk without any fuss.

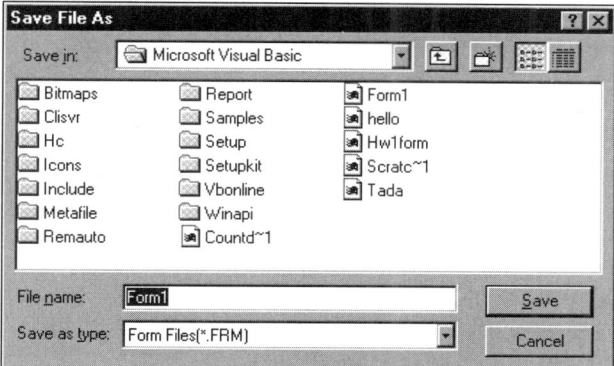

Figure 1-7: The first time you save the project, Visual Basic asks for a file name for each form.

You don't have to wait for us to remind you to save your work. Click Save Project often as you work on the projects in this book.

ADDING GRAPHICS TO YOUR MESSAGE

We promised you at the beginning of this chapter that we'd add a little visual pizzazz to the Hello World message. Visual Basic includes a lovely set of icons for you to use in your programs, including the Earth icon shown here. Let's replace the o's in *Hello, World!* with this icon.

To do this, you need to place two Image controls on your form. An *Image control* is a control that can display a graphic. In the process of creating these controls, you'll learn the other two techniques for creating a new control: dragging and copying.

Creating a Control by Dragging

You created the Label control by double-clicking the Label tool, which popped a small copy of the control into the center of your form. Then you had to resize the control. Another way to create a control is to drag it onto the form. You'll use the drag method to add the first Image control to your form.

1. Find the Image tool (shown here). Make sure you find the Image tool, not the Picture Box tool; these two look a lot alike.

2. Click the Image tool once (don't double-click it). Nothing appears on the form yet, but you'll see the result shortly.

3. Enlarge (but don't maximize) the form so that you can see the "o" in "Hello."

4. Move your pointer over the "o" in "Hello." It turns into crosshairs, indicating that you can now drag the selected control onto the form.

5. Imagine a box enclosing the "o" and drag the crosshairs from any one corner of the box to the diagonal corner. (Most people drag from upper right to lower left.) You'll see a box grow as you drag. When you finish, the box turns into a dotted outline with handles.

6. Move and resize the control so it exactly covers the "o" (see Figure 1-8).

Figure 1-8: The Image control appears as a dotted box until you insert a graphic in it.

Now you need to insert the Earth icon into the Image control. To do that, you change its Picture property.

1. In Visual Basic's toolbar (directly below the menu bar), locate and click the Properties icon shown here to bring the Properties window to the top.

2. Make sure the Properties window shows the properties for Image1 Image. If not, drop down the list at the top of the Properties window and choose *Image1 Image.*

3. The *Stretch* property stretches a picture to fit the size of the control. It's a drop-down list with two values, True or False. Set it to *True.*

4. Select the *Picture* property and click the three dots that appear. Figure 1-9 shows the dialog box that appears, which is a common Windows dialog box for opening files.

5. Starting from your Visual Basic folder, locate and open the *Icons* folder, and then the *Elements* folder. Double-click the Earth icon. The dialog box closes and the icon appears in the Image control, as shown in Figure 1-10.

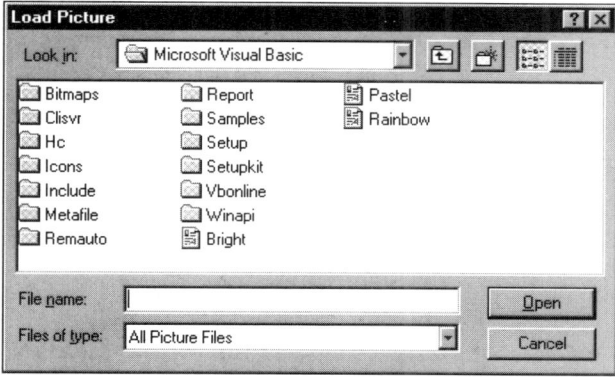

Figure 1-9: The Load Picture dialog box lets you locate and select the picture for an Image control.

If you didn't set Stretch to True, the icon would be the same size as the original graphic, no matter how large the Label control is. It would appear in the upper left corner of the control. The Stretch property makes the icon (or any type of graphic) stretch to fit the control. Note that you can distort a stretched graphic by giving the control different proportions than the original graphic has. You may or may not find this desirable—it's kinda fun with your boss's photograph.

Figure 1-10: Your form looks like this after inserting the Earth icon in the Image control.

COPYING A CONTROL

With one image already on your form, you can quickly create the second one. All you have to do make a copy and position it.

1. Maximize the form so that you can see both o's.

2. Right-click the Image control to select it and pop up a context menu. This handy little menu offers a set of commands that you're most likely to want right now, including the *Copy* and *Paste* commands.

3. Choose *Copy*.

4. Right-click anywhere to pop up the context menu again.

5. Choose *Paste*. Now you get an unexpected message: *Do you want to create a control array?* You'll learn about control arrays in Chapter 12.

6. For now, just say *No*. As soon as you click the *No* button, a copy of the Image control, earth and all, appears in upper left corner of the form.

7. Drag the new copy to cover the "o" in "World," as shown in Figure 1-11.

8. Click the Save Project icon to save your work so far, then press *F5* to see how your program works.

Figure 1-11: Now both o's are replaced by the Earth icon.

CODING AN EVENT

So far, your program doesn't really do much. Most programs also respond to events. An *event* is a user action, such as clicking an icon or pressing a key. Each form and each control can have events associated with them. It's up to you to code the *procedures* that make the events work.

Let's make it a little easier to end the Hello World program. You can make it terminate if the user clicks anywhere on the form.

You code a procedure in the *code window* (see Figure 1-12). There are several ways to open the window, but the easiest is to double-click the desired object. Double-click the Label control now to open a code window on your screen.

You can see that Visual Basic has automatically provided two statements for you. These two statements act like bookends to identify the beginning and end of the procedure. Notice that the first line, the Private Sub statement, identifies the event to be processed: Label1_Click. In other words, this procedure processes a click on Label1. This is confirmed in the Object and Proc boxes above the work area. The last line, the End Sub statement, merely identifies the end of the procedure. You place all your code between these two statements.

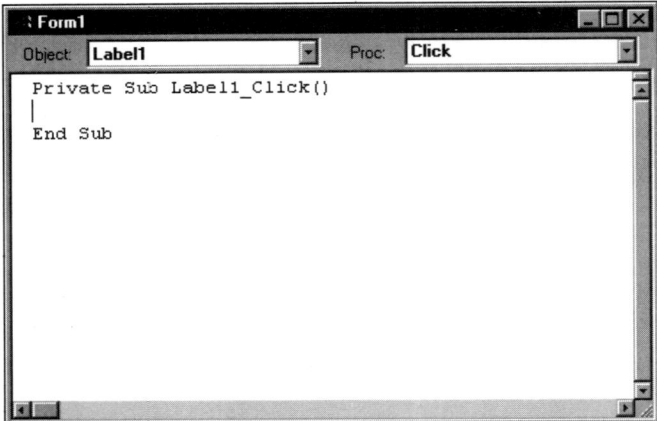

Figure 1-12: Events are coded in the code window, which appears when you double-click a control.

1. Click the blank line between the Private Sub and End Sub statements. This places the typing cursor on the blank line.

2. Press *Tab* to indent the line. Indenting isn't required, but it's a convention that makes code much easier to read.

3. Type the word *End*. The End statement terminates the program. Your procedure should now look like Figure 1-13.

4. Try out your new code by pressing *F5* to run the program.

5. Click anywhere on the Label control. The program ends and you return to the Visual Basic environment.

6. Run the program again, but this time click one of the Image controls. Notice that nothing happens. The only event you have coded so far is Label1_Click, so there is no code for Image1_Click or Image2_Click.

7. Click the Label control to end the program.

8. Save your project by clicking the Save Project icon.

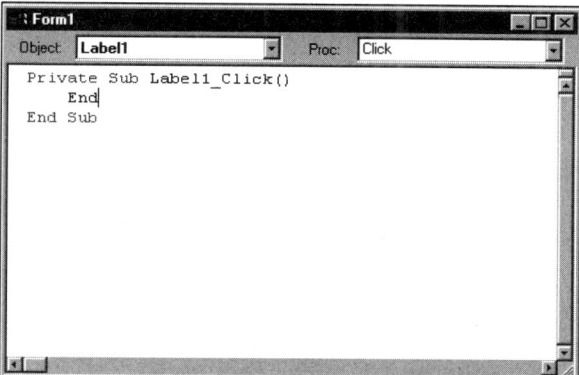

Figure 1-13: You place your statements, such as the End statement shown here, between the Sub and End Sub statements.

Well, that was simple, wasn't it? Go ahead and create procedures for the two Image controls so that the program ends if someone clicks either one of them. That way, the user can click anywhere on the form (except the title bar) to end the program.

SUMMARY

Well, there you have it. You have created a small working program. In the process, you've learned how to create a form, add controls to the form, set properties, write procedures to handle events, and save your project. While it can't be said that you know everything that you need to know about Visual Basic—after all, there must be something in the rest of the book—you have the basic elements in your grasp.

Before you continue, you might want to try writing a few programs on your own. There are so many fun messages that you could create right now, with the skills that you have learned so far. You could, for example, leave an "out to lunch" message for your coworkers, a mushy note for your sweetheart, or a "finish your homework before you play any computer games" note for your kids. The more programs you write, the more comfortable you'll be with the basics. So go ahead and have some fun! (You can tell your boss we said so.)

CHAPTER OBJECTIVES

Until you write Windows programs, you view
Windows with a user's eye. When you see a
window or a dialog box, you tend to think of how
you're going to use it to accomplish your work.
You don't really think of all the operations that are
coordinated behind the scenes to give you useful
output from your programs.

In this chapter, we're going to start training your
eye to see the programmer's view of Windows.
You'll learn:

▶ How windows and controls are related

▶ How Windows and Visual Basic respond to events

▶ The difference between run-time and design-
  time properties

▶ How Windows multitasks among programs

A Programmer's
View of Windows

From the user's point of view, Windows provides a relatively easy way to get your work done. When you start Windows, you're presented with a desktop. With Windows 95 and the latest version of Windows NT, the desktop has icons on it that represent various system resources, and there's a taskbar at the bottom that grants you access to all the programs, documents, settings, disk drives, and other resources on your machine, as shown in Figure 2-1.

When you start one of your Windows applications, it most likely opens up a window on the screen. Each object in the window represents a job that your application can do for you. You can manipulate various tools to edit documents, print reports, chat online with friends, and destroy alien warships — perhaps all at the same time.

A number of these objects are common among Windows programs, so that they quickly become old friends. After you have worked with just a few applications, you immediately recognize the title bar and its icons; the menu bar and the File, Edit, and Help menus (as well as the common commands on those menus); the toolbar and many of its tools, the scroll bars, and the status bar.

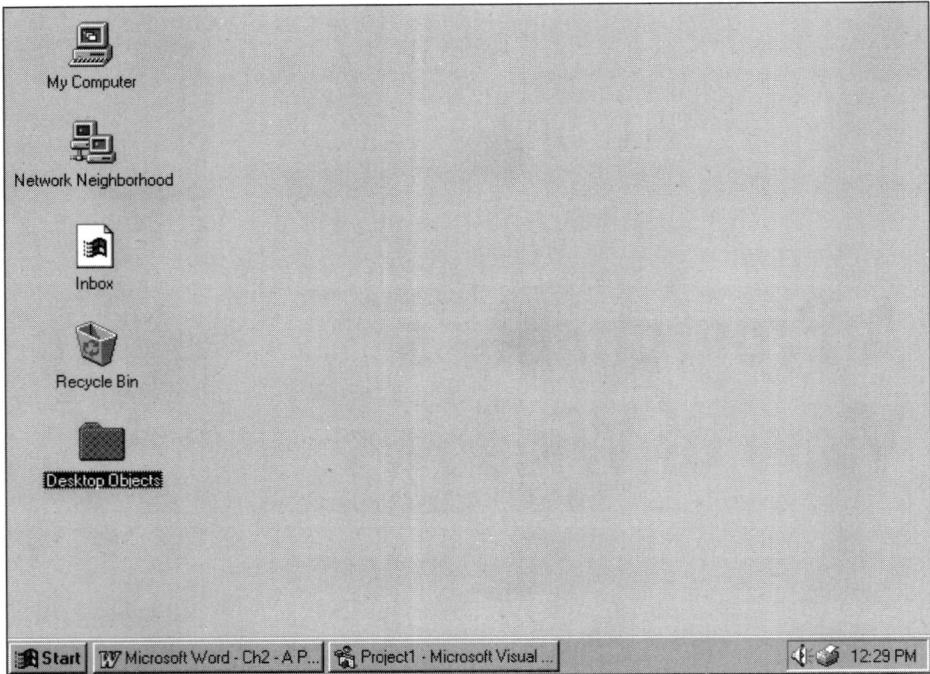

Figure 2-1: Windows 95 presents a desktop with a taskbar and Start button to provide access to all resources on your system.

The File Open and File Save As dialog boxes are familiar features, and you almost instinctively know how to use many of the objects in dialog boxes: CommandButtons, ListBoxes, TextBoxes, CheckBoxes, OptionButtons (also called *radio buttons*), and so on. After a while, you find yourself attempting to use new applications without bothering to read the documentation. You know that you'll be able to use most of the tools without any assistance, and you can find out anything else from the built-in Help system.

THE PROGRAMMER'S POINT OF VIEW

Let's turn around now and look at how a programmer views Windows. How do windows get on the screen? How does a menu bar get into your application? How are controls placed on a form? How do controls do their jobs?

From the programmer's perspective, a window is a blank canvas with two sides. On the front, the side facing the user, the programmer paints forms and controls.

Text boxes, lines, buttons, and scroll bars are all just objects that the programmer places on the window to give the user control over the application.

Putting this pretty face on the application is the "Visual" part of Visual Basic. You simply choose controls from a palette of tools, place them in the desired locations, and set their properties.

On the back of the canvas is the part that's most interesting to the programmer: the code. The code is what tells each control what to do when activated in certain ways. It's the code that differentiates an OK button from a Cancel button, a Help menu from a File menu.

This code is written in a language called BASIC, hence the "Basic" part of Visual Basic. BASIC was originally designed to be an easy-to-learn language that students could use to learn fundamental computer skills. Largely because of Microsoft's efforts, it has become one of the most popular programming languages available today.

Design Time versus Run Time

As a programmer, you must always be aware of the differences between how Visual Basic behaves while you're creating a program and when you're actually running the program. When you're creating, you're working in *design* mode, as shown in Figure 2-2. The various design windows are available to you—the toolbox and Properties windows, for example. In the main Visual Basic window at the top of the screen, the expression *[design]* appears in the title bar.

When you execute the program, you switch into *run* mode, as shown in Figure 2-3. If you're running it from within Visual Basic, for testing and debugging purposes, the expression *[run]* appears in the Visual Basic window. The Debug and the main Visual Basic windows are available to you, but not the design-time windows such as code, Properties, and toolbox. The forms and controls work just as they do for any user of the program.

Later on, when you're ready to release your program and you turn it into an executable program file (an .exe file), it runs just like any other program. No parts of the Visual Basic development environment are available any more.

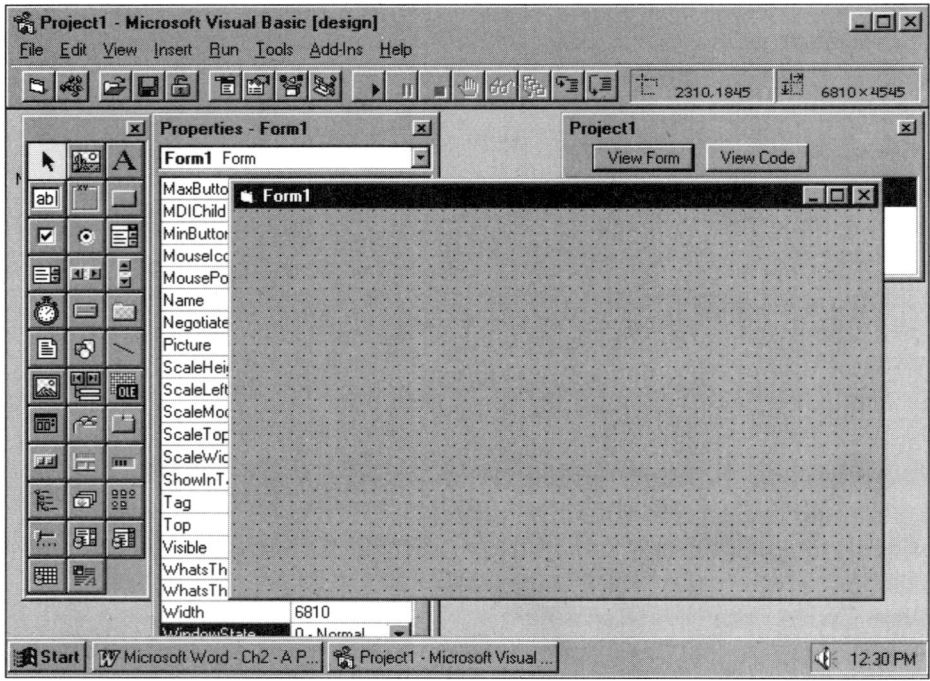

Figure 2-2: In design mode, you can create a new form, add controls to it, set properties, and so on.

Many Visual Basic features work the same at design time and run time. But many others are different at run time. As a simple example, let's explore the resizing capability of a form.

---

1. For this experiment, you'll work with a new project. If Visual Basic is not running, start it up so that a new project is started automatically. If it is already running, save your current project, if desired, and choose *File | New* to start a new project.

2. Experiment with resizing Form1 in design mode. You'll find that you can resize it freely. Make Form1 very small before going on to Step 3.

3. Press *F5* to run the current program. Notice that the initial size of the form at run time is the same small size that you gave it in design mode.

4. Experiment with resizing the form in run mode. Make the form very large before going on to Step 5.

5. Click the Close icon to end the program and return to design mode. What happens to the size of the form? It returns to the same small size that it last had at design time!

6. Run the program again. What is the form's initial size? The same small size that it had before.

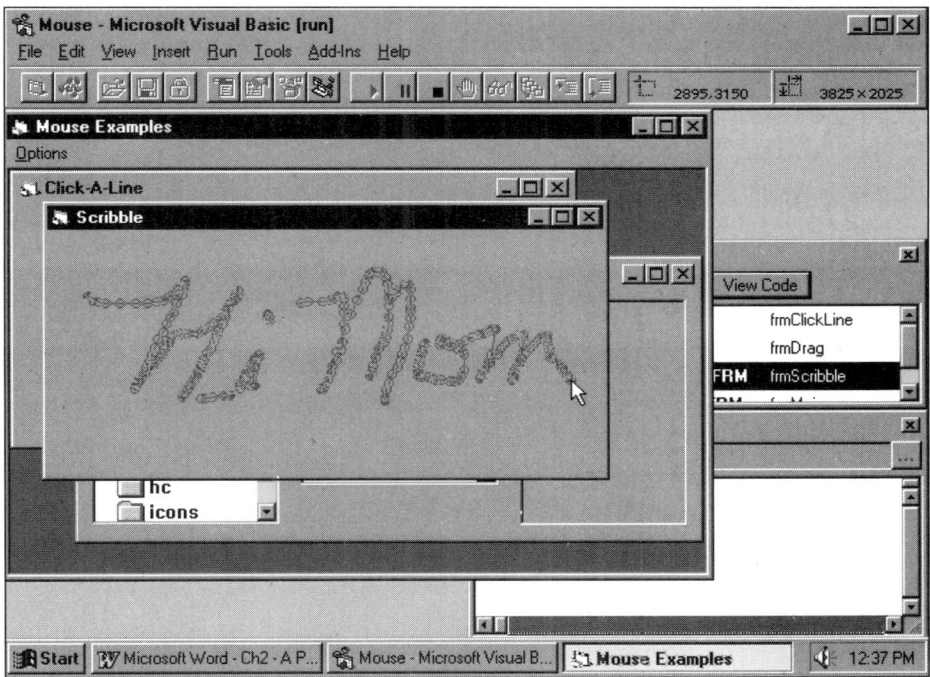

Figure 2-3: At run time, you work with the program just as the eventual user will.

As you can see from this experiment, the changes that you make to the form at design time affect the form at run time, but the reverse is not true. Run-time changes affect only the current run of the program. As soon as you end the program, those changes are forgotten and you revert to design status.

Some properties go into effect only at run time. Do you remember from Chapter 1 that you set the WindowState property for your Hello World form to Maximize? This caused the form to be maximized as soon as you ran the program, but did not affect the form at design time. A similar property is BorderStyle, as you'll see in the following experiment.

1. Change the *BorderStyle* property to *1 - Fixed Single*. This tells Visual Basic that the form's size is fixed (that is, it can't be changed) at run time.

2. Stay in design mode and resize the form. You'll have no trouble changing the size, even though the form's border is now fixed.

3. Run the program and try to resize the border. You can't do it—in fact, the mouse pointer doesn't even change into the resize pointer when you place it over the border. Notice also that the Minimize and Maximize icons have disappeared from the title bar.

4. Click the form's Control-menu icon to drop down the control menu. Notice that the standard Minimize, Maximize, Restore, and Size commands are missing from the menu.

5. End the program and return to design mode. Notice that, as always, you can resize, minimize, maximize, and restore the form at design time.

Throughout this book and the Visual Basic documentation, you'll read about features that are available only at design time or only at run time. As you've seen, design-time features are accessed by setting properties or by direct manipulation of the controls (such as resizing the form). Run-time features are usually controlled by code; you'll learn how to write such code in later chapters.

Windows and Controls

In Chapter 1, we walked you through the process of creating a simple Windows application using Visual Basic. As you recall, after you started Visual Basic, you got a form like the one shown in Figure 2-2. This is the blank canvas upon which you create your masterpiece. (Actually, the canvas isn't completely blank; several controls are already in place, provided automatically by Visual Basic. The form has a border for resizing, a title bar, and title-bar icons.)

The center of the form, covered with dots in Figure 2-2, is the interesting part. This is where you, as a programmer, do your work. You choose what controls you want on the form, where they'll be placed, what their properties are, and what they'll do.

You'll be glad to know that each control knows how to perform its visual action. For example, if the user clicks a button, the button pushes itself in automatically. If the user opens a menu, the menu appears on the screen. If the user clicks a CheckBox, the CheckBox automatically checks or unchecks. If the user selects an OptionButton, the other OptionButtons automatically deselect. You don't have to write a single line of code to make any of this happen.

However much you watch a button depress, or a scroll bar move, or an option button deselect, these visual actions don't get your job done. They're simply feedback mechanisms so that users can see that the computer is paying attention to what they do.

Therefore, it's relatively easy to put together a screen that *looks* quite good, but doesn't *do* anything. In order for your screen to do something, you have to get behind the screen and add the code that tells your computer what you want to happen. But how does your program know what code to execute?

Windows and Events

Every operation you perform on your computer is an *event*. Clicking a button, moving the mouse, selecting a menu item, or pressing a key on the keyboard are all events. Windows is an *event-driven* system. This means that every time the user manipulates a control, an event is generated that Windows must pay attention to, although it may not actually execute any code, as you'll see shortly.

Windows keeps track of which event goes with which application. For example, keypresses go to the active application, and button clicks go to the application that holds the button. When an application is ready, Windows tells it which event to process next. Once you start an application, it initializes itself and then sits idle, waiting for an event.

Let's take the Windows Solitaire game as an example. Start up Windows Solitaire. The program named sol.exe initializes itself, deals a hand, then sits and waits for an event. It never gets tired of waiting; it will wait until your computer shuts down or disintegrates into a pile of dust, if you don't send it an event.

How many different events do you think Solitaire could receive at this point? Probably more than you realize. It's ready to accept any one of *dozens* of different events while it's just sitting there. A partial list of some events that it could process are:

▶ Clicking the draw pile

▶ Dragging a card

▶ Double-clicking a card

▶ Clicking the Minimize icon

▶ Choosing one of the seven choices on the menu bar

▶ Closing the application

Okay, stop playing Solitaire now, and let's go on to the next topic.

Multitasking

While Solitaire is sitting there waiting for its next event, other applications can also be waiting for the next event to process. Each application running on your computer simply waits for events, then processes them as quickly as possible. If a program takes too much time to complete a task, Windows 95 may interrupt it to allow other programs a chance. In this way, programs take turns, and they all appear to run simultaneously, although only one of them at a time can actually use your computer's processor. This method of running multiple programs at once is called *pre-emptive multitasking*.

NOTE

Earlier versions of Windows use *cooperative multitasking*, in which a program returns control to Windows voluntarily when it completes a task. You have to wait for a long-running task to finish before you can do anything else. A malfunctioning task could tie up your entire system, forcing you to reboot to clear it. Windows 95's pre-emptive multitasking circumvents these problems.

Sometimes an application has to do some very lengthy processing in order to handle an event. This is why the mouse cursor sometimes changes to an hourglass. If an application knows that what it's about to do will take more than a moment, it changes the mouse cursor to an hourglass to let you know that this processing will take a while. With Windows 95, you can go on to work on other applications while the processing takes place. (With earlier versions of Windows, you have to wait until the processing finishes and the hourglass clears.)

Program-Generated Events

There are many different types of events that an application can receive. We already told you about some of the ones that the user can generate. The user isn't the only source of events, however. Other sources of events are timers, other applications, your modem, and even Windows itself.

Think about a modern word processor, spreadsheet, database, or other application. Most of them have an automatic save feature that saves the current document every few minutes. The user does nothing to trigger the save action; the event is generated by a timer.

Other applications can control your applications by sending keypress, mouse movement, button click, and similar events to your application. Additionally, Microsoft invented two other ways to let applications interact: *Dynamic Data Exchange (DDE)* and *Object Linking and Embedding (OLE),* which both enable applications to share data with each other. We'll talk more about these two features in Part VI, Advanced Topics.

Communications applications often set up the modem to send events when certain situations happen, such as carrier loss, received characters, and so on.

Finally, Windows itself can send events to your applications. Whenever your program is minimized or maximized, Windows sends an event to your program to resize it accordingly. If a different application obscures your application's window, and then your application is reactivated, Windows sends a message to your application to redraw itself.

How Events Execute Your Code

Here comes the programmer's part. When the user (or another application or whatever) generates an event for your code, Windows hands the event to your program. All that the program needs to do is to figure out what the event is, determine what control the event goes to, and execute the appropriate code.

In some programming languages, particularly C and C++, it can be quite tedious to identify the control and the event. But Visual Basic makes it simple. The only thing you have to do to get your code executed is to name your code the way Visual Basic wants you to.

Your form, and every control on it, has a name. Additionally, each type of event has a name. In order to make Visual Basic execute a particular piece of code in response to an event, you create an *event procedure,* which has the form shown below (where italics indicate generic terms that should be replaced with specific names when you use this form):

```
Private Sub ControlName_EventName()
    [Put your code here]
End Sub
```

The first statement, called the Sub statement, tells Visual Basic when this procedure should be executed by identifying the control and the event. *ControlName* is simply the name of the control for which you're creating an event procedure, such as Label1 or Form1. *EventName* is the name of the event you want to capture, such as Click or Drag. (We'll explain the word *Private* and the empty parentheses in a later chapter. In the meantime, be sure to use them in every procedure.)

For example, suppose you have a button named Button1 and you want to execute a piece of code whenever the user clicks it. You name your code Button1_Click. Your event procedure would look like:

```
Private Sub Button1_Click()
   [Put your code here]
End Sub
```

All you need to do is put the code in the procedure, and every time the user clicks Button1, your code gets executed.

When Windows gives your application an event, Visual Basic automatically determines which control the event goes to, and looks for an event procedure with the appropriate name. If it can find it, then Visual Basic executes your code. Otherwise, it ignores the event and returns control to Windows.

Going back to the metaphor of a program as a two-sided canvas, from the front of the canvas, the user sees a control that can be clicked or otherwise manipulated to accomplish a task. From behind the canvas, the programmer sees a procedure that must be coded and related to the control and the event.

SUMMARY

A user's view of the computer is simple: An application is a tool that does specific tasks. A programmer, however, views the computer as a blank canvas upon which to create a new tool for the user. A user views the windows and controls on the screen as a means to manipulate the application, while the programmer views windows and controls as building blocks with which to construct a program.

In this chapter, you've begun the process of thinking about your computer, Windows, Visual Basic, and applications in programmers' terms. You've learned that there are differences between design time and run time. And you have learned a bit more about how Windows reacts to controls and events, as well as how it manages to run several programs simultaneously.

You've also seen that Visual Basic doesn't make you write unnecessary code. You don't have to make buttons appear to be pressed, the title bar icons work, or the resizing border work. The only code you have to write are the procedures that are unique to your program. But don't worry, you won't be bored. You'll have plenty to do to make use of your time and talents, as you'll see in upcoming chapters.

CHAPTER OBJECTIVES

In this chapter, we'll be taking a closer look at the elements of the Visual Basic programming environment. You'll learn about:

▶ The major windows: the main window, the toolbox, the Properties window, the project window, the code window, and a few windows you haven't seen before

▶ The features and mechanics of each window, and how they interact with each other

▶ The details of programming tasks such as designing forms, creating code, and testing and debugging

As you learn to use the environment, you'll also learn quite a bit more about controls and debugging in particular.

The Visual Basic 4.0 Programming Environment

Let's begin by exploring the various windows that you'll be using to create and test your programs. As you know, Visual Basic initially opens five windows. There are several other windows that you will frequently use.

THE MAIN WINDOW

Stretched across the top of your screen is the main Visual Basic window, as shown in Figure 3-1. This window appears in both design mode and run mode. As you can see, it provides the Visual Basic menus and a toolbar of shortcuts for the most common functions. In addition, it provides the main title bar for your Visual Basic environment, which includes the name of the current project and the current mode, such as *design* or *run*.

Figure 3-1: The main window provides menus and a toolbar for you to use at design time and run time.

Interaction with Other Windows

Sometimes the main window acts independently of the other Visual Basic windows, but some of its actions affect all windows. The following exercise helps you to discover for yourself how these windows interact.

1. Try resizing the main window. Notice that you can change its horizontal dimensions, but not vertical. Size changes don't affect any other windows.

2. Try moving the main window around. You can move it anywhere on the screen, and it will overlap other windows.

3. Try closing every window *except* the main window. Every other window closes independently.

4. To reopen the closed windows, choose the following commands from the View menu: *Form*, *Project*, *Properties*, and *Toolbox*.

5. Now close the main window. You have just exited Visual Basic, because closing the main window ends the program.

6. Restart Visual Basic.

7. Try minimizing the form. It minimizes independently into a button on your screen. Notice that the toolbox, Properties, and project windows can't be minimized independently.

8. Now try minimizing the main window. The entire Visual Basic environment minimizes.

9. Restore the main window.

TIP

If the main window gets buried under your other work, you can quickly pop it to the top by pressing Alt+Tab once. Or in Windows 95 or Windows NT, click the project's icon in the taskbar.

Location and Size Values

Another important feature of the main window appears at the right end of the toolbar (see Figure 3-2), where the location and size of the current object are shown in *twips* (explained shortly).

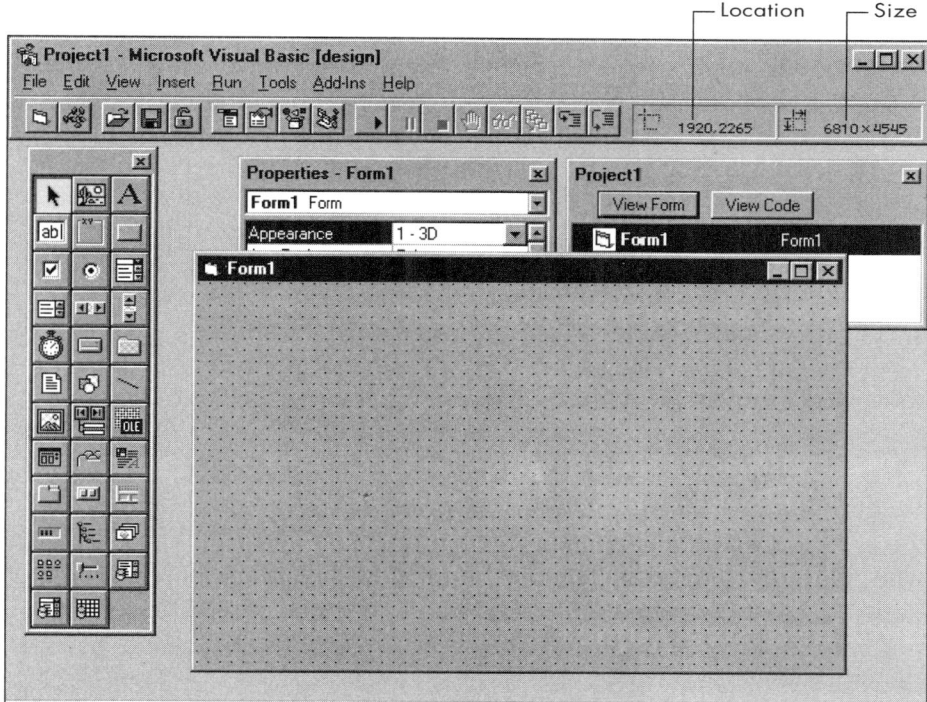

Figure 3-2: The location and dimensions in twips of the current object appear on the right end of the toolbar.

Try moving the form around on the screen and watch the effect on the location value. The location is shown as *left,top*, so a value of 2880,1590 means that the current object is 2880 twips in from the left and 1590 twips down from the top.

Now try resizing the form several times and watch the effect on the size value, The size is shown as *width × height*, so 1320 × 4112 means that the object is 1320 twips wide and 4112 twips high.

Okay, so what's a twip? According to Visual Basic's help, a twip is a unit of measurement defined as 1/1440 of a logical inch. The size of a logical inch, however, depends on the monitor and the resolution. So there's no exact definition of the size of a twip; it's just a very small unit of measure.

For a form, the location is given relative to the screen edges, so a location of 1620,3112 is 1620 twips from the left edge of the screen and 3112 twips down from the top of the screen. For a control, the location is given relative to the edges of the client area — that is, the area bounded by the menu bar or title bar on the top, and the form's border on the left. Try the following exercise to see how the location and size values change.

1. Draw a new Label control on the form. Notice that the toolbar now shows the location and size of the control, not the form.

2. Try switching back and forth between the form and the Label control and watch the effect on the location and size values.

3. Move the Label control around and watch how the location value changes as you move it. When you move a form, the value doesn't change until you drop the form, but when you move a control, the value changes dynamically.

4. Similarly, resize the Label control and watch how both values change as you resize it.

5. Try positioning the Label control at exactly 100,150 and making its size exactly 220 × 350. Even with the dynamic readout, you'll find this very hard to do, as twips are so small that it's difficult to move the mouse that precisely.

TIP A better way to position and size objects exactly is to set their Left, Right, Height, and Width properties.

NOTE You don't have to deal with twips. Every form has a property called ScaleMode that determines how items contained on the form are measured. You can choose points, picas, centimeters, inches, and so on. The form's ScaleMode doesn't affect the measurement of the form itself, only the controls on the form. Feel free to experiment with ScaleMode before going on to the next topic.

THE TOOLBOX

The toolbox (see Figure 3-3) can be moved, closed, and reopened, but it can't be resized, minimized, or maximized. Its size depends on the number of tools it displays and changes automatically as you add and subtract tools from it.

Figure 3-3: The toolbox provides controls and other objects that you can draw on your form.

TIP

If the toolbox gets buried under other windows or closed, a quick way to pop it to the top is to choose View | Toolbox.

The initial toolbox contains the standard tools plus some of the custom controls that are included in the Visual Basic package. You can't remove the standard tools, such as the Label and TextBox controls, but you can remove and add custom controls. You can also add other objects that can be drawn on your forms via OLE, such as sound clips, Lotus 1-2-3 spreadsheets, and Microsoft WordArt. Let's try tailoring the toolbox.

1. Find the Rich Textbox tool (shown here) in the toolbox. You're going to remove this tool, then add it again.

    If you installed the 16-bit version of Visual Basic, you probably don't have a Rich Textbox control. In that case, use any custom control for this exercise.

2. Choose *Tools | Custom Controls* to open the Custom Controls dialog box, shown on the next page.

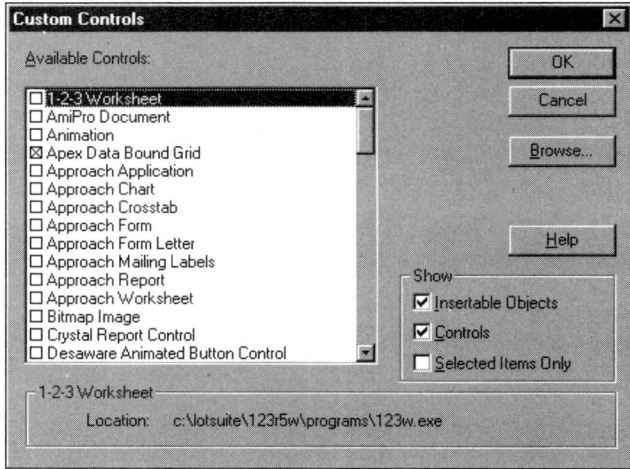

3. Scroll through the list box to see the entire range of items available to you. The check marks indicate items that currently appear in your toolbox.

4. In the *Show* group, uncheck *Insertable Objects* so that only *Controls* is checked. Now scroll through the list box to see the complete list of custom controls available to you.

5. Now uncheck *Controls* and check *Insertable Objects*. Scroll through the list box again to see what objects you can insert on your forms.

6. Check *Controls* and *Selected Items Only*. Notice that the list now shows only the objects that actually appear in your toolbox.

7. Uncheck *Microsoft Rich Textbox Control,* and click *OK* to close the dialog box. Notice that the Rich Textbox tool has disappeared from the toolbox.

8. Restore the Rich Textbox tool by following these steps:

   a) Choose *Tools | Custom Controls*.

   b) Uncheck *Selected Items Only*.

   c) Scroll through the list and check *Microsoft Rich Textbox Control.*

   d) Click *OK* to close the dialog box. Notice that the Rich Textbox tool is now the last tool in the toolbox.

You'll be learning a lot more about custom controls in Chapter 9, and you'll use the Rich Textbox Control in the ScratchPad application that you develop throughout this book. But for now, let's leave the toolbox and examine the Properties window.

THE PROPERTIES WINDOW

The Properties window (Figure 3-4) can be moved, sized, closed, and reopened, but not minimized or maximized. The default size is too narrow to show some complete entries in the property name column on the left and the property value column on the right. Widening the window slightly can make it much more readable.

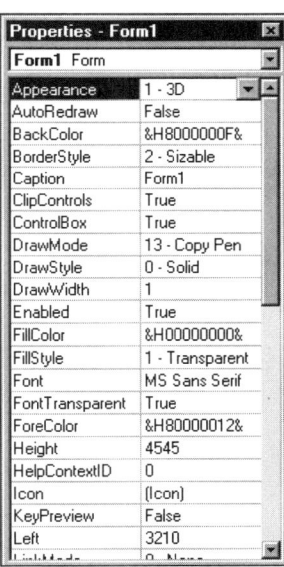

Figure 3-4: The Properties window displays the design-time properties of the currently selected object.

The drop-down list just under the title bar shows all the objects in the current form. When your project has more than one form, only the current form is listed. If Form1 is currently selected and you want to see the objects on Form2, you must activate Form2, then look at the Properties window. To see the properties for a specific object, click the object or select it from the drop-down list.

TIP If your Properties window gets closed or buried under other windows in the Visual Basic work area, a quick way to pop it to the top is to choose View | Properties, press F4, or click the Properties icon (shown here) in the toolbar.

We're not going to get into specific properties here. You'll be learning about the properties for the objects that you use often in upcoming chapters. For now, let's take a look at the project window.

THE PROJECT WINDOW

The project window provides a quick way to access the forms in your project and the code associated with them. The example in Figure 3-5 shows the project window for one of the samples included in your Visual Basic package, called Atm, which emulates the features of a bank's automated teller machine. We'll use this example to explore the features of the project window.

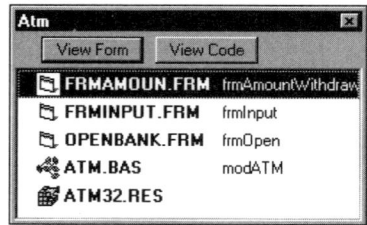

Figure 3-5: The project window lists all modules (form, standard, and class) along with the project's resource file, if any.

1. Choose *File | Open Project*. (Save the current file and project, if desired.)

2. In the Open Project dialog box, locate your Visual Basic folder. Then open the *Samples* folder, followed by the *Resource* folder. The project file named Atm (or Atm.vbp) should be located in Resource.

3. Double-click *Atm* to open it.

The project window gives you a quick and easy way to access all the forms belonging to the project. Forms are identified by the Form icon and file names ending in .frm. The right-hand column shows the

Form icon

name of the form, taken from the Name property. The three forms in the Atm project have been renamed from the default Form1, Form2, and Form3 to frmAmountWithdrawn, frmInput, and frmOpen. Let's take a look at them.

1. In the project window click *frmOpen* to select it.

2. Click *View Form* in the project window. The form appears on your screen, partially covering the project window.

3. Press *Ctrl+R* to pop the project window to the top.

4. Another way to view a form is to double-click its name in the project window. Try double-clicking *frmAmountWithdrawn*. The form appears on the screen.

5. Click the Project icon in Visual Basic's toolbar (shown here) to pop the project window to the top.

6. Double-click *frmInput* to add that form to the display. It covers frmAmountWithdrawn.

7. The project window also provides a quick way to bring a covered form to the top. Click the Project icon, then double-click *frmAmountWithdrawn* in the project window. The form pops to the top of the pile.

What are those other items in the Atm project window? The project window shows all the modules belonging to the project. A form represents one type of module. Atm.bas is a *standard module* — a section of code that is not related to any form. A third type, not shown in the Atm project, is a *class module*, which is used to create new objects. You'll learn more about modules in Chapter 5.

The item name atm32.res is a *resource file* — a file containing data for the project. Resource files are also displayed in the project window.

TIP Visual Basic gives you several ways to access the project window. The formal way is to choose View | Project, but no one ever does that. It's faster and easier to press Ctrl+R or click the Project icon in the toolbar. If the window is already open and is partially showing, you can simply click it, of course.

You've seen how to view forms from the project window. You also use the project window to access code. For code associated with forms, you select the form and click the View Code button. For code in standard or class modules, you can select the module and click View Code or simply double-click the module name in the window. In either case, the selected code appears in the code window, which we'll talk about next.

THE CODE WINDOW

The code window is used for creating and viewing code. The code window is actually an editor so that you can create new code, modify existing code, and view existing code. Code is divided into procedures, with one procedure at a time being displayed in the window.

In Figure 3-6, you can see the code for a procedure named cmdOKEnd_Click. Many of the lines are wider than the window. The editor does not word wrap lines, as each Visual Basic statement must be on a single line. So as you can see in the figure, you have to either make the window wider or scroll right and left to read entire wide lines. When you're typing lines, the editor scrolls automatically so that you can always see the cursor position.

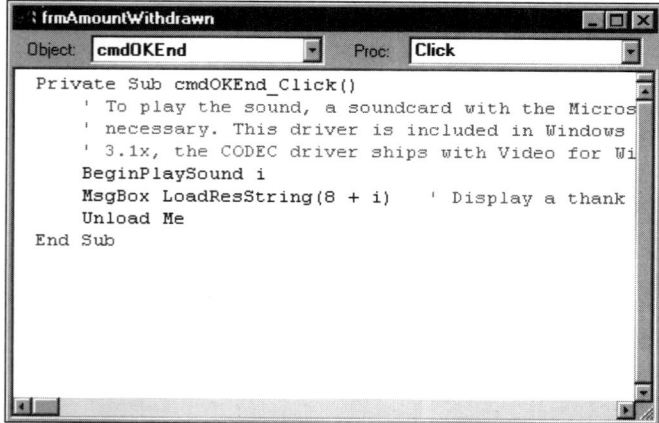

Figure 3-6: The code window provides an intelligent editor to assist you in developing your code.

Before we put the Atm project away, let's look at how you locate procedures in the code window.

1. In the project window, select *frmOpen* and click the *View Code* button to open the code window, as shown in step 1 screen. Notice that the name of the form appears in the title bar, as this code window is specifically related to the frmOpen module.

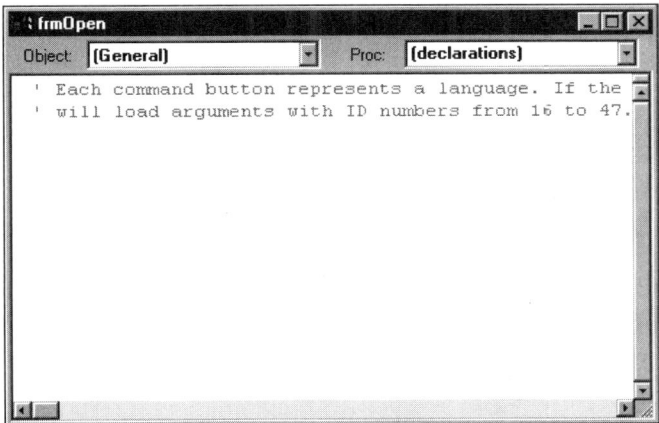

2. Drop down the *Object* list to see all the objects on this form, as shown in step 2 screen. Scroll through the list to see all the objects on the form, including the form itself.

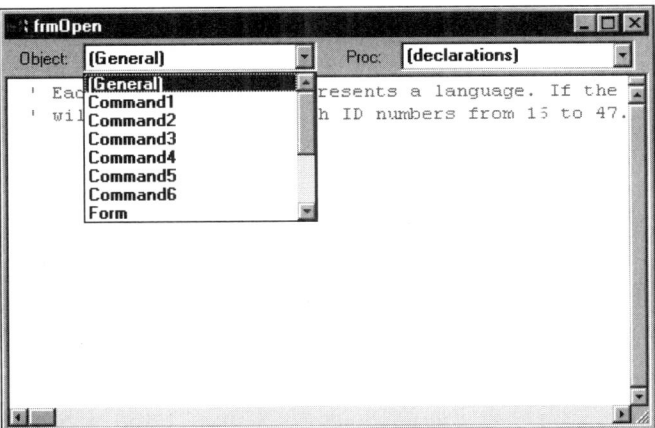

The (General) procedure, shown at the top of the list of objects, represents code that belongs to the form but is not related to any specific object.

3. Choose *Command1* (the first CommandButton on the form). The Command1_Click() procedure appears in the window of the following screen.

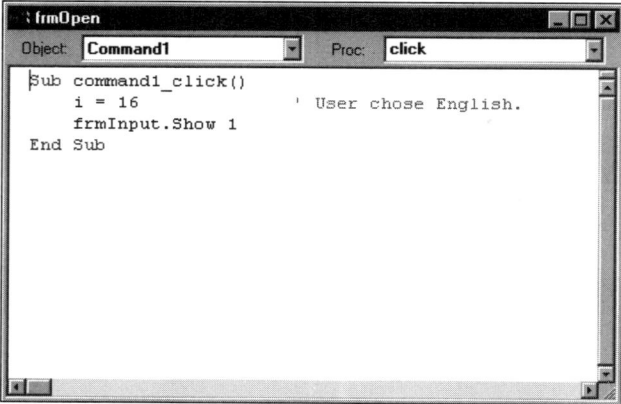

4. Now drop down the *Proc* list to see all the possible events that could be coded for the Command1 button as shown in the following screen. Scroll through the list.

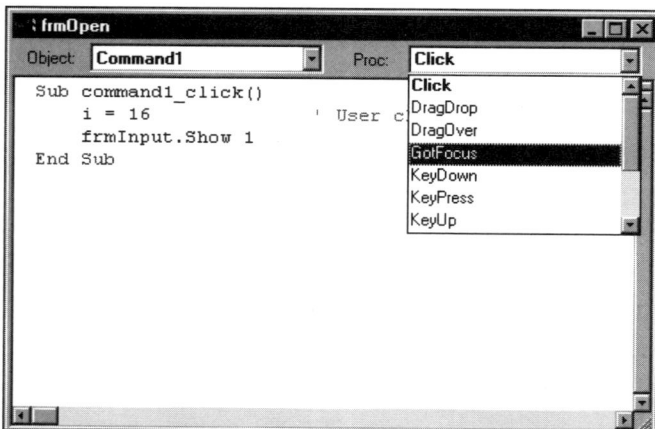

5. Notice that the Click event is shown in bold, but all other events are not in bold. This tells you that the Click event has a coded procedure; the other events do not.

6. On your own, try selecting other items in the Object box, finding out what events are available for an object, and which events already have code associated with them.

Visual Basic's Intelligent Editor

When you're writing code, the editor works alongside you, helping you get your code right the first time. Here are some of the things the editor does to help you:

▶ Predicts what indentation you want when you start a new line

▶ Scans your code as you write it and warns you immediately of any syntax errors

▶ Turns the keywords (such as Private Sub) blue

▶ Turns comments green

▶ Corrects capitalization of names

▶ Standardizes spacing

To try out some of these features, you're going to create a procedure for a new project. You'll type the code shown below in the code window. Then you'll run the program.

```
Private Sub Form_GotFocus()
Dim Count As Double
    Count = 500000
    While Count > 0
        Count = Count - 1
    Wend
    End
End Sub
```

Don't worry if you don't understand these statements now. You're not expected to. You'll learn how they work in later chapters. For now, concentrate on the process of typing them in the code window's editor.

---

1. Start a new project. (Do not save any changes to Atm.)

2. Open the code window for Form1. You can do this by double-clicking the form or by clicking the *View Code* button in the project window.

3. Drop down the *Object* list and choose *Form*. The editor displays an empty Form_Load() procedure.

4. Drop down the *Proc* list and choose *GotFocus*. The editor displays an empty Form_GotFocus() procedure.

5. Position the cursor on the blank line between the Sub and End Sub statements.

6. Press *Tab* once to indent, then type the first line, the *Dim* statement, and press *Enter*. Notice that the editor turns the words *Dim* and *As Double* blue, indicating that it recognizes these keywords.

7. Press *Enter* to start a new line. Notice that the editor automatically indents the new line to the same position as the previous line.

8. Type *count = 500000*, deliberately using a lowercase "c." When you press *Enter*, the editor automatically changes the "c" to uppercase so that it matches the word *Count* in the preceding line.

9. Type the *While* statement but don't put spaces around the > sign. When you press *Enter*, the editor automatically adds spaces around the >.

10. Press *Tab* to indent, then type the statement *Count = Count - 1*. For faster typing, you can use lowercase "c" and omit spacing around the equals and minus signs. The editor will correct the capitalization and insert the spaces.

11. Press *Shift+Tab* to outdent. Then type the *Wend* statement, which the editor turns blue.

12. Type the *End* statement, which the editor turns blue.

13. Press *F5* to run your new procedure. You should see Form1 on your screen for a few seconds, then the program should end and the design environment return. (If you get an error message instead, click *OK* to clear the message and choose *Run | End* to end the program.)

When you select an object in the code window, the editor tries to display the event that you will most likely want. If no events have been coded, it selects the most common event for the object type. For CommandButtons, for example, it chooses the Click event. For forms, it chooses the Load event. If one event has been coded already, it displays that event. If several events have been coded, it displays the most common one.

The editor automatically indents each new line to the same level as the previous line. This is the indentation that you will *most likely* want. As you saw in the previous exercise, you use Tab to indent and Shift+Tab to outdent.

Automatic Syntax Error Detection

If you make a syntax error (that is, an error in the structure of the Basic language), the editor pops up a warning message. Some of the messages are pretty cryptic, but they tell you that there's *something* wrong with the line you just typed. Rereading the line usually reveals the error. Let's try out this feature by intentionally introducing an error into the Form1_Load() procedure.

1. In the While statement, change the > sign to a period (.).

2. Press the *down arrow* key to move the cursor out of the While statement. The editor immediately turns the While statement red and pops up an error message, as shown below.

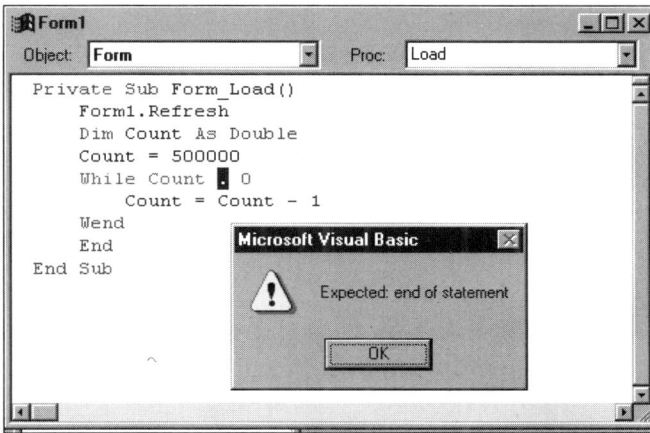

3. Click *OK* to clear the error message.

4. Change the period back to a > sign. The editor immediately removes the red.

5. Press the *down arrow* key to move the cursor out of the While statement. The editor rescans the statement, finds no errors, and turns the word *While* blue.

Using the Edit Menu while Writing Code

Writing code is much like using a word processor. You can cut, paste, delete, and copy text using the Edit menu, just like any other Windows application.

The Edit menu also provides a few more options that you can use while writing code:

▶ *Undo* allows you to undo a change, in case you decide that it isn't what you wanted.

▶ *Redo* allows you to put the change back in if you change your mind.

▶ *Find* helps you find a selected word in your code, so you can locate the place you want to change your code.

▶ *Replace* lets you change a word throughout your code.

▶ *Indent* lets you move the cursor right a tab stop, just like pressing the Tab key.

▶ *Outdent* lets you move your code back a tab stop, just like pressing the Shift+Tab keys.

Customizing the Editor

Visual Basic provides control over how the editor looks and works. When you select Tools|Options from Visual Basic's main window and click on the Editor tab, you'll see the Editor page in the Options dialog box, as shown in Figure 3-7.

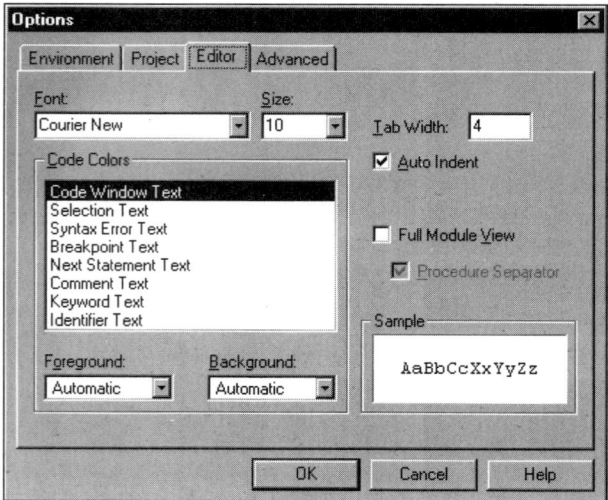

Figure 3-7: You can use the Editor page of the Options dialog box to customize your code window.

You can select the font and size you want to use in the editor using the Font and Size list boxes.

TIP

Your tabs won't line up properly if you use a proportional font, so you'll probably want to use a monospaced font like Courier New or System.

You've already seen how the editor turns keywords blue, errors red, and comments green. The Code Colors group lets you select the colors that you want to use for these and other features in the code window. If you click Keyword Text and look at the Foreground box, it shows a blue color swatch, indicating that the current color selection for keywords is blue. You could drop down the Foreground list and select a different color. And you could select a contrasting color for the background behind the keywords.

Some of the other Code Colors options are shown in Table 3-1.

Table 3-1: Code Colors Options

Option	What Is Affected
Code window text	Text as you type it and before it is scanned
Selection text	Selected text
Syntax error text	Text containing a syntax error
Comment text	Text in comments
Identifier text	Names such as Count and Form1_Load

Four very useful controls in the Editor page of the Options dialog box are: the Tab Width TextBox, the AutoIndent CheckBox, the Full Module View CheckBox, and the Procedure Separator CheckBox.

The *Tab Width* TextBox tells how many characters to indent your code when you press the Tab key. In this book, we use four spaces. If you choose too small a number, then indented code doesn't stand out very well. A number that's too large causes the code to quickly move too close to the right margin of the window. Three and four are very common values to use.

The *AutoIndent* CheckBox also controls code indentation. If it's checked, then when you press the Enter key, Visual Basic inserts a new line in your code window, and automatically tabs over the same amount as the line you were just editing. If you don't have it checked, you can wear out your left pinky by repeatedly tapping the Tab key.

The *Full Module View* CheckBox determines whether to display only one procedure in your code window, or as much code as will reasonably fit. So far, all the code windows you've seen display only one procedure at a time because that's the default setting. But take a look at Figure 3-8, which shows what happens when you check Full Module View.

```
Private Sub Command1_Click()
    Dim i As Integer
    For i = 1 To 20
        If i = 10 Then
            DoIt
        End If
        Command1.Caption = Str$(i)
    Next i
End Sub

Public Sub DoIt()
    Beep
End Sub
```

Figure 3-8: Checking the Full Module View and Procedure Separator CheckBoxes lets Visual Basic fill the code window, separating procedures with lines.

If you check Full Module View, then you have the option of checking *Procedure Separator*. If it's checked, then Visual Basic draws a line between procedures in your code window. Since we have the Procedure Separator box checked in Figure 3-8, there's a line between the procedures.

Code Practice

Later in this chapter, you're going to practice some debugging techniques, and you'll need some code to work on. The following exercise gives you a chance to practice using the editor while you enter the code that you'll use later on. You're going to write code for a CommandButton, so that each time the user clicks it, it counts up from 1 to 20 and beeps when it reaches 10.

In Part III we cover the Basic language in greater detail, so we're not going to describe how the code works here.

NOTE

1. Start a new project in Visual Basic.

2. Paint a CommandButton on the form.

3. Change the button's caption to *Click here!*

4. Double-click the CommandButton to open the code window.

5. Change the code so it looks like this:

```
Private Sub Command1_Click()
    Dim i As Integer
    For i = 1 To 20
        Command1.Caption = Str$(i)
        Command1.Refresh
        If i = 10 Then
        DoIt 'This calls another procedure, named DoIt
        End If
    Next i
End Sub
```

6. From the main window's *Insert* menu, select *Procedure, then* type *DoIt,* and click the *OK* button. Notice that Visual Basic put the following code in the code window for you:

```
Public Sub DoIt()

End Sub
```

7. Insert a Beep statement, like this:

```
Public Sub DoIt()
    Beep
End Sub
```

8. Save your project under the name *CodePrac.*

This is the first time that you have created a procedure that is not associated with a specific object and event. Notice that the editor used the word *Public* instead of *Private* on the Sub statement; that's because you used Insert | Procedure to create the procedure. Public makes the procedure available to all the other procedures in the project, so now you can call DoIt from many other places in your project. In this particular example, of course, you're just calling it from Command1_Click. You'll learn more about public and private procedures in Chapter 12.

THE COLOR PALETTE

You saw in Chapter 1 how you can change the colors of the current control by setting properties such as BackColor and ForeColor. Another way makes use of the color palette, shown in Figure 3-9, which you open by selecting View | Color Palette from the main window. Because the color palette window stays on the screen until you close it, it is particularly handy when you plan to color several controls in a row, especially if you need to experiment a bit to find the most effective color scheme.

Figure 3-9: You can use the color palette to change the foreground and background colors of the currently selected control.

The block on the left, built of two concentric squares, tells the color palette whether it's working on the foreground or background color. If you click the center square, then the color palette is ready to change the foreground color. Likewise, if you click the outer square, the color palette is ready to change the background color. Then, all you need to do is select the color you want from the palette.

Let's set the colors for the small program that you're now working on.

---

1. Close the code window.

2. Choose *View | Color Palette* to open the color palette window.

3. Arrange Form1 and the color palette so you can see them both at once.

4. Select *Form1*.

5. In the color palette, click the outside part of the square to select the BackColor feature, as shown here:

Click here for BackColor

6. Choose a light color for the form. You'll see the form change as soon as you select a color. If you don't like your first color choice, try another one.

Despite the fact that Visual Basic gives you a BackColor property for CommandButtons, you'll find that you can't change the background color of a CommandButton.

Well, we've talked about several windows so far in this chapter—the main window, toolbox, project, Properties, code, and the color palette. You'll meet a couple of new ones later on, but for now, let's turn our attention to how you, as a programmer, use the windows to accomplish your programming tasks.

USING THE ENVIRONMENT TO CREATE PROGRAMS

You had a small taste of your programming tasks in Chapter 1, when you developed your Hello World program. As you recall, you designed a form, wrote some code, and tested your program. We'll dig more deeply into these tasks in this section, as well as another crucial programmer responsibility—debugging.

Designing the Form

The easiest part of Visual Basic is designing the forms. When you write a program with Visual Basic, you start out by creating the main form for your application. To do so, you move the form to a convenient place and resize it by dragging its border. Then you're ready to paint on some controls.

Using the Toolbox

An artist painting a picture has a palette of colors to choose from. You have a palette of tools to work with: the toolbox. As you may remember from Chapter 1, you can use one of two methods to draw a control onto the form. You can double-click the control in the toolbox, which places the control in the center of the form; or, you can click the control in the toolbox once to select it, put the mouse at the place where you want one corner of the control, hold down the left mouse button, and drag the mouse to the desired location of the opposite corner of the control. Once your control is on the form, you can customize it by dragging it to a new location or resizing it. The status area on the toolbar shows you the exact location and size of your new control.

Using the Properties Window

You can customize more than just the size and location of your controls. Each control has a set of properties that affect the way it looks or operates. The Properties window lets you examine and/or change the properties of the currently selected control.

One property that every control has is Name, which determines the name of the control (see Figure 3-10). Visual Basic assigns a default name to each control, such as *Form1* or *Label1*, but most programmers replace these names with more meaningful ones, such as *frmOpen* and *lblHello*. The control name is important, because you may have several of the same type of control on the form, and remembering which one is Command1, for example, which is Command2, and which Command3 can be difficult. Giving controls meaningful names such as cmdOK, cmdCancel, and cmdApply lets you tell them apart in your code.

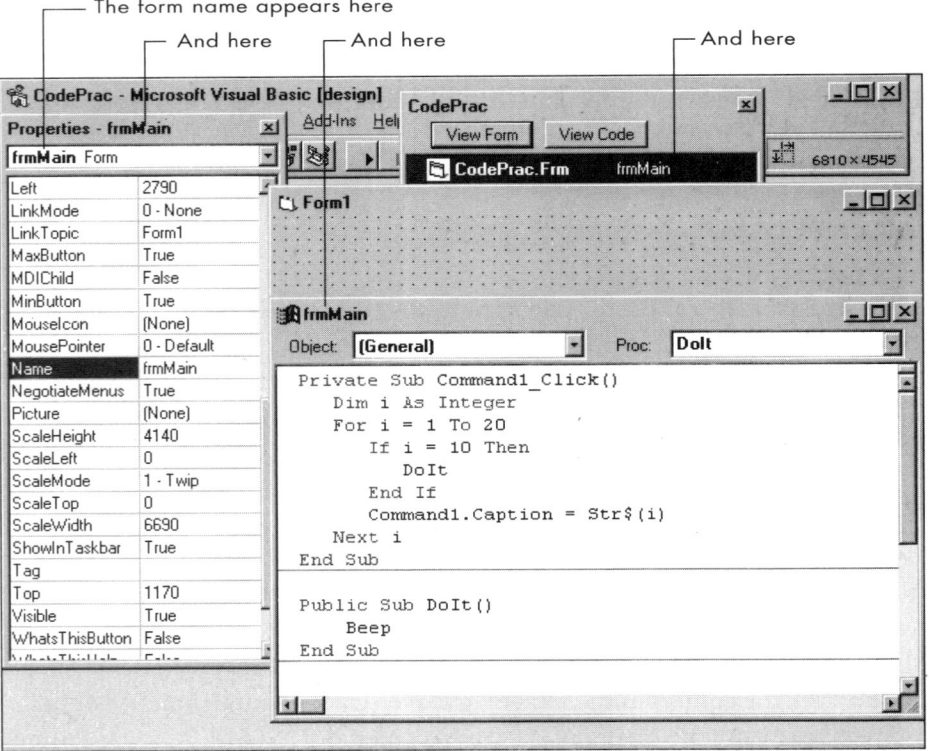

Figure 3-10: The name that you assign to a control appears in many places in the Visual Basic environment.

It's conventional, but not required, to assign names that start with a lowercase, three-character indication of type, as in chkBold (for a CheckBox), optMax (for an OptionButton), and txtUserName (for a TextBox).

Using the Edit Menu while Designing a Form

The Cut, Copy, Paste, and Delete commands on the Edit menu work just about as you'd expect. If you select a control on a form, and copy it, it will be left on the form, but another copy of it will be placed in the Clipboard.

If you find that you're going to put many of the same type of control on a form, and they're supposed to have similar properties, here's a quick tip to save you some time: Draw one of the controls on the form and customize its properties. Then you can copy the control and paste it onto the form as many times as you need. Each of the new controls will have the same properties as the first one.

The Edit menu contains four other useful items when you're painting controls onto a form. The *Bring to Front* option tells a control that it's on top. This is useful when two controls overlap. The one on top is wholly displayed, and the one in back is partially obstructed. The *Send to Back* option tells a control that it's in back.

The *Align to Grid* option tells a control to put its corners on grid dots. This is useful when you're cleaning up a form and you want to ensure that all the controls line up. Once your form is laid out exactly as you want, you might choose the *Lock Controls* option. When you do so, controls on the form can't be moved or resized. To unlock the controls, just select the Lock Controls option again to uncheck it.

Another way to lock and unlock controls is to use the Lock Controls icon from the toolbar. When you do so, the icon changes to an Unlock Controls icon. The Unlock and Lock Controls icons are shown here.

Customizing the Design Environment

Visual Basic draws the grid of dots on your form so you can line up controls in a pleasing way. You can change the grid spacing very easily. Visual Basic also lets you decide whether all controls must align to the grid or not. You can change these parameters by choosing the Tools | Options command from the main window. When you do, you'll see the Options dialog box, shown in Figure 3-11.

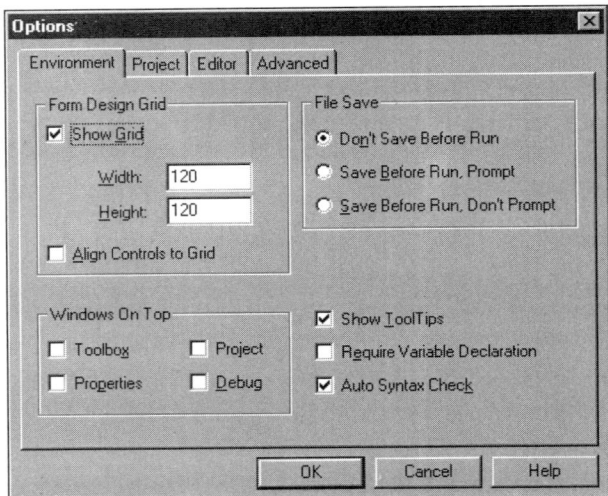

Figure 3-11: From the Options dialog box, you can change some aspects of how Visual Basic works.

The frame labeled *Form Design Grid* controls these parameters. Checking the *Show Grid* CheckBox tells Visual Basic to display the grid on forms. If you check the *Align Controls to Grid* CheckBox, Visual Basic forces you to place the corners of controls on a grid point.

You should make sure the CheckBox labeled *Show ToolTips* is checked while you're here. This is what controls whether Visual Basic prints the names of icons in the toolbox and toolbar when you rest the mouse on them.

Debugging

You'll almost never write perfect code the first time. Professional programmers must fight program bugs all the time. Some programmer a long time ago described programming as "Putting bugs into a program." So don't be discouraged if your programs don't work correctly the first time.

Once you have written some code, you need to test your program to find out where the errors are and then remove them. Then you may have to do it again, because removing some errors often reveals others.

Visual Basic provides quite a bit of support for program debugging. Visual Basic can check for many common errors while you're typing your code. Other errors you have to check for while you're running your code.

Automatic Syntax Checking

You've already seen how Visual Basic automatically scans a statement as soon as you complete it, reporting any syntax errors immediately. You can turn this feature off if you wish (you turn the Auto Syntax Check off or on from the Environment tab of the Tools | Options window you saw in Figure 3-11), but you would be foolish to do so.

Logic Error Checking

The rest of your error checking occurs while you're running your program to identify errors in logic. Logic errors are often difficult to pin down. You know something went wrong because you got an erroneous result, but you don't know at which point the mistake was made. To help you home in on a logic error, Visual Basic allows you to control which statements to execute and when to execute them. It also allows you to examine the values for your data items step-by-step; this can often pinpoint the moment at which a wrong result appears and hence, the statement that produced it.

The Run Menu

Normally, when you run your program, it runs extremely fast. After all, your computer is capable of processing millions of instructions per second. Each Basic statement might result in hundreds of instructions to the processor, so a Basic program containing 100 statements will still produce far less than a million instructions. Theoretically, it runs in a flash, but because it must access agonizingly slow devices such as the disk drive, the printer, and the keyboard (along with the slowest "device" of all, the user), it takes much longer in reality. Even programs that don't otherwise access such devices have to be loaded from the hard disk, so there's always a long wait at the beginning.

Processor speeds are often reported in *MIPS*—millions of instructions per second.

Since computers are so much faster than we are, we can't possibly watch what's going on in a computer and detect what's going wrong unless we can slow down the computer. That's what the options on the Run menu, shown in Figure 3-12, do for us.

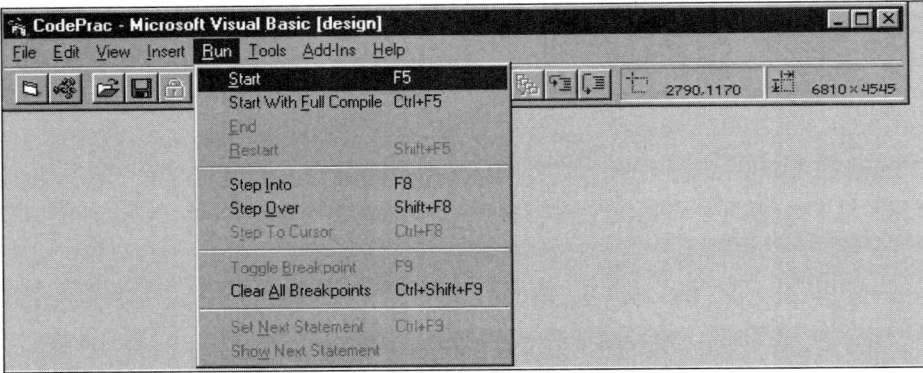

Figure 3-12: The commands on the Run menu help you test and debug your program.

Let's try running the program that you created earlier, called CodePrac. (In the step-by-step instructions, keypresses in parentheses are the shortcut keys for commands.)

1. If CodePrac isn't currently open on your screen, open it now.

2. Choose *Run | Start* (F5).

3. Click the CommandButton. You'll see the caption change from 1 to 20 (although it probably changes so fast that you can't read all the numbers). You'll also hear it beep when it reaches 10.

4. Try clicking the CommandButton several more times. The same thing happens each time.

5. Pull down the *Run* menu and notice that the first item is now called *Break*. When a program is running, *Start* is replaced by *Break*, which forces your program to pause. Choose **Break** (Ctrl+Break).

6. Try clicking the CommandButton again. All you get is a beep. Why? Because the program is paused.

7. Pull down the *Run* menu again and notice that the first item is now called *Continue*. When a program is paused, *Continue* ends the pause and lets it continue from exactly where it was when it was paused. Choose *Continue* (F5).

8. Click the CommandButton again. It should function as before.

9. Now choose *Run | Restart*. Notice that the CommandButton is once again labeled *Click here!*. That's because the Restart command started the program again from the beginning.

10. Choose *Run | End* to terminate the program and return to the design environment.

What's the difference between Break and End? *Break* pauses execution without losing your place in the program, so that you can pick up and go on with the Continue command. But *End* terminates the program, returning you to the design environment. Similarly, *Continue* resumes where you paused, but *Restart* goes back to the beginning.

TIP It pays to know your shortcut keys when testing a program, as they'll save you a lot of time. F5 is the shortcut key for both Start and Continue. So to start the program, you press F5. While it's running, you pause it by pressing Ctrl+Break. And to continue after the pause, you press F5 again. You can start and pause program execution as many times as you want.

While your program is stopped, the statement that Visual Basic intends to run next is highlighted, as shown in Figure 3-13.

The next group of items on the Run menu, *Step Into*, *Step Over*, and *Step To Cursor*, let you run your program a limited amount. Let's try out Step Into.

1. Choose *Run | Step Into.* Visual Basic starts the program and displays the form.

2. Arrange your screen so that you can see both the form and the code window.

3. Visual Basic won't start executing any procedures until you give it an event to process. Click the **Command1** button to invoke the Command1_Click procedure. The code window pops to the top and Visual Basic highlights the statement it will execute next.

4. The shortcut key for Run | Step Into is F8. Press **F8** once to execute the next statement. Nothing happens on the form, because the statement did not affect the form. Visual Basic executed the statement and highlighted the next one.

5. Keep pressing **F8** and watch the results on the form. Eventually, you should see the CommandButton's caption change from 1 to 2 to 3 and so on. When it reaches 10, the DoIt procedure is called and the computer should beep.

```
Form1                                           _ □ ×
Object: Command1            ▼   Proc: Click               ▼
    Private Sub Command1_Click()
        Dim i As Integer
        For i = 1 To 20
            Command1.Caption = Str$(i)
            Command1.Refresh
|           If i = 10 Then
                DoIt
            End If
        Next i
    End Sub
```

Figure 3-13: The line of code with the box around it is the next line that Visual Basic intends to execute.

Step Into and Step Over are very similar. Each one executes just one statement at a time, which is called *stepping* through a program. The difference lies in what happens when the current procedure calls another procedure, as our sample program calls the procedure named DoIt. *Step Into* executes the called procedure one step at a time (that is, it steps *into* the called procedure). But *Step Over* executes the called procedure as if it was one statement (that is, it steps *over* the called procedure). If you need to debug the called procedure, you use Step Into. When you know that the called procedure works because you've already tested and debugged it previously, you use Step Over.

As you step through a program, notice also the effect on Visual Basic's main window, where the expressions *[run]* and *[break]* alternate in the title bar and the icons on the toolbar constantly change. You'll learn about the toolbar icons a little later.

If you only had the Step Into and Step Over menu items, it could take you hours of debugging to get to the point where you identify the error. Fortunately, Visual Basic provides several more options for executing your program up to a certain point, then pausing. *Step To Cursor*, for example, executes the program until it reaches the statement containing the cursor.

A *breakpoint* is a statement where Visual Basic pauses during execution until you choose Continue. The *Toggle Breakpoint* command identifies the current statement as a breakpoint. When you run the program using the Run and Continue commands, it pauses when it reaches a breakpoint. If the current statement is already a breakpoint, the Toggle Breakpoint command clears it so that it is no longer a breakpoint. *Clear All Breakpoints* turns off all the breakpoints you have set.

Visual Basic highlights breakpoints in dark red by default. You can change the highlight color by choosing Tools | Options and clicking the Editor tab.

Once you execute a line that has a bug and fix it, you may want to run the line over again to see if the change you made really fixed the bug. You don't necessarily want to restart the program—it could take too long. Fortunately, Visual Basic provides a method for you to choose the next statement to execute. The next selection on the Run menu is *Set Next Statement*. You can simply place the cursor on the line you want to run next, and choose Set Next Statement to tell Visual Basic to execute that line next.

When you debug code, sometimes you have to move the code window around to look at other code in your program. When you do, it's easy to lose your place. If you want to find the next line that Visual Basic is going to execute, just choose the *Show Next Statement* command from the Run menu, and Visual Basic will adjust the code window to display the next statement.

Now you know all the tools Visual Basic provides for controlling which statements to execute. However, you can't tell if a program is failing just by seeing what code it executes. You also need to look at the values the program is using, so you can see if these values are correct.

The Debug Window

When you run your program, Visual Basic opens a new window on your screen, the Debug window, shown in Figure 3-14. The top part of the Debug window shows the status of the program: what procedure is currently running and whether the program is running or paused.

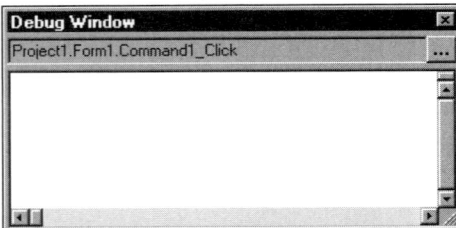

Figure 3-14: The Debug window gives you feedback from Visual Basic's built-in debugger.

The bottom pane has two uses: It displays any values that you're watching, and it displays any messages your program sends to it.

The Tools Menu

The Tools menu, shown in Figure 3-15, is a catch-all menu. As you can see, it has five divisions. The first division is the one that interests us right now. It has four options that let you examine and change the values that your program is using.

The *Add Watch* command lets you tell Visual Basic that you want it to continually display the value of a data item in the Debug window. When you do so, Visual Basic displays the Add Watch dialog, in Figure 3-16, to prompt you for the data you want to watch. Every time your program stops or pauses, Visual Basic displays the data in the Debug window.

The Tools | Edit Watch command brings up a similar dialog box, shown in Figure 3-17. With the Edit Watch dialog box, you can change a watch expression or delete it altogether by clicking the Delete button.

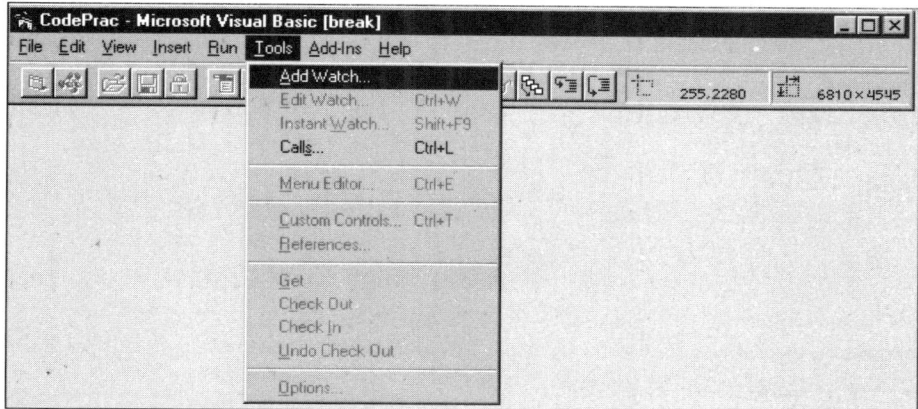

Figure 3-15: The top section of the Tools menu provides access to the data your program is using.

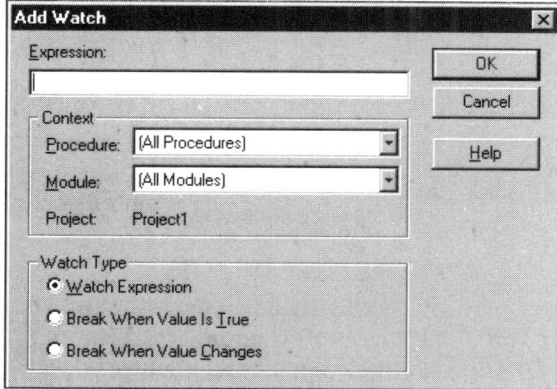

Figure 3-16: The Add Watch dialog allows you to choose the data you want to watch in the Debug window.

The *Instant Watch* command is available only at run time. It allows you to instantly see the value of an expression. You select the expression in the code window, then choose Instant Watch. Figure 3-18 shows the Instant Watch dialog box after we've selected the text "i" in a Visual Basic program.

If you decide that you want to add the expression to your list of watch expressions after you examine its value initially, you can click the Add button to add it to your list.

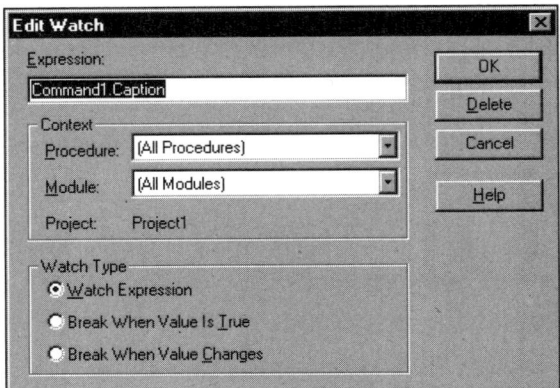

Figure 3-17: You can use the Edit Watch dialog to change or delete existing watch expressions from the Debug window.

Figure 3-18: The Instant Watch dialog box allows you to select a part of your code and immediately see its value.

The toolbar in the main window has some of the common menu equivalents as shortcuts. Figure 3-19 shows a section of the toolbar, labeled with its equivalent menu selections.

Now that you've met the debugging commands, let's work an example to get our feet wet. We're going to continue with the code we used in our last step-by-step exercise.

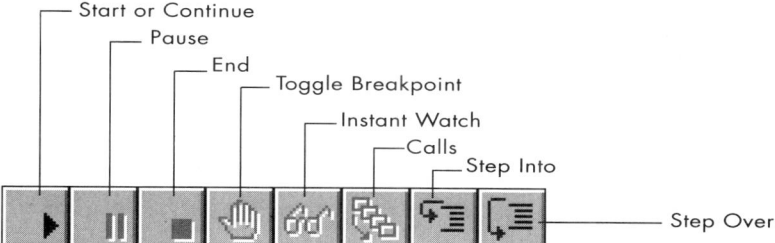

Figure 3-19: The toolbar in the main window offers these buttons as shortcuts to the indicated menu selections.

1. Click the mouse cursor on the line that says:

```
Command1.Caption = Str$(i)
```

2. Select *Run | Step To Cursor* (Ctrl+F8), and your program will start running.

3. If you can't see your form, move the windows around so that you can see the CommandButton. Notice that it says *Click here!* on it. Click the CommandButton icon to generate the Command1_Click event.

   Now your program should pause, and Visual Basic is ready to execute the statement you just selected.

4. Select *Run | Step Over* (Shift+F8) from the main window, or click the Step Over icon (shown here) on the toolbar. Notice that the CommandButton now says 1 and the highlight has moved down one line in the code window. Visual Basic executed one line.

5. Now click the mouse cursor on the line that says *DoIt*, and set a breakpoint by selecting *Run | Toggle Breakpoint* (F9 or the Toggle Breakpoint icon).

6. Select *Run | Continue* (F5 or the Continue icon) to continue executing the program.

   Notice that your program immediately stopped again, but now the CommandButton says *10*, and Visual Basic is ready to execute the line that says DoIt.

7. Let's inspect the value of the variable named *i* by selecting i in the previous line. Now select *Tools*|*Instant Watch* (Shift+F9 or the Instant Watch icon). When you do, you'll see the dialog box that follows:

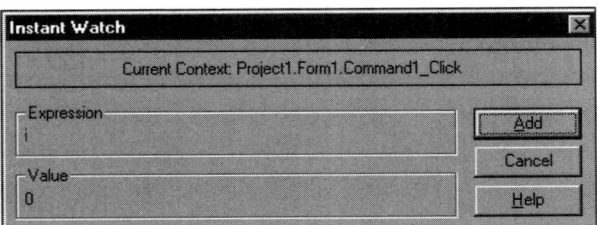

8. As you can see, the value of i is 10. Click the *Add* button, and notice that the Debug window has a watch added to it as shown here:

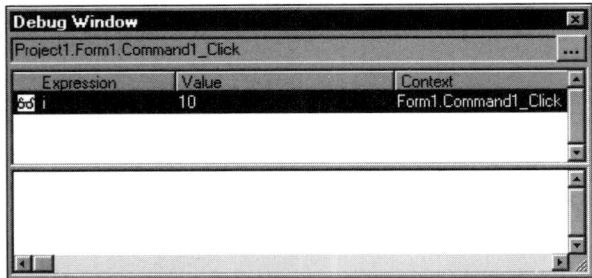

9. Let's also tell the debugger to watch the caption of the CommandButton. To do so, select *Tools*|*Add Watch* to get the Add Watch dialog box. Enter *Command1.Caption* in the Expression box, and click *OK*. Now the Debug window will watch the values of both i and Command1.Caption.

10. Now step over the program by repeatedly pressing Shift+F8 or clicking the Step Over icon and watch the effect on the CommandButton and on the expressions in the Add Watch dialog box. Stop when i reaches 20.

Window Management

Programming is an iterative process. You don't just sit down, draw a form, add all the code at once, compile it, and you're done. You develop one feature at a time, test and debug that, save it to disk, then start to work on the next feature.

You'll typically bounce around between the form, the code window, the Debug window, the Properties window, and so on. You probably don't have a 50-inch monitor to work on, so you're going to run out of screen space, as you have probably already experienced in this chapter. You use the View menu (see Figure 3-20) to help you navigate among all the windows you can access from Visual Basic.

The first two options, *Code* and *Form*, allow you to switch between the code and form windows for a particular form that you're working on. If you're on a code window, and want to see the form associated with it, just select View | Form. Conversely, selecting View | Code shows the code window for the form you're working on. These two commands duplicate the function of the View Form and View Code buttons in the project window.

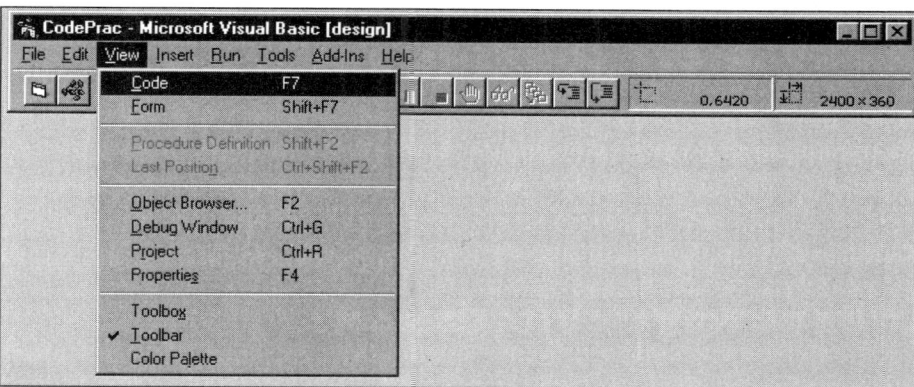

Figure 3-20: The View menu allows you to access all the windows that Visual Basic offers.

The *Procedure Definition* option helps you find a procedure, given a reference to it in a code window. If you're working on a piece of code that calls a procedure, and you want to see the procedure definition, just highlight the procedure name and select View | Procedure Definition. Visual Basic will then display the procedure definition in the code window.

Last Position allows you to backtrack through the last four lines of code you edited. If you're editing or debugging code and you want to track backward through the lines you've been working on, you can use the View | Last Position (Ctrl+Shift+F2) command. Remember, though, it only works for the last four lines you've worked on. Let's try out the Procedure Definition and Last Position commands right now.

1. In the code window, click anywhere in the expression *DoIt*.

2. Choose *View | Procedure Definition* (Shift+F2). The DoIt procedure appears in the code window.

3. Choose *View | Last Position* (Ctrl+Shift+F2). Remember that it only works for the last four lines you've worked on. Try it several times to see what happens.

The remaining commands on the View menu allow you to display the various Visual Basic windows. The last three selections allow you to view the toolbox, toolbar, and color palette. We haven't talked about the Object Browser window yet, so let's do that now.

The Object Browser

The Object Browser window, shown in Figure 3-21, is a powerful management tool in itself. From the Object Browser window, you can easily determine what events and properties are supported by any object in your project. Additionally, it can take you to the source code for any event procedure you have in your project. Finally, it can take you directly to the help screen for any object or property that has a help screen defined for it.

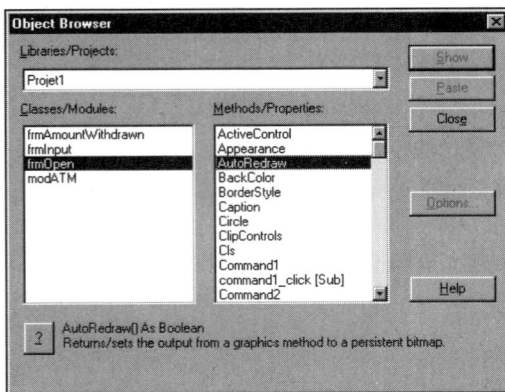

Figure 3-21: You can use the Object Browser window to navigate through your project.

By default, the Libraries/Project box holds your project name in it, so you can examine your own code. You can select the module in your project that you want to examine from the Classes/Modules box, and all the event procedures and methods that the selected module understands appear in the Methods/Properties box.

Once you select something in the Methods/Properties box, text appears to the right of the Help (question mark) button that briefly describes the item you selected. If the Help button isn't grayed out, then clicking it will take you to the help screen appropriate to the method or property. If you select an event procedure on the form, then the Show button becomes active. Clicking this button opens the code window and positions the cursor in the selected procedure.

To access the Object Browser, choose View | Object Browser (F2) or click the Object Browser icon (shown here) in the toolbar.

CONTEXT MENUS

You're hard at work designing forms for a new application. You've got three forms open on your screen, the toolbox, the Properties window, and the color palette. Now you want to add a custom control to your toolbox, so you reach for the Tools menu—where the heck is it? The main window is buried somewhere under the mess, and it will take several moves to find it. But there's an easier way to access the Custom Controls command—just pop up the toolbox's context menu, as shown in Figure 3-22.

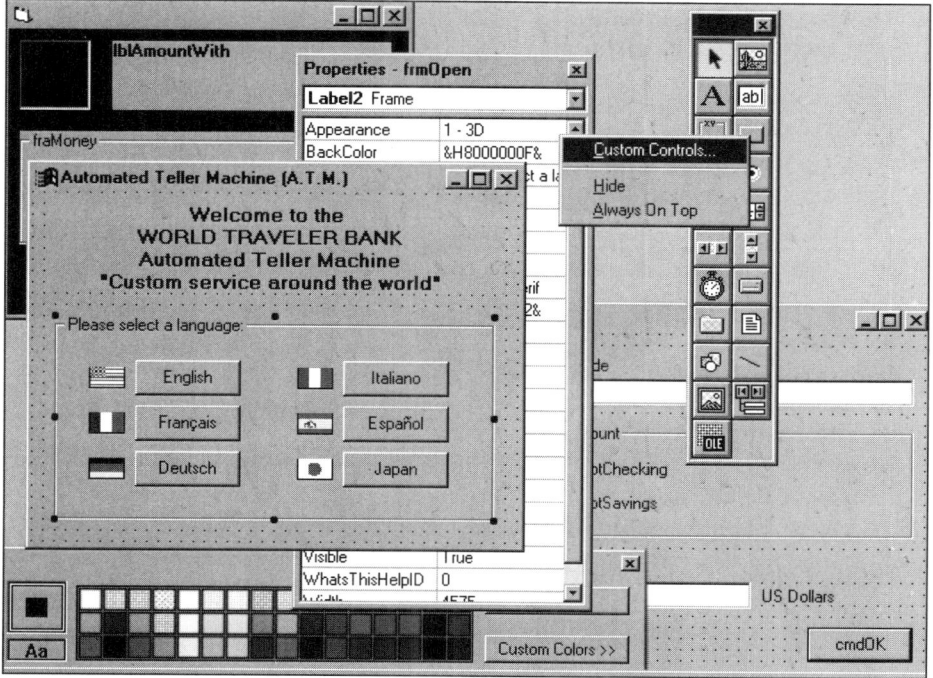

Figure 3-22: Context menus, accessed by right-clicking various parts of the screen, provide the commands you're most likely to want right now.

A *context menu* is a floating menu that provides a collection of commands specific to your current task. They might come from several different menus in the menu bar. You pop up a context menu by right-clicking the area where you are working. Let's take a look at a few of Visual Basic's context menus.

1. Right-click the toolbox to see the context menu shown in Figure 3-22. (In Windows 95, if you right-click the title bar of the toolbox, you get a different context menu, identical to the control menu.)

2. Choose *Always On Top*. Then try to cover the toolbox with another window. It can't be done.

3. Right-click the toolbox again and unselect *Always On Top*.

4. Right-click the Properties window. Notice that it also offers an Always On Top feature.

5. Right-click the project window. This context menu includes several file management commands plus the Hide and Always On Top options.

6. Right-click a blank area on the form. You get commands to view the code window, edit menu items for the form, lock the controls, paste something from the Clipboard, and view the Properties window.

7. Now click a control on the form. Some of the commands on this menu are the same as the form's context menu, such as View Code and Properties, but you also get commands to Cut, Copy, or Delete the control, Align to Grid, and Bring to Front or Send to Back.

8. The context menus provide a very quick and easy way to copy controls:

   a) Right-click a control and choose *Copy*.

   b) Right-click the form and choose *Paste*.

   c) When Visual Basic asks if you want to create a control array, answer *No*.

   It's as easy as that.

9. Right-click the code window. The context menu provides some familiar commands, such as Copy, Paste, and Toggle Breakpoint. The three Break options are advanced features that we won't cover in this book.

SUMMARY

We hope you're feeling a little more comfortable with the Visual Basic environment now. You've learned a lot in this chapter about the features and the mechanics of the various windows and how you pull them together to achieve your programming tasks.

Don't worry if typing code and debugging still seem awkward to you. Practice makes perfect, and you'll get a lot more practice as you continue with this book. We'll occasionally remind you in Notes and Tips of some of the things you read about here.

There are a few nooks and crannies that we didn't explore, but we covered all the features that you're going to need to get familiar with Visual Basic. There's one major feature of the environment that we have yet to discuss — the help facility. That's covered in the next chapter.

CHAPTER OBJECTIVES

There's no way we can cover all of Visual Basic in this book. And there's no way you'll remember every detail of what we do cover. But we can show you how to find information on your own when you need to. That's what this chapter will do. You'll learn about:

 The Help library: What's in it and how you use it

► Visual Basic Books Online

► Learning Microsoft Visual Basic (the tutorial provided with Visual Basic)

► Getting outside help: Microsoft Product Support Services, Microsoft Knowledge Base, Microsoft Software Library, and a lot more

Getting Help

When you want to look up details on the Visual Basic statements, controls, environment, and so on, you'll reach for the Help library first.

THE HELP LIBRARY

The Help library contains:

▶ A complete language reference so you can look up statements such as Sub, events such as Click, and controls such as Label

▶ A section on how to use Visual Basic, with topics such as Setting Properties and Writing and Debugging Code

▶ A glossary of terms such as *bit* and *breakpcint*

▶ A section on the development environment, which explains how to use such things as the color palette and the Propert:es window

▶ How to access data in databases

▶ How to access outside Help

▶   Additional topics for the Professional edition, such as Custom Controls, Crystal Reports, and VisData

▶   Additional topics for the Enterprise edition, such as SourceSafe and Remote Data Objects

▶   Lots and lots of programming examples throughout the library

The Visual Basic Help library actually comprises several .hlp files in your Visual Basic folders. For example, there are separate files for Visual Basic itself, the control reference, the Enterprise edition, the samples that are included in the Help library, and so on.

As an experienced Windows user, you probably know a lot about using Help libraries, so we're not going to spend much time on the details. We'll just highlight the basics, then concentrate on lesser-known features such as Bookmarks and Annotations.

Accessing the Help Library

You can access the Help Library from the Help menu, the F1 key, or the Object Browser. Some dialog boxes also have a Help command button. Once you have entered the system by any of these means, you can travel to any topic in the library.

The Help menu includes two commands that act as a gateway into the library: *Contents* and *Search for Help On*. In Windows 95, both commands open the window named Help Topics: Visual Basic Help, as shown in Figure 4-1.

Your Help library might have different contents from what we show here, depending on which edition of Visual Basic you have installed. For example, if you installed the Standard edition, you won't have Custom Control Help or Enterprise Help. If you're using an earlier version of Windows, your Contents screen will look different but contain essentially the same topics.

The Search For Help On command takes you to the Index page of the same window, whereas the Contents command arrives at the Contents page or the Find page, whichever you used last. No matter which page you start on, you can access the others by clicking their tabs.

Figure 4-1: The Help Topics window gives you three ways to find a Help topic.

Contents Page

The Contents page uses three icons to represent types of entries:

▶ A closed book represents a closed category; you double-click the entry to expand it so that its contents are visible.

▶ An open book represents an expanded category; its contents are indented underneath it; double-click the entry to hide the contents again.

▶ A page with a question mark represents an actual topic; you double-click the entry to read the topic. This opens the topic window and closes the Help Topics window.

The Index Page

It's often faster and easier to find a topic from the index, shown in Figure 4-2, which is much like an index in a book. You can locate a topic by scrolling through the list or by typing the word or phrase you're looking for in the text box at the top.

Figure 4-2: The Index page provides an index to the topics in the Help library.

You often don't have to type a complete word because the list scrolls with each letter you type. By the time you have typed two or three letters, the topic you want usually appears on the screen or you'll be able to see from the visible entries that it's not in the list.

The Find Page

Help indexes are created by the people who create the Help library, often the same programmers who create the application. We don't want to knock their abilities; after all, we're programmers, and you may be or soon will be. Let's just gently say that people who know an application inside-out often don't understand how users will approach it—especially how they'll try to use the Help index. The very words users want to look up often don't appear in the index.

Windows 95 offers a marvelous solution to this dilemma, called Find. Find provides a searchable index of *every word* in the Help library, including *a*, *an*, and *the!* If the word you want is mentioned anywhere in the library, Find will locate it.

Find also includes two other helpful search features:

▶ Searching for complete phrases, such as *Bill Gates* or *custom controls*

▶ Searching for words or phrases that are similar to the one you enter

The first time you use Find, Windows 95 must create the index. You get to choose from optional features like the two listed above.

The more features you choose, the longer it takes to create the index, the larger the index file will be on your hard disk, and the slower Find will work.

Let's find out if your index already exists. (Skip this exercise if you don't have Windows 95.)

1. Choose *Help | Contents*.

2. Click the *Find* tab. If you see an animated message *Loading Word List*, your index has already been created, and you can skip the rest of this exercise. If you see the Find Setup Wizard window, shown here, your index has not been created and you should go on to Step 3.

3. If you don't want to create the index now, click *Cancel* and skip the rest of this exercise. If you do want to create the index now, click *Next* and go on to Step 4.

4. The Setup Wizard next asks how much of the Find facilities you want to install. Your choices are:

   a) *Minimize database size* saves disk space but omits features such as phrase searching and similarity searching.

   b) *Maximize search capabilities* creates a much larger database but provides the full set of search capabilities.

   c) *Customize search capabilities* lets you choose which facilities you want to install, and is not covered here.

   Click the option you want to install, then click *Next*.

5. If you did not select the Customize option, the next window merely tells you to click *Finish* to create the index. If you selected the Customize option, the Setup Wizard walks you through the process of selecting features. Then you arrive at the Finish page.

   When you click Finish, you'll see an animated message while the index is created. (It could take several minutes.) Finally, the Find page appears in the Help Topics window.

Figure 4-3 shows what the Find page looks like. To use the Find index, type the word that you are looking for in Box 1. In Box 2, Find lists every word in the index starting with the letters that you typed. In Box 3, it lists every topic containing those words. You can often shorten the list in Box 3 by selecting only one or two of the words in Box 2.

If you type two or more words, Box 2 builds a list for each word. For example, if you type "hard drive" (don't include the quotes), the first list shows words such as *hard, hardly,* and *harden,* and the second list shows words such as *drive, drives, driver,* and *drivers.* Only the last list is displayed. The other lists are represented by three dots.

Box 3 then shows all topics containing at least one word from each list, not necessarily as a phrase. Eligible topics might contain *hard* and *driver, hardly* and *drive,* or *harden* and *drives.*

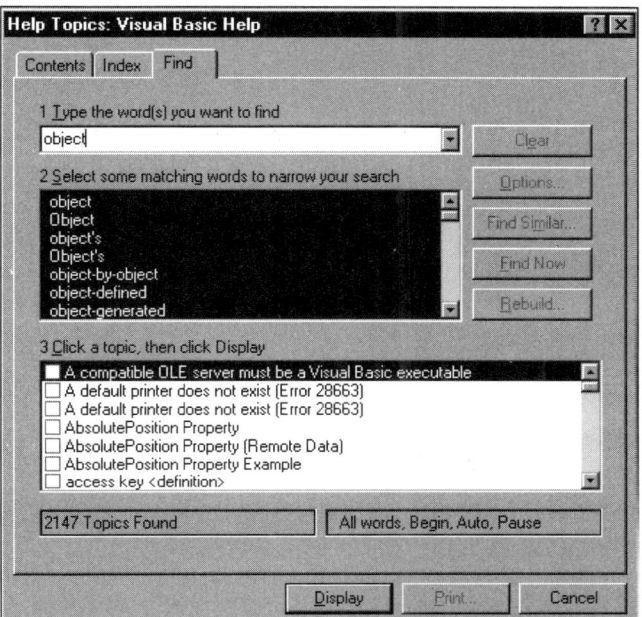

Figure 4-3: By default, Find lists every Help topic containing a word starting with the letters that you type.

You can limit each list to useful words. As you type "hard", for example, and before you type the space following it, you can see the list of words starting with *hard*. Select the ones you want to search for. Then type the space and the word "drive" to see the second list. Again, select the words you want to search for, and you'll produce a much more reasonable list.

If instead you want to search for the phrase *hard drive* and you have installed the phrase-searching capability, you can click the Options button to open a dialog box where you can check the phrase option.

If you still can't find the topic you want and you have installed the similarity searching feature, you can select topics in Box 3 (so that an X appears in their check boxes), then click the Find Similar button. Find then lists all topics related to the selected topics.

With all these search capabilities at your fingertips, if you can't find the topic you want, it probably doesn't exist.

The Object Browser

Suppose you're designing a form and you want to find out more about the
BorderStyle property. You could use the Contents, Index, or Find feature, but
another quick way to get there uses the Object Browser, shown in Figure 4-4.

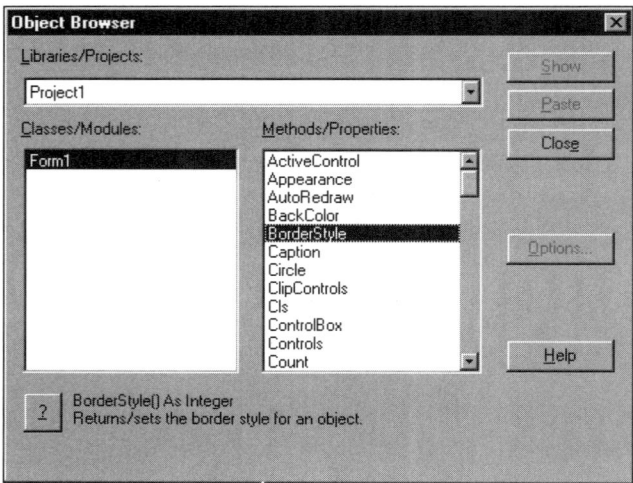

Figure 4-4: The Object Browser makes it easy to find Help topics for objects in your
application.

Let's try out this facility.

1. Choose *View|Object Browser* or click the Object Browser icon.

2. In the *Classes/Modules* box, if *Form1* is not already selected, click
   it. The properties for Form1 appear in the Methods/Properties
   box. Methods are explained in Chapter 6.

3. Click the *BorderStyle* property. A brief and somewhat cryptic
   explanation of BorderStyle appears next to the Help icon.

4. Click the Help icon to open the Help topic for BorderStyle.

In rare cases, the Help icon is dimmed, indicating that the selected item does
not have a Help topic.

Navigating among Topics

Once a topic is on your screen, you can easily travel to other topics. Figure 4-5 shows a typical topic window and the types of navigation features it provides.

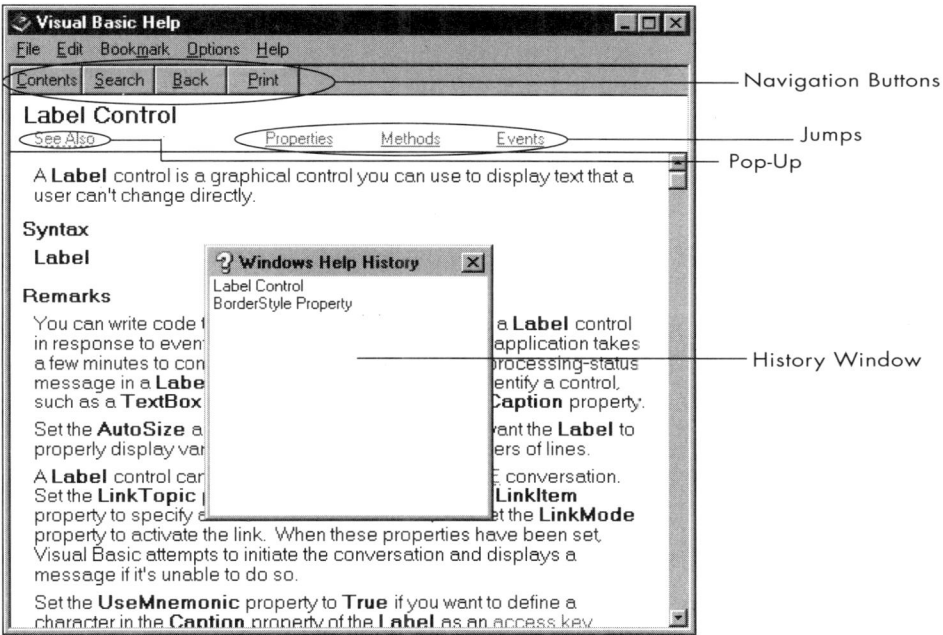

Figure 4-5: A topic window contains several navigational features.

Navigation Buttons

Directly underneath the menu bar is a button bar, containing these navigation buttons:

▶ *Contents* returns you to the Contents page or the Find page, whichever you used last.

▶ *Search* returns you to the Index page.

▶ *Back* returns you to the previous topic that you viewed. If it's dimmed, this is the first topic you have viewed since opening the Help library.

Some windows also include >> and << buttons, which move forward or backward one topic in the list of contents. (<< is not the same as the Back button, which returns to the previous topic that you viewed.)

The History Window

The Options | Display History Window command pops up a list of all the topics you have displayed since opening the Help library. You can return to any topic by selecting it in the list. After you have displayed half a dozen or more topics, using the History window can be faster than repeatedly pressing the Back button to return to an earlier topic.

Jumps and Pop-Ups

Phrases displayed in green are *jumps* or *pop-ups*. If a phrase has a solid underline, it's a jump to another topic. Clicking it either opens a secondary window or replaces the current topic with the new topic.

Phrases with dotted underlines are pop-ups. When you click a pop-up, a box opens containing additional information. You click the box to close it and return to the main topic. Pop-ups often contain glossary definitions, but they can contain any information, including more jumps and pop-ups.

Many of the Visual Basic topics provide the row of pop-ups and jumps just under the topic title that you can see in Figure 4-5. This row doesn't scroll, so it's always available to you as you scroll around in the topic. *See Also* pops up a list of jumps (and sometimes pop-ups) for related topics. *Methods*, *Properties*, and *Events* each open a secondary window with a list of jumps to the methods, properties, or events related to the current topic. Figure 4-6 shows an example of the Properties window secondary to the Label Control topic.

Bookmarks

When you find a topic that you'll refer to often, you might want to mark it with a *bookmark*. A bookmark makes it simple to return to the topic. Let's insert a bookmark at the Label Control help topic.

Figure 4-6: When you click the Properties jump in the Label Control window, a secondary window opens providing a list of properties for the Label control; each item is a jump to the Help topic for that property.

---

1. Open the Label Control topic. (Use any method you'd like to open it.)

2. Choose *Bookmark|Define* to open the Bookmark Define dialog box, shown here.

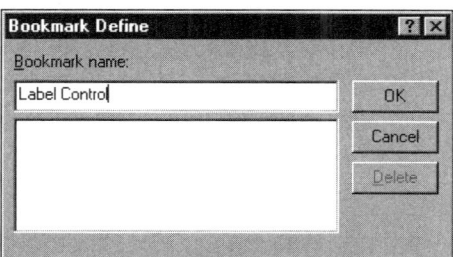

3. Help suggests the topic name, Label Control, as the bookmark name. You could replace the name if you want. But for now, let's just accept it and go on. Click *OK* to create the bookmark.

4. Close the Help window.

5. Now start up Help again and open the Print Method topic.

6. Pull down the Bookmark menu. Notice that your new bookmark, Label Control, appears as an item on this menu, as shown here.

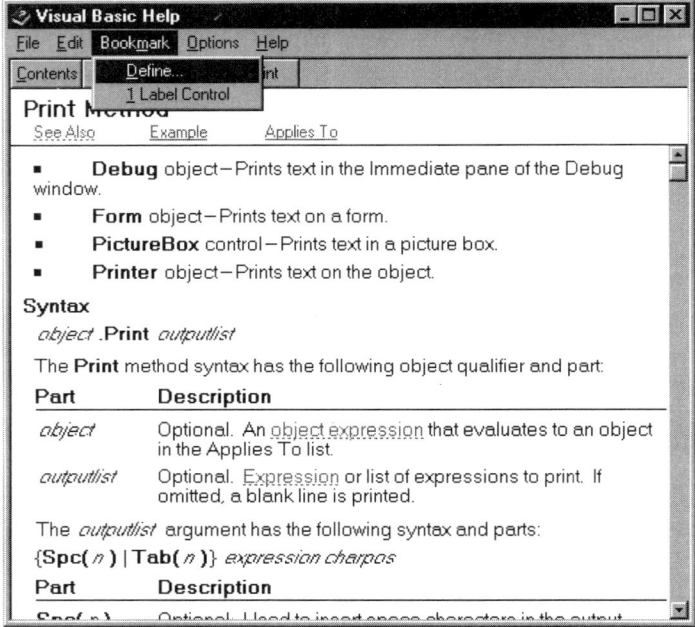

7. Choose the *Label Control* option to jump to that topic. It's as easy as that!

8. If you want to delete the Label Control bookmark, follow these steps:

   a) Choose *Bookmark | Define*.

   b) Click the *Label Control* bookmark to select it.

   c) Click *Delete* to delete the selected bookmark.

   d) Click *OK* to close the dialog box.

It's unfortunate, but you can't jump to a bookmark from the Help Topics window. You have to open a topic—any topic—in order to access the Bookmark menu. You can create as many bookmarks as you like, but there's no sense in duplicating the index. Stick to the few topics to which you want easy access.

Annotations

As you gain experience with Visual Basic, you'll discover tips and solutions that aren't documented in the Help library. You might want to add your own notes to some topics, so you don't forget what you worked so hard to discover.

Annotations can be especially helpful if you share your computer with someone else or you're in a workgroup, as you can see each other's notes in your Help library. A workgroup leader, for example, might insert notes on how objects are to be used (or not used) on a project.

Let's create and use an annotation for the Label Control topic.

1. Display the Label Control topic.

2. Choose *Edit | Annotate* to open the Annotate dialog box, shown here.

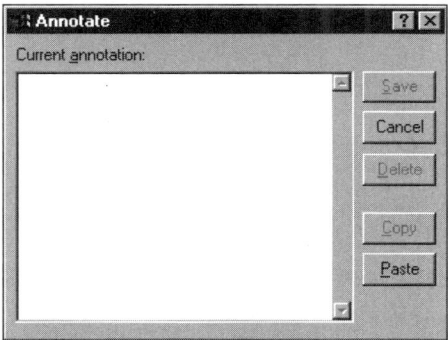

3. In the TextBox, type *This is the first control I used in my Hello World program.* (If you don't like our rather dull note, feel free to type anything you'd like here.)

4. Click *Save* to close the dialog box. Notice the green paper clip in front of the topic title. This is the Annotation icon.

5. Click the paper clip to read the annotation. At this point, you can edit it, copy all or part of it to the Windows Clipboard, paste text from the Windows Clipboard, and/or delete the annotation.

6. Click *Delete* to delete the annotation. Notice that the paper clip disappears from the topic window.

Annotations go into a separate .ann file in the same folder as the help file. For topics in vb.hlp, for example, annotations are stored in vb.ann. If all your annotations disappear from a particular help library, the .ann file was deleted, moved, or renamed.

To share your annotations with co-workers, copy your .ann file to their computers; be sure to put it in the same folder as the related .hlp file. To eliminate all annotations at once, delete the .ann file.

Other Help Features

You might find occasion to print or copy a help topic. To print, just click the Print button. To copy, choose Edit | Copy or press Ctrl+C.

Use File | Open to open a different Help library. You can browse for and open any .hlp file in your system. For example, while working in Visual Basic, you could open Windows 95's Help library to look up some Windows information.

If you find the Help window hard to read, you can use the Options | Font command to select a larger or smaller font. (Your only choices are Small, Medium, and Large; you can't select a different typeface.) You might also try changing the colors on your screen with the Options | Use System Colors command.

If you want to keep the Help window on your screen while you follow a list of steps, choose Options | Keep Help on Top | Always on Top. When you're done following the Help topic, you'll probably want to return the window to its normal (not on top) status. Choose Options | Keep Help on Top | Default to return to the normal status.

The Default setting lets topics keep themselves on top if they're set up that way. If you don't want any topics to be on top, choose Options | Keep Help on Top | Not on Top.

Exploring the Help Library

Now that you have a grip on the mechanics of working with the Help library, let's explore some of those Help library sections that we mentioned earlier.

At the beginning of the Contents, you'll find the Readme files. These are files containing information that didn't make it into the documentation, either because it was discovered after the documentation was sent to the printer or because it is too hardware specific. When you open the *ReadMe* topic, you see a list of jumps to all the Readme files, as shown in Figure 4-7. From there, you can access all the Readme information included with Visual Basic.

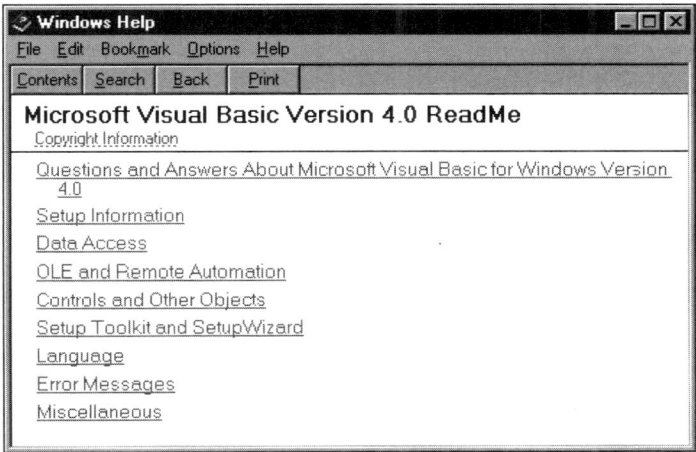

Figure 4-7: The Help library's ReadMe topic provides c list of jumps to all the Readme files included in your Visual Basic package.

Look also for the topic called *Text Files* in the Visual Basic Help category. This topic lists some text files included in your Visual Basic package that contain additional information. You have to use a word processor or editor to read these files, which are located on the installation disk.

When you expand the Visual Basic Help category, you'll find an entry labeled *Contents Topic* that opens the topic shown in Figure 4-8. This topic provides jumps to the other sections in the Visual Basic category. You can also reach those sections from the Contents page, but the information is organized differently here, along with notes about the major sections, and you might find it easier to find what you're looking for in this section.

The language reference is found by expanding *Visual Basic Help* and then expanding *Programming Language*. At the top of this section, you'll find an entry named *Programming Language Summary* which opens the topic shown in Figure 4-9.

This topic provides jumps to every article in the language reference, which includes every standard control, property, event, and method in Visual Basic. The alphabet buttons at the top help you scroll in the list. To quickly find Label Control, for example, you would click the *L* button.

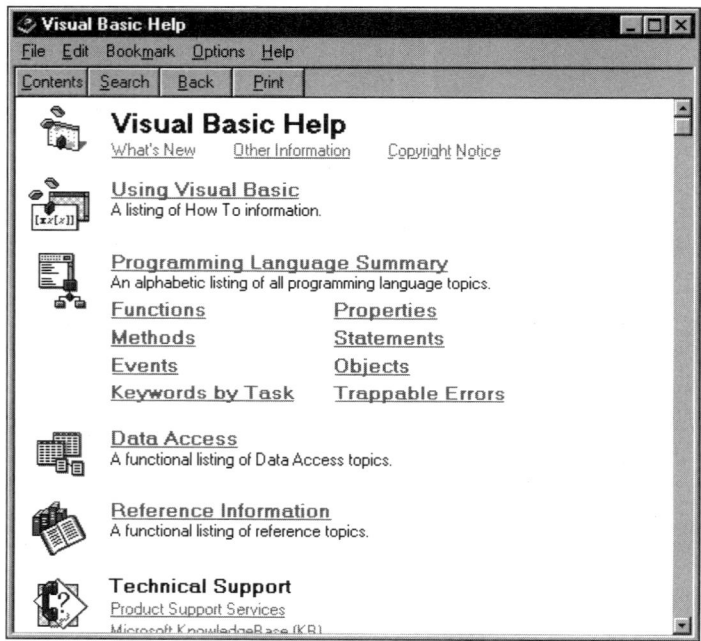

Figure 4-8: The Contents Topic category provides jumps to the other sections in the Visual Basic category.

The section called *Using Visual Basic* provides how-to information that guides you step-by-step in specific procedures, such as adding a menu bar to a form. At the top of the section is a topic called *How To Information Summary*, which displays a complete list of the procedures that are covered in the section. Figure 4-10 shows the beginning of this list. As you can see, it provides alphabet buttons to speed scrolling through the list.

You can see the complete Glossary by choosing the *Glossary* topic under Visual Basic Help (see Figure 4-11). The alphabet buttons help you scroll quickly to the term that you want to look up. Each entry is a pop-up definition; click the entry to read the definition, then click it again to close the definition.

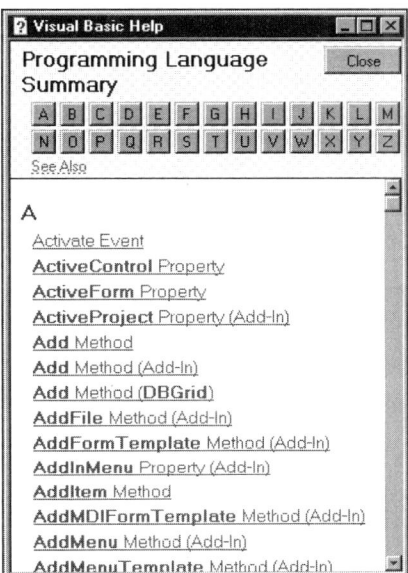

Figure 4-9: The Programming Language Summary topic provides an alphabetized list of jumps to each topic in the Programming Language section.

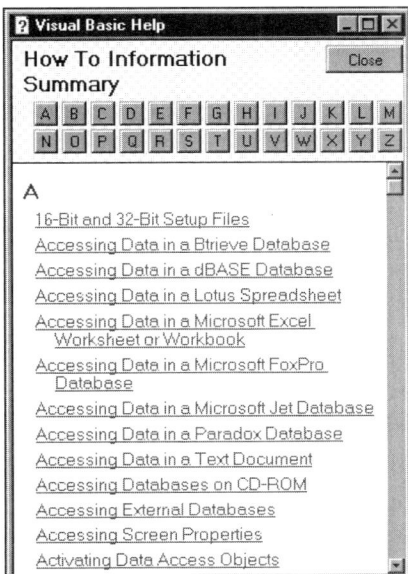

Figure 4-10: The How To Information Summary provides an alphabetical list of jumps to all the how-to topics in the Using Visual Basic section.

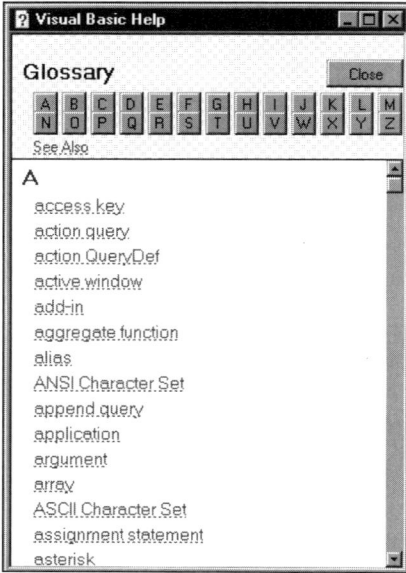

Figure 4-11: The Glossary topic provides a complete list of all the terms that have pop-up definitions in the Visual Basic Help Library.

Some of the other topics and categories that you'll find in the Help library are shown in Table 4-1.

Table 4-1: Other Visual Basic Help Topics

Topic/Category	Description
What's New	Overviews new features in Visual Basic 4.0
Development Environment	Provides a list of jumps to all the windows, dialog boxes, menus, and commands that make up the Visual Basic environment
Data Access	Provides a list of jumps to topics on accessing data in databases
Using the Microsoft Knowledge Base	Explains how to access and use this massive collection of articles on all Microsoft products. The Knowledge Base is described in more detail later in this chapter.
Miscellaneous Information	Provides a list of jumps to topics such as Accessibility for People with Disabilities, Character Set, and Keyboard Guide
Other Help Files	Provides a list of jumps to the other help files in the Help library, including Samples (programming examples)
Custom Control Help	Provides topics that document each of the custom controls included in the Professional edition
Enterprise Help	Provides topics that document features included in the Enterprise edition, such as Remote Data Objects and Component Manager

LEARNING MICROSOFT VISUAL BASIC

Included in your Visual Basic package is an online tutorial called *Learning Microsoft Visual Basic*. The tutorial provides nine lessons and a set of instructions. It's actually a Help library, so you should recognize the interface.

Rather than try to describe what a lesson is like, let's just walk through one. Each lesson takes about ten minutes to complete.

1. Choose *Help | Learning Microsoft Visual Basic*. The contents page appears on your screen, as shown here.

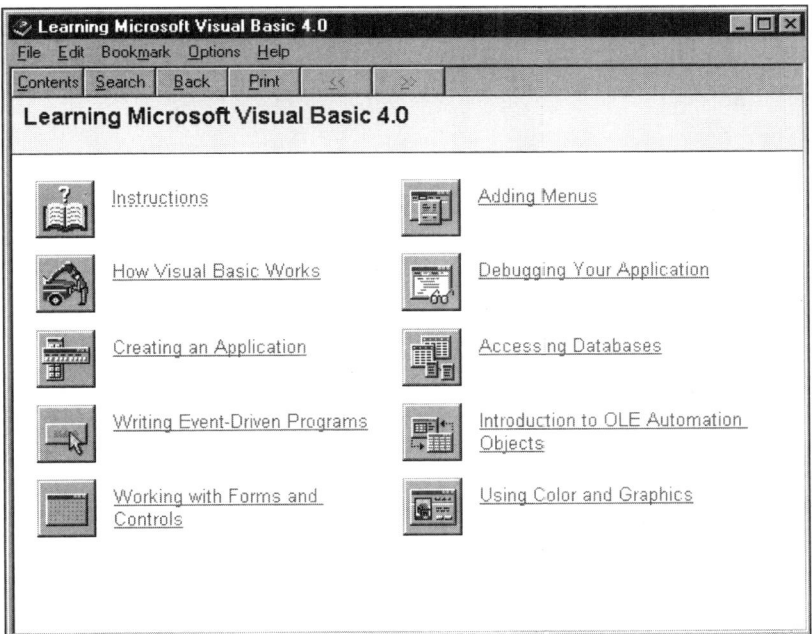

2. Click *Instructions* to see a quick summary of how to navigate within a lesson.

3. Click the pop-up box to clear it.

4. Click *Creating an Application*. The first page of the lesson appears on your screen, as shown on the next page.

5. When you're done reading the first page, click the **>>** button to go on to the next page.

6. Click **<<** to return to the preceding page.

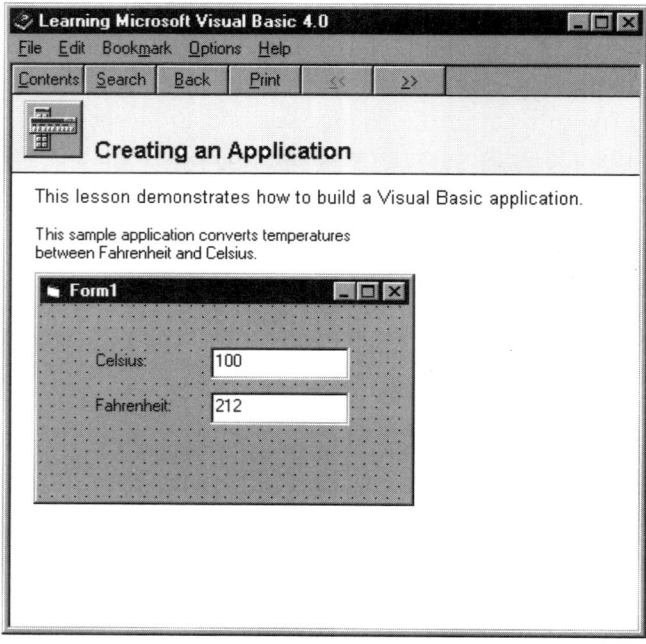

7. Click **Contents** to return to the table of contents.

8. Go ahead and explore the rest of the tutorial on your own. When you're done, click the **Close** button to close the window and return to Visual Basic.

The tutorial isn't really meant to be searchable; you're supposed to read each lesson in sequence. Although the window provides a Search button that takes you to the Index page of the Help Topics window, there's only one item in the index, *Contents*. You could create a Find index if you wish, but there's very little reason to do so.

VISUAL BASIC BOOKS ONLINE

If you're the person who actually bought Visual Basic and carried it home, you know that it comes with a huge (and heavy) stack of documentation. All of that documentation has been reproduced on the installation CD as Visual Basic Books Online (see Figure 4-12). The online books are actually a much more convenient way to access the documentation, not only because they don't take up any desk space (and they aren't in someone else's office), but also because of the software features that paper documentation can't provide.

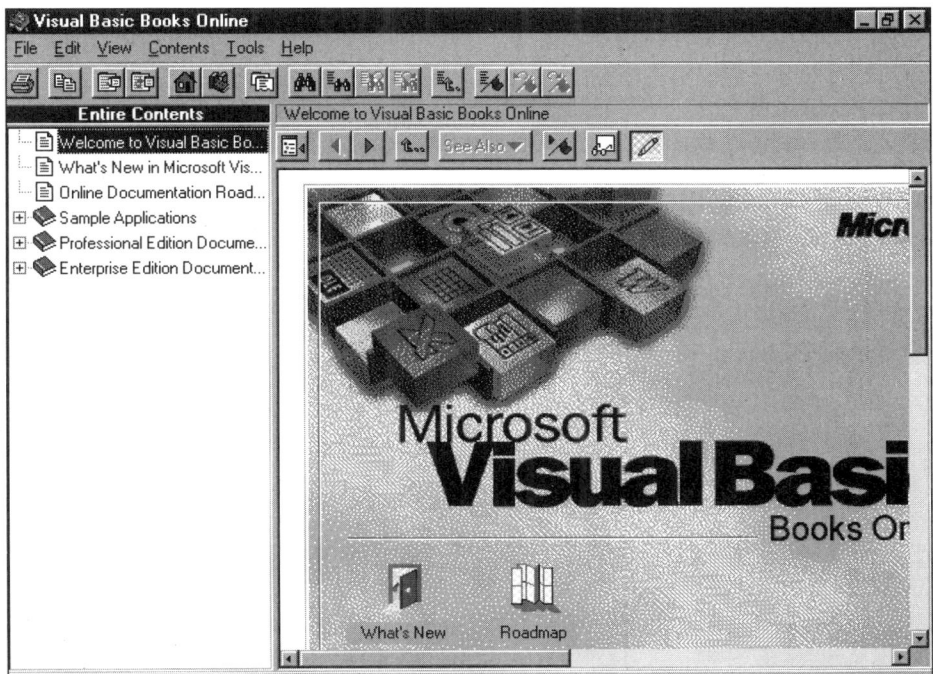

Figure 4-12: Visual Basic Books Online provides an electronic copy of the Visual Basic documentation.

You have to insert the Visual Basic CD in the CD-ROM drive in order to use Books Online. So put the CD in, and let's explore the interface.

1. Choose *Help|Visual Basic Books Online* to open the window shown in Figure 4-12.

2. You can adjust the sizes of the two main panes. Try dragging the dividing line between the Contents pane and the Topic pane so that the Contents pane is wider.

   When the Topic pane is displaying text instead of graphics, it wraps paragraphs to fit the width of the pane so that you don't have to scroll sideways to read. It can't wrap graphics such as the Books Online logo, however.

3. ToolTips are available in Books Online. Pause your mouse over some of the buttons to see the ToolTips.

4. You also have a feature called TitleTips. Make the Contents pane narrow so that the entire titles don't show. Then pause your mouse over an abbreviated title. The entire title pops up.

5. Choose *Help|Contents* to open the Help library. This is another source of information on how to use Books Online.

6. Close the Help window.

The View Menu

The View menu (see Figure 4-13) offers several commands for tailoring the Books Online window. In the following exercise, we'll explore the top two sections of the menu. You'll learn about the items in the bottom sections a little later.

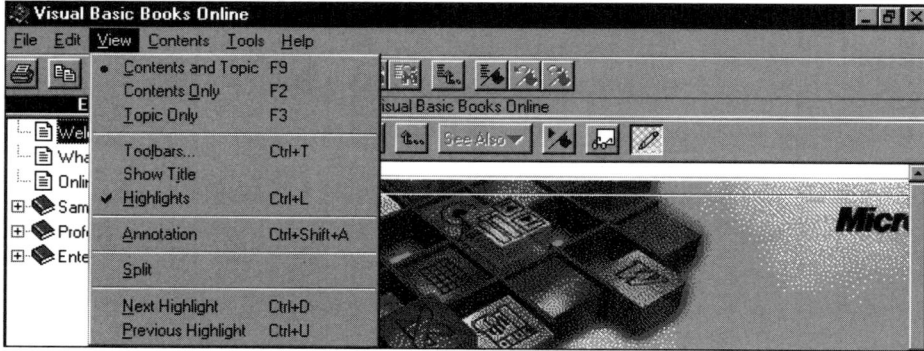

Figure 4-13: The View menu controls which features appear in the Books Online window.

1. Choose *View|Contents Only* (F2). The Topic pane disappears.

2. Choose *View|Topic Only* (F3). The Contents pane is replaced by the Topic pane.

3. Choose *View|Contents and Topic* (F9). Now you're back to the standard view.

4. Choose *View|Toolbars* to pop up the dialog box shown on the next page. Notice that both toolbars are enabled, along with ToolTips. You'll probably want to keep all these features, so click *Cancel* to close the dialog box.

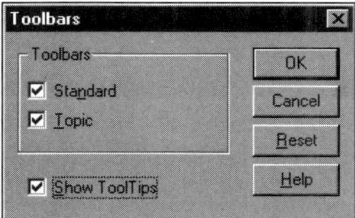

5. Choose *View | Show Title* to add the topic title to the Topic pane.

6. Do you want to keep the topic title? It's easy to forget what topic you're reading and the title helps to remind you, but it steals space from the topic pane. If you decide you don't want it, go ahead and turn it off now by choosing *View | Show Title* again.

The Contents Pane

The Contents pane works much like Visual Basic's Contents page. Figure 4-14 shows the Contents pane with some categories expanded.

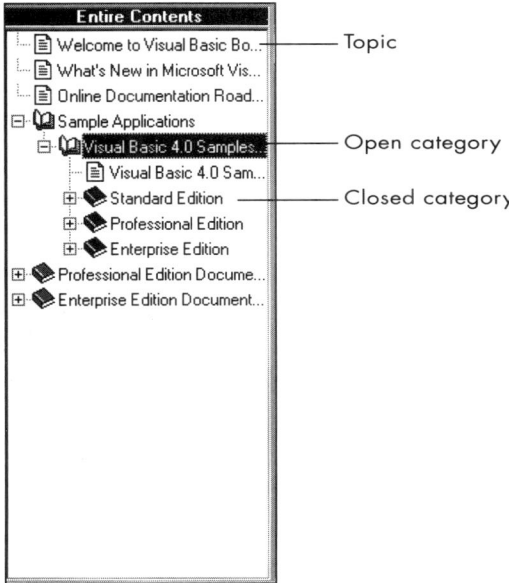

Figure 4-14: The Contents pane acts like an interactive table of contents to help you find the topics you want.

A closed book icon indicates a closed category; in Books Online, it also has a plus icon. You can expand the category by double-clicking it or by clicking the plus icon. An open book icon indicates an expanded category. You can close it by double-clicking the category itself or by clicking the minus icon. A page icon indicates a topic that you can read by double-clicking it.

Let's try navigating around in the topics.

1. Click the Next in Contents icon, shown here, which switches to the next topic (What's New in Microsoft Visual Basic 4.0).

2. Click the Next in Contents icon several more times.

3. Click the Previous in Contents icon, shown here, which switches to the previous topic.

4. Try *Ctrl+>* and *Ctrl+<*, which are equivalent to Next in Contents and Previous in Contents.

5. Click the Home Screen icon to return to the Books Online logo.

6. Another way to open a topic is to double-click it. Double-click *What's New in Microsoft Visual Basic 4.0.*

7. Click the Go Back icon (in the Topic toolbar), which returns you to the screen you viewed before this one.

NOTE Many topics contain jumps to other topics. As always, jumps are displayed in green and underlined. (You can change the color by choosing Tools | Options.) Some topics contain pop-ups, displayed in gray. If the See Also icon becomes available, click it to see a list of jumps to related topics.

The History Window

You'll often find that you want to return to topics that you read before. Books Online keeps tracks of the topics that you display, just as the Help library does. You can return to former topics easily by selecting them in the History window.

1. Click the History List icon (in the main toolbar). The History window appears on your screen, as shown in the following screen.

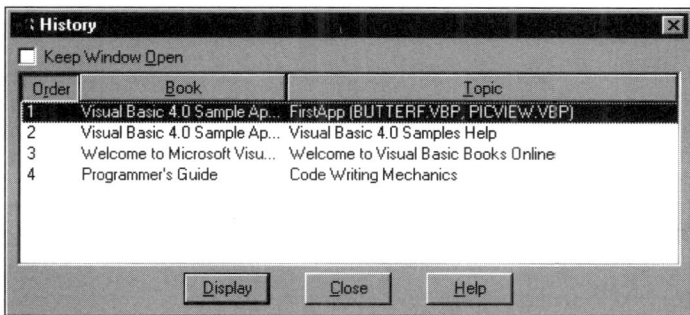

2. The button bar controls the order of the list. The Order button is selected by default; it displays the list in the same order that you viewed the topics. Try clicking the *Topic* button to display the list in alphabetical order by topic. Sometimes this is the easiest way to locate a topic that you want to reread.

3. Click the *Book* button to display the list in alphabetical order by book.

4. Make the window wider by dragging a side border.

5. You can resize the individual fields to make them easier to read. Drag the dividing line between the Book button and the Topic button to make the Book field wider, as shown here.

Drag this line

6. Double-click a topic to return to it and close the History window.

When you select a topic, the History window closes by default. If you want it to stay open while you read the topic, check Keep Window Open near the top of the History window.

The Keyword Index

The Contents pane is just one way to locate a topic in Books Online. Another way is to look up a word or phrase in the keyword index. Let's try looking up the BorderStyle property.

1. Click the Keyword Index icon in the main toolbar. This opens the Keyword Index dialog box shown here.

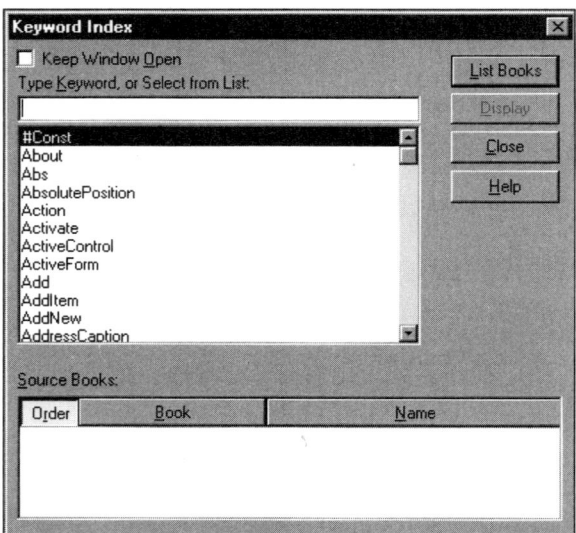

2. You could scroll through the list box until you reach BorderStyle, but it's easier to just type part of the word in the textbox. Type *bor* and you'll scroll to BorderColor. BorderStyle is directly below BorderColor.

3. Double-click *BorderStyle* to list all topics containing that keyword, as shown on the next page.

4. In the *Source Books* list box, double-click the only entry to open the topic and close the Keyword Index.

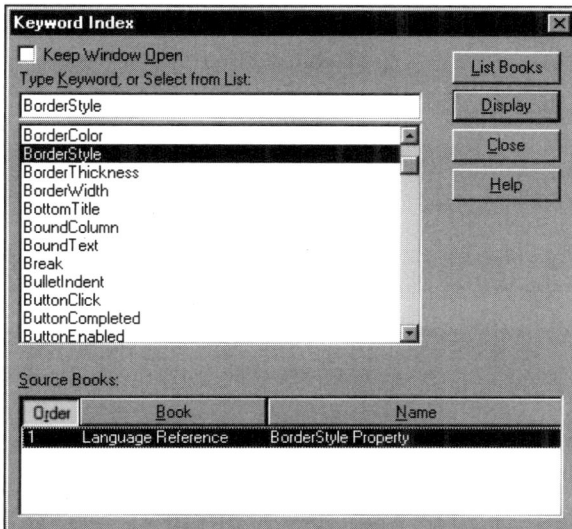

The buttons in the Source Books list box work just like the buttons in the History window. You can drag the dividing line between them to change the width of the fields. And when the list contains more than one item, you can click a button to sort the list in that order. If you want to keep the Keyword Index open while you read topics, check Keep Window Open near the top of the window.

Queries

Another very powerful way to locate topics is to search for them using Books Online's Query feature. A query locates all topics containing specified words or phrases.

Let's try out a basic query, then we'll get into some of the more complex features of this facility.

1. Click the Query icon on the main toolbar. This opens the Query dialog box.

2. Type *ole* in the text box and click *Run Query*. The Query Results dialog box displays the topics that contain the expression *ole* or *OLE* as shown on the next page.

3. Make the window larger and adjust the size of the fields so that you can see the complete titles of the books and the topics.

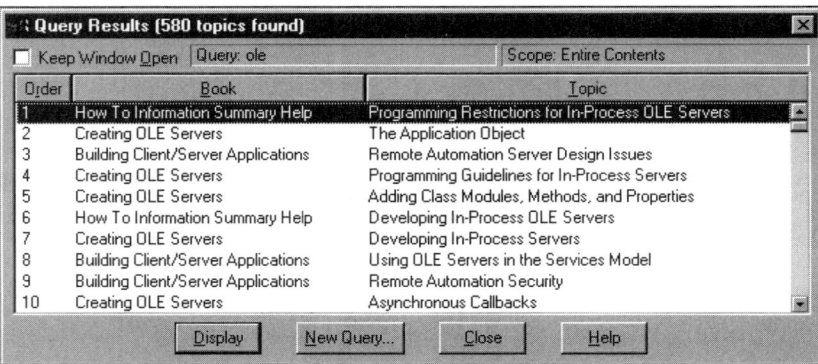

4. Double-click a topic — any topic — to display that topic and close the Query Results dialog box.

5. Now click the Query Results icon in the main toolbar. This icon reopens the Query Results dialog box.

6. Display another topic.

When you do a query, you'll probably need to read several of the topics that are identified in the Query Results dialog box. You might want to use the Keep Window Open feature so that you don't have to reopen the dialog box every time you want to select another topic.

TIP If you want to read the topics in sequence, click the *Next in Query Results* icon to see the next topic in the list. To return to the previous topic, click the *Previous in Query Results* icon. The Query Results dialog box does not need to be open for these icons to work.

Did you notice that the entries in the Query Results dialog box are displayed in numeric order? This is not just an arbitrary order. (Computers have difficulty being arbitrary.) It indicates the number of occurrences, or *hits*, of the search word in each article. The number 1 represents the most hits and therefore the article you are most likely to want. You might also have noticed that the hits were highlighted in the articles you displayed. We'll look at the highlighting feature next.

Highlighting Hits

By default, the Query feature highlights the hits in each found article. This helps you find the desired areas in a long article. To scroll rapidly to the next hit, choose View | Next Highlight or press Ctrl+D. View | Previous Highlight (Ctrl+U) scrolls to the preceding hit. Ctrl+D and Ctrl+U are easy to remember, as they stand for Down and Up.

If you don't like the highlighting feature, you can turn it off by choosing View | Highlights (Ctrl+L) or by clicking the Highlights icon, shown here, in the Topic toolbar.

More Elaborate Searches

When you entered "ole", the Query feature searched for those letters as a whole word. But suppose you want to search for all words beginning with *drive*, as in *drive, drives, driver,* and *drivers*. No, you don't have to do four separate searches. By adding an asterisk after "drive", as in "drive*", you ask Query to locate any word starting with *drive*.

To locate all articles containing both *hard* and *drive*, not necessarily as a phrase, enter "hard and drive". To locate *hard drive* as a phrase, enter "hard drive" (include the quotes). To locate articles containing *hard* and *drive* fairly near each other, as in *hard IDE drive*, enter "hard near drive".

You can control how near is near by choosing Tools | Options. By default, near means within eight words.

To locate articles containing either *hard* or *drive* or both, enter "hard or drive". To locate articles containing *hard* but not *drive*, enter "hard not drive".

In the Query dialog box, the *Scope of Search* group and the *Topic Area to Search* group determine where the Query feature looks for the search words. By default, it looks in all articles in all books, examining both titles and contents of the articles. In other words, the entire Books Online library. To save time and limit the number of articles that are found, you can limit the search. Selecting *Title Only* shortens the search considerably, as it searches just the titles of topics, not the topics themselves—ensuring that any topics found really address the desired topic. *Current Topic Only* limits the search to the topic that is currently displayed and provides a handy way to locate the areas you're interested in within the current topic.

Suppose you're looking for articles that contrast the features of OLE and DDE. You searched for *ole* but found too many articles—it will take too long to open each one to find out if it contains the information you need. You can narrow the search by searching only the articles that also contain DDE. Just enter "dde" as the search word and select Last Topics Found in the Scope of Search group.

The subset feature lets you select a group of articles to be searched. We talk about subsets in the next section.

Subsets

The entire contents of Visual Basic Books Online might contain much more information than you need. For example, if you don't have the Enterprise edition, why include that book in your Contents pane or in your searches? You can define a *subset* of the Contents that doesn't include the Enterprise edition documentation.

Let's define a subset containing just the Programmer's Reference and the Language Reference from the Professional edition.

1. Close any dialog boxes so that you're looking at the main Books Online window.

2. Choose *Contents | Define Subset* or click the Define Subset icon shown here. This opens the Define Subset dialog box, as shown here.

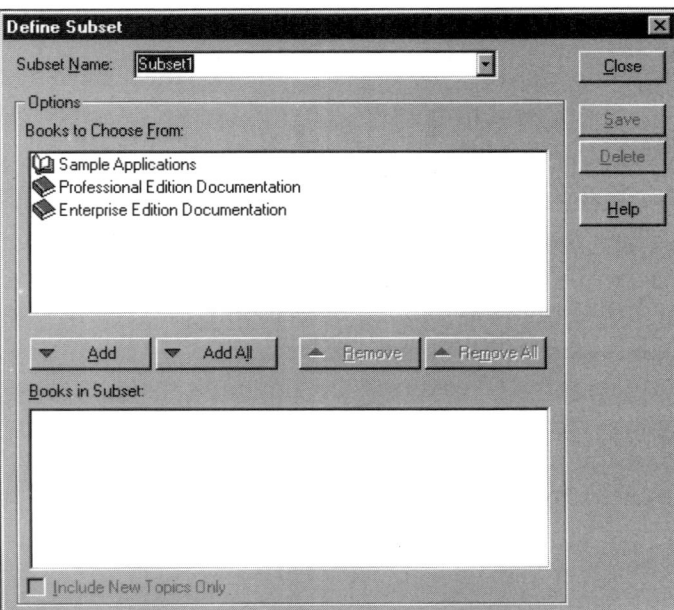

3. Type *Practice Subset* in the *Subset Name* box.

4. In the *Books to Choose From* box, double-click *Professional Edition Documentation* to expand its contents.

5. Click *Programmer's Guide* to select it, then click the *Add* button.

6. Click *Language Reference* and click *Add*. Your dialog box should now look like the following:

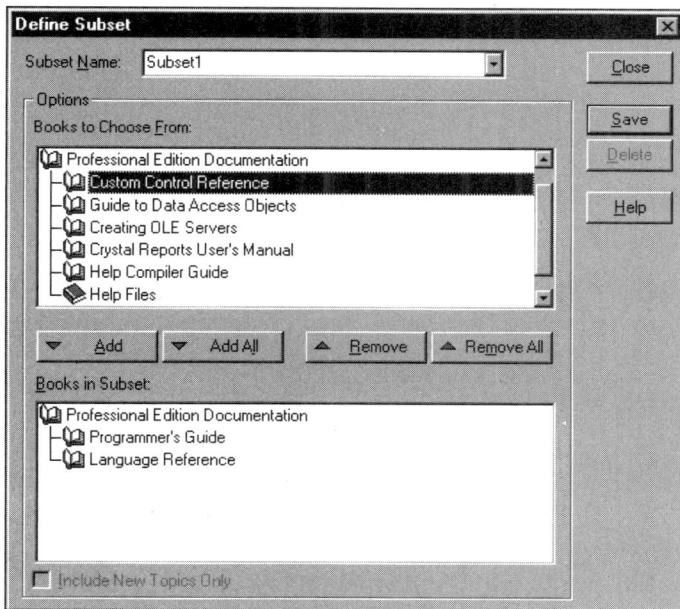

7. Click *Save* to create the subset. Notice that the dialog box stays open so that you can define more subsets if you wish.

8. Click *Close* to close the dialog box.

Notice the immediate effect on your Books Online window. The Contents pane now shows only the subset you just defined; its title bar says *Practice Subset* instead of *Entire Contents*, as before.

Let's try switching back and forth between the entire contents and your subset.

1. Choose *Contents|Select Subset* or click the Select Subset icon to open the dialog box shown here.

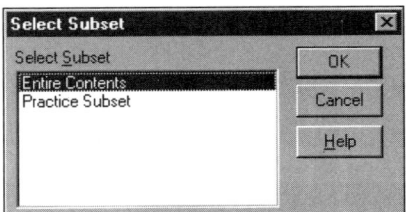

2. Double-click *Entire Contents* to return to the complete contents.

3. Click the Select Subset icon and double-click *Practice Subset*.

Queries ignore the current subset and search the entire contents unless you choose Subset of Contents in the Query dialog box. You can also define a new subset from the Query dialog box by clicking the Define Subset button, which opens the same Define Subset dialog box that you just learned how to use.

Annotations and Bookmarks

You can add your own notes (annotations) to the Books Online topics, and you can insert bookmarks on topics that you want to return to easily.

To create an annotation, you choose *View|Annotation* (Ctrl+Shift+A) or click the View Annotation icon. The Topic pane splits into two panes, as shown in Figure 4-15. The bottom pane is the Annotation pane. You can drag the dividing line between it and the Topic pane to change the sizes of the two panes.

Once you open the Annotation pane, it stays open until you close it again, even when you change topics. You can type and edit the text in the pane as desired.

To insert a bookmark in a topic, choose *Edit|Bookmarks* (Ctrl+M) or click the Add Bookmark icon. There are several ways to locate a bookmark:

▶ Choose *Edit|Bookmarks* or click the Bookmark List icon, which displays your bookmark list, where you can select the bookmark you want to jump to.

▶ Once you have jumped to a bookmark, the Next Bookmark in List icon becomes available. Click it to jump to the next bookmark without opening the list.

▶ When you jump to the next bookmark, the Previous Bookmark in List icon becomes available. Click it to return to the previous bookmark without opening the list.

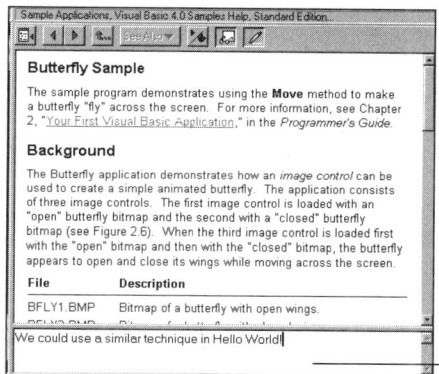
Annotation pane

Figure 4-15: The Annotation pane lets you insert, read, and edit your own notes attached to Books Online topics.

OUTSIDE HELP

With the Help library, the tutorial, and Visual Basic Books Online, you can probably find the answers to 99 percent of your Visual Basic questions and problems. But what about that other one percent—the control that doesn't work the way the documentation says, the error message that won't go away, the loop that won't end? When you can't find the answer you're looking for in your Visual Basic package, you still have lots of resources available, although they're not quite as convenient as the Help library and Books Online.

In general, Microsoft provides support for all of its products via several routes:

▶ The Internet, CompuServe, and America Online

▶ Phone and fax

▶ Consultants

▶ Membership in the Microsoft Developers Network

Product Support Services and the Microsoft Support Network

Microsoft's product support engineers are available by phone to work with you in solving problems that you can't solve via your online documentation. Be sure to be at your computer when you call for product support. The engineer may want information from your Help | About box as well as from diagnostic programs that are included in your Visual Basic package.

You may also need to provide:

▶ Your Visual Basic version number

▶ A description of your hardware (processor, RAM, type of network card, and so on)

▶ The exact wording of any messages you received

▶ A complete and detailed description of what you did, what the computer did, how you tried to fix it, what happened next, and so on

Within the United States and Canada, the Microsoft Support Network provides product support. The standard service is available for no charge (except long distance fees) between 6:00 am and 6:00 pm Pacific time, Monday through Friday (except on holidays). For Microsoft Visual Basic, call (206) 646-5105.

In Canada, standard support is available between 8:00 am and 8:00 pm Eastern time, Monday through Friday, (except on holidays). For Microsoft Visual Basic support, call (905) 568-3503.

You can use the standard service for 30 days after you make your first call. After that, you're expected to pay for support by using one of the higher-level support services:

▶ Priority Support is designed for individuals and small companies. It charges generally by the incident, but you can buy plans that cost less if you'll be using the service often.

▶ Premier Support is intended for large companies. It provides a higher priority of response and is paid for by an annual fee.

▶ Premier Global Support is intended for huge, multinational organizations. It provides an account manager and a world-wide response team, and you pay for it by an annual fee.

Microsoft FastTips makes available an up-to-date brochure for the Microsoft Support Network that explains each of these services in detail, including pricing and telephone numbers. So let's talk about FastTips next.

Microsoft FastTips for Developers

If you have a problem with Visual Basic, it's likely that other people have had the same problem. Microsoft maintains a Technical Library of articles on Visual Basic as well as its other development systems. An easy way to order items from the Technical Library is via FastTips, an automated phone system. FastTips also provides information on the Microsoft Support Network (MSSN) and Microsoft Sales and Service.

At the time we're writing this, the phone number for FastTips is (800) 936-4300. Then you work your way through the menu system until you have ordered everything that you want to order. Orders can be mailed or faxed to you, whichever you prefer. We received our fax order within three minutes.

The first time you call FastTips, you'll need to order the catalog of the Technical Library, as all articles are ordered by catalog number.

You might also want to order a map of the FastTips menu system, which gives you a good overview of the available features. It also saves you from having to listen while a voice reads you each menu as you work your way around the system.

When you receive your first catalog, you'll find that it doesn't actually have any Visual Basic articles in it. Instead, it itemizes more specific catalogs that you can order. For example, if you're having problems with installation, you would order the catalog on VB Setup and Installation. If you need to know more about custom controls, you would order the catalog on VB Programming: Custom Controls. A few of the other catalogs are:

▶ VB Run-Time Environment

▶ VB Design Environment

▶ VB Programming: Forms/Standard Controls

▶ VB: OLE

Microsoft on the Internet

Figure 4-16 shows Microsoft's home page at Web site http://www.microsoft.com. Each area of the graphic is a link to another page. To get to the Visual Basic section, for example, you would click *For Developers Only*. Then you click *Visual Basic* on the developers' page (not shown).

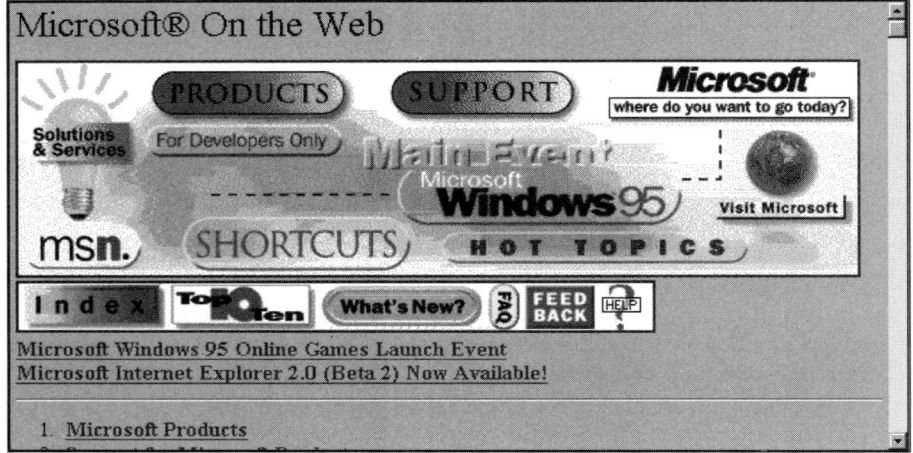

Figure 4-16: On Microsoft's Web site, you would click For Developers Only to access information about Visual Basic.

If your Web browser does not display graphics, scroll to the bottom of the page for a text representation of the same topics.

The gopher site at gopher.microsoft.com, shown in Figure 4-17, also provides a wealth of information for Microsoft product users. We'll be talking in detail about the Knowledge Base, the Developer's Network, the Software Library, and the Support Network at the end of this chapter.

Microsoft also maintains an FTP site at ftp.microsoft.com, although the last time we looked at it, it was several months out of date.

Online Services

You can reach Microsoft on CompuServe or America Online. To access the Knowledge Base on CompuServe, type "go mskb". For the Support Library, type "go msl". For the BASIC forum, which includes a Visual Basic area, type "go msbasic".

Figure 4-17: Microsoft's Internet gopher site provides easy access to information such as the Knowledge Base, the Developer's Network, and the Software Library.

You access the Microsoft area on America Online via keyword "microsoft", which opens the dialog box shown in Figure 4-18. Both buttons lead to Microsoft Web pages.

Figure 4-18: To access the Microsoft area on America Online, enter the keyword "microsoft".

Microsoft Knowledge Base

The Microsoft Knowledge Base is a huge collection of over 55,000 technical articles on all aspects of Microsoft products. The Knowledge Base is updated daily, so you'll find the latest information there. The Microsoft customer support engineers use the Knowledge Base when helping customers solve problems. You also have access to the Knowledge Base via the Internet—you'll find it at Microsoft's Web site or FTP site.

The Knowledge Base provides a search feature to help you find the articles you need. Articles that mention software fixes or examples provide links to the necessary software in the Microsoft Software Library (described next) so that you can download the software easily.

Before you try to access the Knowledge base at either site, you should read the information in your Visual Basic Help library on the Knowledge base. It includes detailed instructions on how to access the sites and how to use the Knowledge Base.

Microsoft Software Library

The Microsoft Software Library (MSL) provides software such as new drivers, patches or upgrades to eliminate bugs in your software, utilities, programming examples, Help files, and application notes. You can access the library via the Internet, CompuServe (use "go msl"), the Knowledge Base, or Microsoft Download Service, which is described next.

Microsoft Download Service

Microsoft Download Service (MSDL) is a bulletin board service (BBS) providing access to the Microsoft Software Library.

To access MSDL, you must have a modem and a telecommunications program such as Windows 95's HyperTerminal. Set up your modem for 1200 to 14,400 bps, no parity, 8 data bits, and 1 stop bit. Then call (206) 936-6735.

You can request complete instructions on how to use MSDL from FastTips. If you need them right away and don't have a fax machine, you can listen to them being read to you.

Member Networks

Microsoft provides two membership organizations with somewhat similar services. The Visual Basic Help library contains detailed information on additional benefits and how to join both organizations.

▶ The *Microsoft Developers Network (MSDN)* is a membership program for people who develop Windows applications. When you join, you receive quarterly updates of the Development Library CD. You also get a bimonthly newsletter.

▶ *TechNet* is an information-subscription service. Members receive monthly CD-ROMs containing the current Knowledge Base and the Software Library. There is also a TechNet forum on CompuServe ("go technet").

Consulting Services

If you feel like you need help from real live consultants, you might want to learn more about these two programs:

▶ *Microsoft Authorized Support Centers (ASCs)* offer customized support services such as planning, implementation, and maintenance of your system.

▶ *Microsoft Solution Providers* are independent consultants who provide consultation systems development and training.

Both of these services are more fully described in the Help library.

SUMMARY

Are you surprised at how much help is at your fingertips when you're working with Visual Basic? You can get most answers within just a couple of minutes, by looking in the various reference sources that come with Visual Basic. But when you need to turn to outside sources, the help is there, although it might take a little longer (and cost a little more).

The most important message of this chapter is: The help is there! No matter how tough a problem you run into, you can seek out the solution.

CHAPTER OBJECTIVES

As you have already seen in the first few chapters, a new Visual Basic project starts with the form and its controls because they provide the interface between the user and the software. In this chapter, you'll learn a lot more about forms:

▶ How to add a menu bar to a form

▶ How to add a second form to a project

▶ How to create an application that handles multiple documents

▶ How to create a dialog box

▶ The relationship between forms and modules

Forms, Menus, and Modules

5

In this chapter we introduce the application that you will be developing throughout the rest of this book, ScratchPad. We'll discuss what ScratchPad will do, and you'll create the basic forms, add a menu bar, and create the About dialog box. You'll continue to add features to ScratchPad in the upcoming chapters.

We wanted to give you a program to work on with a little more meat than "Hello, World!" — something that you might actually find useful. But we didn't want something that was so complex that a beginning programmer couldn't hope to accomplish it in a reasonably short period of time. We think that ScratchPad fills the bill.

INTRODUCING SCRATCHPAD

ScratchPad is simply a place where people can jot down any notes that appeal to them. This tool should be easy to use spontaneously and might even replace those sticky yellow notes all over your monitor! Users can save their notes in a file or as a database, edit them, and print them. In the 32-bit version of Visual Basic, they can format their notes with fonts and color and insert OLE objects such as sound and video clips, spreadsheet excerpts, and pictures. ScratchPad will also have the ability to query a database and paste the results into the ScratchPad window. It will also provide online help, with a Help library and ToolTips.

The main window for ScratchPad simply provides a half-sheet of "paper," somewhat like a small notebook or notepad, as you can see in Figure 5-1. At the top are a menu bar and a toolbar; then the client area consists of a large TextBox where users jot down their notes.

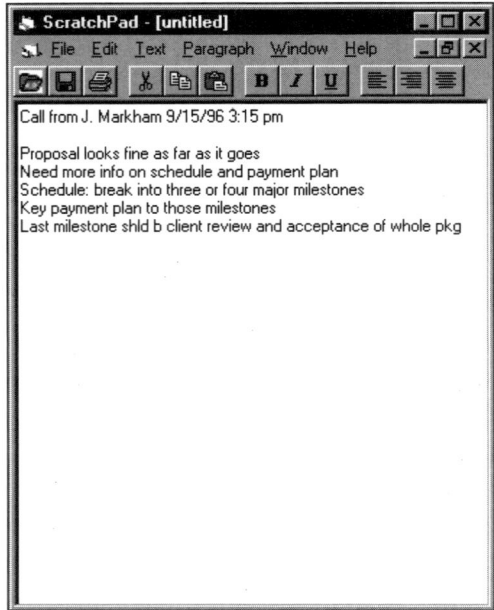

Figure 5-1: ScratchPad's window provides a large TextBox where users can jot down notes.

THE MULTIPLE DOCUMENT INTERFACE

Like all word processors and editors, ScratchPad creates and edits documents. You can work on several documents at once in ScratchPad. Figure 5-2 shows an example where we're working on a shopping list, a to-do list, notes for a presentation, and a list of expenses, all at the same time. This example demonstrates several important characteristics of an application that handles multiple documents:

▶ Each open document occupies its own window, called a *child* window, that remains within the client area of the application's MDI window. (*MDI* stands for "multiple document interface," which we discuss shortly).

▶ You can open numerous child windows, but there is only one parent window.

▶ Only one child window can be active; its title bar is highlighted.

▶ A child window can be moved and sized, but it must remain within the parent window's work area.

▶ When the active child window is maximized, it fills the parent window's work area, *not* the entire screen. Its caption is added to the parent window's caption.

▶ Frequently, a Window menu provides commands to manage the child windows, such as Tile and Cascade, along with a WindowList.

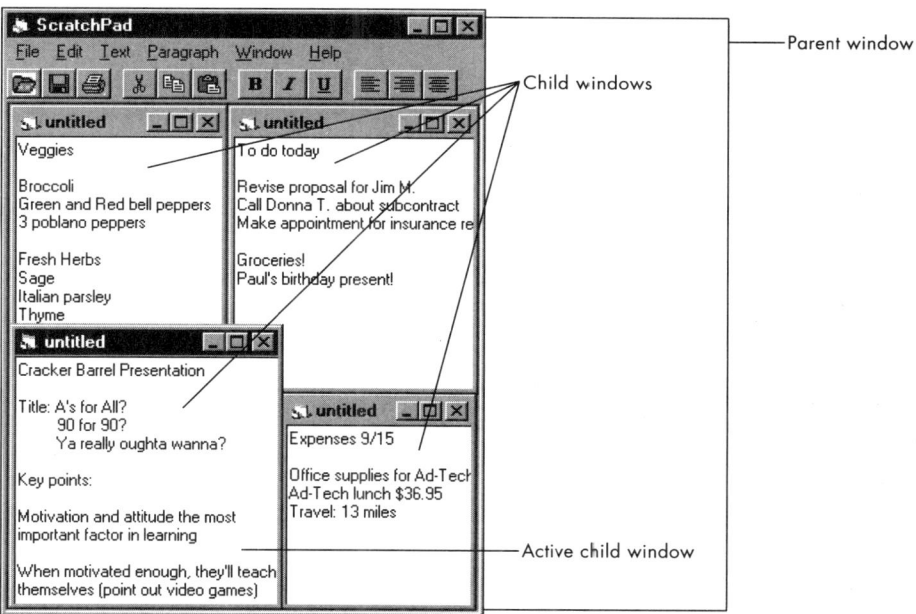

Figure 5-2: ScratchPad uses Visual Basic's Multiple Document Interface to let you work on several documents at once.

NOTE The only limit to the number of child windows that can be opened is determined by how much memory is on the system and how many resource-heavy application windows are open at the time. But some applications place a numeric limit on the number of open children.

To create an application that handles more than one document at a time, you use Visual Basic's Multiple Document Interface (MDI). It's almost ridiculously easy to do, because Visual Basic does most of the work for you. You create the parent form, called the MDI form, and one child form. Visual Basic does all the work of making the parent and children interact with each other properly. But it's your responsibility to create the Window menu and the commands on the File menu for opening, saving, printing, and closing the files that appear in the child windows.

Let's start our work on ScratchPad by creating the child form. We'll just create the form itself now; we'll add the menu bar later in this chapter, and the other controls in later chapters.

1. Start a new project. Visual Basic displays Form1, which you'll use as the child form.

   Don't worry about the size or location of the form. Because this is a child form, Visual Basic will manage its size and location.

2. Change the *Caption* property to *untitled*.

3. Change the form's *Name* property to *frmDocument*.

4. Change the *WindowState* property to *2 - Maximize*d. This maximizes the document when it first appears in the parent window. (The user can restore it if desired.)

5. Change the *MDIChild* property to *True*. This tells Visual Basic that this form is a child form.

6. Save the form file as *frmDocument.frm* and the project as *ScratchPad.vbp*.

Were you surprised that we used Form1 for the child form instead of the parent? That's because you have to create a parent form using a special command: Insert | MDI Form. Let's do that now.

1. Choose *Insert|MDI Form*. A form captioned MDIForm1 appears on your screen. The dark gray background reminds you that this is an MDI form.

2. Position and size the form so that it fits in the right half of the screen, stretching from the top to the taskbar. (Use the examples in Figures 5-1 and 5-2 as a guide.)

3. Change the *Caption* to *ScratchPad*.

4. Change the *Name* to *frmScratchPad*.

5. Save the form as *frmScratchPad.frm*.

6. Run the program. The child form appears maximized within the parent window. Notice the child's caption, untitled, in the parent's title bar.

7. Experiment with restoring, resizing, and minimizing the child window. You can see how much work Visual Basic is doing for you.

8. End the program to return to the design environment.

ADDING A MENU BAR

You use menus in your programs to let your users execute commands. While you can make menus simple or complex, it is a good idea to stick to certain design norms so that your users don't have to spend too much time trying to figure out strange-looking menus.

Designing Good Menus

Since you're already familiar with Windows, you're probably pretty much aware of normal menu design. Figure 5-3 shows a typical example, the File menu from ScratchPad that you'll create very soon.

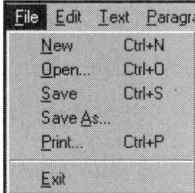

Figure 5-3: ScratchPad's File menu demonstrates many characteristics common to menus in Windows applications.

The menu bar is located beneath the title bar. Selecting a menu causes a drop-down list of menu options (or commands) to open. The menu options are often separated into smaller groups of related commands by separator bars.

The menu bar usually contains at least two menus—the File menu and the Help menu. Applications that edit files usually have an Edit menu, too. When an application permits multiple documents, it usually provides a Window menu. Two other common menus are View, which contains commands to customize the appearance of the work area, and Tools, which provides access to features such as spelling checkers, calculators, and drawing tools.

Notice in the menu bar in Figure 5-3 that there is an underline under one letter in each menu. The underlined letter is the *access key* for that menu. Pressing Alt plus the access key pulls the menu down. Usually the access key is the first letter of the menu item, but this is not always the case. You might choose another letter because another menu is already using the first letter.

In the File menu itself, each of the options has an access key. Once the menu is pulled down, a user types the access key (without Alt) to choose an option. In Visual Basic, you don't have to write code to make the access keys work. All you do is designate the access keys—we'll show you how in a minute—and Visual Basic makes them work.

Some of the items are followed by an ellipsis (...). The ellipsis indicates that this command requires additional information to be executed. When the user chooses the command, a dialog box appears to collect the additional information.

Let's look at another menu example. Figure 5-4 shows Microsoft Excel's Format menu. Notice that several of the options are followed by an arrowhead. When you highlight one of these items, a submenu (or cascading menu) appears. In the example, the Row option is highlighted and the submenu contains options that pertain to that option: Height, AutoFit, Hide, and Unhide.

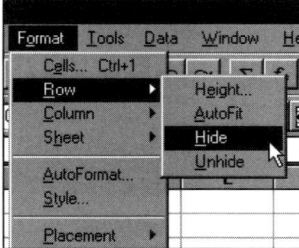

Figure 5-4: This example from Microsoft Excel shows how a submenu appears when you highlight a command with an arrowhead.

Figure 5-4 also shows an example of a *shortcut key*. Notice the message Ctrl+1 next to the Cells command. A user can press Ctrl+1 to trigger the Cells command without pulling down the Format menu. For most users, it's faster to press Ctrl+1 than to pull down the menu and click a command; that's why the key combo is referred to as a shortcut.

Another feature that you can see in both Figures 5-3 and 5-4 is the horizontal line that separates commands into groups. This line is known as the *separator line*.

Using Menu Editor to Create Menus

You use Menu Editor to create and update menus for your Visual Basic application. Figure 5-5 shows the Menu Editor's window. Let's build a standard File menu for our ScratchPad program. After we finish the File menu, you can practice what you learn by building the other menus.

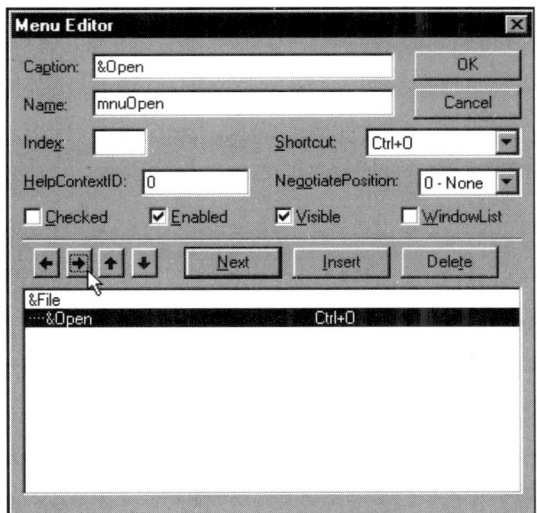

Figure 5-5: Visual Basic's Menu Editor lets you add menus to your Windows applications.

1. Click the MDI form *(frmScratchPad)* to make sure it is the selected object.

2. Click the Menu Editor icon (shown here) on the Visual Basic toolbar. The Menu Editor window should open on your screen.

   You can also open Menu Editor by choosing Tools | Menu Editor.

3. The Caption box identifies the word or phrase that will actually appear on the menu. Since we're starting with the File menu, type &*File* in the *Caption* box. The ampersand (&) precedes the access key, which is F in this case. You'll see the word &File appear in the large list box near the bottom of the dialog box, where your menu captions are displayed.

4. The Name box is where you set the Name property that you'll use in your code to refer to this menu. For *Name,* type *mnuFile.*

5. Leave Menu Editor open while you read the next section.

That's all the properties that you need to set for the File menu. You'll use some of the other properties in the next section.

Adding Commands to the Menu

Now that we have created the File menu, let's add the commands to it. We'll define the commands in the order that we want them to appear, beginning with New.

1. Click the *Next* button. The line beneath File becomes selected in the ListBox, and all the properties return to their default values.

2. Type *&New* in the *Caption* box.

3. Type *mnuFileNew* in the *Name* box.

4. The Shortcut box provides a drop-down list where you can select a shortcut key for the menu command. Select *Ctrl+N* in the *Shortcut* box.

5. The outline buttons (see Figure 5-6) control the placement of the current item in the ListBox. Try clicking the up button to move New up one line.

6. Click the down button to move New down one line.

7. Try the left and right buttons, which indent and un-indent the item.

8. Now click the right button so that New is indented one level under File. With this indentation, New will appear on the File menu rather than the menu bar.

9. Leave Menu Editor open while you read the next section.

NOTE

We're employing a common naming scheme for menu items. Each name starts with *mnu,* followed by the name of the menu, followed by the name of the option, as in mnuFileNew. The hierarchy continues to another level for a submenu. For example, if Format | Paragraph leads to a submenu containing an option called Borders, that option would be named mnuFormatParagraphBorders.

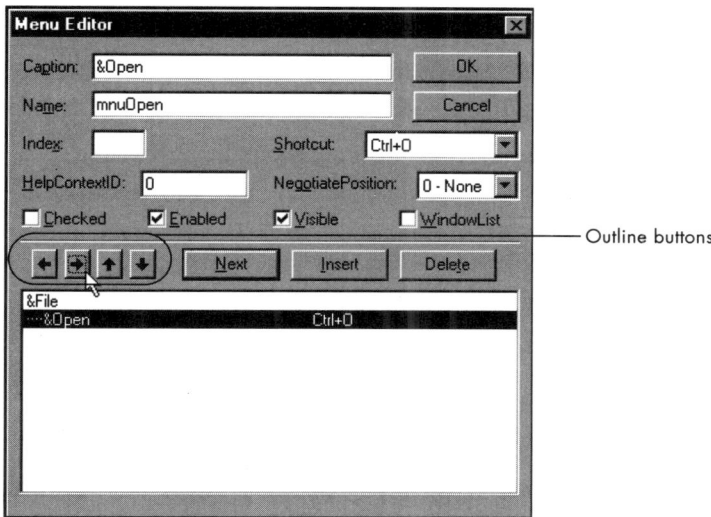

Outline buttons

Figure 5-6: These four outline buttons let you control the placement of the current caption in the list box.

When a command leads to a dialog box, we place an ellipsis (...) after its name. In our File menu, the Open, Save As, and Print commands all have ellipses. So when you create their captions, be sure to type the three dots after the name. Let's create the rest of the first group of commands now.

1. Click *Next* to start a new line. It is automatically indented to the same level as the preceding line.

2. Type *&Open...* (don't forget the ellipsis) for the *Caption*, type *mnuFileOpen* for the *Name*, and select *Ctrl+O* as the *Shortcut*.

3. Click *Next* to start a new line. Type *&Save* (no ellipsis) for the *Caption*, type *mnuFileSave* for the *Name*, and select *Ctrl+S* as the *Shortcut*.

4. Click *Next*, type *Save &As...* for the *Caption*, and type *mnuFileSaveAs* for the *Name*. (No shortcut.)

5. Click *Next*, type *&Print...* for the *Caption*, type *mnuFilePrint* for the *Name*, and select *Ctrl+P* as the *Shortcut*.

6. Leave Menu Editor open while you read the next section.

Separator Bars

A separator bar helps to group similar commands together. Our current example has a separator bar before the Exit command. To create a separator bar, you type a single hyphen (-) as the Caption of the menu item. You must give this bar a name, just like any other menu item. We usually call the bars mnuFileSep1, mnuFileSep2, and so on. In this case, since there is only one bar on the File menu, we'll just call it mnuFileSep. Let's finish the menus now.

---

1. Click *Next* to start the next item.

2. Type one hyphen (-) for the *Caption*. This caption tells Menu Editor that you want a separator bar.

3. Type *mnuFileSep* for the *Name*.

4. Click *Next*. Type *&Exit* for the *Caption* and type *mnuFileExit* for the *name*.

5. Now you should be able to create the rest of the menus on your own. Create the menus shown below.

   Use the left arrow button to un-indent the Edit item, so that it is not a part of the File menu. Names are shown in parentheses after each item.

   ```
   Edit (mnuEdit)
     Copy (mnuEditCopy) Ctrl+C
     Cut (mnuEditCut) Ctrl+X
     Paste (mnuEditPaste) Ctrl+V
   Text  (mnuText)
     Font... (mnuTextFont) Ctrl+F
     Color... (mnuTextColor) Ctrl+H
   Paragraph  (mnuParagraph)
     Left (mnuParagraphLeft) Ctrl+L
     Right (mnuParagraphRight) Ctrl+R
     Center (mnuParagraphCenter) Ctrl+M
     _____ (mnuParagraphSep)
     Bullet (mnuParagraphBullet) Ctrl+B
   Window (mnuWindow)
     Tile (mnuWindowTile)
     Cascade (mnuWindowCascade)
   Help (mnuHelp)
     ScratchPad Help Topics... (mnuHelpTopics)
   About ScratchPad...  (mnuHelpAbout)
   ```

6. Click *OK* to close Menu Editor. The menu bar appears on your form.

7. Pull down each menu and examine its contents. If anything looks wrong, reopen Menu Editor and fix it.

8. When all is well, save your project.

9. Run your project and try out the menus. You can pull them down, but nothing happens yet when you choose an option.

Other Menu Properties

As you can see in Menu Editor, a menu item has several properties in addition to Caption, Name, and Shortcut. Only Caption and Name are required. All the others are optional. Table 5-1 briefly describes each property.

Table 5-1: Menu Item Properties

Property	Effect
Caption	Specifies the exact text to appear on the menu; required.
Name	Specifies the name by which you reference this item in your code; required.
Index	Indicates the item's position in a control array.
Shortcut	The key combo that triggers this option.
HelpContextID	Identifies the help topic related to this option.
NegotiatePosition	Indicates how the menu bar displays menu items from applications that are included in this application via OLE.
Checked	When True, a small check mark appears to the left of the item.
Enabled	When False, the item is dimmed and cannot be selected.
Visible	When False, the item does not appear on the menu.
WindowList	For applications that handle multiple documents via MDI, displays the list of open child forms at the bottom of the current menu.

When you set these properties in Menu Editor, they affect the initial appearance of the menus when you start up the application. But you can also access each property by name at run time to change its setting. For example, suppose you want the Edit|Paste command to be disabled unless something is on the Clipboard. You would uncheck its Enabled property in Menu Editor so that it is disabled when the application starts. Then, when the user cuts or copies some text to the Clipboard, you would use the following statement to enable it:

```
mnuEditPaste.Enabled = True
```

The only property that you can't change at run time is the item's name.

Adding a Window List

When an application handles multiple documents, the Window menu often displays a list of open windows, as you can see in Figure 5-7. Let's add this list to our Window menu now.

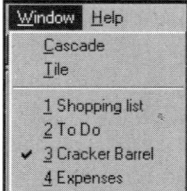

Figure 5-7: You can activate a window by selecting it from the Window list.

1. Click the MDI form (the parent form) to make sure it is selected.

2. Open Menu Editor. (Hint: Click the Menu Editor icon or choose *Tools | Menu Editor.*) The menus we defined previously appear in the ListBox.

3. Click the *Window* item in the ListBox. The Window item's properties appear in the various boxes.

4. Click *WindowList* so that a check mark appears in its box. This tells Visual Basic that you want a window list on this menu. Visual Basic will do the rest.

5. Click *OK* to close Menu Editor.

6. Pull down the *Window* menu. You won't see a window list while in design mode.

7. Run the program and pull down the *Window* menu. You'll see the window list with one item on it: the untitled window.

8. End the program and save your project.

In ScratchPad, we placed the menu bar on the parent form because we're going to use the same menus all the time. Some applications have more than one type of child form, each with their own menu bar. For such applications, you would define the menu bar on each child form. At run time, Visual Basic automatically moves the active child's menu bar to the parent form, overlaying the parent's menu bar, if any.

Making Menu Items Work

As soon as you create a menu, its physical features work. That is, menus and submenus appear when they're supposed to, options are dimmed when their Enabled properties are False, and so on. And when someone chooses a menu command at run time, Visual Basic generates an event. Now all you have to do is write the code to process the events.

In this chapter, we'll write the code for the File | New and Help | About commands. You'll be writing the code for the other ScratchPad commands in upcoming chapters.

OPENING A NEW DOCUMENT WINDOW

When the user selects File | New, a new ScratchPad window should appear into which the user can type text. How do we make the new window appear? First, we declare a new form object, then we show that object. Here's what the code looks like:

```
Dim objNewDoc As New frmDocument
objNewDoc.Show
```

The Dim statement creates a new instance of frmDocument called objNewDoc. The *New* keyword is important, as it tells Visual Basic that objNewDoc is another instance of a frmDocument object, not some type of variable. Then the Show method displays the new object.

Let's add this code to ScratchPad and try it out.

1. In design mode, click *File | New* on the parent form. This opens up the code window for mnuFileNew_Click. (Click is the only available event for menu items.)

2. Enter the two lines of code shown in the text before this exercise to the procedure.

3. Save your project.

4. Run the program. Visual Basic displays the first child document maximized inside the parent window.

5. Restore the document to unmaximized size.

6. Choose *File | New*. A new maximized document appears in the window.

7. Restore the new document to unmaximized size. You should now see two forms in the window.

8. Add as many new documents as you'd like.

9. Take a look at the *Window* menu to see what the window list looks like.

10. When you're done experimenting, end the program.

CASCADING AND TILING THE CHILD WINDOWS

Now let's turn our attention to the two commands on the Window menu: Cascade and Tile. Once again, Visual Basic makes it very easy to make those two commands work. Because frmScratchPad is an MDI form, it has a method called Arrange, which looks like this:

```
object.Arrange arrangement
```

The value of *arrangement* determines how the open windows on the form are arranged. You can use one of these special words: vbCascade, vbTileHorizontal, vbTileVertical. What's the difference between tiling horizontally and vertically? If you have six windows tiled horizontally, there are two windows on each row, and three rows. If the same six windows are tiled vertically, you get three windows on each row, and two rows. In other words, the horizontally tiled windows are short and wide, while the vertically tiled windows are tall and skinny. To tile the open windows in frmScratchPad horizontally, you would code:

```
frmScratchPad.Arrange vbTileHorizontal
```

Let's make the Window menu commands work now.

---

1. In design mode, click *Window|Cascade* to open the code window for mnuWindowCascade_Click.

2. Add the following statement to the procedure:

```
frmScratchPad.Arrange vbCascade
```

3. Click *Window|Tile* to open the code window for mnuWindowTile_Click.

4. Add the following statement to the procedure:

```
frmScratchPad.Arrange vbTileVertical
```

5. Save your project.

6. Try out your new commands:

    a) Run the program.

    b) Use *File|New* to create several child forms.

    c) Choose *Window|Cascade*.

    d) Choose *Window|Tile*.

7. End the program.

ADDING AN ABOUT DIALOG BOX

All the forms we've developed so far have been windows. But dialog boxes are also forms, with a few different properties:

▶ They are usually not resizable.

▶ They don't usually have a control menu or Minimize or Maximize icons.

▶ They usually offer at least one CommandButton.

In the next exercise, we'll create the dialog box that appears when someone chooses Help|About ScratchPad. Figure 5-8 shows an example of the window we'll create. You can, of course, be as creative as you want with this dialog box—perhaps adding your own photograph, a video clip, a sound clip (music or a greeting), or whatever. (Adding multimedia is covered in Chapter 8.)

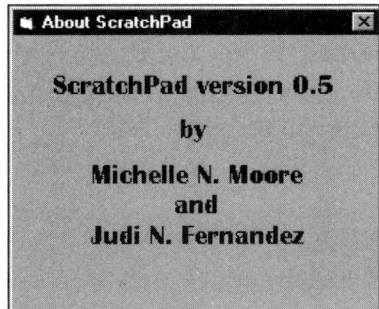

Figure 5-8: The About dialog box contains authorship and copyright information for your program.

First, let's create the form for the dialog box.

1. To add another blank form to your project, click the form tool in the toolbar (shown here) or choose *Insert | Form*.

   The new form is captioned Form1.

2. Change the *Caption* to *About ScratchPad*.

3. Change the *Name* to *frmAbout*.

4. For *BorderStyle*, choose *3 - Fixed Dialog*. This fixes the border of the form so it can't be resized.

   This is the most important property, as it tells Visual Basic that you're creating a dialog box. Visual Basic automatically sets MaxButton and MinButton to False, so there won't be a Maximize or Minimize icon on the title bar.

5. Place whatever Labels, Images, and other controls you'd like on the form.

6. Save the new form as *frmAbout.frm*. Save your project, too.

We'll use the Show method to display this dialog box, in much the same way that we used Show to display the child form before. But this time, we want to consider *modality*. When a form is *modal*, the user must deal with it. She or he can't click another window or dialog box in the same application until the modal form is closed. When a form is *modeless*, on the other hand, the user can switch away from it without closing it. Most windows are modeless; most dialog boxes are modal—although there are exceptions in both cases.

You determine whether a form is modeless or modal when you display it via the Show method. To make it modal, you code something like this:

```
object.Show 1
```

To make it modeless, you use a 0 or nothing instead of the 1. All the forms that we have shown so far have been modeless because we have omitted the 0 or 1. Now, we're going to make the About dialog box modal. Let's write the code to show the dialog box.

1. In design mode, click *Help|About* to open the code window for *mnuHelpAbout_Click*.

2. Insert the following statement in the procedure.

   ```
   frmAbout.Show 1
   ```

3. Save the project.

4. Run the program and choose *Help|About*. The dialog box appears.

5. Try to choose another menu command in the ScratchPad application. You can't do it because there is a modal dialog on your screen. You can switch to other applications, however.

6. Close the dialog box by clicking its Close icon.

7. End the program.

MODULES

Take a look at your project window. Notice that each form has its own entry in the window (see Figure 5-9). The file name of the form is shown on the left, and the Name property on the right. The icon indicates the type of object: a plain old garden-variety form, a child form, and an MDI form.

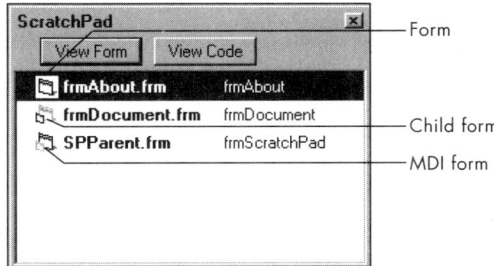

Figure 5-9: The project window shows a separate entry for each form module.

Each of the items in the Project window represents not just a form but a *form module* — a form and the code that belongs to it. When you add a new form to a project, Visual Basic automatically creates a new form module for it. As you write code for the various objects on the form, Visual Basic stores the code in the form module. When you save the information as a .frm file, you save the entire module.

Each module has its own code window. When you're looking at the code window for the child form, for example, the only objects in the Object drop-down list are the ones on that form. To see the procedures for a different form, you must open its code window. The title bar of the code window shows the name of the module.

TIP

To open a module's code window, select the module in the project window and click View Code.

Similarly, the Properties window shows only one form at a time. When you're looking at the properties for the child form, for example, the window's drop-down list shows only the objects on that form. But unlike the code windows, there is only one Properties window. If you select another form, the window also switches to that form. The title bar of the window shows the name of the current form.

Form modules are the most common type of module, but you can have two other types: standard and class. A *standard module* contains procedures that are not related to a form. A *class module* contains the code that defines a new class of objects. You'll learn how to work with modules in later chapters.

SUMMARY

Well, you've begun your work on ScratchPad, and in the process, you've learned quite a bit about forms, menus, and modules. You now know how to create an MDI form, a related child form, and a dialog box. You can define a menu bar with all the features that you're used to seeing in your Windows applications. You know how to attach code to a menu item, and you've learned how to implement several commands that are common to an MDI application:

▶ File | New

▶ Window | Cascade

▶ Window | Tile

▶ Help | About

You've also learned that Visual Basic stores code in modules, and you've seen that each form has its own module. You'll be learning much more about modules in upcoming chapters.

And speaking of upcoming chapters, you'll also continue to work on ScratchPad. You'll add controls to the forms, including text boxes and a toolbar, and you'll learn how to implement the input and output commands on the File menu (Open, Save, Save As, and Print) as well as the commands on the Edit, Text, Paragraph, and Help menus.

PART

II

Building Programs from Objects

A Windows application is built around objects: windows, dialog boxes, controls, menus, and so on. In this part, you'll learn how to use many of the objects available to you in Visual Basic 4.0. We'll start with some very familiar objects: windows, dialog boxes, menus, TextBoxes, CheckBoxes, and the like. Then you'll learn how to create and manage those dialog boxes that seem so ubiquitous in Windows: Open, Save As, Print, Font, and Color. We'll explore multimedia, where you'll learn to add animation, sound, and video to your applications. And finally, you'll learn about many of the custom controls included in Visual Basic 4.0, such as 3D CheckBoxes, ProgressBars, TabStrips, and Rich TextBoxes.

CHAPTER OBJECTIVES

You've played a bit with controls in earlier chapters, but we haven't gotten into them very deeply—until now. In this chapter, you'll learn many of the details of the *standard* controls—the ones you're most familiar with from your own work with Windows applications, such as the TextBox, the CheckBox, the ListBox, and the OptionButton. (The custom controls are discussed in Chapter 9.) You'll also meet a few controls that you might not have noticed before, such as the Timer, the Shape, and the Line. You will learn:

▶ What each control is, what it looks like, what it does, and when to use it

▶ The most important design-time properties for each control (there's no way we can cover all the properties for all the controls)

▶ What run-time properties are and how to set them

▶ Which events are associated with each control and a bit more about how events are coded

▶ What methods are and how you code them

CHAPTER

The Standard Controls

6

In this chapter, you're going to create several small, hopefully fun programs to demonstrate the features of the various controls, their properties, events, and methods. In addition, you'll add a text box to ScratchPad.

TEXT BOXES

The TextBox control allows a user to enter free-form text such as name and address information, numbers, notes, file names, and the like. When a TextBox already contains information, you can change it by editing the value in the box. We're going to use a TextBox as the main work area in ScratchPad, so let's add it to the form now.

1. Start up your ScratchPad project if it isn't already on your screen.

2. Select a child form (from Document).

3. Locate the TextBox tool (shown here) in the toolbox and double-click it. A TextBox control appears in the middle of your form.

4. Resize the TextBox to fill the form.

5. Bring the Properties window to the top and make sure it's showing the properties for Text1 TextBox.

6. Change the TextBox's name to *txtTextEntry*.

7. Notice that there is some default text in the TextBox: Text1. This is determined by the Text property. Find the *Text* property and delete the default text.

8. Change the *Appearance* property from 3D to *Flat* and notice the difference in how the border of the TextBox looks. (If you can't see the difference at first, switch it between 3D and Flat a couple more times.)

TextBox Properties

Every TextBox starts out with default text that is the same as the default name of the control: Text*n*. When you change the box's name, as you saw in the exercise, the default text does not change to match. If you want the TextBox to have a default value, you edit the Text property to show the desired value. If you want it blank, you delete the default Text value, as you did here.

Many controls have an Appearance property so that you can choose between a 3D border, which is always the default, and a flat border. You'll probably want to go with the 3D style in most cases—it looks more sophisticated and has become a Windows standard. In this case, we chose the flat style because we don't want this TextBox to look like a control—just a place where you can type your ScratchPad note.

So far so good, but will it fly? Yes, but not very well, as it turns out. Try it for yourself and you'll see the problems immediately.

1. Press *F5* to run your program.

2. The cursor automatically appears in the TextBox. (You'll learn why later in this chapter.)

3. Try typing the following paragraph as sample text:

   This is the first paragraph. It consists of several sentences. But the TextBox doesn't wrap as I type, and . . . hey, where's the ScrollBar?

4. You've identified one problem. Now try pressing *Enter* to start a new paragraph, and you'll discover the second problem. All you get is a beep.

5. Click the Close icon to end the program so we can fix these problems.

6. Set the *MultiLine* property to *True*. This causes word wrapping when you reach the end of a line, and it permits you to press Enter to start a new line.

7. With wrapping, you don't need a horizontal scroll bar, but you still need a vertical one when you reach the bottom of the box. So set the *ScrollBars* property to *2 - Vertical*.

8. Try out these new features:

   a. Start the program. Notice the ScrollBar!

   b. Type an entire paragraph (any text you want). Notice that it wraps!

   c. Select the entire paragraph and press *Ctrl+Insert* to copy it to the Windows Clipboard.

      (Yes, Clipboard functions are built into the TextBox control. You don't have to do anything special to make them work.)

   d. Start a new line and press *Shift+Insert* to paste from the Clipboard.

   e. Repeat Step 8d until the box is filled and the ScrollBar becomes active.

   f. Scroll up and down in the box. It works!

9. Click the Close icon to end the program.

Many TextBoxes do not need or want multiple lines or ScrollBars, but for this type of application, you need them.

Changing Properties at Run Time

We've mentioned several times that you can set properties through code. Let's take a look now at how that works. We'll put ScratchPad away for a while and start a new project called FontDemo. Here's what it does:

▶ Lets the user type up to ten characters in a TextBox and click a font button.

▶ Displays the contents of the TextBox in the indicated font.

The form looks like Figure 6-1. You already know how to create this form, but just in case, let's walk through the steps anyway.

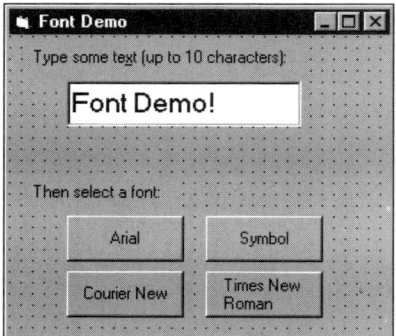

Figure 6-1: The form for FontDemo includes a TextBox and four CommandButtons.

The fonts in this example are supplied by Windows and appear on most systems. Feel free to use whatever fonts are available on your computer.

1. Start a new project.

2. Change Form1's Caption to *Font Demo.*

3. Double-click the TextBox tool to place a default size TextBox in the middle of the form.

4. We'll use "Font Demo!" as a default value, so set the Text property to *Font Demo!.*

5. Change the name of the box to *txtDemoText* and the font size to 14 points.

6. Set the *MaxLength* property to *10*. This prevents people from typing more than ten characters in the box.

7. Add the first CommandButton, change its caption to *&Arial,* and change its name to *cmdArial.* The ampersand in front of the letter "A" makes that letter the access key for the control. When you run the program, you'll see an underline below the A. When you press Alt+A, you'll select the Arial button.

8. Copy the CommandButton (click *No* when Visual Basic asks if you want to create a control array). Change the caption to *&Courier New* and the name to *cmdCourier.*

9. Repeat Step 8 for the *&Times New Roman* and *&Symbol* CommandButtons. Name them *cmdTimes* and *cmdSymbol.*

10. Add the two Label controls. Be sure to put an ampersand before the "x" in the Label above the TextBox.

11. Position and size everything to make a nice-looking form.

    Hint: Having trouble lining up the CommandButtons neatly? Choose *Tools|Options* and on the *Environment* page, check *Align Controls to Grid*. Now when you move a control, it snaps to the nearest grid points.

12. Save the form as *FontDemo.frm* and the project as *FontDemo.vbp*.

We'll start working on the code soon, but first let's talk about how we'll reference a particular property in our code. A reference takes this general form:

```
control.property
```

So to refer to the Top property of the txtStartNumber control, you would write:

```
txtStartNumber.Top
```

Similarly, Label1.Caption refers to the Caption property of the Label1 control, while Form1.BackColor refers to the BackColor property of Form1 (which is treated like a control in this instance).

To set a property at run time, you write an assignment statement like this:

```
property = value
```

So to set the Top of Label1 to 100 twips, you write:

```
Label1.Top = 100
```

With these techniques in hand, let's start writing our code. We'll write similar procedures for each of the CommandButtons, so let's write one procedure, then copy and adapt it for the other buttons.

Here's the code for cmdCourier_Click:

```
txtDemoText.Font = "Courier New"
```

This statement sets the name of the font for the TextBox to Courier New. Let's add it to our program.

1. Double-click the *cmdCourier* button to open the code window. Notice that Visual Basic displays the cmdCourier_Click procedure.

2. Type the statement shown above in the procedure.

3. Press *F5* to test your new program.

4. Type whatever you'd like in the TextBox. Notice that you can't type more than ten characters.

5. Click the *Courier New* button. The text in the TextBox should change to the Courier New font.

6. Try the other buttons. They have no effect.

7. Click the Close icon to end the program.

If the Courier New button didn't work, you probably made a typing error, either in the code or in the properties box. Locate and fix the error and try it again.

Now copy the code to the other buttons, changing the name of the font as appropriate. Test your program again.

TextBox Events

Our FontDemo program didn't give us much opportunity to explore the events associated with TextBoxes, as it used the CommandButtons to trigger events. TextBoxes do have events, but you'll find that you don't use them very often; most programs just don't trigger events from TextBoxes.

The events associated with a TextBox handle user actions with the keyboard (Change, KeyDown, KeyPress, KeyUp), actions with the mouse (Click, DblClick, MouseDown, MouseMove, MouseUp, DragDrop, DragOver), and actions that change the focus (GotFocus, LostFocus). There are also several events having to do with DDE links.

The Change event is triggered as soon as the user changes a character in the TextBox. The MouseDown event is triggered if the user presses the mouse button while over the box. The GotFocus event is triggered each time the TextBox receives the focus (the cursor) from some other place. GotFocus is also triggered when the program begins if the cursor starts out in the TextBox.

TIP

Don't forget that you can find out more details about a TextBox's properties, events, and other features by looking up TextBox in your Visual Basic Help library.

TextBox Methods

We've mentioned methods a few times but have never discussed them in detail. A *method* is an action that a control can perform. You don't have to write code for the details of the method; Visual Basic has already provided the details. All you have to do is mention the name of the control and the method, like this:

```
control.method
```

Here are some examples of methods:

▶ *Form3.Show* — Causes Visual Basic to display Form3

▶ *Form3.Hide* — Causes Visual Basic to hide Form3

▶ *txtName.Refresh* — Causes Visual Basic to repaint the control named txtName on the screen

▶ *txtName.SetFocus* — Moves the focus (cursor) to the control named txtName

Some methods require parameters to identify exactly how the method is to be applied. For example, the Move method must have parameters showing where the control is to be moved. The following example moves the control to 100 twips on the left, 200 twips on the top, with a width of 3000 twips and a height of 500 twips:

```
txtName.Move 100 200 3000 500
```

Like most controls, TextBoxes have a few methods associated with them, including Refresh, SetFocus, and Move. Several of the methods have to do with DDE.

COMMAND BUTTONS

You've already used several CommandButtons in the programs you have written—especially FontDemo. And so you know how to create, position, size, and caption them. You also know how to write code for a button click event. But what other events can a CommandButton have? How do you designate the default button? And how do you make the Cancel button work? We'll answer these questions in this section.

CommandButton Properties

Many of the CommandButton properties are already familiar to you from working with other controls. You already know what Appearance, Caption, Font, Name, and the size and location properties (Top, Left, Width, and Height) do. To explore some of the other CommandButton properties, we'll make some changes to the FontDemo program:

▶ We'll eliminate the default text and disable (dim) the CommandButtons until the user types at least one character in the TextBox.

▶ We'll make Times New Roman the default font.

Disabling CommandButtons

First, let's disable the CommandButtons. The Enabled property controls this feature. When it's set to True, which is the default, the button is available and can be clicked. But when it's set to False, the button is dimmed, cannot be tabbed to, and cannot be clicked — even if there's a Click event procedure for it.

1. Click any one CommandButton to select it. Then hold down *Ctrl* while you click the other three buttons. This selects all four buttons at once. Notice that the selection handles are gray, indicating a multiple selection.

   Another easy way to select neighboring controls is to enclose them in a dotted selection box. To do this, make sure no tool is selected in the toolbox; you can click the selection tool (the arrow) in the upper left corner of the toolbox to make sure nothing else is selected. Then position the mouse pointer slightly above and to the left of the first control to be selected, press and hold down the mouse button, and drag the pointer down and to the right. You'll see a dotted box enclose controls as you drag. When all the desired controls are enclosed in the dotted box, release the mouse button to select them.

2. Bring the Properties window to the top. Notice that only a few properties are available. These are the properties that can be set simultaneously for all the controls that are currently selected.

3. Set *Enabled* to *False*.

4. Try out your revised program. Notice that all four CommandButtons are dim, as shown here, and you can't click them.

5. End the program.

Enabling CommandButtons at Run Time

Now let's write the code that enables these buttons when the user types something in the TextBox. We'll create a procedure for the txtDemoText_Change event, which is triggered the moment the user changes a character in the TextBox. As soon as this event is triggered, we'll change the Enabled property of all four buttons to True.

1. Select the TextBox and delete the default value in the Text property.

2. Double-click the TextBox to open the code window. Notice that Visual Basic automatically opens the Change event, because this is the default event for TextBoxes.

3. Add this code to the procedure:

```
cmdArial.Enabled = True
cmdCourier.Enabled = True
cmdTimes.Enabled = True
cmdSymbol.Enabled = True
```

4. Try out your new version of the program. Notice that the buttons become available as soon as you type the first character.

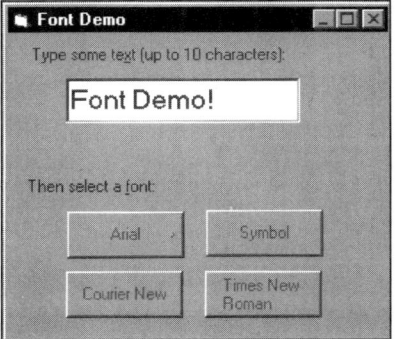

5. End the program and save your project.

We haven't done a very sophisticated job of disabling and enabling these CommandButtons. If someone erased the characters they typed, the buttons would remain enabled. But we're concerned here with how the Enabled property works, and this little program should suffice for that purpose.

Let's move on to the next task, making Times New Roman the default button. We'll use the Default property to accomplish this. Only CommandButtons have this True/False property. Only one button on a form can have Default set to True. When you set Default to True for one button, Visual Basic automatically sets it to False for all other buttons on the form.

1. Switch the cmdTimes and cmdArial buttons, so that cmdTimes is the first button.

2. Set the *Default* property to *True*.

3. Run the program.

4. Type any character to enable the buttons. Notice that the Times New Roman button is now identified as the default button.

5. Press *Enter* to trigger the default button. The text changes to Times New Roman font.

6. Leave the program running while you read the next section.

Controlling the Tab Order

When you moved the Times New Roman button, you created a problem we often run into in our Visual Basic programs. Watch what happens to the focus in the following exercise.

1. Notice where the focus is on your window. If it's in the TextBox, it takes the form of a typing cursor. If it's on one of the CommandButtons, it appears as a dotted box near the edges of the button.

2. Press *Tab* repeatedly and watch the focus move in the window. It goes from control to control in the order that you created them, not the order that they now appear on the screen.

3. Try pressing *Shift+Tab* to reverse the order. You'll see the same problem in the reverse order.

4. Close the program and save your project.

Two properties control what happens when you press Tab: TabStop and TabIndex. TabStop is a True/False property. When it's True, the Tab key moves the focus to the control. When it's false, you can't tab to the control.

The TabStop property is available for controls that can receive the focus. Controls such as Labels or Frames, that can't receive the focus, do not have the TabStop property.

For controls where TabStop is True, TabIndex indicates the control's position in the tabbing order. Visual Basic assigns default TabIndex values as you create your controls, giving TabIndex 0 to the first control you create, TabIndex 1 to the second control, and so on.

Visual Basic automatically places the focus on the control with TabIndex 0 when you start up a program, so it's especially important to control this particular item. Disabled and invisible items are removed from the tabbing order until they are enabled or displayed.

When you change a TabIndex, Visual Basic automatically renumbers all the other TabIndexes for the form.

Since we often move controls around and insert additional controls during program development, the default order is often not the best order. Let's correct the tabbing order by changing the TabIndex values.

1. Select the TextBox and select the *TabIndex* property. If you created the TextBox first, the TabIndex is 0. If not, change it to 0 now.

2. Set the *TabIndexes* for the CommandButtons in the order that you want them.

3. Now try the program again.

4. Close the program and save your project.

Cancel Buttons

There's one more CommandButton property that you should be aware of, but we can't demonstrate it with FontDemo. When the Cancel property is set to True for a button, that button acts as the Cancel button. That is, when a dialog box is open and you have made changes in it but have not yet applied those changes, the Cancel button eliminates the changes and closes the dialog box. It has the same effect as the Esc key.

Like Default, the Cancel property applies only to CommandButtons. Only one button in a dialog box can have Cancel set to True. The caption of the button should probably be "Cancel," but that is not a requirement. Also, in dialog boxes that make irreversible operations, such as deleting files or deleting records from a database, the Cancel button should probably be the default button.

Now why can't we demonstrate the Cancel button with FontDemo? Because FontDemo has one form, the main application window. The Cancel button has no effect in the main application window—it will not close the window and terminate the program. You'll be creating dialog boxes later in this book, and you'll have plenty of opportunity to create Cancel buttons then.

CommandButton Events

By far the most common event for a CommandButton is the Click event. Several other events are available, however, including GotFocus, LostFocus, KeyDown, KeyPress, KeyUp, MouseMove, MouseDown, and MouseUp. Your typical Windows applications don't use these events. But if you're writing an application for kids, for example, and you want the shape of the pointer to change as it passes over a CommandButton or a sound clip to play when the button is activated by a keypress, the events are available for you to make these things happen.

CommandButton Methods

CommandButtons have very few methods. The two that you are familiar with are Move and Refresh. Many applications change the caption of a command button in response to other activities. You've probably seen this happen in applications you have used. If you change the caption of a CommandButton, you might want to follow up with a Refresh method to make sure that the new caption gets repainted on the screen.

LABELS

You've already worked with Label controls, and their common properties, events, and methods are familiar to you now. Properties that you should now recognize are Alignment, Appearance, BackColor, BorderStyle, Caption, Enabled, Font, ForeColor, Name, TabIndex, Visible, WordWrap, and the location and size properties. Familiar events are Change, Click, DblClick, MouseDown, MouseMove, and MouseUp. Methods include Move and Refresh.

But wait a minute. Why does a Label control have a TabIndex property when a Label can't receive the focus? For that matter, why do we put an access key in a Label caption when it can't receive the focus? Read on to find out the answers.

Creating Access Keys for Controls without Captions

Several types of controls don't have Caption properties: TextBoxes, ComboBoxes, and ListBoxes are common examples. We use Label controls to place "captions" above or next to these other controls. We also use these Labels to create access keys for controls that can't have their own Captions.

When you try to put the focus on a Label control or any other control that can't receive it, the focus goes instead to the next item in the tab order. So when you press the access key for the label above a TextBox, for example, or if you tab to it, the focus goes to TextBox. Of course, you must arrange the TabIndexes to make it happen.

Check this out for yourself. Run the FontDemo program and press the access key for the Label above the TextBox (Alt+X). The focus goes to the TextBox. (If not, then you need to set the TabIndex for the Label.)

Setting Label Properties at Run Time

Let's take a brief look at how you would change a label control at run time. The following procedure moves and sizes a Label control named lblMovable, changes its caption to read "Click Here!", and sets its colors.

```
lblMovable.Move 10 10 4000 3000
lblMovable.Caption = "Click Here!"
lblMovable.BackColor = vbRed
lblMovable.ForeColor = vbWhite
lblMovable.Refresh
```

In the first line, the Move method positions and sizes the control. It saves us from having to write four separate statements to set the Left, Top, Width, and Height properties. The second line sets the caption; notice the use of quotes around the string value. The third and fourth lines set the background and text colors; the terms vbRed and vbWhite are explained in the sidebar on "Specifying Colors in Visual Basic." The last line forces Visual Basic to repaint the modified label before going on to the next statement in the program.

TIP

There's a shortcut for writing a series of statements for the same control. It saves you from having to type the name of the control over and over again. It looks like this:

```
With lblMovable
   .Move 10 10 4000 3000
   .Caption = "Click Here!"
   .BackColor = vbRed
   .ForeColor = vbWhite
   .Refresh
End With
```

▶ Specifying Colors in Visual Basic

Visual Basic's native method of identifying colors is the RGB (Red-Green-Blue) method, in which the color is defined by the amount of red, green, and blue it contains. An RGB value is a four-byte number. From right to left, these four bytes show:

▶ The lowest byte shows the amount of red in the color, from 0 (none) to 255 (full intensity).

▶ The second byte shows the amount of green in the color.

▶ The third byte shows the amount of blue in the color.

▶ The fourth byte is always 0. It may or may not be shown on your screen, as Visual Basic suppresses leading zeros in some cases.

RGB values are almost always written in hexadecimal. In Visual Basic, hexadecimal values are indicated with "&H" at the beginning and "&" at the end, as in &H001099FF&. The digits 0 through F are used to express the values. Every two digits make up a byte, with 00 representing zero and FF representing 255. So the RGB value &H001099FF& has full red (FF), a lot of green (99), and just a touch of blue (10). The result is a medium orange.

The reason hexadecimal is used for RGB values is because we can see the three separate bytes in the number. The value &H001099FF& expressed in decimal is 1,087,999. This number will produce the same result in Visual Basic, but is much harder for humans to interpret, as we can't see the three color bytes in it. If you enter a decimal value in a property field such as BackColor, Visual Basic immediately translates it to hexadecimal.

When you're writing a color value in a statement, you don't have to write the hexadecimal value yourself. You can use the RGB function instead. The RGB function lets you specify the three color values as decimal numbers, as in RGB (10, 150, 255).

An even easier way to specify a color in code is to use the QBColor function, which calls upon one of 16 previously defined Quick Basic colors, as shown in the following table:

0	Black	4	Red	8	Gray	12	Light Red
1	Blue	5	Magenta	9	Light Blue	13	Light Magenta
2	Green	6	Yellow	10	Light Green	14	Light Yellow
3	Cyan	7	White	11	Light Cyan	15	Bright White

For example, to set the BackColor of txtName to Gray, you could code:

```
txtName.BackColor = QBColor(8)
```

Another way to accomplish the same function is to use one of the Visual Basic color constants. A *constant* is a Visual Basic name that has a value permanently assigned to it, as opposed to a variable, which is a name that can have various values. Visual Basic provides eight standard color constants: vbBlack, vbBlue, vbRed, vbGreen, vbCyan, vbMagenta, vbWhite, and vbYellow.

For example, if you would like to set the BackColor property of txtName to a standard yellow color, you could code:

```
txtName.BackColor = vbYellow
```

Visual Basic also provides constants for the user's system colors. These names refer to the various Windows elements, as in vbActiveTitleBar and vbMenuBar. When you refer to one of these constants, you access the user's current setting for that element. For example, suppose you want to set the BackColor of txtName to whatever color the user is currently using for the desktop:

```
txtName.BackColor = vbDesktop
```

There are too many system color constants to list here. If you want to use this feature, look it up in the Object Browser under VB - Visual Basic Objects and Procedures.

CHECK BOXES

Even though you haven't created a CheckBox control yet, you'll find that you already know enough to use them easily. By way of example, we'll add a new function to FontDemo, as shown in Figure 6-2. The CheckBoxes are used to determine the style of the text in the TextBox. Let's start by adding the CheckBoxes to the form:

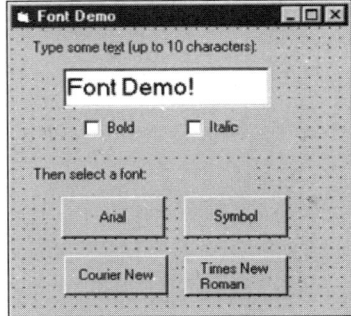

Figure 6-2: We added CheckBoxes to the FontDemo form.

1. Double-click the CheckBox tool (shown here) to add the first CheckBox to the form.

2. Change the *Caption* to *&Bold*.

3. Change its name to *chkBold*.

4. Copy the CheckBox and say *No* when Visual Basic asks if you want to create a control array.

5. Caption the second CheckBox *&Italic* and name it *chkItalic*.

6. Set the CheckBox *TabIndexes* to *2* and *3*.

7. Save your project.

Check marks appear and disappear automatically when users click CheckBoxes, so we don't have to worry about coding Click events to make those check marks work. But we do have to set or clear the Bold and Italic properties when someone clicks one of these boxes.

When a CheckBox is checked, its Value property is set to 1. When it's not checked, Value is 0. You can set Value yourself to check or uncheck the box, either at design time (to control the initial state of the box) or at run time. And you can test Value to see whether it is currently checked or not.

NOTE

When the CheckBox is dimmed, Value is 2.

We use an If statement to test the Value property. A simple If statement looks like this:

```
If condition Then
   [statements to execute if the condition is true]
Else
   [statements to execute if the condition is false]
End If
```

You can see that everything hinges on the condition that follows the word If. When we're testing CheckBoxes, our condition is stated as *CheckBox.Value = 1* (which means that it is checked). You'll learn all about If statements and conditions in Chapter 12, but for now, let's look at how we test our two CheckBoxes.

```
If chkBold.Value = 1 Then
   [set bold font]
Else
   [clear the bold font]
Endif

If chkItalics.Value = 1 Then
   [set italics font]
Else
   [clear the italics font]
End If
```

Now the question becomes, how do we set the bold and italic font for the TextBox? Any object that has a Font property has these run-time properties:

object.Font.Name

object.Font.Size

object.Font.Bold

object.Font.Italic

object.Font.Underline

object.Font.StrikeThrough

Technically, the Font itself is an object and Bold, Italic, and so on are run-time properties of the Font object, but you can ignore that technicality. It's important that the word Italic be singular; Visual Basic does not recognize *object*.Font.Italics (plural) as a property.

Font.Name has a value equivalent to a font name such as Courier New or Times New Roman. Font.Size is the font's size in points. The other four properties, relating to the font's style, have True/False values. So to turn bold type on, you would code *object*.Font.Bold = True. To turn it off, you would code *object*.Font.Bold = False.

Now you know everything you need to know to make those CheckBoxes work.

1. Double-click the *Bold* CheckBox to open chkBold_Click.

2. Add the code shown here:

```
If chkBold.Value = 1 Then
   txtDemoText.Font.Bold = True
Else
   txtDemoText.Font.Bold = False
End If
```

3. Copy the new code to the Windows Clipboard.

4. Paste the new code into *chkItalic_Click* and adapt it for the Italic CheckBox.

5. Try out your revised program. Be sure to test every combination of the two CheckBoxes and the four fonts.

6. End the program and save your project.

FRAMES

Frame controls serve to group other controls together by placing a frame, or box, around them. Figure 6-3 shows an example of a dialog box from Visual Basic itself that uses several Frame controls. Frames are especially important for grouping OptionButtons, as the Frame identifies the limits of the group.

Frames can be simply aesthetic devices, serving to group controls to enhance the readability of a form. Or a Frame can act as a *container*, actually owning the controls inside it, in the same way that a form contains the controls within its borders.

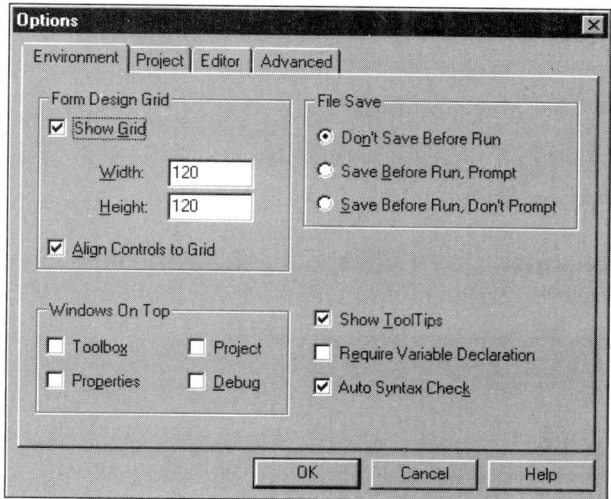

Figure 6-3: This dialog box uses three Frame controls to group related controls together.

When a Frame contains the controls it encloses, they can't be moved outside the Frame, and if you move the Frame, they move with it. That's about the only advantage of using a Frame as a container unless you're dealing with OptionButtons, as in the Frame labeled File Save in Figure 6-3. As you know, one and only one OptionButton in a set must be selected; when you select one, Visual Basic automatically deselects the previous one. The Frame tells Visual Basic which OptionButtons comprise the set.

To make a Frame into a container, you must draw it first, then draw its contained controls inside it. If you draw a control elsewhere and drag it onto a Frame, the control merely sits on top of the Frame and is not contained by it. You'll get a chance to practice this technique when we discuss OptionButtons, next.

Like Labels, Frames cannot receive the focus, but they can have Captions with access keys. When you try to place the focus on a Frame, it goes to the next control in the tabbing order. Ordinarily, you arrange the TabIndexes so that the next item is the first control inside the Frame. Frames can help to provide access keys for controls that don't have Captions, such as ListBoxes and TextBoxes.

You are familiar with most of the properties for a Frame: Appearance, BackColor, Caption, Enabled, Font and all the run-time Font properties such as Font.Bold and Font.Italics, ForeColor, Height, Left, Name, TabIndex, Top, Visible, and Width. Methods include Move and Refresh. Events include Click, DblClick, MouseDown, MouseUp, and MouseMove.

OPTION BUTTONS

OptionButton controls are used in groups to provide a set of mutually exclusive choices. Visual Basic automatically manages a group of OptionButtons for you. You don't have to worry about writing code to turn off the former selection when a new selection is made, for example.

OptionButtons must appear in some kind of container so that Visual Basic knows which buttons belong together. A Frame is usually the container, as in the File Save group in Figure 6-3. But the form itself can also be a container, as you can see in the examples in Figure 6-4 and 6-5. In Figure 6-4, which is taken from MS Word for Windows, it's easy to identify the group, as they are the only controls on the form. In Figure 6-5, which we made up to illustrate the point, there are two groups of OptionButtons: the group contained by the form itself (Option1 through Option3) and the group contained by the Frame (Option4 through Option7).

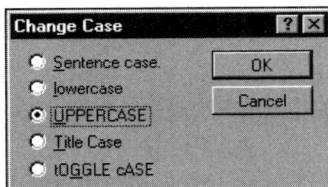

Figure 6-4: This dialog box uses the form itself to contain the OptionButtons.

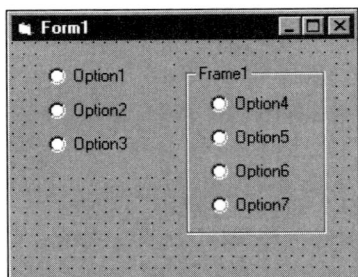

Figure 6-5: In this dialog box, the form contains one set of OptionButtons and the Frame contains another set.

When you're creating a set of OptionButtons inside a Frame, it's very important that they actually are contained in the Frame. If you accidentally contain some in the Frame and some on the form, you'll create two sets of buttons. To make sure that they're contained properly, you must draw the Frame first, then draw the OptionButtons inside it. The real test comes when you move the Frame. If the OptionButtons move with it, they're contained by it.

NOTE

PictureBoxes, which you'll meet soon, can also be used as containers.

Let's revise FontDemo to use OptionButtons instead of the four font CommandButtons. The revised form looks like Figure 6-6. We'll redraw the form first, then talk about how the code has to be revised to make it work.

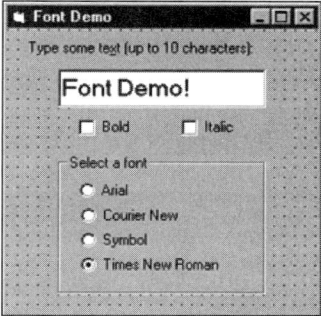

Figure 6-6: We have replaced the CommandButtons with OptionButtons.

1. Select all four CommandButtons and press the *Delete* key to eliminate them. Also delete their Label.

2. Draw a Frame on the form and change its *Caption* to *Select a font:*. Make it more than big enough to hold the four OptionButtons.

3. Click the OptionButton tool (shown here) in the toolbox, then draw the first OptionButton inside the Frame, as illustrated.

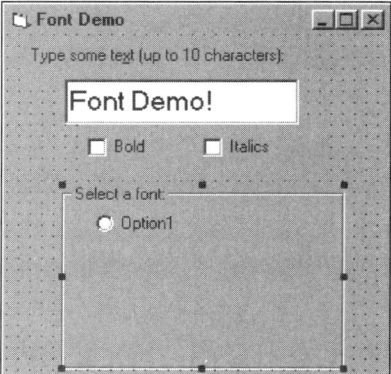

4. Change the OptionButton's *Name* to *optArial* and its *Caption* to *Arial*.

5. Repeat Steps 3 and 4 for the Times New Roman, Courier New, and Symbol OptionButtons.

6. Try moving the Frame. Do all four OptionButtons move with it? If so, they are correctly contained by it. If not, delete the ones that didn't move and try again.

7. Arrange and size the form and its controls to be attractive and easy to read.

8. Examine and set the TabIndexes to provide a logical tabbing order for all the controls on the form.

9. Save your project.

Now the question becomes, which OptionButton will be selected by default when we start the program? The Value property determines whether or not an OptionButton is selected. When you set Value to True for one OptionButton, Visual Basic automatically sets it to False for all the other OptionButtons in the set. Let's make the Arial button the default button for FontDemo.

1. Click the *Arial* button to select it.

2. Set *Value* to *True*. Note that Visual Basic adds the black selection dot to the button.

3. Just as an experiment, click the *Symbol* button and set its *Value* to *True*. Notice that Visual Basic shifts the black selection dot to the Symbol button.

4. Set Arial's *Value* to *True* again. Visual Basic shifts the black selection dot to the Arial button.

5. Set the TextBox's *Font* to *Arial*. This makes Arial the initial (default) font for the TextBox.

6. Save your project.

Now, how do we use these OptionButtons to change the font for the TextBox? Right off the bat, of course, we need to delete any code referring to the old CommandButtons, as it would now cause error messages. Let's delete that code now.

1. Double-click the TextBox to open the code window for txtDemoText_Change.

2. Delete all the code from this procedure.

3. Drop down the *Object* list. Notice that the CommandButtons have disappeared from this list because you deleted the buttons themselves.

4. Choose the *(General)* section. You'll find that Visual Basic has moved the CommandButton procedures there.

5. Delete the code for CommandButtons from the (General) section.

6. Save your project.

Next, we need to create Click events for each of the four OptionButtons. When someone clicks the Courier New button, for example, we want to switch to the Courier New font.

1. Double-click the *Courier New* button to open the *optCourier_Click* procedure.

2. Insert this line in the procedure:

```
txtDemoText.Font = "Courier New"
```

The procedure should look like the following:

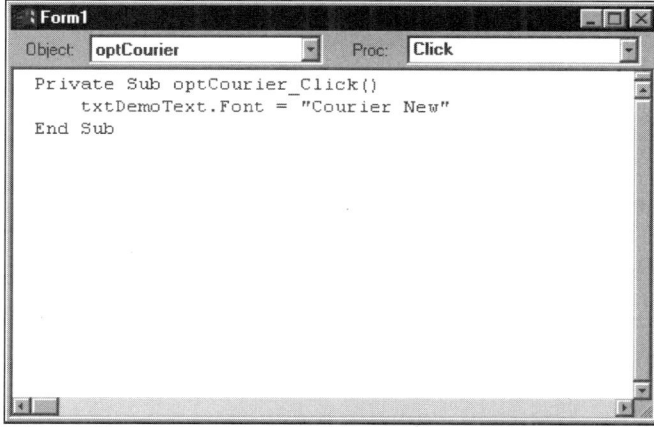

3. Copy the line of code and adapt it for the other three OptionButtons.

4. Try out your revised program. Be sure to test all combinations of font and style.

5. Close the program and save your work.

LIST BOXES

A *ListBox* provides a list of options for users to choose from, such as Figure 6-7. When someone highlights an item in a ListBox, either by clicking or by moving the focus with the cursor control keys, a Click event is generated. You can process the event or wait for the user to actually select an item by double-clicking it, which produces both Click and Double-Click events.

Creating a ListBox

Once you have drawn a ListBox on your form, you use the List property to create the contents of the list. Figure 6-8 shows what the List property looks like when you drop it down and type a list in it. The list doesn't appear in the ListBox itself until you press Enter to close the drop-down. You can go back and revise the list as many times as you'd like until you're satisfied with it.

We'll experiment with a ListBox by replacing FontDemo's OptionButtons with a ListBox as shown in Figure 6-9. Let's do that now, then talk about how to code the events for it.

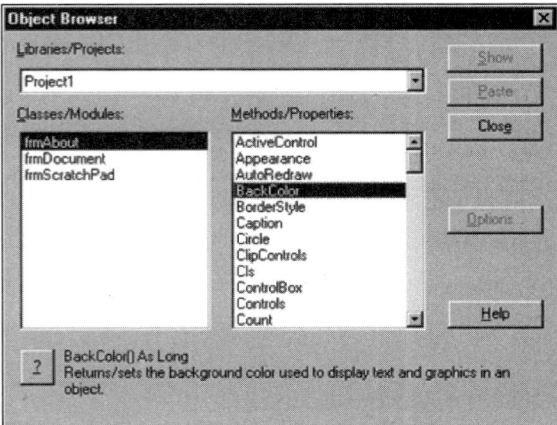

Figure 6-7: Visual Basic's Object Browser provides two typical ListBox examples; the contents of the second box change according to the item selected in the first box.

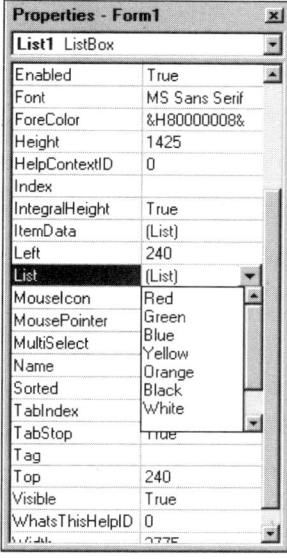

Figure 6-8: The List property provides a drop-down area where you type the initial items for your ListBox, if any.

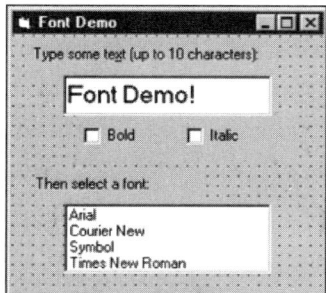

Figure 6-9: In this version of FontDemo, users select the font from a ListBox.

1. Delete the Frame. Notice that its OptionButtons go with it.

2. In the code window, delete the procedures for the OptionButtons from the *(General)* section.

3. Click the ListBox tool (shown here) and draw a blank ListBox on the form as shown.

4. Name the ListBox *lstFonts*.

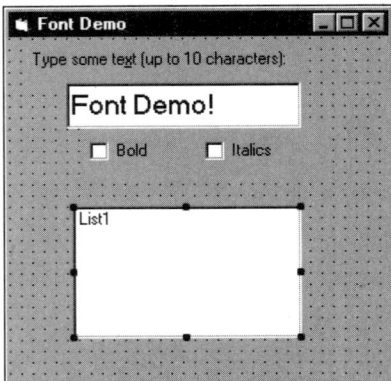

5. Select the *List* property and click the drop-down arrow to display the blank list, as shown here. Notice that the typing cursor is waiting for you on the first empty line.

   For a wider typing area, make the Properties window wider.

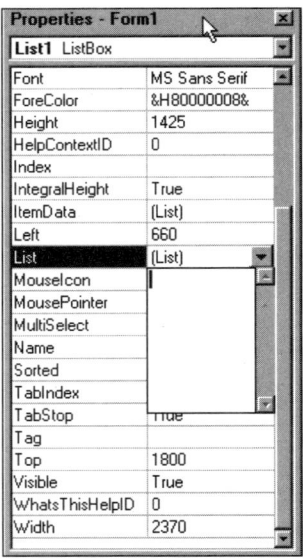

6. Type *Arial* and press *Ctrl+Enter*.

   If you just press Enter, Visual Basic closes the drop-down. To start a new line in the list, be sure to press Ctrl+Enter instead of just Enter.

7. Finish the list with *Courier New, Symbol,* and *Times New Roman.*

8. When you press *Enter* after you finish the last line, Visual Basic closes the list and displays it in the ListBox.

9. Add the Label above the ListBox and set all the TabIndexes to the correct order.

10. Size and position all the controls to make a readable, attractive display.

11. Save your project.

Coding Procedures for a ListBox

Once again, we're faced with the problem of how to make our new control work. When the user clicks the list, how do we know which font was selected so that we can set the TextBox? The solution lies with a run-time property called Text, which Visual Basic sets to the contents of the selected item. In our example, Text always contains the name of the desired font, so setting the TextBox to the desired font is as easy as this:

```
txtDemoText.Font = lstFonts.Text
```

Now let's add the code that processes our ListBox.

1. Double-click the ListBox to open the code window for the *lstFonts_Click* procedure.

2. Add the statement to the procedure as shown here.

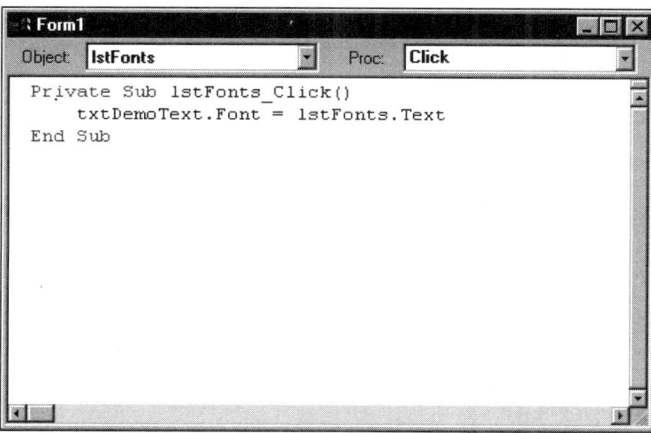

3. Try out your program. Be sure to test all possible combinations of font and style.

4. Close the program and save your project.

Additional ListBox Features

Here are some things you should know about ListBoxes:

▶ Visual Basic automatically adds ScrollBars to ListBoxes when needed.

▶ If you didn't type the list in alphabetical order, or if you add items at run time, you can use the Sorted property to have Visual Basic sort it for you.

▶ ListBoxes don't have Captions, so you need to use a Label to create a caption and an access key for a ListBox.

▶ The ListCount property tells you the number of items currently in the list, and the ListIndex property tells you the sequential number of the currently selected item. (Visual Basic numbers the items 0, 1, 2, 3, and so on, for ListIndex.) Both of these properties are run-time properties only.

▶ The AddItem method lets you add an item to a ListBox at run time.

▶ The RemoveItem method lets you delete an item from a Listbox at run time.

▶ The Clear method deletes all items from a ListBox at run time.

COMBO BOXES

Have you noticed that there's no tool for a simple drop-down list in your toolbox? That's because a drop-down list is a type of ComboBox. The ComboBox's Style property determines which type of box you get. All three types are shown in Figure 6-10.

▶ *Style* = *0* for a standard ComboBox, which provides a drop-down list combined with a text box.

▶ *Style* = *1* for a simple ComboBox, where the list doesn't drop down; use the Height property to determine whether the list shows or just the text box.

▶ *Style* = *2* for the plain drop-down list, with no text box. The box at the top looks like a text box, but it merely displays the current choice; typing in it triggers one of the choices from the list.

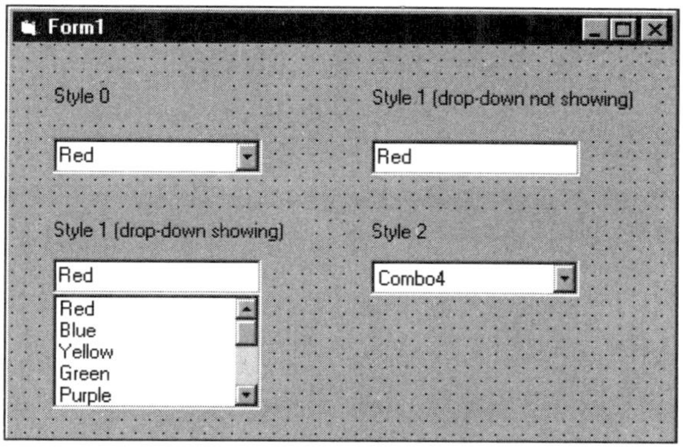

Figure 6-10: Three different styles of controls can be created with the ComboBox control.

For Styles 0 and 1, the initial (default) selection is determined by the Text property. Style 2 has no initial value; its Text property is available only at run time. In all three cases, you can use the Text property to determine the user's current choice, just as you did with the ListBox.

For Style 0, where the user can type a value in the text box or select from the list box, you need to provide procedures for both possibilities. For the list box, process the Click event. For the text box, process the KeyPress event. The KeyPress event is triggered when the user presses a character key (not the auxiliary keys such as Shift and Ctrl). The numeric value of the key is passed to the procedure, and Visual Basic automatically includes the (KeyAscii as Integer) expression in the Sub statement, so that you can access the key value. Don't remove that expression or you'll end up with an error message. You can change the name KeyAscii to another name if you wish, but there's little need to do so. In the following example, we retain the name KeyAscii.

```
Private Sub ComboBoxName_KeyPress(KeyAscii as Integer)
```

In this case, we want to set the font when the user presses Enter (KeyAscii = 13) to indicate that he or she is finished typing. The procedure might look like this:

```
Private Sub cboFonts_KeyPress(KeyAscii as Integer)
  If KeyAscii = 13 Then
    txtDemoFont.Font = cboFonts.Text
  End If
End Sub
```

We won't take the time to walk you through a ComboBox example since all the techniques involved are familiar to you from other types of controls. But if you want to do it on your own, try replacing the ListBox on the form with a ComboBox and coding the Click and KeyPress events to make it work.

THE SPECIAL LIST BOXES

The standard controls also provide three special ListBoxes, for use in displaying drives, directories (folders), and files:

▶ *DriveListBox* – Displays the user's drives in a Style 2 ComboBox

▶ *DirListBox* – Displays the current drive's folder hierarchy (directory structure) in a list box

▶ *FileListBox* – Displays the current folder's file list in a list box

These controls make it easy for you to create a dialog box where the user can select one or more files for whatever reason. In Figure 6-11, we have created an Insert File dialog box to demonstrate all three types of controls.

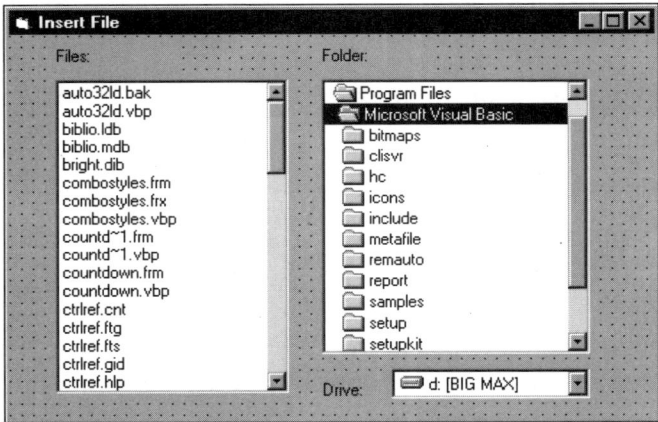

Figure 6-11: The standard controls include these special ListBoxes for listing drives, directories (folders), and files.

You don't have to do anything special to make information appear in these ListBoxes. Visual Basic fills them in automatically. In fact, it fills them at design time, as soon as you create the controls. What you have to code are the procedures that make things happen when the user makes a choice in one of the boxes.

Without any code, if someone selects drive A, for example, the DriveListBox changes, but the other two ListBoxes do not. To make the changes, you use three run-time properties. For the DriveListBox, the property called Drive shows the name of the currently selected drive. For the DirListBox and the FileListBox, the Path property shows the currently selected folder. The FileListBox also has a run-time property called FileName that shows the path and name of the currently selected file.

The DriveListBox and DirListBox do not have Click events. You use the *Change* event to identify when the user has selected a different drive or directory. Suppose the user selects a different drive and you want to change the DirListBox and the FileListBox accordingly. You would create these two procedures:

```
Private Sub Drive1_Change()
  Dir1.Path = Drive1.Drive
End Sub

Private Sub Dir1_Change()
  File1.Path = Dir1.Path
End Sub
```

The second procedure is triggered by any change to the Dir1 box, whether the change comes from the user or from the Drive1_Change procedure.

GRAPHICS CONTROLS

You have already learned how to use the Image control to add some graphical interest to your Hello World form. Visual Basic offers several other types of graphical controls:

▶ The *PictureBox* control is much like Image, but offers more properties and features; consequently, it consumes more system resources and takes longer to draw. The tool for PictureBox is shown here.

▶ The *Line* tool, shown here, draws a straight line on the form.

▶ The *Shape* tool, shown here, draws a geometric shape on the form; its Shape property determines whether the shape is a rectangle, square, circle, oval, and so on.

For Line and Shape, you control the color, the style of the line (solid, dotted, and so on), and the thickness of the line with properties such as BackColor, BorderColor, BorderStyle, and BorderWidth. You draw the object on the form with your mouse, and you can change its size and location by dragging its selection handles.

How does the PictureBox control differ from the Image control? First, it gives you a lot more say-so over the appearance of the control: its location on the form (Align, CurrentX, CurrentY), its colors (BackColor, ForeColor, FillColor, DrawMode), how often it is redrawn on the screen (AutoRedraw), and its size (AutoSize). Second, you can display more types of things in it: bitmaps, icons, metafiles, and text. Third, you have more control over how things are displayed inside the control with properties such as ClipControls (for clipping an image), DrawStyle and DrawWidth (to control the lines used for drawing), Font and all the font properties such as Font.Bold and Font.Italic, and setting the scale of the image (twips, inches, or whatever).

The PictureBox can act as a container for other controls, such as OptionButtons. It offers both the TabStop and TabIndex properties, which the Image control doesn't have. And you can create a DDE link between its contents and a source location for the contents.

From this brief list of the differences, you can see why the PictureBox is much more flexible and powerful than the Image control, but also why you'd use the Image control whenever possible — it's a lot easier to use and doesn't eat up your users' system resources.

TIMER

The Timer control generates Timer events at specified time intervals. For example, you could set it to generate a Timer event every second. Then you code a procedure for the Timer event to control what happens each time the event is triggered. Let's make our form flash red and blue every second.

---

1. Start a new project. (We're finally finished with FontDemo!)

2. Double-click the Timer tool, shown here.

   This adds a Timer control to the form, like the following:

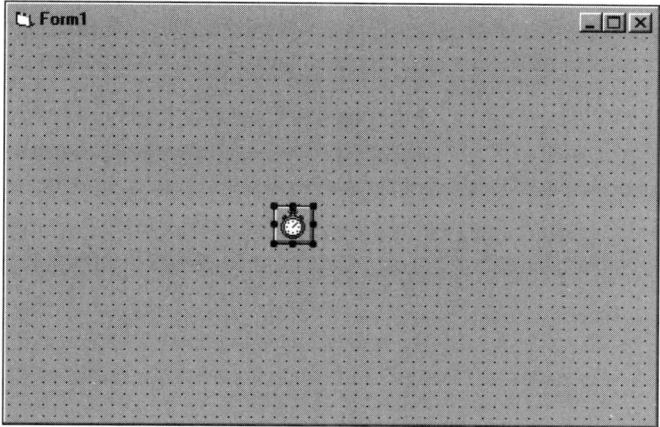

3. Set the Timer's *Interval* property to *1000* milliseconds (which is one second). This determines how often the Timer event will be triggered.

4. Double-click the Timer to open the *Timer1_Timer* procedure.

5. Add the code shown to the procedure:

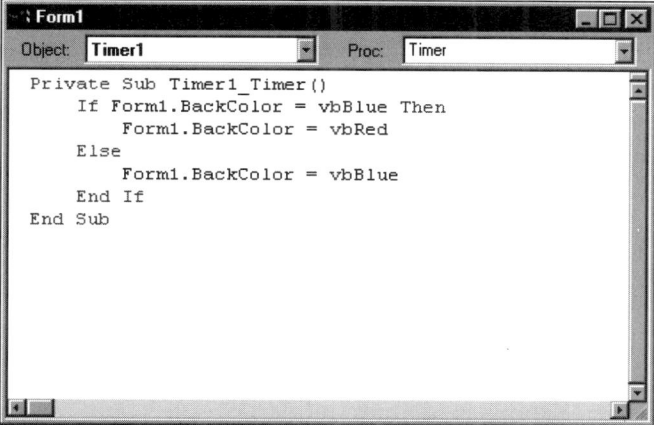

```
Private Sub Timer1_Timer()
    If Form1.BackColor = vbBlue Then
        Form1.BackColor = vbRed
    Else
        Form1.BackColor = vbBlue
    End If
End Sub
```

6. Run your program. The form should flash blue, then red, then blue, then red, until you end the program. Fun, huh?

The Timer control is our first encounter with an *invisible* control. You can see it on the form at design time, but it disappears at run time. There's no way to make it visible at run time. So when you draw it on the form, you don't worry about location or size. Just plunk it down anywhere.

How do we use Timer controls? Here are some examples:

▶ To create an AutoSave feature that saves the user's current work every so many minutes

▶ To create an animated image by changing the picture in an Image control every so many milliseconds

▶ To create an animated image by moving a graphic control every so many milliseconds

▶ To create a flashing warning message

OTHER STANDARD CONTROLS

The other controls in the standard toolbox are:

▶ *HScrollBar* and *VScrollBar* – provide horizontal and vertical ScrollBars for objects that don't ordinarily have them

▶ *Data* – provides access to data in databases and is described in Chapter 15

▶ *OLE* – lets you insert OLE objects into your form at run time and is described in Chapter 19

SUMMARY

You've met a lot of controls in this chapter. Most of them were old familiar friends; you've used them hundreds of times in other people's applications. We hope you had fun stepping behind the scenes to learn how they work. You might have also encountered a few strangers, especially that invisible control, Timer.

In a relatively short period of time, you've learned how to use TextBox, CheckBox, Label, Frame, OptionButton, ListBox, ComboBox, DriveListBox, DirListBox, FileListBox, PictureBox, Image, Line, Shape, and Timer. You have seen how to draw them, how to set their major properties at design time and run time, some of their events, and some of the methods. You've also briefly met the HScrollBar, VScrollBar, Data, and OLE controls.

Will you remember all this new information? You'll be using many of these controls as you progress through this book, and of course you'll use them in your real-world programs too. The ones you use, you'll remember. The ones you don't use, you might begin to forget. But you have an important skill: you know how to look them up in your online references. So don't worry about memorizing every detail in this chapter. (We had to look up details, too, while we were writing the chapter. We even learned a few things we didn't know before.)

We're not done with controls yet. In the next chapter, we'll begin exploring some of the custom controls provided by Visual Basic. In particular, Chapter 7 is concerned with the CommonDialog control, which makes it (almost) simple for you to create Open, Save As, Print, Font, and Color dialog boxes.

CHAPTER OBJECTIVES

Have you ever noticed how most Windows applications use the exact same dialog box for File Open? File Save As is also common to most applications, as is Print. These applications aren't just copy-catting each other. Windows provides a set of *common dialogs* for functions such as these that save you the trouble of creating them. All you do is indicate which common dialog you want to use and Visual Basic adds it to your program.

In this chapter, you'll learn how to use the common dialogs to create dialog boxes for these functions:

► File Open

► File Save As

► Print

► Select Color

► Select Font

The Common Dialogs

7

We said in the introduction that Windows, not Visual Basic, provides the common dialogs, and that's true. They're contained in a dynamic-link library (.dll) file called commdlg.dll. This file must be present in your Windows\System folder before you can use the common dialogs. Before we delve into the common dialogs, let's review the basics of .dll files. (You can skip this section if you're already familiar with .dll files.)

.DLL FILES IN A NUTSHELL

A *.dll (dynamic-link library) file* is a portion of a program that is loaded into memory only when a main program (stored in an .exe file) requests it—hence, the word "dynamic" in its name. Most .dlls contain generalized code, such as the code for the common dialogs, that are useful to many applications.

When you install a new application, it usually installs the .dlls it needs in your Windows\System folder. These new .dlls might upgrade older versions of the same .dlls that other applications were already using. Most of the time, the upgraded code works just fine with the other applications too. However, there is a chance that one of your older applications will malfunction because of the changed .dll. In that case, your best bet is to talk to the vendor of the older applications; they probably have an upgrade that works with the newer .dll.

It can also happen that a new installation replaces a .dll with an *older* version of the same .dll, in which case some of your other applications will probably malfunction. Reinstalling the malfunctioning application usually solves the problem, as it reinstalls the newer version of the .dll.

The primary reason that it's so hard to uninstall a Windows application is because of the .dlls that were installed with the application. Since they're placed in the Windows\System folder, they don't get erased when you delete the application's folders. You probably have many unused .dlls in your Windows\System folder right now—but which ones are they? You can now get small utility programs that will identify and delete .dlls that are not currently being used. There are several of them available in software stores or as downloadable shareware from online services and BBSs.

THE WINDOWS COMMDLG.DLL FILE

Commdlg.dll is a standard part of Windows, and it's probably in just the right place on your system—otherwise many of your applications would not work correctly. Your version of commdlg.dll determines what your common dialogs look like. The ones you'll see in this chapter come from Windows 95.

When you include one of the common dialogs in an application that you write, your users must also have commdlg.dll in their Windows\System folders. It's unlikely that it will be missing, but it could be a different version than the one on your system. You should consider whether you want to include a copy of the .dll file when you distribute your software. If you decide to include it, make sure it gets installed in the user's Windows\System folder. If you use Visual Basic's SetupWizard to create a standard Setup program for your application, as explained in Chapter 21, SetupWizard will include the appropriate code to install all the .dlls needed by your application in the user's Windows\System folder.

THE .OCX FILE

Windows provides the common dialogs, but Visual Basic provides the CommonDialog control, which displays and manages the common dialogs. This is a custom control and, like all custom controls, is contained in a separate file called an *.ocx* file. Like .dlls, .ocx files are usually installed in the Windows\System folder. The CommonDialog custom control resides in comdlg16.ocx or comdlg32.ocx, depending on whether you have installed the 16-bit or 32-bit version of Visual Basic.

When you use a custom control to create an application, then copy that application to another computer, the necessary .ocx file must also be copied to the other computer. So if you distribute an application that uses custom controls, you must be sure to distribute the .ocx files, too. If you distribute an application that uses the CommonDialog control, you must ship either comdlg16.ocx or comdlg32.ocx with it, depending on which control you used to develop the program. As with .dll files, Visual Basic's SetupWizard will create a Setup file that installs all the necessary .ocx files on the user's system, as explained in Chapter 21.

ADDING A COMMON DIALOG TO YOUR APPLICATION

Visual Basic provides a common dialog control that lets you use Windows common dialogs. However, this is a custom control, so it might not appear in your toolbox. Let's find out if it's in your toolbox.

1. Your default toolbox is reloaded whenever you start a new project, so start one now.

2. Look for the CommonDialog tool (shown here).

3. Even if it's there, choose *Tools|Custom Controls* to open the Custom Controls dialog box:

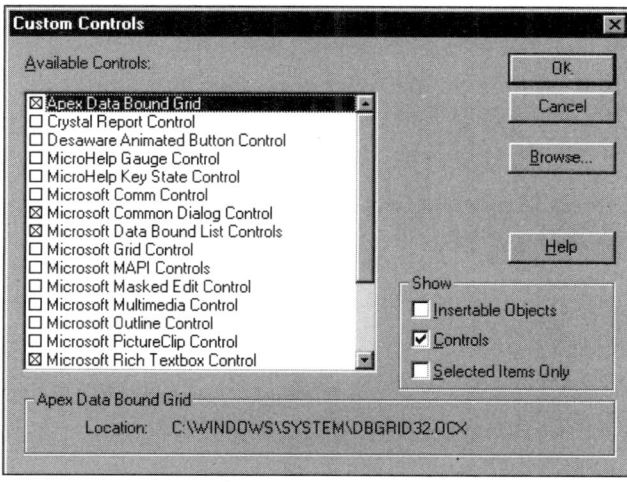

4. Make sure the Controls CheckBox is checked. This adds the custom controls to the list box.

5. Find the custom control named *Microsoft Common Dialog Control.* When this control is selected and has an X in its CheckBox, the CommonDialog control appears in your toolbox. Make sure that it is selected now.

6. Close the Custom Controls dialog box.

To add any of the common dialogs to your application, you double-click the CommonDialog tool in your toolbox. This places a CommonDialog control on the current form. This is another one of those invisible controls, so you don't have to worry about placing or sizing it. You can just shove it off to a corner where it's out of the way.

We'll use several of the common dialogs in ScratchPad, so let's add the control to the form now.

1. Open your ScratchPad project and make sure the CommonDialog tool is in your toolbox.

2. Double-click the CommonDialog tool. Visual Basic adds the CommonDialog control to your form.

THE COMMON DIALOG METHODS

Now that the control's on your form, how do you use it to create the various types of dialog boxes? The CommonDialog control provides six methods, which you use to display each of the dialogs:

▶ ShowColor

▶ ShowFont

▶ ShowHelp

▶ ShowOpen

▶ ShowPrinter

▶ ShowSave

To display the File Open dialog box, for example, you would use the ShowOpen method. Let's try it.

1. In your ScratchPad form, pull down the *File* menu and click the *Open* command. This opens the code window for *mnuFileOpen_Click*.

2. Insert the ShowOpen statement shown:

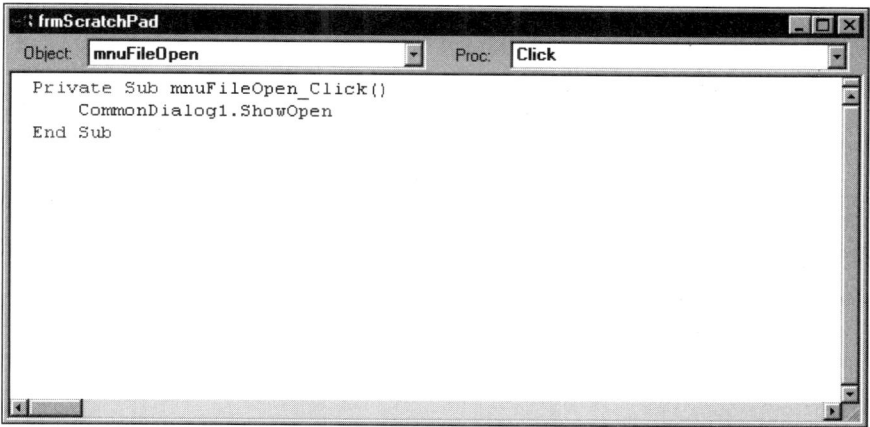

3. Run the program.

4. Choose the *File | Open* command. The Open dialog appears.

5. Cancel the dialog box and end the program.

It's as simple as that to make one of the common dialogs appear. You do have some control over how the dialog looks by setting its properties, either at design time or at run time. We'll explore the CommonDialog properties in the next section.

COMMON DIALOG PROPERTIES

The Properties window for the common dialogs, shown in Figure 7-1, displays the design-time properties for all the various dialogs that can result from this control. Properties include such things as the caption in the title bar and the default file name extension for the dialogs that access files.

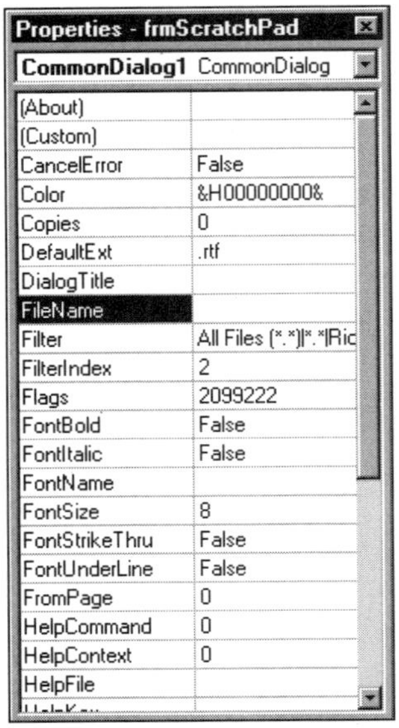

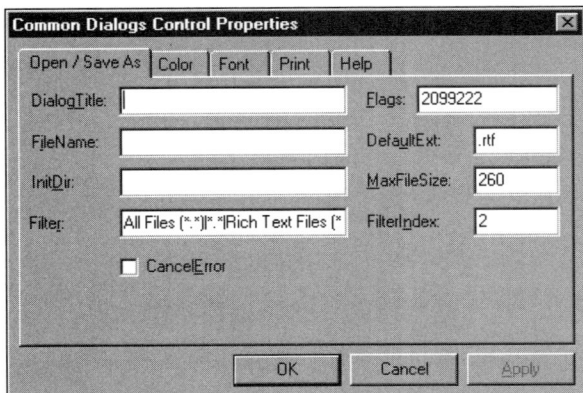

Figure 7-1: The CommonDialog design-time properties include properties for each of the common dialog boxes.

Notice that the first property is called *(About)*. Choosing this property displays an About dialog box that tells you the version number of your CommonDialog control. To find out what version you have, click (About) now, then click the three dots that appear.

Figure 7-2: An easier way to set properties for the common dialogs is provided by clicking the (Custom) item in the Properties window.

Most custom controls have an (About) item in the Properties window.

Directly below (About) is a feature that we're going to use, called *(Custom)*. When you click this item, a dialog box appears where you can set the properties for each type of common dialog. Figure 7-2 shows the first page of this dialog box, where you can set the design-time properties for the Open and Save As dialogs.

The Open and Save As Properties

By default, the caption in the title bar for the Open dialog is *Open* and the caption for Save As is *Save As*. But sometimes we use these dialogs for other functions, such as Insert File or Compare Files, where the default caption might not be appropriate. You can specify your own caption in the DialogTitle box.

Whatever title you enter for DialogTitle is used as caption for both Open and Save As, so if you're using both of these dialogs in your project and want to have a different caption for each one, you'll have to set the caption at run time.

The FileName box determines the initial contents of the FileName field in the common dialog. It's blank by default. If you supply a specific file name, it acts as the default file name. If you supply a global file name, it acts as a filter to determine which files are displayed in the dialog.

Another way to create filters uses the Type drop-down list, as shown in Figure 7-3. You create a list like this by placing a string of values in the Filter box. To create the list, type a description such as "Sound files" followed by a vertical bar (|) and the filters for those files separated by semicolons (;), as in "*.wav; *.mid". Then type another vertical bar, and type the next description, a vertical bar, and the filters for those files. If you want a description to include the filters, as in "Sound files (*.wav *.mid)", be sure to include them in the description section *and* the filter section.

The following example shows how the filters were created for the example in Figure 7-3:

```
All files (*.*)|*.*|Sound files (*.wav *.mid)|*.wav; *.mid|Video
files (*.mpg *.avi)|*.mpg; *.avi
```

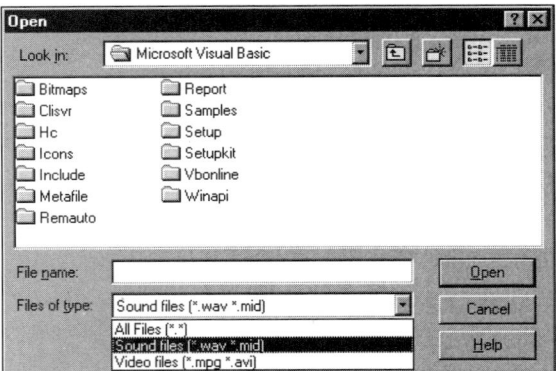

Figure 7-3: You create a filter list for the Files of Type drop-down by entering a string of values in the Filter text box.

If you would like to specify a default filter for the Type drop-down, enter its number in the FilterIndex box. In the above example, *All files* is number 1, *Sound files* is number 2, and *Video files* is number 3. To make Sound files the default filter, you would enter a 2 in FilterIndex.

Many applications supply a default extension for their document files, such as .doc for Microsoft Word files or .vbp for Visual Basic project files. If you would like to supply a default extension, enter it in the DefaultExt box.

The Flags property uses numbers to select options for the dialog such as whether or not the user can select multiple file names or create long file names. Table 7-1 shows a selection of flags for the Open and Save As dialogs.

Table 7-1: Some CommonDialog Flags for the Open and Save As Dialog Boxes

Flag	Effect
1	The Read-Only CheckBox will be initially checked when the dialog is displayed
4	Hides the Read-Only CheckBox
16	Displays the Help button in the dialog box
2	The Save As dialog box will generate a message if the specified file name already exists, and the user must confirm to overwrite the file
512	Lets users select multiple file names
2048	Displays a warning message if a user enters an invalid path
4096	Displays a warning message if the user enters a nonexistent file name in the FileName box
2097152	Permits users to create long file names

Your Visual Basic documentation describes the complete set of flags under the topic Flags Property. Unfortunately, the documentation shows these flags in hexadecimal numbers such as &H8000& instead of decimal, as we've used here. You can't use the hexadecimal values in the Common Dialogs Control Properties box, so you have to convert every value above 9 to its decimal equivalent. Complain to Microsoft.

If you don't have a hexadecimal converter handy, here's a quick-and-dirty way to translate a hex number to its decimal equivalent. Type the hex number in the Flags property in the Properties window (not in the properties dialog box). Be sure to include the &H at the beginning; you can omit the trailing &. It will be converted to its decimal equivalent as soon as you press Enter or select another property.

Now obviously, these are not mutually exclusive options, so how do you tell Visual Basic that you want two or more of them? You add their numbers together. To hide the Read Only CheckBox and generate the Save As overwrite message, you would enter 6 in the Flags box. To display the Help button (16), hide the Read-Only CheckBox (4), and permit long file names (2097152), you would enter 2097172.

Let's set up the properties for ScratchPad's Open and Save As dialog boxes.

1. Click (*Custom*) to open the Common Dialogs Control Properties dialog box.

2. Set the properties listed below:

```
FileName: *.rtf
Type: All files (*.*)|*.*|Rich Text Files (*.rtf)|*.rtf
Filter Index: 2
DefaultExt: rtf
Flags: 2099222
```

Note: The flags you have just set are confirm overwrite (2), hide Read-Only check box (4), display Help icon (16), invalid path warning (2048), and long file names (2097152).

3. Click *File|Save As* to open the code window for *mnuFileSaveAs_Click*.

4. Enter the statement shown here:

```
CommonDialog1.ShowSave
```

5. Save your work.

6. Run the program and try out the File|Open and File|Save commands. Notice that they don't actually open or save any files yet, but they do show the desired dialog boxes.

The Print Properties

The Print dialog box (see Figure 7-4) is used to collect options for a pending Print job. Ordinarily we display it when users choose our File|Print command. We may or may not show it when they click a print icon, as we might want to speed up the process by taking all default options in that case. The ShowPrinter method displays the Print dialog.

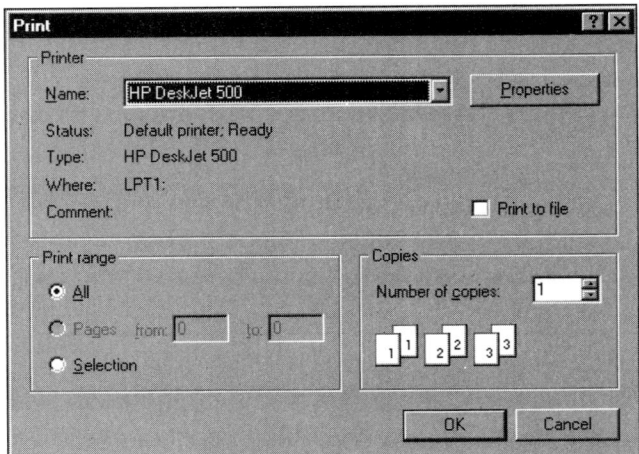

Figure 7-4: Windows automatically fills in the user's current printer setup when you show the Print common dialog.

NOTE

Even though the dialog is named Print, the method is named ShowPrinter.

Figure 7-5 shows the Printer page in the Common Dialogs Control Properties dialog box. Here you can set initial values for the number of copies and the *from* and *to* pages. You can also set minimum and maximum amounts for the print range. When PrinterDefault is checked, any values entered by the user are used to change the system's default print values.

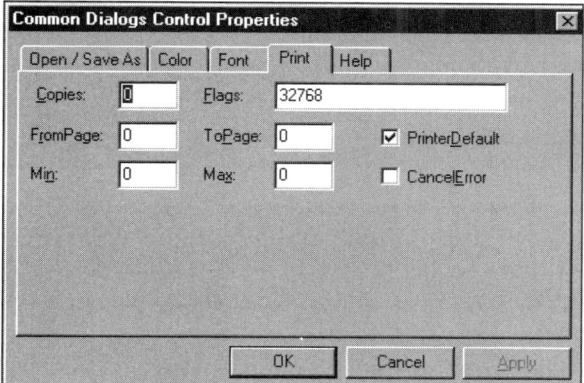

Figure 7-5: On this page, you can set the design-time properties for the Print common dialog.

Table 7-2 shows some of the printer flags; the rest, as you know, are documented in your Help library.

Table 7-2: Some Useful Flags for the Print Dialog

Flag	Effect
0	Selects the All OptionButton in the Print Range group
1	Selects the Selection OptionButton
2	Selects the Pages OptionButton
4	Disables the Selection OptionButton
8	Disables the Pages OptionButton
16	Checks the Collate CheckBox
64	Displays the Print Setup dialog rather than the Print dialog
2048	Displays the Help button

Now let's set up the Print dialog box for ScratchPad.

1. Click *File | Print* to open the code window for *FilePrintCommand_Click*.

2. Enter the statement shown here in the procedure.

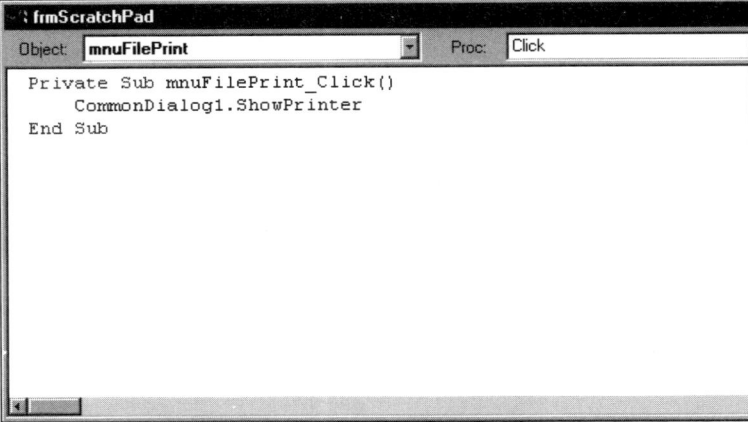

3. In the Properties window, view the properties for CommonDialog1.

4. Replace the default value in *Flags* with *2048,* to display the Help button in the title bar.

5. Run ScratchPad and choose *File | Print.* The Print dialog box should open. You can set the various settings, but it doesn't actually print anything yet.

6. Close the dialog box and end the program. Save your project.

TIP

Why did we use the Properties window instead of the (Custom) feature to set the Flags? When you're going to set just one property, it's faster to just set it in the Properties window.

Would you like to add a Print Setup command to your File menu? You know everything you need to add the command to the menu and make it display the Print Setup dialog box. Feel free to try it on your own.

The Font Properties

We use the Font common dialog to let users select a font. When we display the dialog, Windows automatically fills in the list of fonts that have been installed on the user's system, as shown in Figure 7-6.

As with the other common dialogs, you can set the properties of the Font dialog via the Common Dialogs Control Properties dialog box, shown in Figure 7-7. The

FontName box provides a default name. Likewise, FontSize provides a default size. Min and Max let you specify a minimum and maximum font size, but you have to set the size limit flag (value 8192) in order to put the size limits into effect.

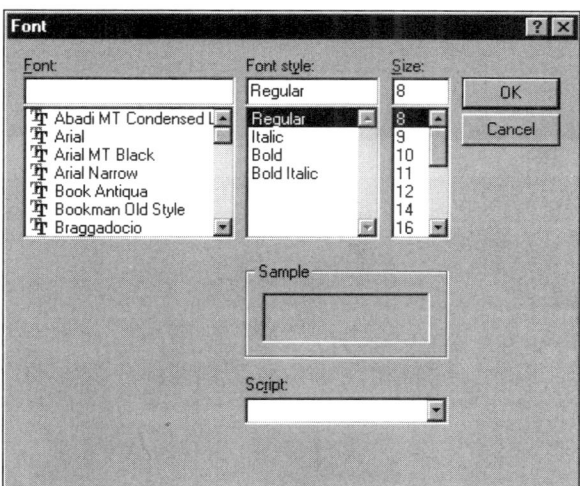

Figure 7-6: The Font common dialog lets users select from the fonts that are installed on their system.

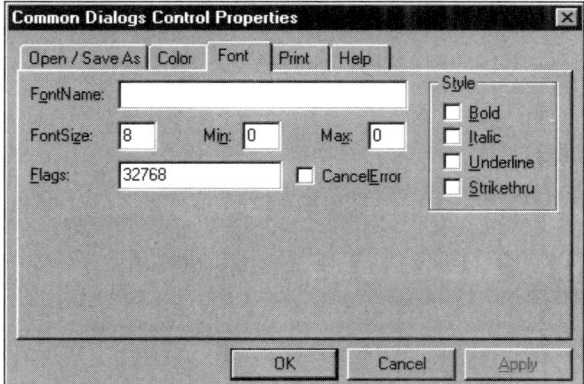

Figure 7-7: You use this page to set design-time properties for the Font common dialog.

The flags are especially important for the Font dialog, because if you don't set one of the three flags in Table 7-3, you'll get the error message *No fonts are installed* when you try to show the dialog.

Table 7-3: Essential Flags for the Font Common Dialog

Flag	Effect
1	Lists screen fonts only
2	Lists printer fonts only
3	Lists both screen and printer fonts

Table 7-4 shows some of the other flag options; the rest are documented in your Visual Basic Help library.

Table 7-4: Other Common Flags for the Font Common Dialog

Flag	Effect
4	Displays the Help button in the dialog box
256	Includes the underline, strikethough, and color effects in the dialog box
262144	Displays TrueType fonts only

Now let's add the Font dialog box to ScratchPad.

1. Choose *Text|Font* to open the *TextFontCommand_Click* procedure in the code window.

2. Add the statement shown to the procedure.

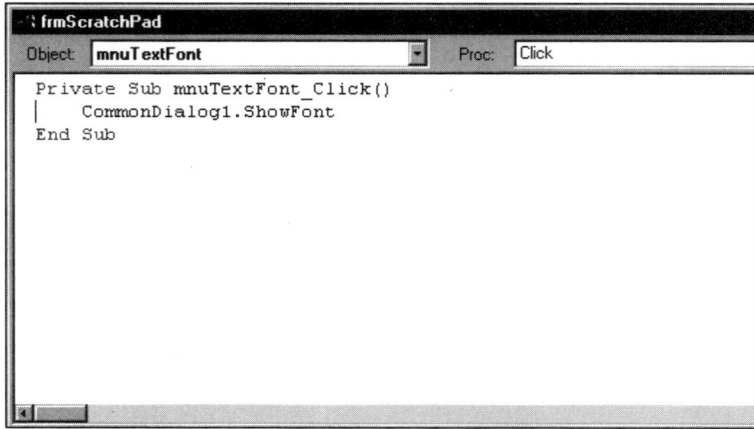

3. Click (*Custom*) and click the three dots.

4. Enter *7* in the *Flags* box to display screen and print fonts and the Help icon.

5. Run the program and choose the *Text|Font* command. You should see the Font dialog box.

6. Close the dialog box and end the program. Save your project.

The Color Properties

The Color common dialog lets users select a color for their current work. Figure 7-8 shows what the dialog box looks like when it is completely open. When it is only partially open, the right half of the box, where users can create their own colors, does not appear. The user clicks the Define Custom Colors button (dimmed in the figure) to open the other half.

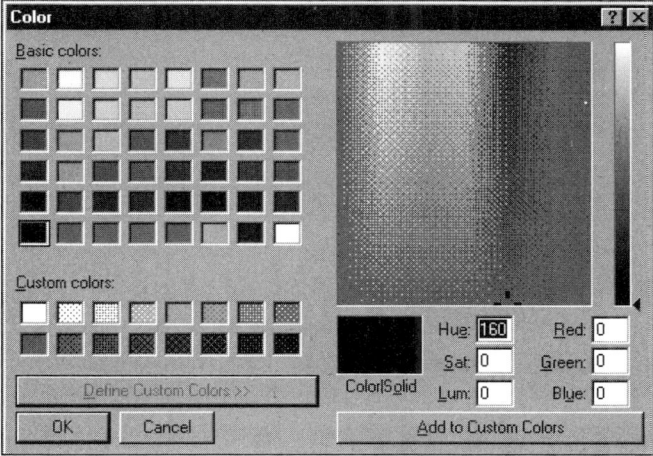

Figure 7-8: The Color common dialog lets users select colors for fonts, lines, and so on.

As with all the other common dialogs, you can set properties for the Color dialog in the Custom Dialogs Control Properties dialog box, shown in Figure 7-9.

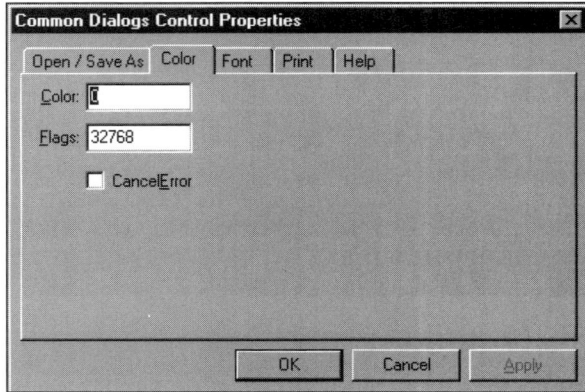

Figure 7-9: The Color page of the Common Dialogs Control Properties dialog box lets you set properties for the Color dialog.

The Color property sets a default color, but you must enable the initial color flag (value 1) to make the default color take effect. The default color is specified as an integer. Table 7-5 gives some common color integers:

Table 7-5: Common Color Integers

Color	Value
Black	0
White	16777214
Red	255
Blue	16711680
Yellow	65535
Cyan	16776960
Green	65280
Magenta	16711935

Table 7-6 shows all the flags for the Color dialog.

Table 7-6: Flags for the Color Common Dialog

Flag	Effect
1	Enables the default color
2	Opens the full Color dialog
8	Includes the Help button in the dialog

The sidebar in Chapter 6 on "Specifying Colors in Visual Basic" explains in more detail how colors are specified.

Now let's add the Color dialog to ScratchPad.

1. Click *Text|Color* to open the *TextColorCommand_Click* procedure.

2. Add the following statement to the procedure:

```
Private Sub mnuTextColor_Click()
    CommonDialog1.ShowColor
End Sub
```

3. In the Properties window for CommonDialog1, set *Flags* to *0*.

4. Run your program and choose *Text|Color*. The Color dialog should open (without the extended part).

5. Click *Define Custom Colors* to open the other half of the dialog box.

6. Close the dialog and end the program. Save your project.

MAKING THE DIALOGS WORK

We've completed only half the task so far. We can display the common dialogs, but they don't open or save any files, print, set colors, and so on. We still have to write the code to make them work. We'll do that in Chapter 9, when we replace the TextBox control with a Rich TextBox, which has facilities for opening and saving files, printing, and setting the font and color of text. A regular TextBox does not have these facilities.

SUMMARY

Now you can use the common dialog boxes: Open, Save As, Print, Font, and Color, in your applications. The biggest problem for most people is figuring out how to set the flags. You know enough about the flags now to create many applications. When you're ready for more advanced applications, you'll have to dig into the Help library and find out what other flags are available.

In the next chapter, we're going to take a look at another powerful custom control, MMControl, which you use to add multimedia to your applications.

CHAPTER OBJECTIVES

You'll find it relatively easy to add media to your applications with Visual Basic. This chapter starts off with a few tricks for animating graphics, but the bulk of the chapter is concerned with the Microsoft multimedia control, named *MMControl*, which is a custom control included in your Visual Basic kit.

In this chapter you'll:

▶ Create animation with the Timer control

▶ Use the MMControl to play sound, midi sequencer, and video clips

▶ Give the user control over the media (selecting, starting, stopping, playing, recording)

While you're learning about multimedia, you'll go back and visit a few old friends, such as Hello World. But for most of the chapter, you'll build an application called EasyWave that lets you record and play .wav (pronounced "wave") sound files. It's a very simple application compared with the ones that come with Windows 95 and most sound boards. Those sophisticated products took hundreds of person-hours to develop, and EasyWave should take you about an hour and put you well on the road to understanding and controlling media.

Multimedia

Without question, the biggest growth surge in personal computing is in multimedia—adding sound, graphics, animation, video, and other bells and whistles to applications. Everyone wants sound and video, at least, in their new products. People are spending billions of dollars every year on multimedia hardware and software—some manufacturers can barely keep up with the demand. Windows 95 includes a wide variety of multimedia facilities, and so does Visual Basic 4.0.

CREATING ANIMATION WITH TIMER

You've already seen in Chapter 6 how the Timer control generates a Timer event at regular intervals. So far, we've used fairly long intervals—half a second or a whole second. But it's not hard to imagine how you can create the appearance of animation by using shorter intervals.

To give you a chance to try out this technique, we're going to develop a program that spins an arrow from north to east to south to west and back to north again. The form, shown in Figure 8-1, is very simple. The graphics that you'll use are Arw08up.ico, Arw08rt.ico, Arw08dn.ico, and Arw08lt.ico. You'll find them in the Microsoft Visual Basic\Icons\Arrows folder.

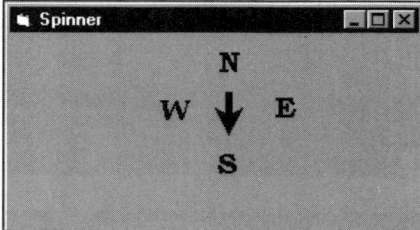

Figure 8-1: In the Spinner application, the arrow spins north, east, south, and west, controlled by Timer events.

Setting Up the Form

Let's start by creating the form.

1. Start a new project.

2. Add an Image control to the form. Name it *imgSpinner*.

3. Set up the initial picture for the Image control as *Arw08up.ico*.

4. Also insert the four labels on the form for *N, E, S,* and *W.* Use whatever color and fonts you'd like.

5. Insert a Timer control on the form. Set its *Interval* property at *250* milliseconds so that it will generate a Timer event every quarter second.

6. Size and arrange everything neatly.

7. Save your project as *Spinner.*

Swapping Pictures

You'll make the arrow appear to spin by changing the picture displayed by the Image control for each Timer event. But first, you need to learn how to load a picture into an Image control at run time. There are several ways to do this, but the easiest is to actually store the four pictures on the form, making them invisible. Then we can use their Picture properties to set the Picture property for imgSpinner. For example, when we want to insert the up-arrow image in imgSpinner, we would use the following statement (assuming that the invisible control containing the up-arrow picture is called imgUp):

```
imgSpinner.Picture = imgUp.Picture
```

Deciding Which Picture to Load

Now we know how to load a picture, but how do we keep track of which picture is currently displayed so we'll know which to load next? There are lots of solutions to this problem, but here's a fairly easy one: Create a variable named PicTracker and set it to 0 when Arw08up.ico is loaded, 1 for Arw08rt.ico, 2 for Arw08dn.ico, and 3 for Arw08lt.ico. Use PicTracker in If statements to determine which one is currently loaded. The whole procedure looks like this:

```
Private Sub Timer1_Timer()

    Static PicTracker as Integer
    If PicTracker = 0 Then
       imgSpinner.Picture = imgRight.Picture
    End If
    If PicTracker = 1 Then
       imgSpinner.Picture = imgDown.Picture
    End If
    If PicTracker = 2 Then
       imgSpinner.Picture = imgLeft.Picture
    End If
    If PicTracker = 3 Then
       imgSpinner.Picture = imgUp.Picture
    End If
    PicTracker = PicTracker + 1
    If PicTracker = 4 Then
       PicTracker = 0
    End If

End Sub
```

Perhaps we should walk through this routine step by step, to make sure you understand what's happening. Each time Timer1 generates a Timer event, this procedure is executed — so it runs once every quarter second. The first time it's executed, the Static statement creates PicTracker and initializes it to 0. The right arrow is loaded and PicTracker is increased to 1. From then on, Visual Basic remembers PicTracker's former value; it does not get recreated or reinitialized. So the next time the event is triggered, PicTracker is 1. The down arrow is loaded and PicTracker increases to 2. The next time the event is triggered, the left arrow is loaded and PicTracker increases to 3. The next time, the up arrow is loaded, PicTracker increases to 4, and is promptly reset to 0 because of that last If statement.

Putting It All Together

Now we have all the elements we need to make that arrow spin. Let's put them all together.

1. Insert four more Image controls on your form. Since they'll be invisible, you can put them anywhere.

2. Select all four controls and make the *Visible* property *False*.

3. Insert the four pictures into the four Image controls.

4. Name the four Image controls *imgUp, imgLeft, imgDown,* and *imgRight*.

5. Double-click the Timer to open the code window for *Timer1_Timer*.

6. Enter the procedure shown in the text before this exercise.

   Remember that you can save time by entering one If statement, then copying it and adapting it to create the others.

7. Try out your new program!

Additional Animation Projects

Before we go on to the multimedia control, you might want to spend some more time exploring animation on your own:

▶ Play with interval for Spinner; make it go faster or slower.

▶ Make it go counterclockwise.

▶ Try some of the other arrow sets provided in the same folder.

▶ Try creating animations using other sets of images in your Visual Basic folder. In particular, try using the eight phases of the moon in the Microsoft Visual Basic\Icons\Elements folder.

▶ Explore the sample application called Butterf.vbp. It's in the Microsoft Visual Basic\Samples\Firstapp folder. Run the application, then look at its code. You should have no trouble understanding how it works.

▶ Butterf.vbp not only alternates images, it also moves the image across the form. See if you can develop your own application that creates animation by moving the image.

Don't worry if you didn't completely understand everything that we did with
Spinner. Chapter 10 covers variables in detail, including integers such as
PicTracker, the Static statement, and assignment statements.

THE MULTIMEDIA CONTROL

Wouldn't it be cool to add some sound (other than beeps) to your animations?
You can if you and your users have a sound board — by playing sound wave
or midi files along with the animation. To do that, you need to use the
Multimedia control.

Adding MMControl to Your Toolbox

Let's start by putting the control into your toolbox, since it's a custom control
and isn't there by default.

1. Choose *Tools | Custom Controls* to open the Custom Controls dialog box,
   shown.

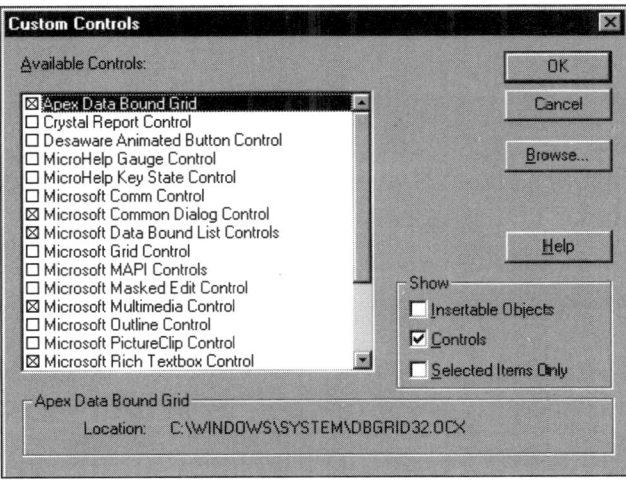

2. Check *Controls* and uncheck the other two CheckBoxes, so that you get a
   complete list of your custom controls, as shown in the illustration.

3. Locate and check *Microsoft Multimedia Control.*

4. Click *OK* to close the dialog box.

5. You should now see the MMControl tool (shown here) as the last tool in your toolbox.

The Multimedia Control Panel

When you draw the control on your form, you get a complete multimedia control panel, as shown in Figure 8-2. If you want to give your user control of the sound media events, you make the control visible and write code for the various buttons. We'll get into that later. But for now, we'll just use the invisible control to play a wave file as part of the Timer event.

Figure 8-2: MMControl places this complete multimedia control panel on your form.

For the sound, we could use any .wav file that makes a click, ding, pop, or other appropriate short noise. Windows' Ding.wav works perfectly. If you installed all the extras that come with the Windows 95 CD-ROM, you might prefer one of the sounds in the Windows\Media folder, such as Utopia Default.wav or Musica Asterisk.wav. And if you're like most people with a sound board, you have probably downloaded and created lots of your own sounds that might do as well.

Let's install the MMControl on our form and set it up for the desired .wav file. Then we'll talk about how to actually play the .wav file.

1. Double-click the MMControl tool to insert an MMControl control on your form. Move it off to the side somewhere, as shown.

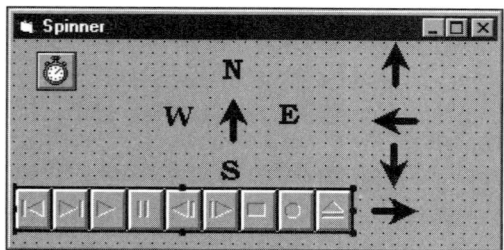

2. In the Properties window, click *Custom* to open the following dialog box:

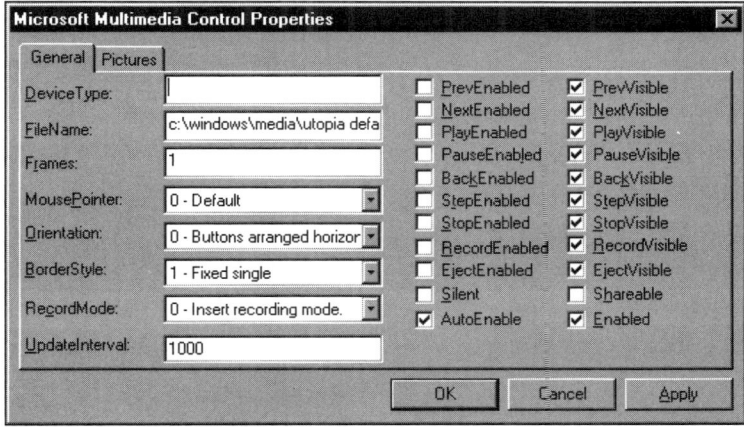

3. Click the *DeviceType* property and type *WaveAudio*. This tells MMControl which type of multimedia device you want to use.

4. In the Properties window, set *Visible* to *False*. (The Microsoft Media Control Properties dialog doesn't have a Visible property.)

5. Click the *FileName* property and enter the complete path and file name of the .wav file you want to use. (You can make the Properties window wider so that you can see the entire FileName property at once.) Our example, using Utopia Default.wav, is shown here:

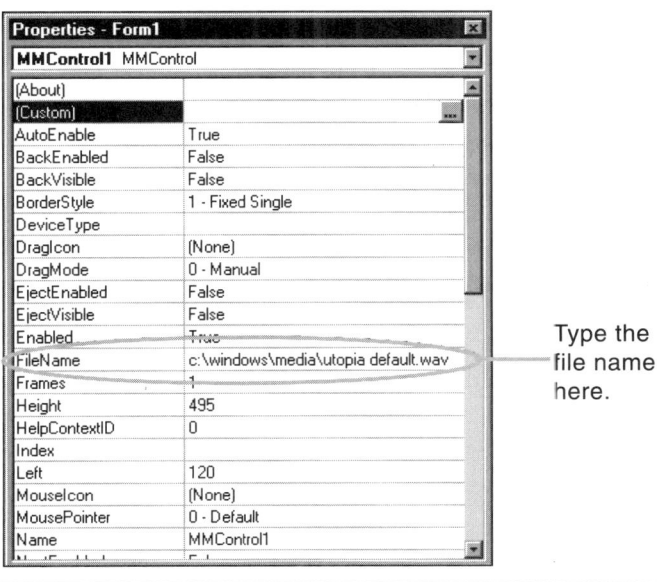

Type the file name here.

The DeviceType Property

Let's look a little more closely at the DeviceType property. MMControl can handle all the major types of multimedia devices, so you have to tell it which one you want to use: AVIVideo, CDAudio, DAT, DigitalVideo, MMMovie, Overlay, Scanner, Sequencer, VCR, Videodisc, WaveAudio, or Other. In this case, we set the property at design time because we're only using one device. You can set it at run time if your application uses more than one device.

TIP You'll find this list online under DeviceType in your Visual Basic Help library.

The MMControl Commands

If we were to run this program now, it would *not* play the indicated .wav file. All it does is set up the properties so that Visual Basic knows which device to open and which .wav file to play when we give the appropriate commands. So how do we give the commands? The regular Visual Basic language has no multimedia commands, as this is a custom control, not a standard one. To provide commands for the custom control, Microsoft gave it a Command property; the commands we need act as values of the Command property. For example, the following statements open and close whatever device is identified by the DeviceType property:

```
MMControl1.Command = "Open"
MMControl1.Command = "Close"
```

The following statement plays whatever sound file is identified by FileName on the currently open device:

```
MMControl1.Command = "Sound"
```

There are a lot more commands, but these are the three we need to play the sound file for Spinner. Let's add them to Spinner and try it out.

1. Double-click the Timer control to open *Timer1_Timer*.

2. Add the Sound command as shown in bold below.

```
Static PicTracker as Integer
If PicTracker = 0 Then
  imgSpinner.Picture = imgRight.Picture
End If
```

```
If PicTracker = 1 Then
   imgSpinner.Picture = imgDown.Picture
End If
If PicTracker = 2 Then
   imgSpinner.Picture = imgLeft.Picture
End If
If PicTracker = 3 Then
   imgSpinner.Picture = imgUp.Picture
End If
PicTracker = PicTracker + 1
If PicTracker = 4 Then
   PicTracker = 0
End If
MMControl1.Command = "Sound"
```

3. Pull down the *Object* list and choose *Form* to open the *Form_Load* procedure.

4. Insert the Open command shown here:

```
MMControl1.Command = "Open"
```

5. Pull down the *Proc* list and choose the *Terminate* procedure.

6. Insert the Close command as shown below.

```
MMControl1.Command = "Close"
```

7. Run your program. Your wave file should play each time the arrow changes. If not, your interval may be too short to allow time for the sound file. Try increasing the Timer interval to see if that fixes it.

Why did we insert the Open command in Form_Load and the Close command in Form_Terminate? Because we only want to open the device once, at the beginning of the program; similarly, we only want to close it once, at the end of the program. Since Form1 is loaded just once, as soon as the program is started, Form_Load provides the ideal opportunity to open the device. And again, since Form1 is terminated once, when we end the program, Form_Terminate is an excellent place to close the device.

ALERT Technically, your program would run just as well if you didn't bother to close the multimedia device. But leaving the device open could stop other programs from accessing the device. A well-behaved Windows program always closes the multimedia devices it opens.

Now that you know how to add a .wav file to an application, you might try a few on your own. Play one of the jungle sounds, or another interesting .wav file, when you start up Hello World.

Playing Midi Sequencer Files

A midi sequencer file is a file that creates music using the synthesizer feature of a sound board, as opposed to wave files, which play an actual recording. Two common types of midi sequence files use the extensions .mid and .rmi.

Playing a midi sequencer file is just as easy as playing a wave file. The only difference is the device name, Sequencer. Also, since .mid and .rmi files tend to run longer, you might want to use the Stop command to stop them if the program ends before the sequencer file does. Let's play a midi file with Hello World. We'll start it when the form loads and stop it when the form terminates.

Pick out the midi file that you want to use. You should have Windows' Canyon.mid, if nothing else. If you installed all the media extras from the Windows 95 CD, you also have a bunch of .mid and .rmi files in your Media folder.

---

1. Save your Spinner project and open Hello World. Notice that Visual Basic returns to the toolbox that you last used with Hello World.

2. Choose *Tools | Custom Controls* and add the *Microsoft Multimedia Control* to your toolbox.

3. Double-click the MMControl tool to insert a multimedia control on your form.

4. Change the *Visible* property to *False*.

5. Set the *DeviceType* property to *Sequencer*.

6. Set the *FileName* property to the name of the midi file you want to use.

7. Open *Form_Load* in the code window.

8. Add the following statements to the procedure.

```
MMControl1.Command = "Open"
MMControl1.Command = "Play"
```

9. Open *Form_Terminate* in the code window.

10. Add the following statements to the procedure.

```
MMControl.Command = "Stop"
MMControl.Command = "Close"
```

11. Try out (and enjoy) your revised program.

Playing AVI Videos

It's almost as easy to play an .avi video along with an application as to add sound waves or midi sequences. The major difference is that a video plays in its own window, and you have very little control over the properties of that window. All you can do is make room for it.

If we add a video to Hello World, in which our main form is maximized, we have to make sure to load the video second so that its window appears on top of the maximized form. Otherwise, it would be covered by the form. So instead of opening and playing the video from the Form_Load event, which would load the video first, we do it from the Form_GotFocus event, which is triggered immediately after the form is loaded.

Select the video that you want to display with Hello World. You should have Skiing.avi available to you, as it comes with Windows. You might have other .avi files as well, depending on what you have installed with your software and what you have created or downloaded yourself. When you're ready, do the following exercise to display the video with Hello World.

1. For MMControl1, change the *DeviceType* property to *AVIVideo*.

2. Change the *FileName* to the name of the file that you want to display.

3. In the code window, move the Open and Play commands from *Form_Load* to *Form_GotFocus*.

4. Try out your revised program. When the video finishes, you can click its Close icon to remove its window.

Letting the User Control the Media

So far, we've been playing our multimedia automatically. Suppose we want to give users control over the device? We can display any kind of icon, button, graphic, or whatever for people to click to start and stop the media. Or we can display all or part of the MMControl panel. We'll try each of these techniques in this section.

Displaying a Separate Image

First, let's give the user an image to click, as shown in Figure 8-3. The computer picture is Pcomputr.wmf in the Metafile\Business folder. You can use any .wav file you'd like with this application.

Figure 8-3: In this small application, clicking the computer graphic causes a sound file to be played.

---

1. Start a new project and add MMControl to the toolbox.

2. Create the Image control for the computer graphic.

3. Name it *imgComputer*.

4. Create the Label.

5. For the form itself, set the *BackColor* to light blue and the *Caption* to *Message*.

6. Add MMControl to the form and make it invisible. Name it *mmcMessage*.

7. Set the *DeviceType* to *WaveAudio* and set the *FileName* for the .wav file you want to play.

8. Open *imgComputer_Click* and add this statement:

```
mmcMessage.Command = "Sound"
```

9. Open *Form_Load* and add this statement:

```
mmcMessage.Command = "Open"
```

10. Open *Form_Terminate* and add this statement:

```
mmcMessage.Command = "Close"
```

11. Try out your new program. Notice that you can play the sound as many times as you want by clicking the computer image.

Okay, we admit that was kind of a silly application, but it takes only a little imagination to see how you could use similar techniques to add sound and/or video to any application. You can add a clicking sound to CommandButtons, for example. If you can record your own .wav files, your CommandButtons can say "Ouch!" or "Hey, stop that!" when clicked. When you terminate Hello World, you could make it say "Good-bye, cruel world."

Displaying and Coding MMControl

Let's get to work on a more serious application, a WaveAudio recording and playback program called EasyWave. We'll start by developing the playback feature, then add the recording feature. By that time, you'll know enough to be able to add additional recording and playback facilities for the hardware you have on your system.

Creating the Play Feature

First, let's set up the main window for WaveAudio playback, as shown in Figure 8-4. The File menu lets users select a .wav file, the box above the Play button displays the name of the current file, and the Play button plays it.

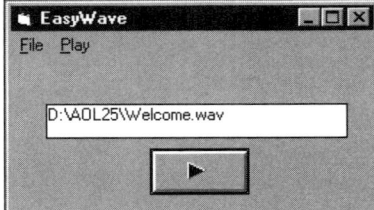

Figure 8-4: The first phase of EasyWave lets users open and play a wave file.

1. Start a new project and add MMControl to the Toolbox. Also make the form's caption *EasyWave*.

2. Add an MMControl named *mmcPanel* to the form.

3. Set up the control's properties as shown. This makes only the Play button visible and enabled. All the other buttons are suppressed.

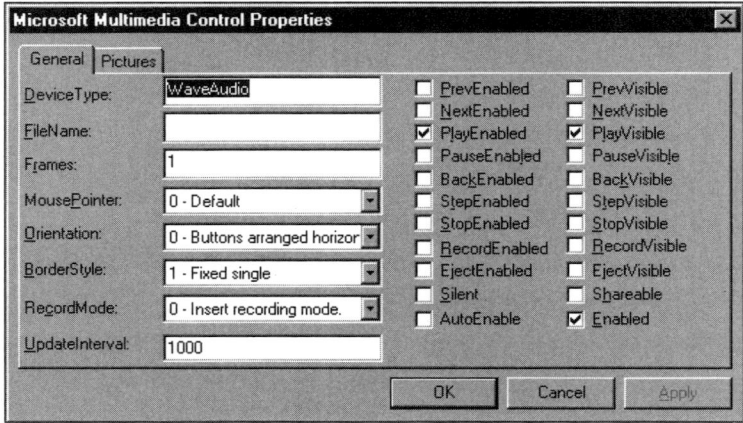

4. Add a menu bar with these menus and commands (their names are shown in parentheses):

```
File (mnuFile)
   Open... (mnuFileOpen)
   Exit (mnuFileExit)
Play (mnuPlay)
   Play (mnuPlayPlay)
```

5. Add a Label control with these properties:

Appearance: 0 - Flat

BorderStyle: 1 - Fixed Single

Name: lblFileName

6. Add a CommonDialog control named *cdlFiles* to the form. Set up its properties as shown:

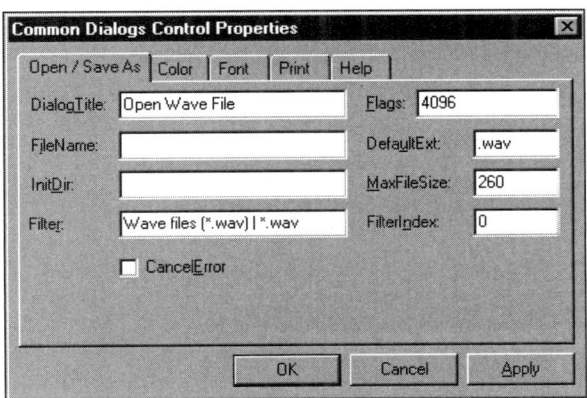

The Flags for the CommonDialog force the user to select an existing file. If someone enters a nonexistent path or file name in the Name box, an error message appears.

The procedures associated with the multimedia control object are named *object_buttonevent*, as in MMControl1_PlayClick and mmcPanel_RecordGotFocus. When you open the code window for a *button*Click event, the editor automatically includes in the Sub statement the expression (Cancel as Integer), as shown below:

```
Private Sub mmcPanel_PlayClick(Cancel As Integer)
```

This expression means that Visual Basic expects any statement that calls mmcPanel_PlayClick to pass it an integer value, which this procedure will refer to as Cancel. The calling statement passes it an integer value by including the integer immediately after the name of the called procedure. The following statement calls mmcPanel_PlayClick and passes it a 1:

```
mmcPanel_PlayClick 1
```

The integer value tells the *button*Click event whether or not to execute the default action for that particular button. For example, the default action for the PlayClick event is to issue a play command for the currently selected device. If the integer is 0 or False, the default action is executed (after executing any statements in the *button*Click procedure). Any other integer is interpreted as True, and the default action is canceled. If it isn't cancelled, the default action is performed after processing all other statements in the *button* click procedure.

ALERT

If you call a MMControl *button*Click event without including an integer on the calling statement, the procedure won't work properly and your entire program could malfunction.

When someone clicks one of the multimedia control panel's buttons, the *button*Click procedure is invoked without being called from someplace else in the program. If that's a possibility in your program, you can set the Cancel integer from within the *button*Click routine, as in the following example, which cancels the default action:

```
Private Sub mmcPanel_PlayClick(Cancel As Integer)
   Cancel = 1  'To cancel the default Play action
   mmcPanel.Command = "Sound"
End Sub
```

Now let's add the code to make this application work.

1. For *mnuFileExit_Click*, add an End statement.

2. For *mnuFileOpen_Click*, add the following statements, which display the Open common dialog, set mmcPanel's FileName property equal to the file name selected by the user, display that file name in the label, and open the WaveAudio device.

```
cdlFiles.ShowOpen
mmcPanel.FileName = cdlFiles.FileName
lblFileName.Caption = cdlFiles.FileName
mmcPanel.Command = "Open"
```

3. For *mmcPanel_PlayClick*, add the following statements, which cancel the default action and play the sound file:

```
Cancel = 1
mmcPanel.Command = "Sound"
```

4. Add the following command to *mnuPlayPlay*:

```
mmcPanel.Command = "Sound"
```

5. For *Form_Terminate*, add the following command:

```
mmcPanel.Command = "Close"
```

6. Save your project as *EasyWave*.

7. Try out your new program!

Adding the Record Feature

When we add the next function, which lets people record WaveAudio files, we'll add Record and Stop buttons to the control and comparable commands to the Play menu. Also, we'll add the Save As common dialog and New, Save Recording, and Save Recording As commands to the File menu.

The Save Recording and Save Recording As menu items and the Record button and Record command become enabled only when the user selects the New command. The Stop button and Stop command become available only during recording.

Let's start by revising the form. Then we'll worry about the changes to the code.

1. Modify the menu bar so it looks like the following. New items are shown in bold, their names are shown in parentheses. Some of them should not be enabled, as shown in parentheses.

```
File
   New... (mnuFileNew)
   Open...
   Save Recording (mnuFileSaveRecording; not enabled)
   Save Recording As... (mnuFileSaveRecordingAs; not enabled)
   _____ (separator line; mnuFileSep)
   Exit
Play
   Play
   Record (mnuPlayRecord; not enabled)
   Stop Recording (mnuPlayStopRecording; not enabled)
```

2. Modify mmcPanel's properties as shown, so that the Record and Stop buttons are visible but dimmed:

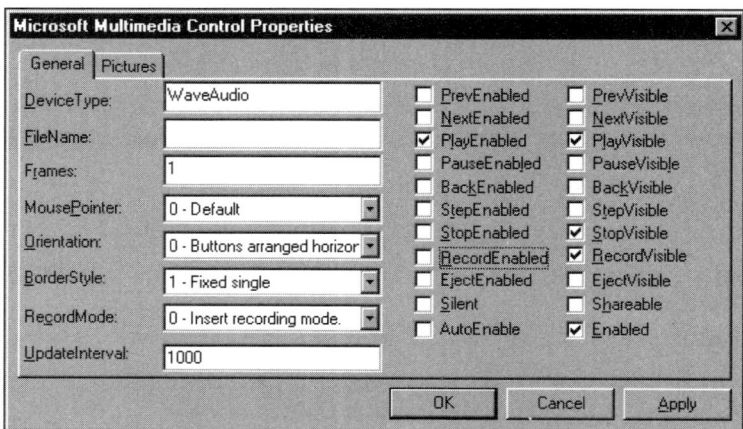

3. Set cdlFiles' *Flags* property to 0.

Because we need different flags for the Open and Save dialogs, we'll have to set the flags at run time. We'll use the same flags for the Open dialog that we used before: the selected file must exist (4096). For the Save As dialog, we'll use the two flags shown below, for a total of 6:

▶ If a user selects an existing file name, display a message to confirm that the file should be overwritten (2)

▶ Hide the Read Only CheckBox, which makes no sense when you're saving a file (4)

Now let's make these features work.

1. Add the statements shown below to *mnuFileNew_Click*. These statements force the user to establish a new file name for the wave to be recorded, then make the recording feature available. We also set the caption in the common dialog title bar to avoid confusing the user.

```
cdlFiles.Flags = 6
cdlFiles.DefaultExt = "wav"
cdlFiles.Caption = "Create a New Wave File"
```

```
cdlFiles.ShowSave
lblFileName.Caption = cdlFiles.filename
mmcPanel.filename = cdlFiles.filename
mmcPanel.RecordEnabled = True
mnuPlayRecord.Enabled = True
```

2. Add the statement shown below to *mnuPlayRecord_Click*:

```
mmcPanel_RecordClick 1
```

3. Add the statements shown below to *mmcPanel_RecordClick*. These statement disable the Play and Record buttons and Play | Play and Play | Record commands and enable the Stop button and Play | StopRecording command. Then the last statement starts recording.

```
mmcPanel.StopEnabled = True
mnuPlayStopRecording.Enabled = True
mnuPlayPlay.Enabled = False
mmcPanel.PlayEnabled = False
mnuPlayRecord.Enabled = False
mmcPanel.RecordEnabled = False
Cancel = 1
mmcPanel.Command = "Record"
```

4. Add the following statements to *mnuPlayStopRecording_Click*. This statement calls the mmcPanel_StopClick procedure.

```
mmcPanel_StopClick 1
```

6. Add the following code to *mmcPanel_StopClick*. These statements stop the recording, disable the Stop button and the Play | StopRecording command, enable the two Save commands on the File menu, enable the Record and Play buttons and the Play | Play and Play | Record commands.

```
Cancel = 1
mmcPanel.Command = "Stop"
mnuPlayStopRecording.Enabled = False
mmcPanel.StopEnabled = False
mnuFileSaveRecording.Enabled = True
mnuFileSaveRecordingAs.Enabled = True
mnuPlayPlay.Enabled = True
mnuPlayRecord.Enabled = True
mmcPanel.PlayEnabled = True
mmcPanel.RecordEnabled = True
```

7. Add the following statement to *mnuFileSaveRecording_Click*:

```
mmcPanel.Command = "Save"
```

8. Add the following statements to *mnuFileSaveRecordingAs_Click*:

```
mnuFileNew_Click
mnuFileSaveRecording_Click
```

9. If you have a sound board and a microphone or CD-ROM drive, try out your revised program. Use the following steps as guidelines.

   a. Set up your microphone or your CD-ROM drive.

       You might have to start up the software that came with your sound board and adjust the input volume/balance of the microphone or CD-ROM drive.

   b. Start EasyWave.

   c. Choose *File | New* and give the wave file a new name, such as Practice or MyNewWave.

   d. Click the Record button or choose *Play | Record* and talk (or sing) into the mike or play the CD track that you want to record.

   e. Click Stop or choose *Play | Stop.*

   f. Click *File | Save* to save the recording.

   g. Click Play or choose *Play | Play* to hear your new recording.

10. One more thing remains to be done. We must set the flags and the caption for the Open common dialog. Add the following statements to the beginning of *mnuFileOpen*:

```
cdl Files.Flags = 4096
cdl Files.Caption = "Open a Wave File"
```

Adding a Flashing "Recording" Message

It's nice to have a message to remind you that you're recording. In this section, we'll add a red "Recording" message to the main window, as shown in Figure 8-5, and make it flash by using the Timer control. This provides a interesting new use of Timer for us, as we've always run it for the duration of the program before. This time, we'll enable it when recording goes on, then disable it when we stop recording. We'll use the Timer control's Enabled property to do this.

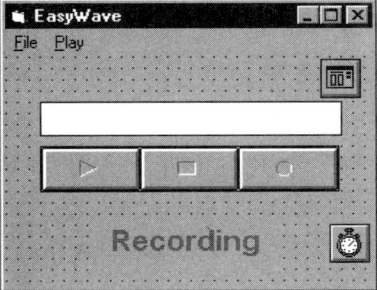

Figure 8-5: The Timer control causes the "Recording" message to flash on and off when you're recording a new wave file.

1. Add a Timer control to your form and name it *tmrFlasher*. Set its properties as follows:

   Enabled: False
   Interval: 250

2. Add a second label to your form and name it *lblRecording*. Set its properties as follows:

   Alignment: Center
   Font: 16 point Arial
   ForeColor: Red
   Caption: Recording
   Visible: False

3. Add the statement shown below to the end of *mmcPanel_RecordClick*:

   ```
   tmrFlasher.Enabled = True
   ```

4. Add the statement below to *tmrFlasher_Timer*:

   ```
   lblRecording.Visible = Not lblRecording.Visible
   ```

5. Add the statement shown below to the end of *mmcPanel_StopClick*:

   ```
   tmrFlasher.Enabled = False
   ```

6. Save your project.

7. Try it out. Start a new recording to see your flashing message. When you stop recording, the message should go away.

Keeping Track of Changes

How often have you tried to close a file or end a program, only to receive a message something like the one shown in Figure 8-6? This is an important feature to add to any program that creates and/or modifies files. Since EasyWave does create files, this is a good time to learn how to create the feature.

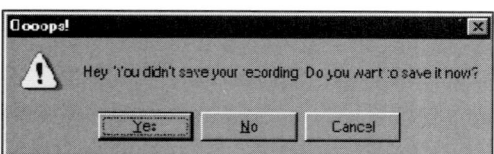

Figure 8-6: Most programs that create and modify files warn you if you are about to lose your unsaved changes.

To make it work, we need to add use the MsgBox function, which creates a message box, just like the one shown in Figure 8-6. (Actually, you can make it say anything you'd like, as long as it warns users that they have not saved the current file and lets them save, not save, or cancel the operation.) We'll also create a variable called ChangeFlag that we'll set to True or False, depending on whether the current recording has been saved.

Because several procedures need to access the current value of ChangeFlag, we'll declare it in the (General) section. As you'll see in Chapter 10, variables declared in the General section are available to all procedures in the module. We'll use the statement shown below to create ChangeFlag. The expression *Boolean* means that ChangeFlag can have a True/False value.

```
Dim ChangeFlag as Boolean
```

How will we use ChangeFlag? We'll initialize it to False when the program starts. When the user starts a new recording, we'll change it to True. When the user saves the recording, we'll change it back to False again.

When the user chooses any command that would lose the current recording — such as File | Open, File | New, or File | Exit — we'll check the flag. If it's false, no problem. But if it's true, we'll display the message box and proceed accordingly.

The MsgBox function is fairly easy to use. We have somewhat simplified its syntax below; for the complete syntax, see your online help library:

```
MsgBox(prompt[, buttons][, title])
```

The *prompt* is the text that you want to display in the message box, such as "Hey! You didn't save your recording. Do you want to save it now?" The *buttons* is an integer that indicates which buttons (and other options) should be included in the box. You can create the buttons value by adding together the button integers from Table 8-1, or by adding together the button constants, as in vbOKCancel + vbSystemModal. If a feature has a 0 value, that means it is a default, so if you omit buttons altogether, you'll get an OK button, the first (and only) button will be the default button, and the user can't continue the application until responding to the message.

Table 8-1: MsgBox Buttons

Constant	Value	Description
vbOKOnly	0	Display OK button only.
vbOKCancel	1	Display OK and Cancel buttons.
vbAbortRetryIgnore	2	Display Abort, Retry, and Ignore buttons.
vbYesNoCancel	3	Display Yes, No and Cancel buttons.
vbYesNo	4	Display Yes and No buttons.
vbRetryCancel	5	Display Retry and Cancel buttons.
vbCritical	16	Display Critical Message icon.
vbQuestion	32	Display Warning Query icon.
vbExclamation	48	Display Warning Message icon.
vbInformation	64	Display Information Message icon.
vbDefaultButton1	0	First button is default.
vbDefaultButton2	256	Second button is default.
vbDefaultButton3	512	Third button is default.
vbApplicationModal	0	The user must respond to the message box before continuing work in the current application.
vbSystemModal	4096	All applications are suspended until the user responds to the message box.

The *title* is the text that should be displayed in the title bar, such as "Oooops!" To create the message box shown in Figure 8-6, we used the following statements:

```
Dim SaveMessage as String
SaveMessage = "Hey! You didn't save your recording. Do you want to
save it now?"
Decision = MsgBox(SaveMessage, vbYesNoCancel + vbExclamation,
"Oooops!")
```

When the user closes the dialog, Visual Basic returns a code indicating which button the user clicked, as shown in Table 8-2.

You test the returned value to decide what to do next.

Table 8-2: Values Returned by MsgBox

Constant	Value	Description
vbOK	1	OK button pressed.
vbCancel	2	Cancel button pressed.
vbAbort	3	Abort button pressed.
vbRetry	4	Retry button pressed.
vbIgnore	5	Ignore button pressed.
vbYes	6	Yes button pressed.
vbNo	7	No button pressed.

Let's create the code to make the warning system work.

1. Add this statement to the (General) section:

```
Dim ChangeFlag As Boolean
```

2. Create a new procedure in the *(General)* section, as shown below:

```
Public Sub CheckSave()
  Dim SaveMessage As String
  Dim Decision As Integer
  SaveMessage = "Hey! You didn't save your recording. Do you
    want to save it now?"
  Decision = MsgBox(SaveMessage, vbYesNoCancel + vbExplanation,
    "Oooops!")
  If Decision = vbYes Then
    mmcPanel.Command = "Save"
  End If
End Sub
```

3. Add the statements shown below to the beginning of *mnuFileNew_Click*:

```
ChangeFlag = False
```

4. Add the statement shown below to the end of *mmcPanel_RecordClick*:

```
ChangeFlag = True
```

5. Add the statement shown below to the end of *mnuFileSaveRecording_Click*:

```
ChangeFlag = False
```

6. Add the statement shown below to the beginning of *mnuFileOpen_Click*:

```
If ChangeFlag = True Then
   CheckSave   'Calls the CheckSave procedure
End If
```

7. Copy the new statements from *mnuFileOpen_Click* and paste them at the beginning of *mnuFileNew_Click* and *Form_Terminate*.

8. Save your project.

9. Try out your revised program.

SUMMARY

As you've seen in this chapter, although Visual Basic does most of the work for you, it can still be quite complex to add multimedia to an application. Perhaps by Visual Basic 5.0 or 6.0, many of the complexities will have been cleared up. But in the meantime, you'll have to keep your wits about you when you're coding multimedia procedures.

You have learned how to animate an icon by using the Timer control. And you've learned how to play waves, midi sequences, and .avi videos using the MMControl control. You've also learned a bit about how to give the user control of the media by displaying the MMControl panel. There's a lot more to be learned in that area. The MMControl commands call on the Windows MCI commands, and if you want to learn more about handling multimedia, you should spend some time learning about those commands in an advanced text or reference manual. (They are not included in the Visual Basic reference material.)

Now you have learned two of the most important custom controls: CommonDialog and MMControl. More custom controls are discussed in the next chapter.

CHAPTER OBJECTIVES

When we talked about the standard controls, did you wonder what happened to some of your favorites, like the spin button, the slider, and the progress bar? Those are custom controls, and you'll find them in the Custom Control dialog box (if you have the Professional or Enterprise edition of Visual Basic), along with about 25 others.

In this chapter, we'll overview all the custom controls that come with the Professional edition. Then we'll take a more detailed look at the controls that people use most often:

► Slider
► TabStrip
► ProgressBar
► StatusBar
► Rich TextBox
► Toolbar
► ImageList

Custom Controls

If you've worked with custom controls in former versions of Visual Basic, you know that they were provided in .vbx files. With Visual Basic 4.0 and its increased implementation of OLE, the .vbx format has been improved and called *.ocx* (OLE control extension). The .vbx files work only on 16-bit systems; .ocx files work on both 16-bit and 32-bit systems. However, .ocx files can be used only with Visual Basic 4.0 and beyond; they can't be used with earlier versions.

Normally, .ocx files are installed in the Windows\System folder. That's where Visual Basic 4.0 Setup places the ones included in the Professional and Enterprise editions. If you have gotten custom controls from some other place and they're not installed in your Windows\System folder, you can still use them. When you're ready to install one in your toolbox, use the Browse button in the Custom Controls dialog box to locate the controls anywhere on your system.

Figure 9-1 shows what the Add Custom Control dialog box looks like immediately after you click Browse. You can see that it shows you all the .ocx files in the System folder. From there, you can change to other folders, locate and select the desired .ocx file, and its custom controls will be added to the list in your Custom Controls dialog box.

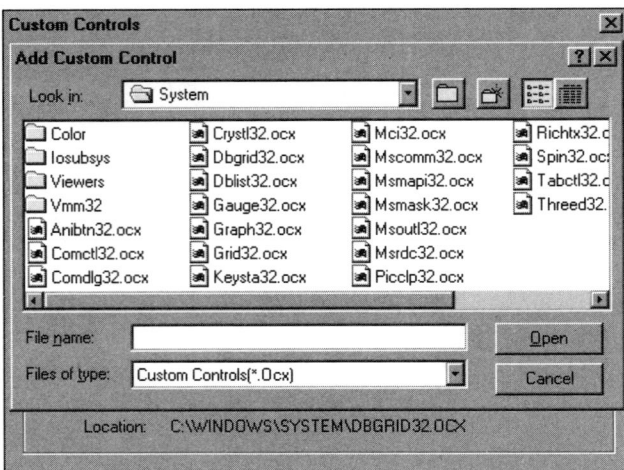

Figure 9-1: This Add Custom Control dialog box, which opens when you click Browse in the Custom Control dialog box, lets you locate an .ocx file anywhere on your system (including the floppy drives).

HELP FOR CUSTOM CONTROLS

The custom controls included in the Visual Basic package are documented in a Help library (Custom Control Help) and the Professional Edition and Enterprise Edition online books. You'll find descriptions of their properties, events, and methods in the documentation.

Third-party custom controls probably come with Help files too. If not, you can at least get lists of their features from your Visual Basic windows. The Properties window displays their design-time properties. The code window displays their events (in the Proc drop-down). The Object Browser lists all their properties, including run-time properties, and their methods—but only if the control is included in the Object Browser's library list.

Since this might be your only way to find out what properties and methods a custom control has, you should know how to add a control to the library list. You use the Tools|References command to add a control to the library list. Let's look at how that's done. We'll add the 3D controls to the Object Browser.

1. Click the Object Browser icon or choose *View | Object Browser* to open this dialog box:

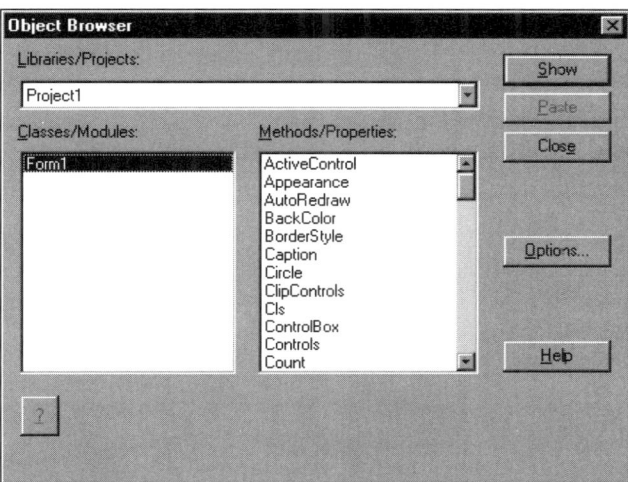

2. Drop down the *Libraries/Projects* list and scroll through it looking for *Sheridan 3D Controls*. You'll find that it's not there.

3. Close the Object Browser and choose *Tools | References* to open the References dialog box:

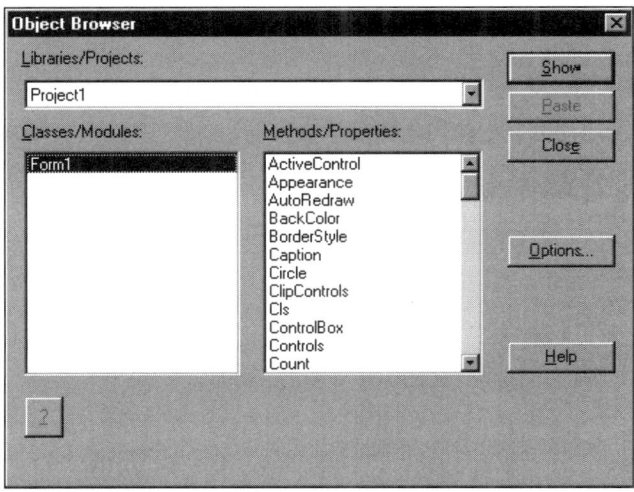

4. Scroll through your list looking for Sheridan 3D Controls. It's not there.

5. Click the *Browse* button to open the Add Reference dialog box shown:

6. Change *Files of type* to *Ole controls (.Ocx)*, as illustrated in Step 5.

7. Scroll and find the file called *Threed32.ocx*. This contains the 3D controls.

8. Double-click *Threed32.ocx*. The Add Reference dialog box closes and Sheridan 3D Controls appears in the References dialog box, already checked.

9. Click *OK* to close the dialog box and add Sheridan 3D Controls to your library list.

10. Now reopen the Object Browser.

11. Drop down the *Libraries/Projects* list and choose *Sheridan 3D Controls*. The classes and modules for the 3D controls appear in the Object Browser.

12. Scroll through the list and choose *SSCheck* (the 3D CheckBox). The methods and properties for this control appear in the Methods/Properties list.

When you're trying to locate the methods and properties for an unfamiliar control, you might have to do some guessing to find the correct .ocx file, library name, and control name. In the case of the 3D controls, the words "Threed" and "3D" provided the clues to the .ocx file and library, and the word "check" led us to the CheckBox control. It can be an awkward process, but sometimes it's the only way you can find out about a third-party control's run-time properties and methods.

SUMMARY OF CUSTOM CONTROLS INCLUDED IN THE PROFESSIONAL EDITION

Table 9-1 gives a quick overview of the custom controls provided in the Professional Edition (which means they're in the Enterprise Edition, too).

Table 9-1: Custom Controls in the VB Professional Edition

Custom Control	What It Does
3D controls	These controls are similar to their standard counterparts (CheckBox, Frame, CommandButton, OptionButton) but have a more 3D appearance, can have 3D text for captions, and offer more options as to the placement of the caption. Also included in the 3D controls are the 3D Group, which looks like a toolbar, and the 3D Panel, which displays 3D text on a 3D background.
Animated button	This button uses the same techniques that you learned for animating an Image control. When clicked, it displays whatever series of graphics you designate to create effects such as the pages turning in a book or a pencil writing on a page.
Communications	You use this control to provide serial modem communications services.
Gauge	Displays a thermometer or dial-type gauge.
Graph	This control displays many different types and styles of graphs.
ImageList	An invisible control that provides a list of images to be used by other controls, such as the Toolbar.
Key state	This control displays the status of the CapsLock, NumLock, Insert, and ScrollLock keys. The user can toggle these keys on and off by clicking the various parts of the control.
ListView	This control lists data in four different views: icons, small icons, list, and report.
MAPI controls	These controls give you the ability to add e-mail (MAPI) functions to an application.
Masked edit	This text box control lets you restrict the data entered into the box; you could, for example, refuse to accept nonnumeric characters in a Social Security Number box. Masked edit also provides DDE services and can be linked to a database.
Multimedia MCI	You have already seen how this control provides multimedia recording and playback services

(continued)

Custom Control	What It Does
Outline	This list box lets you display hierarchical lists of information.
Picture clip	You can display just part of a picture with this control.
ProgressBar	This control displays a progress bar, also known as a *fillbar*, and graphically marks progress by filling the bar with "chunks."
Rich TextBox	This TextBox provides rich text features: character formatting (fonts, color, and so on), paragraph formatting (alignment and so on), drag and drop editing, and OLE embedded objects. It can be linked to a memo field in a database.
Slider	This control provides a slider for setting values in ranges.
SpinButton	This control also lets you control the range of a value by letting the user click arrows to raise or lower the selected value.
Status	This control provides a status bar with up to sixteen panels.
SSTab	This control lets you created multiple-page dialog boxes with tabbed pages.
TabStrip	This control is similar to SSTab but provides more functionality (for Windows 95 only).
Toolbar	This control lets you create a button bar or toolbar (Windows 95 only).
TreeView	This control is similar to the Outline control; it lets you display a hierarchical list (Windows 95 only).

THE MICROSOFT WINDOWS COMMON CONTROLS

As we mentioned in the introduction for this chapter, some of the controls are so common that most people think they're standard controls. In this section, we'll show you how to use the tools that are known collectively as the Microsoft Windows Common Controls: TabStrip, Toolbar, StatusBar, ProgressBar, TreeView, ImageList, ListView, and Slider. These controls are all contained in comctl32.ocx.

NOTE

All of controls in comctl32.ocx are 32-bit controls and can be used only with Windows 95 or Windows NT 3.5 or higher.

Before we get into details, let's make sure that you have these controls in your toolbox.

1. Begin a new project.

2. Look in your toolbox for any of the Windows common controls, such as Slider (shown here). If it's there, you can skip the rest of this exercise.

3. Choose *Tools | Custom Controls* to open the Custom Controls dialog box.

4. Check *Microsoft Windows Common Controls* and click *OK*. This adds the eight tools to your toolbox.

TabStrip

When a dialog box contains a lot of options, it can help to organize them into pages so that the user is not confronted with a huge array of controls all at once. Figure 9-2 shows a typical example, this one from Visual Basic itself. The TabStrip control can be used to create the tabs at the tops of the pages.

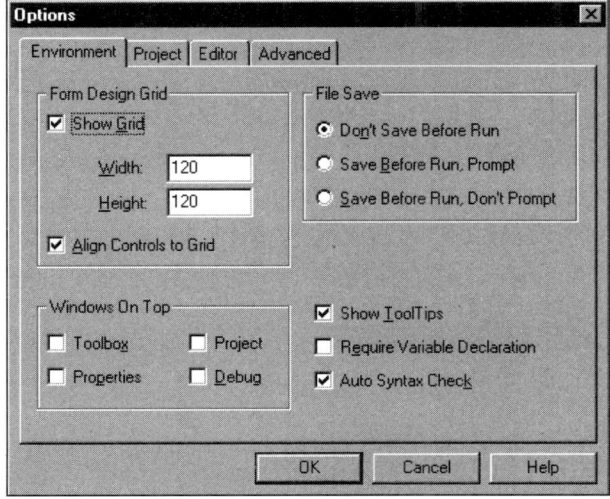

Figure 9-2: Tabbed pages in a dialog box, such as the ones shown here, can be created with the TabStrip control.

How to Create a Tab Strip

Let's walk through the process of creating the tabbed pages shown in Figure 9-2. We won't bother with all the details of the controls on each page, but we'll create the pages, then add a couple of controls to each one so that you can see how it's done.

1. Double-click the TabStrip tool as shown here to place the initial control on your form.

2. Size and position the TabStrip to fill most of the form, as shown:

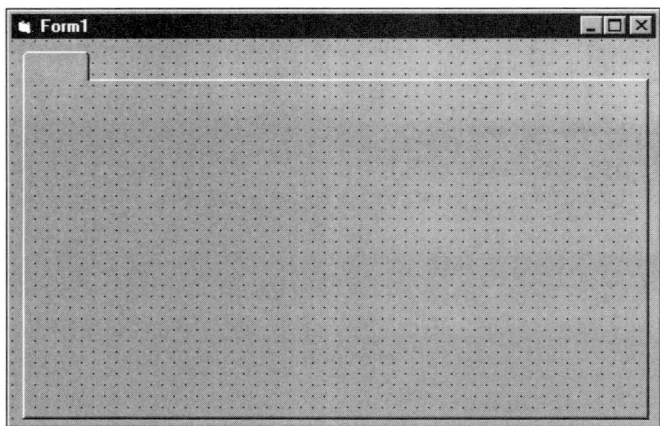

3. Choose (*Custom*) in the Properties window to open the Tabstrip Control Properties dialog box.

4. Click the *Tabs* tab to display the Tabs page:

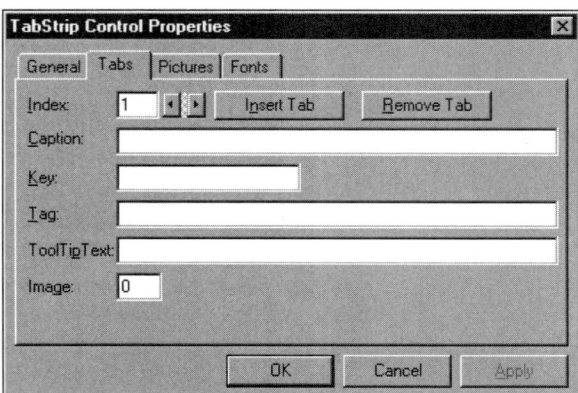

5. Notice that the Index number is 1, showing that you're working on the first tab. Give it a *Caption* of *Environment*.

6. Click *Insert Tab* to add another tab with the *Index* number of *2*. Give it a *Caption* of *Project*.

7. Click *Insert Tab* and give the third tab a *Caption* of *Editor*.

8. Click *Insert Tab* and give the fourth tab a *Caption* of *Advanced*.

9. Click *OK* to close the dialog box. Your form should now look like the following:

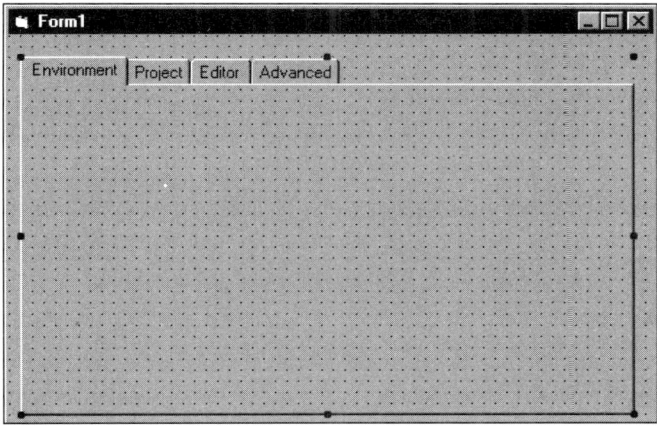

10. Save your form as *TabStrip Form* and your project as *TabStrip Example*.

By the way, you have just created your first *collection*. Each tab is an individual object called a Tab. But you can't access your Tab objects directly. TabStrip has a run-time property called Tabs that represents the collection of individual Tab objects. To access the first Tab in your collection, you would refer to TabStrip1.Tabs(1). The number in parentheses is the index number for the tab.

If you assign a Key property to a tab, you can refer to the Key rather than the Index number. For example, if the Environment tab's key is Env, you could refer to the tab as TabStrip1.Tabs(Env).

NOTE

You can't access the properties for the individual tabs in the Properties window, which shows the properties for the TabStrip only. You have to use the Tabs page in the TabStrip Control Properties dialog box to see the design-time properties, such as Caption and Key, for each tab. At run time, you access the properties of a Tab by expressions such as TabStrip1.Tabs(1).Caption and TabStrip1.Tabs(Env).Image.

Placing Controls on a Tab Page

Now for some bad news. The tabs that you have just created don't really represent separate pages. There's only one page, and you're responsible for changing its contents when the user clicks a different tab.

Want more bad news? The tabbed page cannot act as a container object, so you can't place controls directly in it. You have to draw a container object in the same area as the page and put the controls in that container. People usually use a PictureBox or a Frame to contain the controls on a tabbed page. Let's make some containers for our controls.

1. Draw a Label1, Frame1, and Picture1 on the tabbed page.

2. Draw Label2 inside Frame1.

   Don't forget that you must draw an object inside a container to make sure that it's contained by the container. If you draw the object somewhere else and move it to the container, the container won't contain it.

3. Draw Label3 inside Picture1. Your form should now look something like the following:

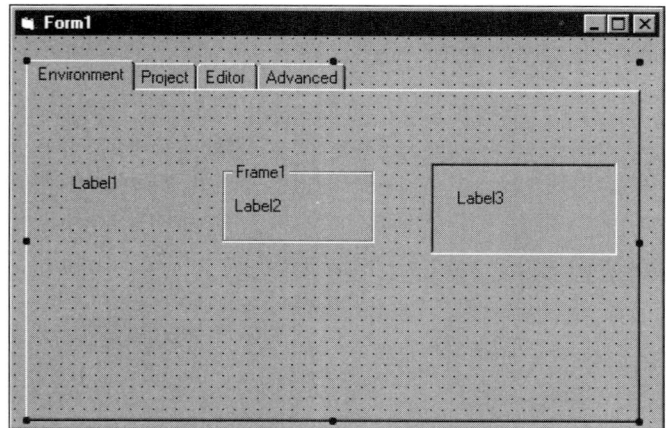

4. Run your program. You'll see Frame1 containing Label2 and Picture1 containing Label3, but you can't see Label1 because it isn't inside a container.

5. End the program.

Okay, now let's get to work on setting up the four separate pages. Here's what we'll do:

▶ Create a PictureBox for the Environment page containing the controls for that page.

▶ Right on top of it, create a PictureBox for the Editor page, containing the controls for that page.

▶ Do the same for the other two pages.

▶ At run time, change the order of the PictureBoxes to determine which one is on top, depending on which tab the user clicks.

Let's create the PictureBoxes first, then work on the code that puts the correct one on top.

---

1. Delete Label1, Frame1, and Label3.

2. Expand Picture1 to fill almost the entire page area.

3. Give it these properties:

Appearance: 0 - Flat
BackColor: Gray
BorderStyle: 0 - None
Name: picEnvironment

Notice that it is now invisible except for the handles (and the absence of a grid).

4. Draw four CheckBoxes on it and caption them *Environment 1* through *Environment 4*. Don't create the CheckBoxes by double-clicking. That places them on the form, not in the current container. Click the CheckBox tool once, then drag the mouse to draw a control in the PictureBox.

5. Now draw another PictureBox right on top of the existing one. Name it *picProject*. Give it the same properties as picEnvironment. PictureBoxes can contain other PictureBoxes. It's very easy to accidentally draw the second PictureBox *inside* the first one. If that happens, the second PictureBox won't show up at run time. To avoid this, always draw your PictureBoxes by double-clicking, then resize them. As you know, double-clicking guarantees that the object will be contained on the form, not inside another container.

6. Draw four OptionButtons on picProject and caption them *Project 1* through *Project 4*.

7. Draw a third PictureBox and name it *picEditor*. Give it the same properties as the other two.

8. Draw four CommandButtons on picEditor and caption them *Editor 1* through *Editor 4*.

9. Draw the last PictureBox and name it *picAdvanced*.

10. Draw four TextBoxes in picAdvanced and set their Text properties to *Advanced 1* through *Advanced 4*.

11. We want to make picEnvironment the box that displays when the program starts, so let's put it on top of the stack:

   a. Click *picAdvanced* to select it and choose *Edit|Send to back* to place it at the back of the four pictures. PicEditor is now on top, although picAdvanced is still selected.

   b. Click picEditor to select it and choose Edit|Send to back. PicProject is now on top.

   c. Click *picProject* to select it and choose *Edit|Send to back*. PicEnvironment is now on top.

12. Save your work.

At design time, we can use Edit|Send to back and Edit|Bring to front to control the order of the PictureBoxes. But what do we do at run time to change the order? We have to use a method called *ZOrder* (pronounced "Zee-order"), which moves an object to the front or the back. Most controls have the ZOrder method so that you can move them around at run time. The ZOrder method

takes a parameter of 1 to move to the back or 0 to move to the front. So if we
want to move picAdvanced to the front, we code this statement:

```
picAdvanced.ZOrder 0
```

We have to deal with one more question: How do we know which tab was
clicked? TabStrip has a run-time property called SelectedItem, which has the
same properties as the Tab that was clicked, so if TabStrip.SelectedItem.Index
is 1, we know that the first Tab was clicked. If TabStrip.SelectedItem.Key is
"Env", we know that the Tab with a Key of "Env" was clicked. We used
Indexes, not Keys, in our example, so we'll use a set of If statements like the
following to determine which Tab was clicked:

```
If TabStrip.SelectedItem.Index = 1 Then
  picEnvironment.ZOrder 0
End If
```

These are the only new statements we need to make the tabbed pages fly. Let's
put them to work.

1. Double-click the TabStrip to open the code window for *TabStrip1_Click*.

2. Insert this code:

```
If TabStrip1.SelectedItem.Index = 1 Then
  picEnvironment.ZOrder 0
End If
If TabStrip1.SelectedItem.Index = 2 Then
  picProject.ZOrder 0
End If
If TabStrip1.SelectedItem.Index = 3 Then
  picEditor.ZOrder 0
End If
If TabStrip1.SelectedItem.Index = 4 Then
  picAdvanced.ZOrder 0
End If
```

3. Try out your new program. Be sure to click each of the tabs. You should
   see the appropriate controls appear for each tab.

The hardest part of creating a set of tabbed pages with TabStrip is drawing the
PictureBoxes and their controls correctly. If one or more of your pages doesn't
show up as it should, you can bet your boots it's because you inadvertently
drew one PictureBox inside another, or you didn't draw the controls inside the
PictureBox correctly.

TIP

Sometimes it helps to give each PictureBox a different background color while you're working on them. Then you can see the difference between them, and it's easier to tell when one is contained inside another.

Other TabStrip Features

TabStrips normally have notebook-style tabs at the top, as you have seen in this sample program, but you can opt to have buttons instead. Just set Style to *1 - Buttons* instead of *0 - Tabs*. You can also create several rows of tabs, as you have seen in some dialog boxes, by setting MultiRow to True. You can set the font for the tabs on the Fonts page and place pictures on the tabs using an ImageList, which is described later in this chapter.

You can add and remove tabs at run time by using the Add, Remove, and Clear methods; Clear removes all the tabs. These methods belong to the Tabs collection, not the TabStrip itself. So to remove the fourth tab from TabStrip1, you would code this statement:

```
TabStrip1.Tabs.Remove 4
```

StatusBar

StatusBar provides a status bar at the bottom of a window, much like the one in Figure 9-3, which is taken from Microsoft Word for Windows 95. StatusBar has a property called Panels which represents a collection of Panel objects. StatusBar can have up to 16 Panels.

A Panel can contain text, a picture (such as an icon), or one of the following standard system items:

▶ The status of the Insert, CapsLock, NumLock, or ScrollLock key

▶ The system time

▶ The system date

When you select one of the system items, Visual Basic automatically provides the status information for you. If you choose to display text (such as status messages, help messages, and hints) or images in a Panel, then you are responsible for writing the code to display whatever you want there.

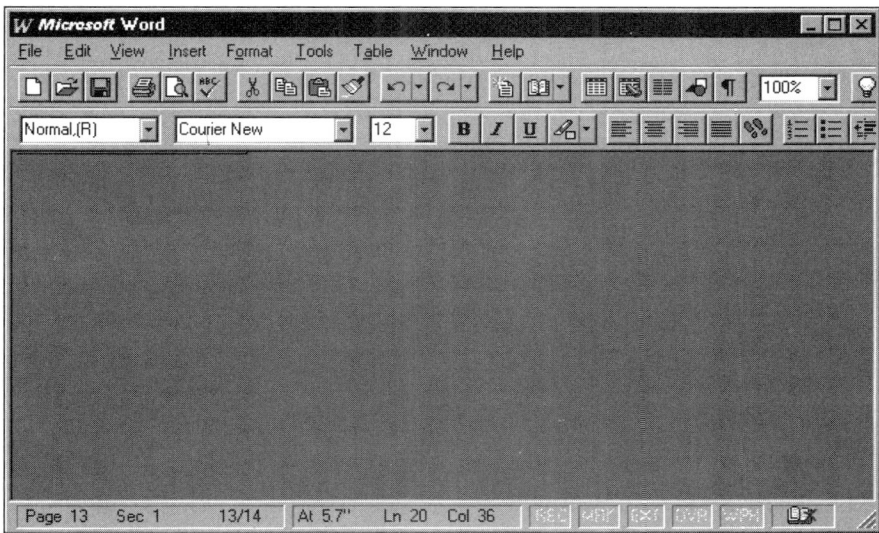

Figure 9-3: The StatusBar control provides a status bar much like the one at the bottom of this window, which is taken from Microsoft Word for Windows 95.

You set up the Panels much like you set up the Tabs in a TabStrip. In the following exercise, you'll set up a StatusBar with text, Caps, Ins, and time panels.

1. Start a new project and make sure that the Microsoft Windows Common Controls are in your toolbox.

2. Double-click the StatusBar tool (shown here) to put a new StatusBar on your form. Notice that it automatically aligns with the bottom of the form. It also contains the first panel.

3. Click *(Custom)* to open the StatusBar Control Properties dialog box:

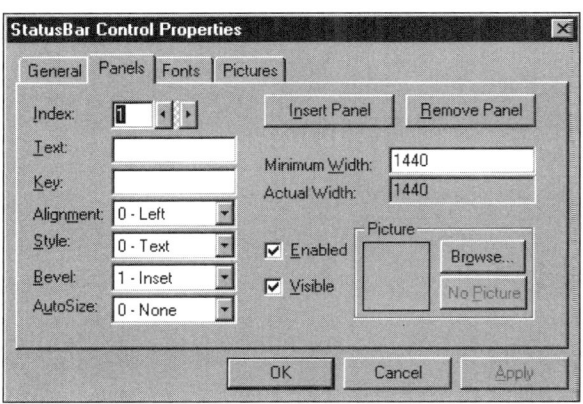

4. Click *Panels* to display the Panels page. It is already set up for the first Panel.

5. This will be your text panel, so in the *Text* box enter the default message *Type any text*.

6. Choose these properties:

   Alignment: 0 - Left (aligns the contents on the left)
   Style: 0 - Text
   Bevel: 0 - None (no 3D effect around the edges)
   AutoSize: 0 - None (the size is fixed)
   Minimum Width: 3000 twips

7. Click *Apply* to see the effect of these properties without closing the dialog box.

8. Click *Insert Panel* to add the second Panel, choose the following properties, and click *Apply*:

   Alignment: Center
   Style: 1 - CAPS (reports the status of the CapsLock key)
   Bevel: 1 - Inset (insets it in the bar)
   AutoSize: 1 - Spring (adjusts the size so that all the panels together completely fill the bar)
   Minimum size: 500 twips

9. Click *Insert Panel* to add the third Panel, choose the following properties, and click *Apply*:

   Alignment: 1 - Center
   Style: 3 - INS (reports the status of the Insert key)
   Bevel: 1 - Inset
   AutoSize: 1 - Spring
   Minimum size: 500 twips

10. Click *Insert Panel* to add the fourth Panel, choose these properties, and click *Apply*:

    Alignment: 1 - Center
    Style: 5 - Time (displays the system time)
    Bevel: 2 - Raised (raises it above the bar)
    AutoSize: 1 - Spring
    Minimum size: 500 twips

11. Click *OK* to close the dialog box. Your form should now look like the following:

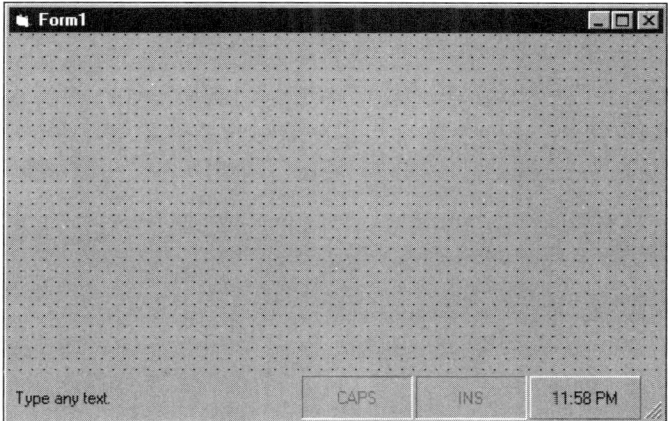

12. Run your program.

   a. Turn CapsLock and Insert on and off so you can see what happens.

   b. Make the window wider and narrower and watch how Visual Basic adjusts the sizes of the Panels that use the Spring AutoSize setting. (If you make the window too narrow, some of the Panels disappear.)

   c. Notice the three types of Bevel: none, inset, and raised. (Does any of this look like the Windows 95 Taskbar to you? It's not quite the same, but it's close.)

13. Close the program and save your form as *Status* and your project as *Status Example*.

If you want to change the message in the first Panel, you can access it this way:

```
StatusBar1.Panels(1).Text = "Whatever message you want"
```

If you want users to be able to click Panels, code a procedure for the StatusBar1_Click event. You can find out which panel was clicked this way:

```
If StatusBar1.SelectedItem.Index = 1 Then
  [statements to process the first panel]
End If
If StatusBar1.SelectedItem.Index = 2 Then
  [statements to process the second panel]
End If
[and so on]
```

Other Features of StatusBar

The third AutoSize feature adjusts the width of the Panel to its contents. This comes in particularly handy when you're letting users tailor the contents of the panels to suit themselves.

The StatusBar is aligned at the bottom by default. You can also choose to align it at the top, the left, the right, or no alignment at all, in which case it floats free in the window and the user can move it around. Use the Align property in the Properties window to select the desired alignment.

If you just want to use the StatusBar as a message area, you can choose to have a single panel that is the width of the bar. Set Style equal to *1 - Single Panel* in the Properties window or on the General page of the dialog box.

You can select the font for the text in the Panels. Use the Font property in the Properties window or on the Fonts page in the dialog box.

If you want to let users tailor the status bar, you can add and remove items by using the Add, Remove, and Clear methods. The following example uses a Key instead of an Index because, when you don't know exactly how many Panels you'll have, a Key can be easier to keep track of.

```
StatusBar1.Panels.Add "CAPS"
With StatusBar1.Panels("CAPS")
  .Alignment = 1   'Centered
  .Style = 1       'This is the CAPS style
  .Bevel = 1       'Inset
  .AutoSize = 1    'Spring
  .MinWidth = 500
End With
```

ProgressBar

When your program must perform a very long operation, such as scanning the hard disk for a virus or merge-printing, a ProgressBar helps to keep your users informed as to the status of the task. Figure 9-4 shows ProgressBar at work.

NOTE

ProgressBar approximates progress. For a more accurate representation, use Gauge.

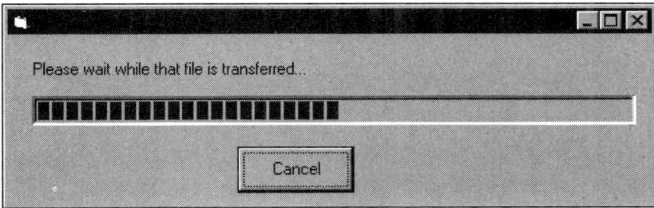

Figure 9-4: ProgressBar displays and fills a fillbar like this while a long-running task progresses.

Figure 9-5 shows the ProgressBar design-time properties. The size of the "chunks" in the bar is determined by the Height property: the taller the bar, the larger the chunks. The number of chunks displayed at any given time is determined by three properties:

▶ *Min* and *Max* are simply arbitrary numbers that establish the range you want to use. Min is usually 0 and Max 100, but if you're dealing with degrees Fahrenheit from freezing to boiling, you might find it easier to think of Min as 32 and Max 212.

▶ *Value* (run time only) determines the current position between Min and Max. For example, if the range is 200 and value is 50, approximate one fourth of the bar will be filled.

Properties - Form1	
ProgressBar1 ProgressBar	
(About)	
(Custom)	...
Align	0 - None
Appearance	1 - 3D
BorderStyle	0 - None
DragIcon	(None)
DragMode	0 - Manual
Enabled	True
Height	315
Index	
Left	255
Max	100
Min	0
MouseIcon	(None)
MousePointer	0 - Default
Name	ProgressBar1
Negotiate	False
TabIndex	2
Tag	
Top	645
Visible	True
WhatsThisHelpID	0
Width	6270

Figure 9-5: The ProgressBar design-time properties include Min and Max, which help to determine the size of the chunks in the bar.

Figure 9-6 compares bars with three different Heights. All bars have the same Width. In all three cases, Min is 0, Max is 100, and Value is 60. You can see what a difference Height makes in the appearance of the bar.

Figure 9-6: These three bars have the same Width, Min, Max, and Value but different Height properties. You can see that the Height determines the size of the chunks in the bars.

Slider

You have probably seen and used a Slider control dozens of times when working with Windows. Figure 9-7 shows a typical example, taken from Windows 95's Control Panel.

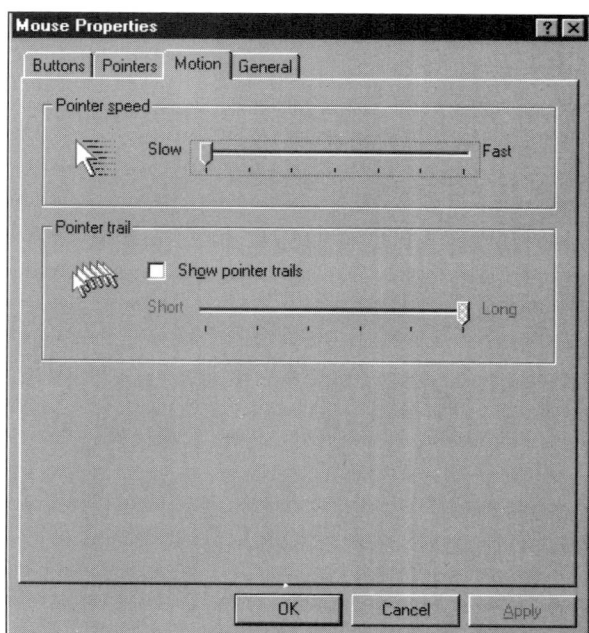

Figure 9-7: These Slider controls let users set the value within a range by dragging the sliding tab.

The Orientation property determines whether the control is horizontal (0) or vertical (1). The TickStyle property determines whether the ticks are on the bottom or left (0), the top or right (1), both (2), or no ticks are displayed (3).

Three properties determine how many tick marks are displayed: Min, Max, and TickFrequency. Min and Max determine the range of values, just as they do for ProgressBar. TickFrequency indicates how often ticks appear in the range created by Min and Max. For example, if Min is 0, Max is 50, and TickFrequency is 10, there will be 6 ticks, at 0, 10, 20, 30, 40, and 50.

The SmallChange property determines how far the slider moves when users press the left or right arrow keys. LargeChange determines how far the slider moves when users press PageUp or PageDown or click the bar to the side of the slider.

As usual, Value indicates the current position of the slider within the bar. You can set the initial position of the slider by setting Value at design time. When a user drags the slider, you can find out the new position from the Value property. For example, the following statement sets a variable called Temperature based on the current Value of Slider1:

```
Temperature = Slider1.Value
```

Rich TextBox

Rich TextBox provides an enhanced text box that is capable of displaying rich text. Rich text is almost as generic as ASCII text, but permits more formatting information. Most Windows applications that handle text can import and export rich text files. Specifically, the difference between ASCII text and rich text is that rich text permits:

► Character formatting: fonts, point sizes, color, bold, italics, underline, strikethrough, subscripts, and superscripts

► Paragraph formatting: alignment, indentation, bullet, and tabs

The Rich TextBox also permits OLE embedded objects, drag-and-drop editing, and linking to a memo field in a database. You can save the contents of a Rich TextBox to a database, an .rtf file (a rich text file), or an ASCII text file (in which case the formatting is lost).

Some of the features of the Rich TextBox are automatic, such as drag-and-drop editing and the OLE connection. As soon as you draw the control on the form, these features are available to you. Others you must provide the code for. For example, for users to select some text for character formatting, you must provide the necessary menu commands or toolbar icons (Font, Color, Bold, Italics, and so on), the necessary dialog boxes, and the code to apply the user's choices to the selected text.

So far, you have used a regular TextBox control as the main work area in ScratchPad. Now, we're going to replace that control with a Rich TextBox and add all the code to make it work. Let's start by placing the control on the form and setting its initial properties.

1. Open your ScratchPad project.

2. Delete the TextBox and draw a Rich TextBox in its place. The Rich TextBox tool is shown here.

3. Name it *rtbPage*.

4. Set *Appearance* to *Flat*.

5. Rich TextBox has a huge right margin by default, much wider than the Width of the box. Set the *RightMargin* property to be about 500 twips less than the Width property.

6. Set *ScrollBars* to *3 - Both*.

7. Run the program and try out your new control.

   a. Type a few paragraphs of text.

   b. Notice that you can select text.

   c. You can move text by dragging it.

   d. And you can copy text by holding down Ctrl while you drag it.

8. End the program and save your project.

Now let's work on letting our users change the font of some selected text. You have already created a Text menu with two items: Font and Color. Both of these commands use the CommonDialog control, so they'll be fairly easy to program.

To actually change the text after a user has selected a font, you need to work with a number of properties in the Rich TextBox and the CommonDialog. Table 9-2 shows the Rich TextBox properties that affect text.

Table 9-2: Rich TextBox Text Properties

Property	Effect
SelFontName	Indicates the font name of the currently selected text
SelFontSize	Indicates the point size of the currently selected text
SelBold	Indicates True or False if the currently selected text is bold or not
SelItalic	Indicates True or False if the currently selected text is in italics or not
SelUnderline	Indicates True or False if the currently selected text is underlined or not
SelStrikethru	Indicates True or False if the currently selected text is struck through or not

Each of these properties can be set from a comparable property of the CommonDialog. When users make their selections in the Font dialog and click OK to close the dialog, the following properties are available:

▶ *FontName* and *FontSize* indicate the user's choices for these two properties.

▶ *Bold, Italic, Underline,* and *Strikethru* indicate whether each of these boxes was checked (True) or unchecked (False) when the dialog ended.

It's a relatively simple matter to apply the user's choices to the selected text:

```
rtbPage.SelFontName = CommonDialog1.FontName
rtbPage.SelFontSize = CommonDialog1.FontSize
rtbPage.SelBold = CommonDialog1.FontBold
rtbPage.SelItalic = CommonDialog1.FontItalic
rtbPage.SelStrikethru = CommonDialog1.FontStrikethru
rtbPage.SelUnderline = CommonDialog1.FontUnderline
```

Let's add this code to our program and try it out.

1. Click *Text|Font* to open the code window for mnuTextFont_Click.

2. Add the following code. Remember that it's important to set the Flags before showing the Font dialog or you'll get an error message saying that no fonts are installed.

```
CommonDialog1.Flags = 3
CommonDialog1.ShowFont
```

```
rtbPage.SelFontName = CommonDialog1.FontName
rtbPage.SelFontSize = CommonDialog1.FontSize
rtbPage.SelBold = CommonDialog1.FontBold
rtbPage.SelItalic = CommonDialog1.FontItalic
rtbPage.SelStrikethru = CommonDialog1.FontStrikethru
rtbPage.SelUnderline = CommonDialog1.FontUnderline
```

3. Try out your new code. You should now be able to select a block of text and set its font, make it bold, and so forth. Easy, eh?

4. Close the program and save your project.

Adding color is even easier, as you'll see in the following exercise.

1. Click *Text | Color* to open the code window for *mnuTextColor_Click*.

2. Add the following code:

```
CommonDialog1.ShowColor
rtbPage.SelColor = CommonDialog1.Color
```

3. Try out your new color feature.

4. Close the program and save your project.

It's also very easy to set the alignment and bullet features of selected paragraphs. In the Rich TextBox, the Alignment property can be set to 0 for left alignment, 1 for right alignment, or 2 for centered alignment. The Bullet property can be set to True or False.

1. Click *Paragraph | Left* and enter this code:

```
rtbPage.SelAlignment = 0
```

2. Click *Paragraph | Right* and enter this code:

```
rtbPage.SelAlignment = 1
```

3. Click *Paragraph | Center* and enter this code:

```
rtbPage.SelAlignment = 2
```

4. Click *Paragraph | Bullet* and enter this code:

```
rtbPage.SelBullet = Not rtbPage.SelBullet
```

5. Try out your new features.

6. Close the program and save your project.

Using the Clipboard with a Rich TextBox

Another great advantage of a Rich TextBox is that it gives you a means to interact with the Clipboard, so that you can create commands to cut, copy, and paste text. To accomplish this, you use the SelText property along with the Clipboard object. SelText contains the currently selected text string. The Clipboard object represents Windows' Clipboard and provides several methods we'll use for cutting, copying, and pasting, as shown in Table 9-3.

Table 9-3: Clipboard Object Methods

Method	Effect
Clear	Clears the contents of the Clipboard
GetData	Pastes a graphic from the Clipboard
GetText	Pastes text from the Clipboard
GetFormat	Returns an integer indicating whether the object(s) on the Clipboard match a specified type, such as text, a bitmap graphic, or a metafile graphic
SetData	Places a graphic on the Clipboard
SetText	Places text on the Clipboard

NOTE

The Clipboard can contain several items at a time, as long as each item has a different format. When you copy a new text item to the Clipboard, for example, it replaces any existing text but does not disturb other items on the Clipboard. Likewise, when you copy a bitmap to the Clipboard, it replaces any existing bitmap but does not disturb the current text or a graphic in another format.

We'll use SetText to copy data to the Clipboard. SetText has this syntax:

```
Clipboard.SetText text
```

The *text* parameter provides the actual text to be copied to the Clipboard. We'll use rtbPage.SelText here. So the statement that copies text from our Rich TextBox to the Clipboard looks like this:

```
Clipboard.SetText frmDocument.rtbPage.SelText
```

To cut the text to the Clipboard, we'll follow this statement with a statement that sets the contents of SelText to null:

```
rtbPage.SelText = ""
```

To paste text, all we have to do is copy from the GetText function to SelText:

```
frmDocument.rtbPage.SelText = Clipboard.GetText
```

Let's add these functions to ScratchPad now.

1. Click *Edit | Copy* to open the code window for mnuEditCopy_Click. Notice that you're in frmScratchPad since that's where the menu is located.

2. Enter the following statement:

```
Clipboard.SetText frmDocument.rtbPage.SelText
```

3. Click *Edit | Cut* to open the code window for mnuEditCut_Click and enter the following statements:

```
Clipboard.SetText frmDocument.rtbPage.SelText
frmDocument.rtbPage.SelText = ""
```

4. Click *Edit | Paste* to open the code window for mnuEditPaste_Click and enter the following statement:

```
frmDocument.rtbPage.SelText = Clipboard.GetText
```

5. Save your work.

6. Try out your new Clipboard functions.

Using Files in the Rich TextBox

One of the reasons we chose a Rich TextBox for ScratchPad is because it has file management capabilities. We can open a file into a Rich TextBox and save the contents of a Rich TextBox as a file. We'll use common Open and Save As dialogs in conjunction with the Rich TextBox to manage the ScratchPad files.

Opening a File into a Rich TextBox

When a user closes a common Open dialog, the property called *filename* contains the pathname(s) of the file(s) that were selected. The path alone is also contained in the Path property and the name of the file without the path appears in the FileTitle property. (If the user closed the dialog without selecting a file, these properties contain null values.)

The Rich TextBox provides a method called LoadFile that opens a designated file. Its syntax is:

```
object.LoadFile pathname[, filetype]
```

You can get the pathname from the CommonDialog's filename property. So to open the file identified by CommonDialog1.filename, you could code:

```
RichTextBox1.LoadFile CommonDialog1.filename
```

The *filetype* parameter is an integer that is used to limit the file's type to either a rich text file (0) or a text file (1). Visual Basic provides two constants for this function: rtfRTF and rtfText. To limit the preceding statement to an .rtf file only, you would code:

```
RichTextBox1.LoadFile CommonDialog1.filename, rtfRTF
```

Saving a File from a Rich TextBox

The Save As common dialog also uses the properties called filename, Path, and FileTitle. The Rich TextBox uses the SaveFile method to save a file; its syntax is shown below:

```
object.SaveFile pathname[, type]
```

For ScratchPad, we will also set the caption of the form to the saved file name whenever the user might have changed the file name. Let's create the procedure for the File|Save As command.

---

1. Click *File | Save As* to open the *mnuFileSaveAs_Click* procedure in the code window.

2. Add the statements shown here to the end of the procedure:

```
frmDocument.rtbPage.SaveFile CommonDialog1.filename, rtfRTF
```

3. Save your work.

4. Run the program.

5. Type some text in the Rich TextBox.

6. Choose *File | Save As* and save the file under the name *Practice.rtf*.

7. Delete the text in the Rich TextBox.

8. Now choose *File | Open* and select *Practice.rtf*. The text should return to the box, proving that both the Save As and the Open procedures worked correctly.

9. End the program.

We also have to make the File | Save command work. Remember that this command simply saves the current file if it has a name. If it has no name, then it should perform the same functions as File | Save As. You'll make that happen in the following exercise.

1. Click *File | Save* to open *mnuFileSave_Click* in the code window.

2. Add the following statements to the procedure:

```
If CommonDialog1.filename = "" Then
   mnuFileSaveAs_Click
Else
   frmDocument.rtbPage.SaveFile CommonDialog1.filename, rtfRTF
End If
```

3. Save your work.

4. Run your program and check out the new code:

   a. Type some text in the empty Rich TextBox.

   b. Choose *File | Save*. You should get the Save As common dialog.

   c. Name your new file *Exercise*.

   d. Make some more changes to the text.

   e. Choose *File | Save* again. This time, Visual Basic should save the file without asking for a name.

   f. Delete all the text in the box.

g. Now use *File|Open* to open Exercise. You should get the version of Exercise that you saved in Step 4e.

5. End the program.

Printing a File from the Rich TextBox

Another nice feature of the Rich TextBox is that you can print from it by using the SelPrint method, although it has an unfortunate problem, as you'll see shortly. SelPrint prints the selected text or, if nothing is seleted, the entire contents of the box. Its syntax looks like this:

```
object.SelPrint(object.hDC)
```

SelPrint does not send text directly to the printer. Instead, it sends it to the device driver identified by the *object*.hDC parameter. The device driver does the actual printing.

 NOTE The expression *hDC* stands for "device context handle." A *handle* is an identifier assigned by Windows to each available object, such as an open file, a printer, a control, or a device context. A *device context* is also an identifier assigned by Windows; it establishes a link between an application and a device driver.

When you use the common Print dialog to collect print parameters such as the number of copies, the best hDC to use *should be* the one associated with the CommonDialog control, as in CommonDialog1.hDC. This would recognize the user's choices without any more work on your part. But unfortunately, as of this writing, SelPrint does not work with the CommonDialog hDC, and we can't get a clearcut answer from Microsoft as to whether they plan to fix it.

Just in case they do fix it, here's how you would use it. You must be sure to set the 256 flag before you display the Print dialog. That flag causes Visual Basic to establish the CommonDialog hDC value that SelPrint needs. Then you display the Print dialog. When the user closes the dialog, you use SelPrint to send the data to the hDC. The whole procedure looks something like this:

```
Private Sub mnuFilePrint_Click()
  CommonDialog1.Flags = 262456 'Includes 256 flag
  CommonDialog1.ShowPrinter
  rtbPage.SelPrint(CommonDialog1.hDC)
End Sub
```

Since the hDC feature of the CommonDialog control isn't working, we'll bypass the common Print dialog and use SelPrint with the Printer.hDC instead. Printer is an object that represents the current default printer, and the Printer.hDC links our application with that device. Before you can send text to the Printer.hDC, you must initialize the printer with this statement, which prints a null value (so nothing prints):

```
Printer.Print ""
```

Let's put this print procedure in ScratchPad.

1. Click *File|Print* to open the *mnuFilePrint_Click* procedure in the code window.

2. Replace the current code with the following two lines:

```
Printer.Print ""                'Initialize the printer
rtbPage.SelPrint(Printer.hDC)   'Print the current selection
```

3. Save your work.

4. Try out the new *File|Print* command. Be sure to try it with text selected and nothing selected.

ToolBar and ImageList

The ToolBar control lets you create a toolbar just like the ones you see in applications like Visual Basic, Microsoft Word for Windows, Lotus 1-2-3, and so on. It can be made up of command buttons, but most people nowadays expect icons. To create a toolbar of icons, you also need to use the ImageList control.

We'll add a toolbar of icons to ScratchPad in this section, to provide quick and easy access to the functions that already exist on the menu bar. Since they've already been coded once, very little additional coding is involved. All we have to do is refer to the procedures that already exist. For example, if someone clicks the Bold icon, the only statement we need is the one shown below, which tells Visual Basic to execute the procedure named mnuParagraphBold_Click:

```
mnuParagraphBold_Click
```

So the major task now is simply to create the toolbar. But before we do that, we have to create the ImageList. An *ImageList* is an invisible control that simply lists a set of pictures that we want to use in another control. Visual Basic provides a perfect set of icons for a toolbar in the folder called Bitmaps\Tlbr_w95. These are the very familiar icons for standard functions such as Open, Paste, Bold, and Left.

---

1. Double-click the ImageList tool (shown here) to place the control on your frmScratchPad form.

2. Click *(Custom)* to open the ImageList Control Properties dialog box.

3. Click the *Images* tab.

4. Click *Insert Picture*. The page sets up for the first image, then the Select Picture browse box opens so that you can choose the first picture.

5. Locate the *Bitmaps\Tlbr_w95* folder and double-click *open.bmp*. This places the New icon in the first position in the ImageList.

6. Click *Insert Picture* and choose *save.bmp* for the second image.

7. Keep inserting images in this order: *print.bmp, cut.bmp, copy.bmp, paste.bmp, bld.bmp, itl.bmp, undrln.bmp, lft.bmp, rt.bmp, cnt.bmp.*

8. Click *OK* to close the dialog box.

Now we'll create the ToolBar control and cross-reference it to the ImageList.

---

1. Double-click the Toolbar icon (shown here) to place the control on your frmScratchPad form. Notice that it is automatically positioned and sized.

2. Click *(Custom)* to open the ToolBar Control Properties dialog box.

3. On the first page, drop down the *ImageList* list and select the name of your ImageList: *ImageList1*.

4. Click the *Buttons* tab.

5. Click *Insert Button* to insert the first button. At the bottom of the dialog box, change *Image* to *1*. This tells Visual Basic to insert image 1 from the ImageList on the button.

6. Click *Apply* to see the effect in your toolbar.

   Move the dialog box so that you can see the toolbar in the background while you work.

7. In similar fashion, insert buttons number 2 and 3.

8. We want to insert some blank space after button number 3, so follow these directions:

   a. Click *Insert Button*.

   b. Drop down the *Style* list and choose *4 - Placeholder*.

9. Now create buttons 5 through 7, using images 4 through 6. (We're one off now because of the placeholder.)

10. Insert another placeholder.

11. Create buttons 9 through 11 using images 7 through 9.

12. Insert another placeholder.

13. Create the final three buttons using images 10 through 12.

14. Save your work.

Now what remains is to make those buttons work. When you double-click the ToolBar to open the code window for it, Visual Basic creates the procedure header shown below:

```
Private Sub Toolbar1_ButtonClick(ByVal Button As Button)
```

The event is called ButtonClick, not just Click. The expression (ByVal Button As Button) is required, so don't delete or change it or you'll get an error message. When someone clicks one of the buttons on the toolbar, Visual Basic passes to this procedure a set of values including the Index and the Key of the button that was clicked. This set of values is referred to as Button, and you can access the Index as Button.Index and the Key as Button.Key.

We're not using Keys in ScratchPad, so we'll find out which button was clicked by testing Button.Index, as in the following statements:

```
If Button.Index = 1 Then
  mnuFileNew_Click    'Process the File|New command
End If
```

With this information in hand, it's a relatively easy matter to process most of these icons, since all we have to do is refer to the associated menu commands. For the menu commands that we haven't coded yet, we'll just program the button to beep and add a comment about which menu command will be invoked eventually. (If we called unprogrammed procedures, we'd get error messages when we tried to run the program.) For the Bold, Italics, and Underline icons, there are no comparable menu commands, so we'll include code in this procedure to format the selected text in the Rich TextBox. Let's create the necessary code now:

1. Double-Click the ToolBar to open the code window. Visual Basic fills in the Sub and End Sub statements, as usual.

2. Type the procedure shown here. (Don't forget that you can use Copy and Paste to save repetitive typing.)

```
Private Sub Toolbar1_ButtonClick(ByVal Button As Button)
   If Button.Index = 1 Then
      mnuFileOpen_click
   End If
   If Button.Index = 2 Then
      mnuFileSave_Click
   End If
   If Button.Index = 3 Then
      mnuFilePrint_Click
   End If
   If Button.Index = 5 Then
      mnuEditCut_Click
   End If
   If Button.Index = 6 Then
      mnuEditCopy_Click
   End If
   If Button.Index = 7 Then
      mnuEditPaste_Click
   End If
   If Button.Index = 9 Then
      frmDocument.rtbPage.SelBold = Not rtbPage.SelBold
   End If
   If Button.Index = 10 Then
      frmDocument.rtbPage.SelItalic = Not rtbPage.SelItalic
   End If
   If Button.Index = 11 Then
      frmDocument.rtbPage.SelUnderline = Not rtbPage.SelUnderline
   End If
   If Button.Index = 13 Then
      mnuParagraphLeft_Click
   End If
```

```
If Button.Index = 14 Then
   mnuParagraphRight_Click
End If
If Button.Index = 15 Then
   mnuParagraphCenter_Click
End If
End Sub
```

3. Save your work.

4. Try it out.

If you're creating an application that allows users to customize the ToolBar by adding and removing icons and moving them around, be sure to use Keys instead of Indexes to refer to the buttons. Once a user has customized a ToolBar, you won't know which Indexes refer to which buttons, but the Key associated with a button moves with the button.

SUMMARY

The custom controls provided in the Professional Edition— also included in the Enterprise Edition, of course—give you most of the tools you need to create applications with the interface that most Windows users expect and want. In this chapter, you have learned to use the Slider, ProgressBar, TabStrip, StatusBar, Rich TextBox, Toolbar, and ImageList. You have added a Rich TextBox and a Toolbar to ScratchPad.

We'll be looking at a few more controls later on in this book, when we discuss databases and OLE, but we're done with controls for now. In Part III we begin to look more closely at the coding aspects of Visual Basic.

III

Programming in Visual Basic

Objects and code—they go together like bricks and mortar to build a Windows application. Now that you've got a good set of bricks—the objects that you learned about in Part II—it's time to turn our attention to the mortar—the code that makes the objects work. You'll learn how to handle the various Visual Basic data types, such as integers and strings. Then you'll learn how to code math, logic, branching, loops, and other Visual Basic statements and functions. And, of course, since no one writes a perfect program the first time, you'll learn a lot more about debugging.

CHAPTER OBJECTIVES

This chapter focuses on what kinds of data Visual Basic can work with. In this chapter, you'll learn:

 The built-in, or fundamental, data types

▶ How to declare variables

▶ How to declare and use arrays

▶ How to create and use your own data types

As we go along, you'll be creating some short programs to give you a hands-on feel for how the various data types are used and how to declare and use variables and arrays.

Data Types

Deep down, computers work with very few kinds of data: bits and bytes. A computer must be programmed to deal with information the way we think of it, such as fractions, currency, and text. Fortunately, Visual Basic handles most of the work for you so that you don't have to worry about the bits and bytes.

A *bit* is the smallest piece of information that a computer deals with, represented by an electronic switch inside the processor, a pulse traveling along a circuit, or a single spot stored in memory or on a disk. It can have one of two values, usually represented as 0 or 1. A *byte* is a group of eight bits, the basic unit in which you can store meaningful data. There are 256 possible combinations of eight bits, from 00000000 to 11111111, so a byte can have one of 256 values. A *word* is the computer's preferred data size. The first personal computers had fairly small words: eight bits, the same as a byte. Today's computers have 32-bit words, and tomorrow's will have words twice that size.

When you buy memory for your computer, you typically buy it by the *megabyte*, which is 1,048,576 bytes—it's easier to think of it as roughly a million bytes. Your hard disk now might store more than a *gigabyte*, which is roughly a billion bytes. In another 10 years (or less), we'll be dealing with *terabytes*, or roughly a trillion bytes!

THE FUNDAMENTAL DATA TYPES

Most of the time, you won't have to deal directly with bits and bytes. You'll want to deal with meaningful data—numbers and text—as simply as possible. Luckily, Microsoft has already done most of the programming for you: Visual Basic provides support for the text and numeric data that we're used to working with.

Visual Basic provides 11 specific ways to store and handle data in your computer, known as *data types*: six numeric data types, a Boolean type, a string type, a date type, an object type, and the variant type. We'll introduce each type, and you'll have a chance to try many of them out.

The Numeric Data Types

Why on earth would Visual Basic have *six* ways to store numeric data? Because some numbers are short and sweet, like page numbers or scores on a pop quiz. Others have a sign, a decimal point, and lots of digits, like the national debt or the electrical charge in a copper ion. And of course, there are all kinds of variations in between. A student's grade point average, such as 3.7, is short but needs a decimal point. City population figures are medium-long with no decimal point or sign. And so on.

We want to store data as efficiently as possible. The smaller the storage area, the less room it takes in memory and on disk, and the less time it takes to transfer it from one place to another inside the computer. So smaller numbers make your programs more efficient. If there was only one data type, it would have to be large enough to hold the biggest number, and the number 3 would take the same amount of storage space and processing time as -1.05602917000365. To avoid such inefficiency, Visual Basic provides six numeric data types. We'll explore them from the smallest to the largest.

The Byte Data Type

The smallest numeric data type is the Byte. As the name implies, it requires only a single byte to store a number. Therefore, it can hold numbers from 0 to 255. If you try to store the number 256 in a Byte, you'll get an error message.

If some people in your organization use older versions of Visual Basic, you may want to avoid the Byte data type. Since it's a new feature of Visual Basic 4.0, it's not available in older versions.

When you create a Byte variable, there's a pitfall that you need to be aware of. A Byte is an *integral* type—it holds only whole numbers, not fractions. So if you copy a fractional value, like 11.2, to a Byte, the value is rounded to the closest integer value first. The resulting value is then copied to the Byte.

Let's stop here and explore the characteristics of the Byte before we go on to the next data type.

1. Start a new project.

2. Create a Label control with no caption.

3. Double-click the form to open the code window for *Form_Load*.

4. Enter this code:

```
Dim x as Byte          'This creates a Byte variable named x
x = 25                 'This stores the number 25 in x
Label1.Caption = x     'This displays the number in the Label
```

5. Run your program. The number 25 should appear on your form, and all is well.

6. Now change x = 25 to *x = 260* and run the program again. You'll get this error message:

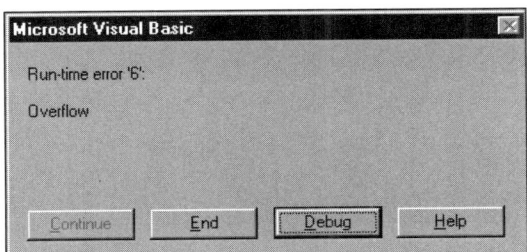

7. Click the *End* icon on the Visual Basic toolbar to end the program.

8. Change x = 260 to *x = 25.9*. When you run the program, Visual Basic rounds off the number, and you'll see 26 on your screen.

9. Change x = 25.9 to *x = -7* and run it again. You get another error message because you can't store a value below 0 in a Byte.

10. Click the *End* icon to end the program.

When you assign a fractional value to a Byte, Visual Basic rounds the value first, then checks for overflow. So you can assign fraction values from –0.5 to just under 255.5 to a Byte without getting an overflow error. But in general, it's better not to play around with the data types. If you want to store a fraction or a negative number, use a different data type.

When you use a Byte to store a number, you're paying a price for the space savings: speed. The processor in your computer works most efficiently on 16- and 32-bit integers; a computer favors its word size. When you operate on single bytes, you can incur a small (very small) time penalty. This is the one exception to the "smaller is faster" statement we made earlier. Those tiny time penalties can add up when you repeat the operation thousands or millions of times. In some programs, it wouldn't matter. In others, it could cause a noticeable delay. It depends on what's being processed.

The Integer Data Type

The fastest data type, and the next smallest, is the Integer. This data type takes two bytes of storage, so it can hold 65536 different values. (That's 256 for the first byte times 256 for the second byte. 256*256 = 65,536.) The Integer includes a sign, so the allowable value range is –32,768 to +32,767. (Why not +32,768? Because the positive numbers start with 0, not 1.) As the name suggests, it's an integer data type and can hold only whole numbers, not fractions. Like the Byte, when you copy a fractional value into an Integer, the value is rounded before the range is checked.

You'll probably use the Integer type often in your programs. When you don't need fractional values, it's a good compromise. It's fast, relatively small, and has a reasonable range.

1. In your program, revise the Dim statement to create an Integer instead of a Byte:

```
Dim x as Integer
```

2. Now run your program. -7 appears on the screen. Unlike Byte, the Integer data type can handle negative numbers.

3. Change x = -7 to *x = -56789*. When you run the program, you get an overflow message.

4. Click the *End* icon to clear the message and end the program.

5. Change the Dim statement to create our next data type, the Long:

```
Dim x as Long
```

6. Run the program now, and you'll see -56789 on your screen, because Long can handle much larger numbers.

The Long Data Type

As you saw in the last exercise, the next larger data type in Visual Basic is called Long. Visual Basic uses four bytes to make a Long, so it can hold 4,294,967,296 different values (256*256*256*256). Because it has a sign, its values range from –2,147,483,648 to +2,147,483,647. Like the first two data types, it holds only integer values.

On current computers, 386DX and above, the Long is only slightly slower than the Integer — about as fast as a Byte. On older computers, 386SX and below, the Long is significantly slower, since those processors access memory only 16 bits at a time.

The Long data type is the last of the integer data types that Visual Basic provides. Now let's take a look at the data types that allow fractions.

The Single Data Type

The Single data type, like the Long, is built from four bytes. Unlike the Long, the Single is formatted to store fractional numbers like 2.7. Therefore, it uses a completely different method of storing its data, and that means that we can't express the range of values as simply as we did before.

The range of a Single is approximately $-3.4*10^{38}$ to $3.4*10^{38}$. How can only four bytes represent such an astronomical number of different values? Visual Basic uses *scientific notation* internally to store the values, just as we used it here to represent them. Scientific notation is a convenient way to represent extremely large and extremely small numbers.

The general form for a number in scientific notation is $1.234*10^5$, where the 1.234 is called the *mantissa*, and the 5 is called the *characteristic*. The mantissa contains the significant digits, and the characteristic indicates where the decimal point is.

A positive characteristic means that you move the decimal point to the right when you want to write the number out. For $1.234*10^5$, you would move the decimal point 5 places to the right, and the number becomes 123,400. A negative characteristic means that you move the decimal point to the left. For $5.6789*10^{-3}$, you would move the decimal point 3 places to the left, and the number becomes .0056789.

As you can see, scientific notation can allow you to conveniently express both large (183,500,000,000,000) and small (0.0000000911) numbers in a more convenient notation: $1.835*10^{14}$ and $9.11*10^{-8}$.

When we're coding a Long number in a statement, we can also use scientific notation instead of writing out all the digits. Visual Basic doesn't have a way to type a superscript, so you can't type a number as $1.234*10^5$. Instead, you replace the *10 with the letter E (either upper- or lowercase) to indicate a value in scientific notation. Thus, for $1.234*10^5$, we write 1.234E+5 in Visual Basic. Negative characteristics aren't a problem either, as $9.11*10^8$ becomes 9.11E-8.

The letter *E* stands for *exponent*, another name for characteristic.

NOTE

In a Single, Visual Basic uses three of the four bytes to hold the mantissa and its sign, giving you room for about 6 or 7 significant digits in the mantissa. The fourth byte holds the characteristic and its sign. The advertised range of the Single is 1.401298E–45 to 3.402823E+38 for positive values, and from –1.401298E–45 to –3.402823E+38 for negative values. Of course, a Single also represents the commonly used value of 0.0 as well.

---

1. In your program, change x = 56789 to *x = 2.123e19*. Notice that the editor changes it to 2.123E+19.

2. Running the program results in an overflow error because you're still using the Long data type.

3. Change the Dim statement to create a Single data type:

```
Dim x as Single
```

4. Now run the program. You'll see 2.123E+19 on your screen.

The Double Data Type

If you need more significant digits or larger exponents than the Single can offer, you can use the Double data type. The Double data type acts almost exactly like a Single, except that it is built from eight bytes. Visual Basic formats it so that a Double holds about 15 significant digits in the mantissa. (This is good enough resolution to hold the distance between the Earth and the Sun with a precision greater than one ten-thousandth of a millimeter — without using an exponent!) While the Single has a characteristic range of −45 to +38, the Double's characteristic range is increased to −324 to +308.

The range of a Double is −4.94065645841247E−324 to −1.79769313486232E308 for negative values, and 4.94065645841247E−324 to 1.79769313486232E308 for positive values.

Rounding Error

One of the compromises you make when you work with a floating-point number (that is, a Single or Double) is the possibility of rounding errors creeping into your calculations. As you know, when you multiply two numbers together, you can get a much larger number. However, a Single has only about 6 digits of precision, and a Double has about 15. For illustration purposes, let's suppose that you can store only three significant digits, and you want to multiply 1.06 and 6.94. The answer should be 7.3564. However, you only get three significant digits, so you have to round the value to 7.36. Now your answer is off by 0.0036, which isn't so bad in itself. The problem comes when you perform hundreds of multiplications and divisions to arrive at a final total. In this case the errors can accumulate, even as far as making the first digit inaccurate!

The Currency Data Type

When you need to work with finances, you don't want to lose track of a single penny. But as we just observed, the Single and Double data types can lose accuracy due to rounding error and loss of significance. Consequently, Visual

Basic offers the Currency data type. This type provides an exact range of −922,337,203,685,477.5808 to 922,337,203,685,477.5807 in steps of 0.0001. This represents a range of $922 trillion, which should be enough to balance your checkbook.

Rounding error is mostly avoided by having a huge range to work in, along with four digits after the decimal point. This allows you to work with accuracy of 1 percent of a penny. Since financial applications rarely have long chains of repeated multiplications and divisions, any error is kept well away from the last penny.

The Nonnumeric Data Types

So far, we've looked only at numeric data types. But most of today's applications are more concerned with nonnumeric data (text, dates, and so on) than with numeric data. In the following sections, we'll explore Visual Basic's nonnumeric data types.

The Boolean Data Type

The Boolean data type holds only two different values: True and False. The Boolean type gets its name from George Boole (1815–1864), the English mathematician who developed a system for analyzing logic problems. You'll be using Boolean data often in your programs: Nearly every time your program makes a decision, it will be based on the value of a Boolean data item.

Since the Boolean holds only two values, you might expect it to need just a single bit. However, it actually takes up two bytes. Why? The machine code to manipulate a single bit is slower and takes more space than treating a Boolean as an integer.

NOTE If you store numeric value in a Boolean, a 0 turns into False, and any other value turns into True. Conversely, when you convert a Boolean data item to a numeric type, True becomes −1, and False becomes 0.

Here's an exercise to try out the Boolean data type.

1. Revise your program to read as follows:

```
Dim x As Boolean
x = True
Label1.Caption = x
```

2. When you run the program, you see True on the screen.

3. Change x = True to *x = False* and run it again.

4. Change x = False to *x = 20*. When you run it, you see True on the screen.

5. Change x = 20 to *x = 0*. When you run it, you see False on the screen.

The String Data Type

Text is another important form of data. In fact, most software is more concerned with storing and manipulating text than numbers. Think of any typical database or word processor, and you'll see what we mean. Even a spreadsheet handles a lot of text.

To help you manage text, Visual Basic provides the String data type. For each text variable, Visual Basic uses a small chunk of memory for bookkeeping, and then it uses one byte to hold each character.

Visual Basic permits two types of String variables: variable length or fixed length. A variable-length String variable can hold up to 2 billion characters, but its length varies according to the text you store in it. You define a variable-length String variable like this:

```
Dim Example As String
```

For Windows 3.1 and earlier, variable-length strings are limited to 64K bytes.

NOTE

A fixed-length String variable has a fixed number of bytes, from 1 to 64K (65,536). You define a fixed-length String by adding the length to the Dim statement, as in this example, which creates a String containing 1048 bytes:

```
Dim Example As String * 1048
```

NOTE Many data items that contain only digits should really be stored as String values. It depends on how you want to process them. If you don't need to perform arithmetic on them but do need to print or display them, they should be treated as strings. Typical examples are post office codes, account numbers, and product serial numbers.

When you're coding a value for a String variable, you must enclose it in quotes, as in "Paul Knudsen" or "Visual Basic 4.0". If you forget the quotes, Visual Basic thinks you're referring to an object or a variable. Let's experiment with Strings.

1. Change your code as follows:

```
Dim x as String
x = "Hi"
Label1.Caption = x
```

2. When you run the program, you'll see the message on your screen, without the quotes.

3. Remove the quotes from around "Hi". Now when you run the program, no message appears.

Why did you get no message when you removed the quotes from around the "Hi"? Because Visual Basic thought you were referring to a variable named Hi. Since it couldn't find one, it created one and gave it a blank value. Hence, the blank message.

The Date Data Type

Another data type that Visual Basic provides is the Date. Visual Basic stores dates in eight bytes, like a Double. In fact, they're very similar to a Double, because Dates are stored as fractional numbers. The part before the decimal point represents the date and the part after the decimal point represents the time. The difference is that, when Visual Basic prints or displays a Date, it translates the numbers into date and time formats that we understand. If you were to see the untranslated number, it might look like 1.3295E+5. Visual Basic knows how to translate that into a date and time value.

The number that represents the date works like this: A 0 represents the date January 1, 1900. A positive number represents the number of days after that. A negative number represents the number of days before that.

For the time, the value indicates the fraction of the day, where .0 is midnight and .5 is noon, or halfway through the day.

When you want to code a particular date or time in a statement, you don't have to figure out the correct day number or time fraction. You can write out the desired date or time enclosed in pound signs, as in *#July 4, 1776#* or *#6:03 pm#*. Let's try it.

---

1. Change your program as shown below. Notice that the editor immediately changes your date to #7/4/1776#.

```
Dim x As Date
x = #July 4, 1776#
Label1.Caption = x
```

2. Run the program. You'll see 7/4/1776 on your screen.

3. Change the second line as shown below. The editor changes the time to #5:00:00 PM#.

```
x = #5:00 pm#
```

4. Run the program, and you'll see 5:00:00 PM on your screen.

5. Remove the pound signs from around the time. You'll get an immediate error message from the editor. It doesn't exactly identify the problem, because you have confused the editor, but it tells you that *something* needs to be fixed before you can successfully run the program.

6. Clear the error message and restore the pound signs.

The Object Data Type

The Object data type represents the most complex type of data: objects. You can access spreadsheets, word processors, other Windows programs, forms, custom controls, and many other things using the Object data type. The data item doesn't really hold the spreadsheet or other object, it simply holds a reference to it.

Using Object variables is an advanced topic, however, so we'll talk about them in detail in Part VI, Advanced Topics.

The Variant Data Type

The Variant data type isn't really a distinct data type so much as it's a shortcut. The Variant can mimic any of the other data types. When you assign data to a Variant, it picks up that data's type and redefines itself to store just that type.

For example, if you put an integer in a Variant, then the Variant becomes an integral, signed data type. Later, if you assign a string to a Variant, it takes on the characteristics of the String data type. There's no limit to the number of times you can change the form of a Variant variable.

Variants are convenient to use and avoid a lot of error messages, but there's a heavy price to pay: Every time you use a Variant data item, Visual Basic has to take some time to figure out what data type to really use. Additionally, the Variant takes more room so that Visual Basic can keep some bookkeeping information about the current data type. In general, while Variant data can be useful in some specialized situations, you should avoid it whenever possible.

DECLARING VARIABLES

The number 7, by itself, doesn't have a type. Yes, it *could* be a Byte or an Integer. But it could just as easily be a Long, Single, Double, Currency, Date, or even a String or a Boolean. A piece of data doesn't have a type by itself. The type of a data item simply determines how the program stores and handles the value.

A *variable* is a named chunk of memory formatted according to one of the data types. Whenever you create a new variable, you're asking Visual Basic to set aside some memory where you can store some data. You might also tell it how much memory to allocate and how to format it by specifying a data type, but you don't have to.

NOTE A constant is also a named chunk of memory that is formatted according to one of the data types. The difference between a variable and a constant is that you can change the value stored in a variable; hence, the name variable. A constant's value cannot be changed; you define the value when you create it, and it retains that value for the life of the program. We'll explore constants in a later chapter.

You have used the Dim statement many times, and you're probably aware that it *declares* (or defines) a new variable; that is, it asks Visual Basic to allocate memory space for the variable. It also assigns a name to the variable, and it may specify the variable's type. You can declare more than one variable in a single Dim statement, like this:

```
Dim Judi, Michelle, Jim, Davida
Dim X as Integer, Y as Single, Z as Boolean
```

ALERT

If you declare a variable and don't specify the type, Visual Basic makes it a Variant. Keep in mind that the Variant type is the least efficient, so you should avoid doing this.

Another way to specify a variable's type is to attach a Type Declaration character to the end of its name. For example, the name Age% represents an Integer variable because the character % is the Type Declaration character for Integers. Table 10-1 shows the complete list of Type Declaration characters. Using these characters to identify your data types has a shortcoming: The Type Declaration character becomes a part of the name and must be included every time you use the name. Another shortcoming is that not all types have a Type Declaration character, as you can see in the table.

Table 10-1: Type Declaration Characters

Type	Character
Integer	%
Long	&
Single	!
Double	#
Currency	@
String	$

NOTE

Don't ask us why $ stands for String, not Currency. Write directly to Microsoft on this one. Well, okay, we'll tell you. The String data type is much older than Currency, and the $ was already in use for String when the Currency data type was created. Microsoft didn't want to make everyone revise their existing programs, so they kept on using $ for String and adopted @ for Currency.

There are five rules that you must follow when you create a variable name:

▶ A variable must begin with a letter, not a digit or a symbol.

▶ It can't contain an embedded period or embedded Type Declaration character.

▶ A variable name cannot be more than 255 characters long.

▶ A variable name cannot be one of Visual Basic's reserved words (the words that the editor recognizes and turns blue); this includes the keywords in statements, the names of the data types, the names of objects, and so on. (A name can include a reserved word as part of its name, however.)

▶ A variable name must be unique within the same scope.

Don't worry about the last one right now. We haven't covered scope yet. We'll talk about it in a later chapter and remind you of the rule.

Here are some examples of legal variable names:

```
Fred/Ethel, George95, Clark-Kent, Mild_Mannered_Reporter
```

Here are a few illegal variable names:

```
1hundred, _ethel_, Dog Breath, Frog.Ears
```

You're probably wondering about the last variable name. As we've worked with sample programs, you've been asked to type things like:

```
txtColor.Text = "Red"
```

Why is Frog.Ears a bad variable name yet txtColor.Text is good? Because txtColor.Text represents *two names* concatenated by the period: Text is a property that belongs to txtColor. When you create a new variable, it must have only one name; hence, no embedded periods are permitted. Let's try out a few variable names.

1. Change your Dim statement to read as follows:

```
Dim _x
```

Visual Basic immediately highlights the underscore and displays an invalid character message.

2. Try out a few of the other invalid names shown above to see what error messages you get.

Out of the box, Visual Basic doesn't require you to declare your variables. However, it's a good idea to declare *all* variables in your program. When Visual Basic doesn't require variable declarations, it automatically creates a variable for you whenever you use a new variable name in a statement. This behavior *seems* convenient, but it actually causes more problems that it's worth. First, if you misspell a variable name, Visual Basic will simply create a new variable, and you won't know about it. Second, when Visual Basic automatically creates a variable for a name that doesn't include a Type Declaration character, it creates a Variant type, which is less efficient than most other variable types.

You can make Visual Basic require variable declarations by selecting Tools | Options to open the dialog box shown in Figure 10-1. Make sure the Require Variable Declaration option is checked. (When you install Visual Basic, it's not checked.) Checking this option inserts the following statement at the beginning of each module:

```
Option Explicit
```

Then, whenever you use a name that hasn't been declared, Visual Basic displays a warning message and requires a Dim statement.

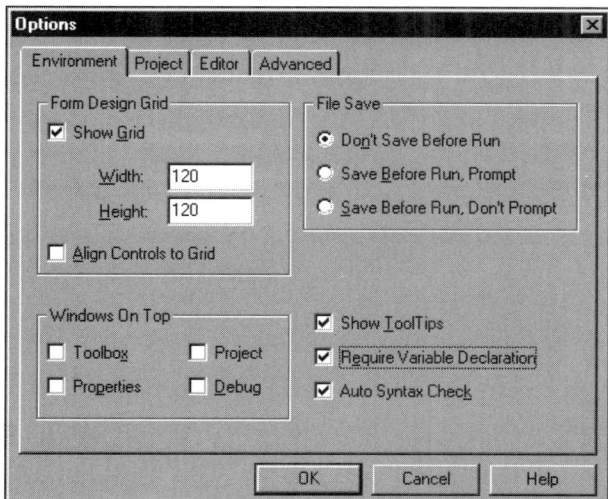

Figure 10-1: By checking the Require Variable Declaration option in the Tools | Options dialog box, you'll save yourself innumerable programming headaches.

AGGREGATE DATA TYPES

The fundamental data types cover most of the data you're likely to need. However, sometimes you're going to need more. In some cases, you're going to want to arrange a big group of sets into an array. In other cases, you can save yourself a great deal of time and typing by creating your own specialized data types.

You'll get a chance to practice using these data types later in the book. For now, we'll just talk about them and not do any exercises.

Arrays

Suppose you have a large collection of variables, all of the same type, used in tabular fashion. For example, you might have a set of student scores on several tests or a sales tax table. You could declare each item as a separate variable, like this:

```
Dim JohnJones_Test1 as Byte, JohnJones_Test2 as Byte,
    JohnJones_Test3 as Byte,....
```

and so on. But if you've got 100 students and 10 tests — which is not an unreasonable example — you'll have to type out 1000 variable names! And to find the average score, you would have to write an assignment statement that sums all 1000 names. You'll quickly look for another way. Fortunately, Visual Basic provides an easy solution to this type of problem, called *arrays*.

An array is a series of data items of the same type. Only the array has a name; the individual items within the array are accessed by appending a numeric index to the array name. For example, suppose you create an array named Scores. The first item in the array is called Scores(1); the second, Scores(2); and so on. To declare the array, you only have to write a very short Dim statement:

```
Dim Scores(1000) as Byte
```

This statement tells Visual Basic to create an array named Scores consisting of 1000 items, each item having the Byte data type. Processing the array is also easier, but we're not going to show you how to do that here. Chapter 12 explains how to process arrays when we discuss program loops.

NOTE

By default, Visual Basic assumes that you want to start numbering your array with item 0. Therefore, the above Dim statement would create an array of 1001 items, not 1000. However, most people include the Option Base statement in their programs so that they can start numbering arrays with 1, not 0. All of the examples in this chapter assume that the program includes an Option Base statement to start arrays at 1. We explain the Option Base statement a little later in the chapter.

All you have to do is specify the upper bound of the array in parentheses when you declare a variable, and it turns into an array. However, each time you declare an array, you can specify the lower bound as well. To do so, just precede the upper bound with the lower bound and the word "To". So if you want to declare an array of Integers named FTemp with the elements numbered from 32 to 212, you could use the following line of code:

```
Dim FTemp(32 To 212) As Integer
```

But wait, there's more! You can have multiple dimensions in your arrays—up to 60. While we can't even imagine an array with 60 dimensions, we have already mentioned two examples of multidimensional arrays. The student test score array involves 100 students (the first dimension) and 10 tests (the second dimension). If you were to print out the test scores, you wouldn't print them in a single column, you'd use a column and row setup, with one dimension in rows and the other in columns:

We defined this array with a single dimension before. Now let's change that definition to reflect the true nature of the array:

```
Dim Scores(10, 100) as Byte
```

Now to access an individual item, we must use two indexes: Scores(2, 4) refers to the second score of the fourth student, or 79 in the above table.

A tax table might have two, three, or even more dimensions. Let's look at a typical three-dimensional example:

```
                      Filing Status
              Single Exemptions      Married Exemptions
Income        1     2     3     4    1     2     3     4
0-5000        400   300   200   0    300   200   0     0
5001-10000    450   385   300   200  385   250   200   0
10001-15000   775   680   534   415  534   315   300   205
```

This particular table has three dimensions: Filing Status, Exemptions, and Income. Assuming that there are five Status categories, four Exemption categories, and ten Income categories, you could declare the array this way:

```
Dim Tax(5, 4, 10) as Integer
```

Now it's easy to look up an individual's tax. If someone is single (that's a 1 on the first dimension), has 1 exemption (a 1 on the second dimension), and earned $14,000 (a 3 on the third dimension), his tax is located at Tax(1, 1, 3).

Visual Basic defaults to using 0 as the first element in an array. So you often get one more element in your arrays than you expect. Most people prefer *natural numbering* — starting with 1 — to *whole numbering* — starting with 0. To accommodate this preference, Visual Basic provides the *Option Base* statement. The Option Base statement may be followed with a 0 or 1, telling Visual Basic to number arrays starting with 0 or 1.

If you specify the Option Base 1 statement in the (General) section of your programs (that is, outside of any procedure), you can make your arrays start at 1 instead of 0. To enter the Option Base statement in the (General) section of one of your programs, select (General) from the Object list in a code window.

Creating Your Own Data Types

Suppose you're writing a work scheduling program and you have to store several names for each shift: the manager, the floor supervisor, counter clerk #1, counter clerk #2, the supply clerk, and the janitor. For each person, you must include the employee number, the first name, the last name, and the phone number, all as separate items. You would have to write a bunch of Dim statements to create all these variables:

```
Dim ManagerEmpNumber as String, ManagerFirstName as String
Dim ManagerLastName as String, ManagerPhone as String
Dim SupervisorEmpNumber as String, ...
```

And so on. Here again, you would quickly look for an easier way. And as usual, Visual Basic provides one. You can create your own data type:

```
Type Staff
   EmpNumber as String
   FirstName as String
   LastName as String
   PhoneNumber as String
End Type
```

This Type declaration creates a new data type that you can use in Dim statements. So you can define the personnel for each shift this way:

```
Dim Manager as Staff, Super as Staff
Dim Clerk1 as Staff, Clerk2 as Staff
Dim Janitor as Staff
```

This Dim statement creates all the storage space you need to store the employee numbers, first names, last names, and phone numbers of all these personnel.

Each item in the type is a property of that type. So to access the manager's first name, you use the expression Manager.FirstName. For the first counter clerk's phone number, you code Clerk1.PhoneNumber.

Why would you create a type like this? Why not just declare the individual variables? Other than saving a lot of typing time and reducing the probability of error, there are several reasons:

▶ You can move the entire data item around as one unit. If you didn't create the data type, it would take four assignment statements to make this change.

▶ When you create a new personnel position, you need only come up with a single new variable name. Without the Staff type, you have to come up with four new variable names.

▶ You can easily use the new data type and functions in related projects, such as the employee benefits program and the employee phone directory.

▶ The most compelling reason is this: Suppose you later add new features to your scheduling program, such as tracking the person's middle initial and employment status (temporary, part-time, full-time). If you use the Staff type, you can simply add the new data elements to the type, and the new fields will be added to all the variables that use that type.

SUMMARY

You've come a long way since the beginning of this particular chapter! You've learned what data types are available for your Visual Basic programs. You also know how to tell Visual Basic which variables you're going to use in your program by declaring them. We also hope you're comfortable with arrays and user-defined data types. The next few chapters will finish what we've started here—you'll see the different operations you can perform on your variables.

CHAPTER OBJECTIVES

In this chapter, you'll learn to use the operators for:

▶ Arithmetic (c = a + b)

▶ Numeric comparisons (a < 5)

▶ String comparisons (txtCity.Text = "Buffalo")

▶ Logic operations (a = not b)

▶ Concatenation (putting strings together)

You'll also learn how to understand and control which operators are processed first when an expression has more than one operand, and to top off the chapter, we'll introduce a variety of functions for solving problems involving:

▶ Mathematics (square root, logarithms, and so on)

▶ Trigonometry (sine, cosine, and so on)

▶ Finance (depreciation, annuities, and so on)

Using Math and Logic

Computers were originally designed for math (number crunching) and logic (making decisions). Even though nowadays we use them more to "crunch" text data, the math and logic operations are still very important.

This chapter is concerned primarily with *operators* — the symbols (sometimes words) that you use to indicate how you want two values to be combined. A lot of these operators are familiar to you, such as + for addition and < for "less than," but you'll also meet some strangers.

ARITHMETIC

In Visual Basic, when you want to do any kind of math, you write an *assignment statement* using the arithmetic operators to perform the math. Suppose, for example, that you want to calculate Area by multiplying Width times Length. You would code this statement, where the asterisk (*) is the arithmetic operator for multiplication:

```
Area = Width * Length
```

Or, if you wanted to increment PageNumber by 1, you would use the plus sign (+) as the arithmetic operator for addition:

```
PageNumber = PageNumber + 1
```

The Arithmetic Operators

Table 11-1 shows all eight of Visual Basic's arithmetic operators.

Table 11-1: The Arithmetic Operators

Name	Operator	Usage	Precedence
Addition	+	a + b	9
Subtraction	−	a − b	9
Multiplication	*	a * b	12
Division	/	a / b	12
Integer Division	\	a \ b	11
Modulus	Mod	a Mod b	10
Negation	−	−b	13
Exponentiation	∧	a ∧ b	14

NOTE

The precedence column shows the order in which operators are executed when you have more than one operator in an expression. We'll explain precedence in detail at the end of the chapter.

As you work through this chapter, you'll try out many of the new concepts in small applications. For the arithmetic operators, you'll work on a form that looks like Figure 11-1. Before we begin examining the arithmetic operators in detail, let's create the basic framework of this program.

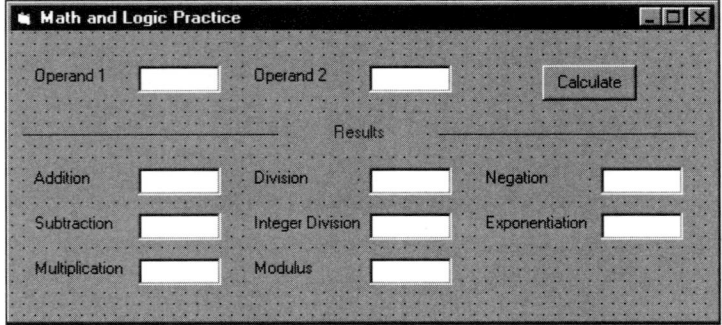

Figure 11-1: We'll create this program to experiment with various math and logic concepts.

1. Start a new project.

2. Create the form. Name the CommandButton *cmdCalculate* and the TextBoxes *txtAddition, txtSubtraction, txtIntegerDivision,* and so on, as shown in Figure 11-1. You don't have to worry about the names of the form itself or the Labels, as we won't refer to those in our code.

3. Open the *cmdCalculate_Click* procedure.

4. Enter these statements:

```
Dim Operand1 as Single, Operand2 as Single, Result as Single
Operand1 = Val(txtOperand1.Text)
Operand2 = Val(txtOperand2.Text)
```

An *operand* is the target of an operation. The operands for addition, for example, are the two numbers that are added together.

5. Save your work as *Math and Logic Practice.*

What does the above code do? First, it declares three Single variables, Operand1, Operand2, and Result. Then it converts the value in the TextBox called txtOperand1 from a text value to a numeric value (the Val function does the conversion), and assigns the result to Operand1. It then does the same thing for the value in txtOperand2.

Why do you have to convert the values from text to numeric? Because you can't type a numeric value, but Visual Basic can't do arithmetic on a text value. So after you type the text value, you have to convert it to a numeric value. Later on, you'll see that, after Visual Basic calculates the result, it has to be reconverted into a text value via the Str function so that it can be displayed. You'll use the Val and Str functions often when doing math. To review:

▶ *Val* produces a numeric value from a text value.

▶ *Str* produces a text value from a numeric value.

Now, with all that in hand, let's look at the first three arithmetic operators, addition, subtraction, and multiplication.

Addition, Subtraction, and Multiplication

The addition, subtraction, and multiplication operators work just as you'd expect: They add, subtract, or multiply the two operands. In the case of subtraction, the second operand is subtracted from the first. Let's try out these three operations in our program:

1. Add the following code to the end of *cmdCalculate_Click*:

```
Result = Operand1 + Operand2          'Adds the operands
txtAddition.Text = Str(Result)        'Displays the result
Result = Operand1 - Operand2          'Subtracts the operands
txtSubtraction.Text = Str(Result)     'Displays the result
Result = Operand1 * Operand2          'Multiplies the operands
txtMultiplication.Text = Str(Result)  'Displays the result
```

2. Run your program.

3. Type *5* in the *Operand1* box and *3* in the *Operand2* box. Then click *Calculate*. You should see 8 in the Addition box, 2 in the Subtraction box, and 15 in the Multiplication box.

   If you got any other results, you probably made a typing error somewhere in your code.

4. Try out some more values on your own. Be sure to try some negative and fractional values.

5. When you're satisfied that it all works as it should, end the program and save your project.

Division

Visual Basic gives you three different division functions. Standard division works just as you'd expect: the second operand is divided into the first operand. The other two division functions handle some rare applications that crop up in pure math and statistics.

Integer division divides the operands as normal, but returns only the integer part of the quotient as the result. If you integer divide 15 by 6, the result would be 2 instead of 2.5. *Modulus* does just the opposite. It divides as normal, then reports only the remainder as the result. If you use modulus to divide 15 by 6, the result is 3. To sum up:

15 / 6 = 2.5   (Standard division)

15 \ 6 = 2   (Integer division)

15 Mod 6 = 3   (Modulus)

Notice that the division (forward slash) and integer division (backslash) operators are very similar. Be careful that you don't accidentally use the wrong one!

What about division by zero? You probably know that a number divided by 0 yields infinity. Computers can't handle infinity, so they punt by creating a "Division by zero" error and terminating. In Chapter 12, you'll learn how to trap errors like this so that your program can handle them without crashing.

Now let's add these three functions to our program:

1. Add the code shown below to the end of *cmdCalculate_Click*:

```
Result = Operand1 / Operand2          'Divides Operand1 by
                                       Operand2
txtDivision.Text = Str(Result)        'Displays the result
Result = Operand1 \ Operand2          'Integer divides Op1
                                       by Op2
txtIntegerDivision.Text = Str(Result) 'Displays the result
Result = Operand1 Mod Operand2        'Modulus divides Op1
                                       by Op2
txtModulus.Text = Str(Result)         'Displays the result
```

2. Run the program.

3. Type *15* in the *Operand1* box and *6* in the *Operand2* box, then click *Calculate.* You should see 2.5 in the Division box, 2 in the Integer Division box, and 3 in the Modulus box.

4. Type *0* in the *Operand2* box and click *Calculate.* You'll get a *Division by 0* error, with an End button in the message box

5. Click *End* to end the program. Then restart the program.

6. Try out some more values on your own. Be sure to experiment with fractional and negative values.

7. End the program and save your work.

Negation

The negation operator simply changes the sign of its single operand. It's the same as multiplying the operand by –1. Note that this is different from making the number negative. It makes a positive number negative, but it makes a negative number positive. We'll practice negation after discussing the final topic, exponentiation.

Exponentiation

Exponentiation means raising a number to a power, as in 5^2. In Visual Basic, you don't write 5^2, you write 5 ^ 2. The following statement calculates the cube of the variable Side and assigns the result to Volume:

```
Volume = Side ^ 3
```

In the following exercise, you'll add negation and exponentiation functions to your program.

1. Add the statements shown below to *cmdCalculate_Click*.

```
Result = -Operand1              'Negates Operand1
txtNegation.Text = Str(Result)  'Displays the result
Result = Operand1 ^ Operand2    'Raises Op1 to the power
                                 indicated by Op2
txtExponentiation.Text = Str(Result)  'Displays the result
```

2. Run your program.

3. Type *5* in *Operand1* and *2* in *Operand2*, then click *Calculate*. You should see -5 in the Negation box and 25 in the Exponentiation box.

4. Try out other values, including fractions and negative numbers.

Keep in mind that exponentiation can create very large numbers. If you use large operands, you're likely to overflow the Single Result variable and get an Overflow error. If this happens, click *End* and restart the program to keep on experimenting.

5. End the program and save your work.

The math operators aren't the only operators in Visual Basic. You also have operators for making comparisons and performing logical functions. The next section explains the comparison operators.

COMPARISONS

Comparisons are used for making decisions in your program. They compare two values and return a result of True or False. They are often used in If statements. In the following example, the Boolean variable named OKFlag is set to True if Operand1 is greater than zero. Otherwise, it is set to False.

```
If Operand1 > 0 Then
    OKFlag = True
Else
    OKFlag = False
End If
```

You can also use comparisons in assignment statements. The following statement accomplishes exactly the same thing as the previous If statement:

```
OKFlag = Operand1 > 0
```

How does this statement work? Visual Basic examines the expression Operand1 > 0 and decides if it is true or false. It then assigns that result to OKFlag.

The Comparison Operators

There are seven comparison operators, as shown in Table 11-2. Six of them can be used to compare numeric values or strings. The Like operator compares strings only.

Table 11-2: The Comparison Operators

Name	Symbol	Usage	Precedence
Less than	<	a < b	7
Less than or equal to	<=	a <= b	7
Greater than	>	a > b	7
Greater than or equal to	>=	a >= b	7
Equal to	=	a = b	7
Not equal to	<>	a <> b	7
Like	Like	a Like b	7

We're not going to get into the details of If statements until the next chapter, so we'll use assignment statements in this chapter to explore the various comparison operators. Figure 11-2 shows the form that we'll use in this section. We'll create the form and some preliminary code now, then go on to discuss and experiment with the operators.

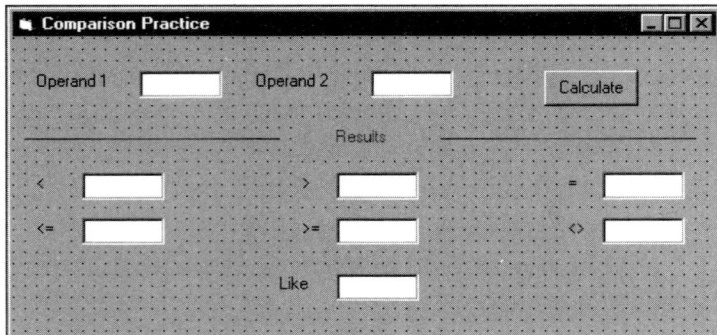

Figure 11-2: We'll use this form to explore the comparison operators.

1. Rather than start a new project, you can save time by adapting the form from the last project. Choose *File|Save File As* to give the form a new name. Then choose *File|Save Project As* to give the project a new name. Use the name *Comparison Practice* for both the form and the project.

2. Adapt the form so that it looks like Figure 11-2. Please name the new TextBoxes as follows:

txtLess   txtGreater   txtEqual
txtLessEqual   txtGreaterEqual   txtNotEqual
                    txtLike

3. Revise *cmdCalculate_Click* so that it looks like the following. Notice that we have eliminated the Result variable. We don't need it now, as comparisons return a text value, which we can store directly in the appropriate TextBox without an intermediary conversion step.

```
Dim Operand1 As Single, Operand2 As Single
Operand1 = Val(txtOperand1.Text)
Operand2 = Val(txtOperand2.Text)
```

4. Save your work.

Numeric Comparisons

Numeric comparisons do exactly what you'd expect: they compare the two operands and return a True or False value. In the following exercise, you'll set up all six numeric comparisons.

1. Add the following code to the end of *cmdCalculate_Click*:

```
txtLess.Text = Operand1 < Operand2
txtLessEqual.Text = Operand1 <= Operand2
txtGreater.Text = Operand1 > Operand2
txtGreaterEqual.Text = Operand1 >= Operand2
txtEqual.Text = Operand1 = Operand2
txtNotEqual.Text = Operand1 <> Operand2
```

2. Run the program and enter *5* in the *Operand1* box and *3* in the *Operand2* box. The results should be:

```
< False      > True       = False
<= False     >= True      <> True
```

3. Try out other sets of values on your own.

4. End the program and save your work.

String Comparisons

These same comparison operators can also be used to compare string values. By default, this will not result in a true comparison of alphabetic order, unfortunately, because all lowercase letters are considered to be less than all uppercase letters. The following five words would be sorted in the order shown:

events
objects
properties
ASCII
ZOrder

NOTE Why does Visual Basic sort strings like this? It's a hangover from the old, geeky days when the BASIC language was first created. Now we're stuck with it because so many older applications were programmed around it. Rather than make people reprogram all their existing applications, Visual Basic provides another solution. You can use the Option Compare Text statement at the beginning of your program to ask Visual Basic to use "normal" alphabetic order—the order that we all expected it to use in the first place. You put the Option Compare Text in the same location where you code the Option Base 1 statement—in the (General) section. When you include Option Compare Text in a program, Visual Basic treats "a" and "A" as the same letter, and puts foreign-language characters like "Â," "Ì," and "Ù" in their appropriate places in the alphabet.

Let's revise the program now so that it makes the string comparisons.

1. Add the following statement to the *(General)* section:

```
Option Compare Text
```

2. Replace all the code in *cmdCalculate_Click* with the following:

```
txtLess.Text = txtOperand1.Text < txtOperand2.Text
txtLessEqual.Text = txtOperand1.Text <= txtOperand2.Text
txtGreater.Text = txtOperand1.Text > txtOperand2.Text
txtGreaterEqual.Text = txtOperand1.Text >= txtOperand2.Text
txtEqual.Text = txtOperand1.Text = txtOperand2.Text
txtNotEqual.Text = txtOperand1.Text <> txtOperand2.Text
```

3. Run the program.

4. Enter *abc* in *Operand1* and *def* in *Operand2*. The results should be as follows:

< True   > False   = False

<= True   >= False   <> True

5. Try out other values, including uppercase strings and strings containing digits and symbols.

6. When you're finished, end the program and save your work.

As you can see, most of the string comparisons do just what you'd expect. But what does the Like operator do? You can use this operator with strings only. Its purpose is to see if a string fits a certain pattern. For example, does the Social Security number entered by the employee in txtSSNum have three digits, followed by a hyphen, then two digits, then another hyphen, then four digits? The comparison expression would look like this:

```
txtSSNum.Text Like "###-##-####"
```

These types of comparisons are wonderfully useful for making sure that users enter data in the appropriate form.

The operand on the left must be a string, as usual. But the operand on the right must be a *pattern*. Patterns can get quite complex. Let's look at the basic rules first:

1. A ? matches *any* single character.

2. An * matches *any* number of characters.

3. A # matches a digit only.

4. Any other character matches that character only.

Thus, the pattern we used for txtSSNum.Text accepts any digits in the first three positions (rule 3), a hyphen only in the fourth position (rule 4), any digits in the next two positions (rule 3), a hyphen only in the next position (rule 4), and any digits in the last four positions.

Let's take a look at a few sample comparisons:

Expression	Result	Rule
"a" Like "a"	True	4
"b" Like "a"	False	4
"x+5" Like "???"	True	1
"abc" Like "a?c"	True	1, 4
"abc" Like "a*"	True	2, 4
"abcba" Like "a*a"	True	2, 4
"abcde" Like "a*a"	False	2, 4
"ab78" Like "??##"	True	1, 3
"ab7a" Like "??##"	False	1, 3

However, these aren't the only rules for using the Like comparison. You can also specify a set or range of characters for a particular position by enclosing them in square brackets. Let's look at those rules.

5. A list of characters appearing in square brackets means that any *one* of the characters can be used. For example, "[abc]" matches a, b, or c, but no other character.

6. If the first character after the opening bracket is an exclamation point, then any character *not* in the list can be used. In other words, "[!a]" matches any character but "a".

7. Inside brackets, the expression *character-character* matches any character within the indicated range of characters. Thus, "[a-g]" matches a, b, c, d, e, f, or g, but no other characters. The first character in a range must be less than the second character, according to the current text sort order. The editor won't catch an invalid range, but you'll get an *invalid pattern string* error at run time.

8. A hyphen (-) at the beginning or end of a bracketed list does not indicate a range. It matches only a hyphen.

9. The pattern "[]" is treated like an empty string and ignored.

When you use Option Compare Text at the beginning of your program, Visual Basic ignores case in Like comparisons, so that "[X-Z]" matches x, X, y Y, Z, or Z. Without Option Compare Text, "[X-Z]" matches only X, Y, or Z.

Let's look at a few more comparisons to see how these rules work:

Comparison	Result	Rule
"a3" Like "[abc][123]"	True	5
"aa" Like "[abc][123]"	False	5
"a3" Like "[abc][!123]"	False	5, 6
"aa" Like "[abc][!123]"	True	5, 6
"abX" Like "ab[W-Z]"	True	1, 7
"abc" Like "ab[W-Z]"	False	1, 7
"abX" Like "ab[!W-Z]"	False	1, 6, 7
"abc" Like "ab[!W-Z]"	True	1, 6, 7
"-" Like "[-$(]"	True	5
"-" Like "[!-$(]"	False	6
"" Like "[]"	True	9

One more set of rules needs to be discussed. What if you want to require a character to match one of the characters that patterns use in a special way (the characters [,], ?, #, -, !, or *)? Here are the rules for special characters.

10. Outside of brackets, a hyphen represents itself just like any other character. Inside of brackets, you have to put it first (or immediately after the exclamation point) or last to make it represent itself, not a range.

11. The exclamation point (!) also acts as itself outside of brackets; inside, if it's not the first character, it represents itself.

12. The right bracket ( ]) represents itself when it's not preceded by a left bracket. For example, the string "a??]d??" requires a right bracket in the fourth position. You can't use a right bracket inside of square brackets.

13. The characters ?, *, [, and # can't be used outside brackets to represent themselves. If you want them to match themselves, you must enclose them in brackets. For example, the string "##[?]" requires two digits followed by a question mark. The string "[[*]]" requires an asterisk enclosed in square brackets.

Let's add a Like comparison to our current application.

1. Add the following statement to the end of *cmdCalculate_Click*:

   ```
   txtLike.Text = txtOperand1.Text Like "a*[1-3]!"
   ```

2. Run the program.

3. Enter *ark2!* in *Operand1* and click the *Calculate* button. The result in the Like box should be True.

4. Try out some other values for Operand1 and watch the result in the Like box.

5. End the program and save your work.

LOGIC OPERATIONS

Logic operations give us the ability to combine two or more comparisons to create a compound condition. For example, the following statement uses the logical And operator to indicate that both comparisons must be true for the ultimate result to be true:

```
Teenager = Age > 10 And Age < 20
```

Logic operations can also be performed on the individual bits of two numeric operands. Computer scientists, mathematicians, and logisticians find such operations useful. The rest of us worry about what they're really up to.

The Logical Operators

Table 11-3 shows the six logical operators in Visual Basic.

Table 11-3: The Logical Operators

Name	Symbol	Usage	Precedence
Not	Not	Not a	6
And	And	a And b	5
Or	Or	a Or b	4
Xor	Xor	a Xor b	3
Eqv	Eqv	a Eqv b	2
Imp	Imp	a Imp b	1

Not

The Not operator needs only one value to work on. The result of the Not operator is opposite of the value on the right. If you give it a Boolean value, it returns the opposite Boolean value to you. We have already used the Not operator in some of our programs to reverse the value of a Boolean variable, in statements similar to these:

```
OKFlag = Not OKFlag
```

And

The And operator returns True if both operands are True. Otherwise, it returns False. In the following statement, EmployeeStatus must be "FT" and Seniority must greater than 13 in order for BonusFlag to be set to True:

```
BonusFlag = EmployeeStatus = "FT" And Seniority > 13
```

Or

The Or operator is similar to the And operator except that it yields a True result if either or both operands are true. In the following example, BonusFlag will be set to True if either EmployeeStatus is "FT" or Seniority is greater than 13:

```
BonusFlag = EmployeeStatus = "FT" Or Seniority > 13
```

Xor

Xor is closely related to Or, but with one major difference. If both operands are true, Xor is false. (Xor stands for "eXclusive or.") In the following example, BonusFlag is set to True if either EmployeeStatus is "FT" or Seniority is greater than 13, but if they're both true, it's set to False:

```
BonusFlag = EmployeeStatus = "FT" Xor Seniority > 13
```

Eqv

Another way to look at the Xor operator is that it simply checks to see if both operands are *different*. The Eqv operator, in this sense, is the opposite of Xor, because it checks to see if both operands are the same. If they're both True or both False, the result is True.

Imp

The final operator is Imp, which stands for "Implies." We use Imp to check if the first condition implies the second. The first condition implies the second in all cases except when the first condition is True and the second is False.

We'll use the form shown in Figure 11-3 to try out the logical operators.

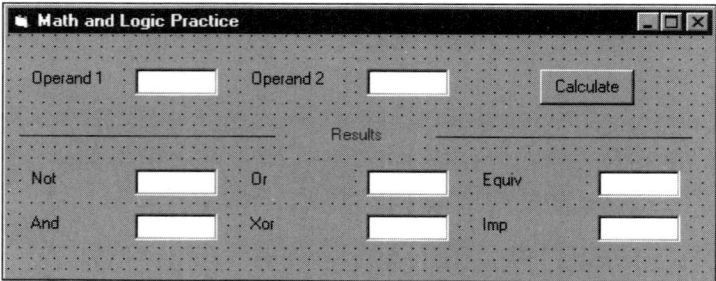

Figure 11-3: We'll use this form to experiment with the logical operators.

---

1. Choose *File | Save File As* and name your form file *Logic Practice.frm*.

2. Choose *File | Save Project As* and name your project *Logic Practice.vbp*.

3. Adapt the form to look like Figure 11-3. Name the new TextBoxes as follows:

   ```
   txtNot       txtOR        txtEqv
   txtAnd       txtXOR       txtImp
   ```

4. Replace all the code in *cmdCalculate_Click* with the following statements. The CBool function converts a text value to Boolean.

   ```
   txtNot.Text = Not CBool(txtOperand1.Text)
   txtAnd.Text = CBool(txtOperand1.Text) And CBool(txtOperand2.Text)
   txtOr.Text = CBool(txtOperand1.Text) Or CBool(txtOperand2.Text)
   txtXor.Text = CBool(txtOperand1.Text) Xor CBool(txtOperand2.Text)
   txtEqv.Text = CBool(txtOperand1.Text) Eqv CBool(txtOperand2.Text)
   txtImp.Text = CBool(txtOperand1.Text) Imp CBool(txtOperand2.Text)
   ```

5. Run the program.

6. Enter *True* in *Operand1* and *False* in *Operand2* and click *Calculate*. The results are shown below:

```
Not False        Or True          Equiv False
And False        Xor True         Imp False
```

7. Try out other combinations of True/False values.

8. End the program and save your work.

CONCATENATION

Concatenation is "geek speak" for joining two items end-to-end. For example, if we concatenate "abc" and "def," the result is "abcdef."

The Concatenation Operators

Visual Basic provides two operators for concatenating strings: + and &. Since + is also an arithmetic operator, most experts recommend that you always use & for concatenation. Both operators do exactly the same thing, so you won't lose any functionality by ignoring the + concatenation operator. Table 11-4 documents the concatenation operators, just to make the chapter's tables complete.

Table 11-4: The Concatenation Operators

Name	Symbol	Usage	Precedence
Concatenation	&	a & b	8
Concatenation	+	a + b	8

 Bug Alert! Be sure to put a space before the & concatenation operator, or Visual Basic will give you an error message: *Expected: end of statement.* Normally, Visual Basic detects operators properly, and puts spaces around them. For some reason, however, Microsoft missed the & operator.

Let's try out the concatenation operator.

1. Replace the six result boxes on your form with a single box, named *txtConcatenate*. Make it fairly large, as shown below:

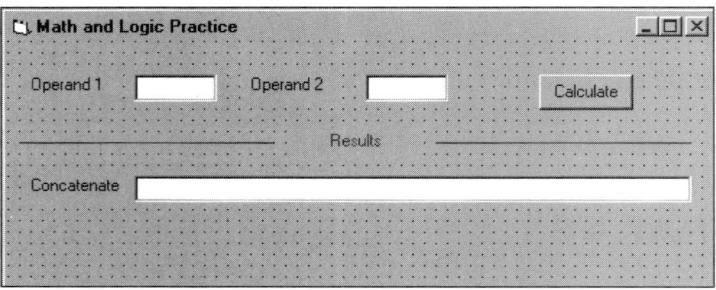

2. Save your form as *Concatenation Practice.frm* and your project as *Concatenation Practice.vbp*.

3. Replace all the code for *cmdCalculate_Click* with the statement shown here:

```
txtConcatenate.Text = txtOperand1.Text & txtOperand2.Text
```

4. Run the program.

5. Type *tree* in *Operand1* and *frog* in *Operand2*. The result should be treefrog.

6. Try some other strings in *Operand1* and *Operand2*.

7. End the program and save your work.

PRECEDENCE

Now you know all the possible operators that you can use with your Visual Basic programs. If you want, you can combine several operations in one statement. For example, the following statement sets OKFlag to True if the result of M*C^2 is greater than the result of Pi*R^2, and if M is greater than zero:

```
OKFlag = M * C ^ 2 > Pi * R ^ 2 And M > 0
```

How do you know which parts of this complex expression Visual Basic will process first? This brings up the topic of precedence that we mentioned briefly earlier in the chapter and that is shown in the Precedence column in Tables 11-1 through 11-4. Table 11-5 is a review of the precedence values for the various operators. Visual Basic handles the operator with the greatest precedence value first. Then it handles the operator with the next greatest value, and so on.

Table 11-5: Operator Precedence in Visual Basic

Operator	Precedence
Exponentiation	14
Negation	13
Multiplication	12
Division	12
Integer Division	11
Modulus	10
Addition	9
Subtraction	9
Concatenation	8
Comparison	7
Not	6
And	5
Or	4
Xor	3
Eqv	2
Imp	1

In the preceding example, the exponentiation operators have the highest precedence (14). Since there are two of them, Visual Basic handles them from left to right: it squares the C first and the R next. Using the symbol # to indicate which parts it has already handled, the expression would now look like this:

```
OKFlag = M * # > Pi * # And M > 0
```

The next highest operator is the multiplication operator (12), so Visual Basic multiplies M times (C ^ 2) and Pi times (R ^ 2). Our expression now looks like this:

```
OKFlag = # > # And M > 0
```

The greater-than operators have the next highest precedence (7), so Visual Basic next makes the comparisons, yielding True/False values. We'll use % to indicate the True/False results in the following expression:

```
OKFlag = % And %
```

We're down to our final operator, which has a precedence of only 5. Visual Basic evaluates this expression to determine the final result, which it assigns to OKFlag.

But what if you want to do the multiplication before the exponentiation? You can put parentheses around the parts of the expression that you want Visual Basic to solve first. Operations in parentheses take precedence over any other operations. You can use as many levels of parentheses as you want to organize your expressions. The rule is that Visual Basic will compute the most deeply nested parentheses first—that is, the part that's inside the most pairs of parentheses. Here's an example that we'll trace through:

```
y = (2 + 3) ^ ((1 + 2) * (3 + 1))
```

Both (1 + 2) and (3 + 1) are the most deeply nested, so Visual Basic would process them from left to right, yielding this expression:

```
y = (2 + 3) ^ (3 * 4)
```

Now (2 + 3) and (3 * 4) are equally nested, so Visual Basic processes them from left to right, yielding:

```
y = 5 ^ 12
```

This calculation yields the final result:

```
y = 390625
```

MATH FUNCTIONS

You can solve a lot of problems with the arithmetic and logical operators, but fortunately, you don't have to write the code for some of the most common arithmetic and logical problems. They have already been coded in the form of functions.

A *function* is a procedure that receives one or more input values, performs an operation on it, and returns a single output value. You call a function by coding its name followed by the input values in parentheses exactly where you want the output value to appear. For example, you could use the Sqr function to assign the square root of Area to Side:

```
Side = Sqr(Area)
```

The function might be part of a larger expression. In the following statement, Visual Basic finds the value for the Sqr function, then multiplies that by 4 and assigns the result to Perimeter:

```
Perimeter = Sqr(Area) * 4
```

The value passed to a function can be a constant:

```
X = Sqr(29.2)
```

It can be an expression:

```
Radius = Sqr(Area / 3.14159)
```

You can even nest functions inside other functions if you keep your wits about you. For example, the Abs function finds the absolute value of a number; that is, it returns the number without a sign. The following statement finds the absolute value of X:

```
Result = Abs(X)
```

The following statement finds the square root of the absolute value of X:

```
Result = Sqr(Abs(X))
```

The Int function returns the integer part of a number, dropping any fractional part. The next statement finds the integer part of the square root of the absolute value of X:

```
Result = Int(Sqr(Abs(X)))
```

We could go on in this fashion, but you probably get the idea.

Visual Basic provides a wide variety of functions for solving problems in mathematics, logic, finance, string manipulation, time and date manipulation, and so on. All the functions are documented in your Visual Basic help library. We'll overview the most common arithmetic and logical functions in this chapter. Additional functions are discussed in other chapters. But for complete details on syntax and usage, and for the remaining functions, look up "functions" in your help library.

Arithmetic Functions

You have already seen a few arithmetic functions: Sqr, Abs, and Int. Table 11-6 shows these functions along with several more.

Table 11-6: Some Useful Arithmetic Functions

Function	Return
Abs	The absolute value of a number
Int	The integer part of a number (without rounding)
Sgn	The sign of a number
Sqr	The square root of a number
Rnd	A random number between 0 and 1
Log	The natural logarithm (base e) of a number
Exp	The base of a natural logarithm (e) raised to a power
Sgn	The sign of a number expressed as an integer (−1 for negative numbers, 0 for zero, 1 for positive numbers)

If you're into logarithms, you might be saying to yourself, "What about a $\log_{10}$ function?" A logarithm to any base can be derived by dividing the natural logarithm of the number by the natural logarithm of the desired base. For example, to find $\log_{10}$ of VarX, you would code:

```
Result = Log(VarX) / Log(10)
```

Trigonometric Functions

Table 11-7 overviews the trigonometric functions.

Table 11-7: Trigonometric Functions

Function	Return
Sin	The sine of an angle
Cos	The cosine of an angle
Tan	The tangent of an angle
Atn	The arctangent of a number

If you use these functions, keep in mind that they work with radians, not degrees. You can convert between radians and degrees by using the following formulas:

```
Radians = Degrees * (pi / 180)
Degrees = Radians * (180 / pi)
```

So to find the sine of a 32-degree angle, you could code:

```
Sine32 = Sin(32 * (3.14159 / 180))
```

There is no standard Visual Basic constant for pi. You can create your own constant by defining pi in the (General) section. To create a constant called Pi that contains the value of pi to ten decimal places you would code the following statement in the (General) section:

```
Constant Pi As Double = 3.1415926536
```

Your Visual Basic help library contains the value of pi to 16 decimal places; look up "pi" in the glossary. You'll also find jumps to "pi" in the descriptions of Sin, Cos, and Tan in the help library.

Where are the other trigonometric functions: secant, cotangent, arcsine, the hyperbolic functions, and the rest? They can all be derived from these four functions. Look up "derived math functions" in the Visual Basic help library for a complete list of formulas. You'll also find jumps to the derived math functions under "See also" in the descriptions of the four trigonometric functions.

The "derived math functions" help topic also includes the formula for deriving logarithms to any base from the natural logarithm, which we discussed in the preceding section.

Financial Functions

Financial functions deal with depreciation, annuities (such as mortgage loans), and investments. Table 11-8 shows the financial functions.

Table 11-8: Financial Functions

Function	Return
IRR	Internal rate of return of an investment
MIRR	Modified internal rate of return of an investment
NPV	Net present value of an investment
SLN	Straight-line depreciation of an asset
DDB	Double-declining balance depreciation of an asset
SYD	Sum of years' digits depreciation of an asset
Pmt	The periodic payment for an annuity
PPmt	The principal payment for an annuity
IPmt	The interest payment for an annuity
Rate	The interest rate for an annuity
NPer	The number of periodic payments for an annuity
PV	The present value of an annuity
FV	The future value of an annuity

Unlike the other functions we have looked at so far, the financial functions have more than one passed value. For example, to calculate the payment for a mortgage loan, you must provide the interest rate, the number of payments to be made, and the amount of the loan. All the passed values must be enclosed in parentheses after the function name, and they must be separated by commas. They must also be in the correct order. Here's an example of a Pmt function for a $7200 loan at 10 percent annual interest (that's a rate of 0.0083 per month), with 48 monthly payments:

```
MonthlyPayment = Pmt(0.0083, 48, 7200)
```

If instead you coded MonthlyPayment = Pmt(7200, 48, 0.0083), Visual Basic would assume that 7200 was the monthly interest rate, 48 the total number of payments, and 0.0083 the total amount of the loan. Visual Basic and the Pmt function have no way of determining that these values don't make sense; they just go ahead and calculate the monthly payments for such a loan. So if you use the financial functions, be sure to look them up in the help library and put the arguments in the correct order.

SUMMARY

Now you have learned the basics of how to do math and logic in your Visual Basic applications. You've learned the operators for arithmetic, comparisons (numeric and string), logic, and concatenation. You've also learned how to control their sequence. In addition, you've been introduced to a number of mathematical functions and you've learned how to use functions in statements.

You created several small applications in this chapter. We won't be using them any more, so go ahead and erase them if you wish.

In the next chapter, you'll see how to control the order in which the statements in a procedure are executed.

CHAPTER OBJECTIVES

In this chapter, you'll explore:

▶ GoTo branches

▶ On Error branches

▶ If decision statements

▶ Select Case decision statements

▶ For . . . Next loops

▶ Do . . . Loop loops

▶ Call statements

▶ How to pass variables to called procedures

▶ How to control the scope of variables

As you learn about these things, you'll create some simple programs that illustrate the various forms of program logic.

Program Logic

So far, each of the procedures you have written has been executed sequentially. That is, Visual Basic proceeded line by line from the first statement to the last. Now we're going to look at some ways of altering the sequential flow. We'll be discussing ways to use conditions to make decisions that select alternate courses of action, or branches. And we'll discuss loops, where a set of statements is repeated several times to accomplish a task.

BRANCHING

A *branch* takes place when you take one of two or more alternate paths in your program, much like coming to a fork in the road. Some branches are unconditional; that is, the branch is taken without considering the results of a condition. Other branches are based on a condition. We'll examine both types of branches in this chapter.

Unconditional Branches

An unconditional branch is a branch that does not involve a decision. It is coded with a GoTo statement, which you'll meet shortly. In earlier programming days, unconditional branches were necessary to create logical structures such as loops, but they made programs very difficult to follow. A programming expert once compared a program full of unconditional branches to a plate of spaghetti. Modern languages such as Visual Basic give you ways to accomplish everything you need without using unconditional branches. We won't go into them any further here, except to mention the use of GoTo in trapping errors (see the next section).

Trapping Errors

The one place where you might want to use a GoTo is to trap an error with the On Error statement. By default, any run-time error is considered *fatal*—that is, Visual Basic displays an error message and ends the program. However, you can override this default behavior by *trapping* errors.

If you provide an On Error statement in a procedure, Visual Basic follows the instructions in that statement when it encounters an error. For example:

```
On Error GoTo ErrorRoutine
```

If this statement is included in a procedure, Visual Basic goes to the line labeled ErrorRoutine if it encounters any run-time error. It's now up to you to write whatever code is necessary to handle all possible run-time errors. You can end the error-handling routine and return to the statement that produced the error with the Resume statement.

Suppose you want to divide Miles by Gallons to find out MPG, but you don't want the program to crash with a Divide By Zero error if Gallons is 0. You could write the following code:

```
On Error GoTo ErrorRoutine
MPG = Miles / Gallons
   .
   .
   .
End
ErrorRoutine:
   frmGallons.Show    'Requires users to enter Gallons
Resume
```

If you don't want the On Error statement to affect the entire procedure, you can place it just above the statements it should apply to. After those statements, you can use another On Error statement to establish a different error-handling routine, or you can use the statement On Error GoTo 0 to indicate that there is no error-handling routine. In the above example, if we want ErrorRoutine to apply only to the division statement, we would add the line shown in bold below:

```
On Error GoTo ErrorRoutine
MPG = Miles / Gallons
On Error GoTo 0
```

In these examples, we included the End statement to make a very important point: you must make sure that control does not fall through to your error handler by accident. The main line of the procedure must end or go to another procedure or return to the calling procedure before the error handler is reached. The only way to reach the error handler should be via a trapped error.

Conditional Branches

A conditional branch occurs whenever a procedure decides between alternate courses of action based on the true/false result of a condition. You can have one, two, or multiple conditional branches depending on the complexity of the decision making.

Single Branches

Suppose the billing manager of your company asks you to make a slight change to the billing program. She wants to print an overdue notice if the customer's payment is less than the previous balance due. But if the payment is equal to or greater than the previous balance, nothing is printed. This is an example of the simplest type of branch, where there's really only one path. If the condition is true, you do something. If it's false, you don't. Figure 12-1 diagrams the logic of the overdue decision. In the figure, the Start and End symbols mark the beginning and end of the decision structure, not the entire program.

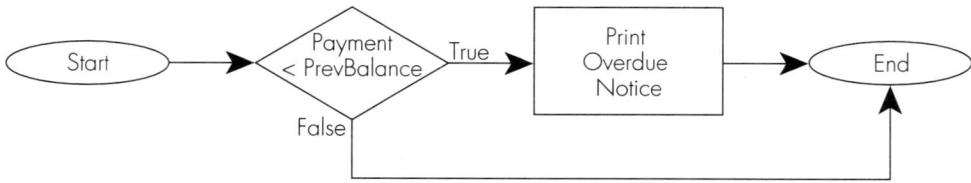

Figure 12-1: A single-branch decision does something if the condition is true but nothing if it's false.

A single branch decision can be coded with an *If . . . Then . . . End If* statement, like this:

```
If Payment < PrevBalance Then
    Print #1, OverdueNotice
End If
```

Indentation is not required, but as you can see, it serves to visually emphasize the logic of the structure, making the If and End If statements stand out. Most experts recommend it, and many bosses demand it.

There's also a shorter version — a one-liner — that harks back to the early days of the BASIC language:

```
If Payment < PrevBalance Then Print #1, OverdueNotice
```

The newer, multiple-line version is preferred for several reasons:

▶ It makes the structure of the branch more explicit, which helps others who must read or edit your program (including yourself a year from now).

▶ You're not limited to one statement if the condition is true; you can execute as many statements as necessary, including more If statements.

▶ It's easier to change into a more complex structure if the logic of the program needs to be revised.

To demonstrate branching, we're going to develop a simple program based on the old game of "Guess a number." We'll add more functions to the game as you learn more about decision structures. The first, very simple version will work like this:

▶ The program selects a number between 1 and 10.

▶ The user types a guess and clicks the Go button.

▶ If the user's guess is right, the program displays "You got it!" in a message box and terminates.

▶ If the user's guess is wrong, nothing happens.

The form, shown in Figure 12-2, is very simple: just a Label, a TextBox, and a CommandButton.

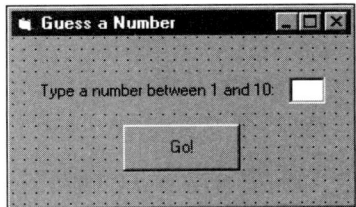

Figure 12-2: We'll use this form to play "Guess a Number."

Computers can't really pick numbers at random—all they can do is follow instructions. However, Visual Basic includes a *Rnd* function that generates a fractional random number that is greater than or equal to 0 and less than 1. In other words, it generates numbers like 0, 0.1254, 0.321, 0.72, and 0.991. Used by itself, the function looks like this:

```
x = Rnd
```

Since we want a number between 1 and 10, we need to multiply its result by 10 and add 1, then use just the integer part of the result, without rounding. Let's take a look at a few examples to see how this works:

Rnd result	(10*Rnd)+1	Integer
0.0	1.0	1
0.1524	2.524	2
0.321	4.21	4
0.72	8.2	8
0.991	10.91	10

The *Int* function returns just the integer part of a number, as in these examples:

```
Int(10.91)  'Returns the value 10
Int(0.)     'Returns the value 0
Int(x)      'Returns the integer part of the value represented by x
```

Putting Int together with Rnd, we get quite a complex expression, but you should now understand all its parts:

```
x = Int((10 * Rnd) + 1)
```

NOTE Now you know how to generate a random number between 1 and 10. But what if you want to generate a number between 1 and 100, or 2 and 50, or 32 and 212? The Help library topic for Rnd explains how to convert the number generated by Rnd into a value within any desired range.

The Rnd function uses a *seed number* to generate its random numbers. You'll end up with the same "random" number every time you play Guess a Number unless you change the seed number, and that requires another statement. The Randomize statement must precede the Rnd function to produce a truly random number. When you don't use any operands with Randomize, it uses the system timer to provide the seed number.

Now let's get started on the Guess a Number program.

1. Start a new project.

2. Create the form shown in Figure 12-2. Name the Label control *lblExplain*. Name the TextBox *txtGuess*. Name the CommandButton *cmdGo*.

3. Double-click the form itself to open the *Form_Load* procedure in the code window.

4. Add the following code to *Form_Load*:

```
Randomize
x = Int((10 * Rnd) + 1)
```

5. Add the following code to *(General)*:

```
Dim x as Integer
```

6. Add the following code to *cmdGo_Click*:

```
If Val(txtGuess.Text) = x Then
    MsgBox("You got it!")
    End
End If
```

7. Try out your new program.

8. When you're done checking out the program, save your work as *Guess.frm* and *Guess.vbp*.

We couldn't really accomplish very much with just single branching, so let's go on to the most common form of branching.

Two Branches

Suppose the billing manager wants another slight change. Now she wants to print a thank-you message if the payment equals or exceeds the previous balance. She still wants to print the overdue notice if the payment is less than the previous balance. Figure 12-3 diagrams the logic of this decision, which typifies a two-branch structure.

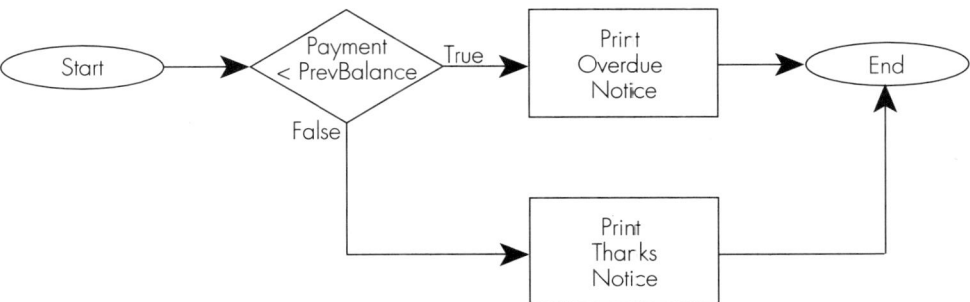

Figure 12-3: In a two-branch structure, the True branch executes one set of statements and the False branch executes another.

When a decision structure has two branches, you do one thing if the condition is true, another if it's false. In Visual Basic, a two-branch structure is created with an *If . . . Then . . . Else . . . End If* structure:

```
If Payment < PrevBalance Then
    Print #1, OverdueNotice
Else
    Print #1, ThanksNotice
End If
```

In the next exercise, we'll add a function to our game: If the user's guess is wrong, we'll sound a Beep and change the message to "Try again." We'll also blank the TextBox so the user doesn't have to erase the old guess to try the next one.

1. Add the code shown in bold below to *cmdGo_Click*:

```
If Val(txtGuess.Text) = x Then
    MsgBox("You got it!")
    End
Else
    Beep
    lblExplain.Caption = "Try again."
    txtGuess.Text = ""
End If
```

2. Check out your revised program.

3. When you're done, save your work.

Multiple Branches

Some decisions need three or more branches to represent all the possibilities. For example, suppose the billing manager likes the new changes so much that she wants to print yet another notice. Now she wants to send an overdue notice if the payment is less than the previous balance, a thank-you note if it equals the previous balance, and a credit notice if it exceeds the previous balance.

NOTE
Programs really do grow this way. The more users like a program, the more improvements they want to make. That's why popular software like Word for Windows and Lotus 1-2-3 are in a constant state of revision. Most programmers spend more time revising/maintaining/upgrading existing software than they spend creating new applications.

Since decisions are binary by nature, being based on true/false conditions, you need a series of conditions to create multiple branches, as shown in Figure 12-4.

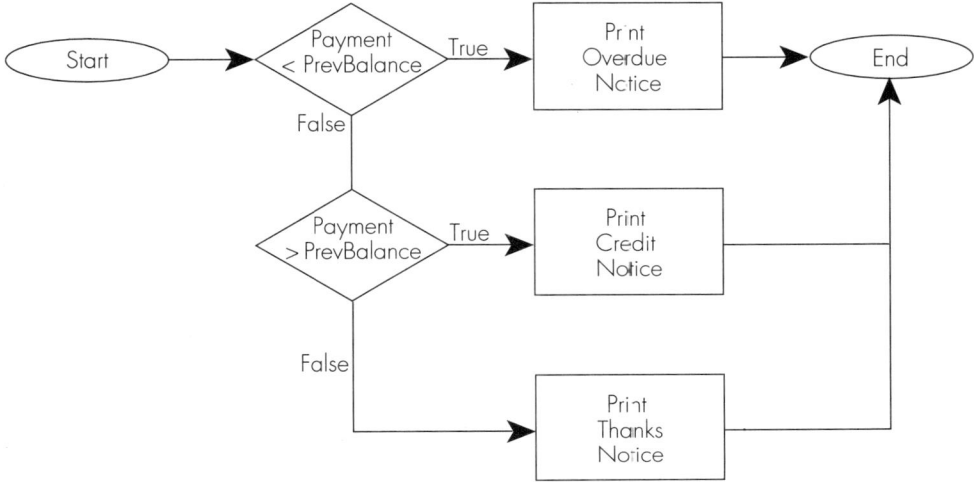

Figure 12-4: You need a series of conditions to create a decision structure with more than two branches.

You code a multiple-branch structure by using the *If . . . Then . . . Elseif . . . Else . . . End If* structure, as in this example:

```
If Payment = PrevBalance Then
     Print #1, ThanksNotice
Elseif Payment < PrevBalance Then
     Print #1, OverdueNotice
Else
     Print #1, CreditNotice
End If
```

Notice that *End If* is two words, but *Elseif* is one word. If you code Else If (as two words), you'll get the error message *Must be first statement on the line.*

With this structure, Visual Basic examines the first condition, then the second condition, and so on until it finds the first true condition. As soon as it finds a true condition, it executes the statements for the True branch, then jumps to the End If statement. No more conditions are examined. If no true conditions are found, it executes the False branch indicated by Else. In the above example, if the payment is equal to the previous balance, Visual Basic prints the thanks notice and jumps to the End If statement. The condition Payment < PrevBalance is never considered.

You might have noticed that we changed the structure somewhat to make Payment = PrevBalance the first condition. Why did we do this? Because this is the most likely condition. By putting it first, we save a wee bit of time with each customer record where it is true, because Visual Basic doesn't have to evaluate the Payment < PrevBalance condition first.

TIP

When you're coding a structure with more than one condition, try to arrange the conditions in order from the most likely to the least likely, as that yields the most efficient processing.

Now let's add some more functions to our program:

▶ If the user's guess is less than x, we'll change the label to read "Higher . . ."

▶ If the user's guess is greater than x, we'll change the label to read "Lower . . ."

▶ Since this makes the game much easier, we'll change the range to 1 to 100.

1. Change the caption of the Label to read *Type a number between 1 and 100.*

2. Change the code in *Form_Load* to read as follows:

```
x = Int((100 * Rnd) + 1)
```

3. Replace the code in *cmdGo_Click* with the following:

```
If Val(txtGuess.Text) > x Then
    Beep
    lblExplain.Caption = "Lower..."
    txtGuess.Text = ""
Elseif Val(txtGuess.Text) < x Then
    Beep
    lblExplain.Caption = "Higher..."
    txtGuess.Text = ""
Else
    lblExplain.Caption = "You got it!"
    End
End If
```

4. Try out your program.

5. When you're done experimenting with it, end the program and save your work.

Nested Ifs

Now the billing manager has another request: Don't send the same notice to everyone whose payment is overdue. If a customer's credit code is less than 3, send a nice notice. But if the credit code is 3 or higher, send a nasty notice.

Notice that this decision is considered only if the condition Payment < PrevBalance turns out to be true. Therefore, the new decision structure is nested inside the True path for that decision. Figure 12-5 diagrams the logic of the revised decision structure.

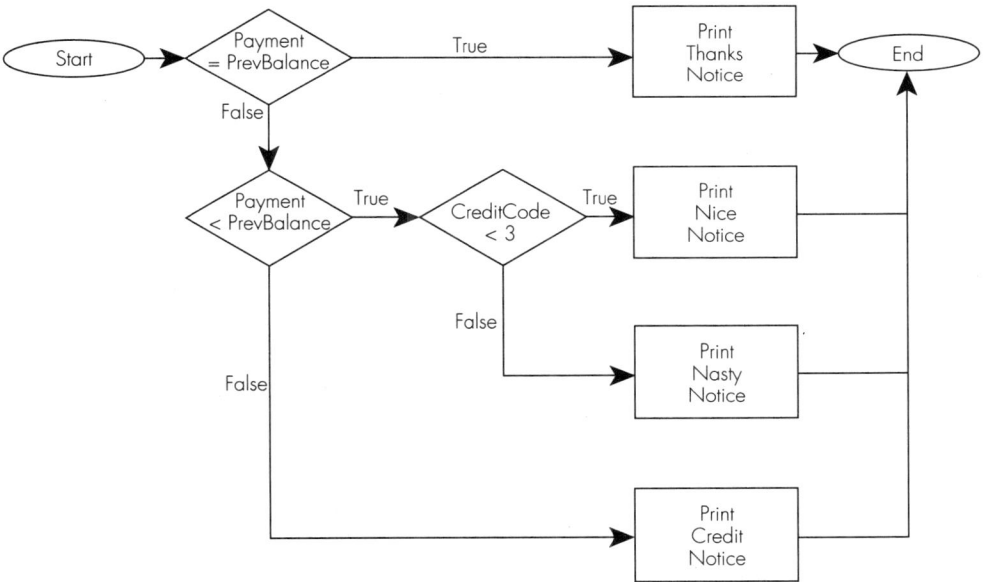

Figure 12-5: The added decision within the second condition requires a nested If.

To create this new structure, we have to code a new *If . . . Then . . . Else . . . End If* statement which is nested inside the other If structure, as shown in bold below:

```
If Payment = PrevBalance Then
    Print #1, ThanksNotice
Elseif Payment < PrevBalance Then
    If CreditCode < 3 Then
      Print #1, NiceNotice
    Else
      Print #1, NastyNotice
    End If
Else
    Print #1, CreditNotice
End If
```

We use the terms *outer If* and *inner If* to refer to the two If statements. The outer If contains the inner If. In this example, If CreditCode < 3 is the inner If and Elseif Payment < PrevBalance is the outer If.

You must be very careful that inner Ifs are complete structures. Suppose you accidentally omitted End If from the inner If in the above example. The code would look like this:

```
If Payment = PrevBalance Then
    Print #1, ThanksNotice
Elseif Payment < PrevBalance Then
    If CreditCode < 3 Then
      Print #1, NiceNotice
    Else
      Print #1, NastyNotice
Else
    Print #1, CreditNotice
End If
```

Visual Basic pays no attention to indentation; that's only for us human readers. Because the inner If statement has no End If, it looks to Visual Basic like the second Else belongs to it, not to the outer If. This will cause an error because an If structure cannot have more than one Else.

The situation is even worse if you omit the End If from an inner If that does not have its own Else statement. Look at this code:

```
If Payment = PrevBalance Then
    Print #1, ThanksNotice
Elseif Payment < PrevBalance Then
    If CreditCode < 3 Then
      Print #1, NiceNotice
Else
    Print #1, CreditNotice
End If
```

Pretend you're Visual Basic and try to figure out when you would print CreditNotice. The answer is, when Payment < PrevBalance and CreditCode is not < 3. Why? Because the inner If does not have an End If statement, the Else appears to Visual Basic to belong to the inner If, not the outer If.

In the next exercise, we'll add more functions to the Guess a Number game. We're going to check to make sure the user actually typed a number between 1 and 100. Any other input should produce a beep and the message *Input error!*

1. Revise the code for *cmdGo_Click*. The new statements are shown in bold below.

```
If Val(txtGuess.Text) >= 1 And Val(txtGuess.Text) <= 100 Then
    If Val(txtGuess.Text) > x Then
        Beep
        lblExplain.Caption = "Lower..."
        txtGuess.Text = ""
    ElseIf Val(txtGuess.Text) < x Then
        Beep
        lblExplain.Caption = "Higher..."
        txtGuess.Text = ""
    Else
        MsgBox("You got it!")
        End
    End If
Else
    Beep
    lblExplain.Caption = "Input error!"
End If
```

2. Run the program and try out values such as 0 and 200.

3. When you're satisfied that the program works, end the program and save your work.

CASES

Sometimes, a whole series of decisions are based on the value of a single variable. We've seen a couple examples of this in past chapters, such as the one shown below (which we used in our animation program in Chapter 8):

```
If PicTracker = 0 Then
    imgSpinner.Picture = imgRight.Picture
End If
If PicTracker = 1 Then
    imgSpinner.Picture = imgDown.Picture
End If
If PicTracker = 2 Then
    imgSpinner.Picture = imgLeft.Picture
End If
If PicTracker = 3 Then
    imgSpinner.Picture = imgUp.Picture
End If
```

Do you remember that we promised that we'd show you an easier way to code this structure? The Select Case statement is set up for just this type of situation. Here's how you would code the same structure using Select Case:

```
Select Case PicTracker
Case 0
    imgSpinner.Picture = imgRight.Picture
Case 1
    imgSpinner.Picture = imgDown.Picture
Case 2
    imgSpinner.Picture = imgLeft.Picture
Case 3
    imgSpinner.Picture = imgUp.Picture
End Select
```

The first line, Select Case PicTracker, tells Visual Basic that the following Cases are going to be based on the value of PicTracker. The line Case 0 indicates that the following statements are to be executed if PicTracker equals 0. Visual Basic executes all statements up until it encounters the next Case statement. Then it skips to End Select.

You can see how much cleaner and neater the Select Case structure is. It's much easier to read than a complex If structure or series of Ifs such as the preceding example, as long as you know how to interpret it.

Let's revise Guess a Number to use a case structure instead of the nested Ifs.

1. Replace all the code in *cmdGo_Click* with the following:

```
Select Case Val(txtGuess.Text)
    Case Is < 1
        Beep
        lblExplain.Caption = "Input error!"
        txtGuess.Text = ""
    Case Is > 100
        Beep
        lblExplain.Caption = "Input error!"
        txtGuess.Text = ""
    Case Is > x
        lblExplain.Caption = "Lower"
        txtGuess.Text = ""
    Case Is < x
        lblExplain.Caption = "Higher"
        txtGuess.Text = ""
    Case x
        MsgBox ("You got it!")
        End
End Select
```

2. Save your work.

3. Try out your revised program. It should work just like it did before. The difference is that now it's easier to read and understand the code.

4. End the program.

LOOPS

A *loop* is a section of code that can be repeated zero or more times. Let's try out a very simple loop, and a very common one. This loop forces the computer to pause, or sleep, for a while. How long depends on the speed of the computer. You can adjust the loop to make it pause shorter or longer on your computer.

1. Start a new project.

2. Create the form shown in Figure 12-6.

3. Name the Label *lblMessage*.

4. Add the following code to *Form_GotFocus*:

```
lblMessage.Refresh
For x = 1 To 500000
Next x
lblMessage.Caption = "Done!"
```

5. Run the program. You should see the message *Waiting* for a while, then *Done!* Appears.

6. Experiment with different values for the number that follows the word *To* in the For statement.

7. End the program and save your work as *Sleeper*.

Figure 12-6: The Sleeper program uses a loop to make the computer "wait."

For . . . Next Loops

The For and Next statements set up a loop. The statements in between them are repeated as many times as the loop is repeated. In the case of the Sleeper loop, we didn't want to do anything in particular, we were just using the loop to tie up the system for a while. Our initial loop was repeated half a million times, which takes the processor a moment or two to accomplish.

What was the system doing during that time? It was adding 1 to x and testing the result against 500000. It did this, of course, 500,000 times. The overall effect, as you saw, was a short pause.

When Visual Basic encounters the above For statement for the first time, it sets x to its initial value of 1. Then the loop is executed for the first time. When Visual Basic reaches the Next statement, it automatically increments x by 1. It then tests to see if x exceeds 500000. If not, the loop is executed again. Each time Visual Basic reaches the Next statement, it increments x and tests it against 500000. If x has not yet exceeded 500000, the loop is repeated from the top. When x reaches 500001, Visual Basic goes on to the statement after Next, and the loop is done.

Many For . . . Next loops have other statements between the For statement and the Next statement. Often the routine uses the For . . . Next variable as part of the processing. In the following example, the loop is used to sum all the elements in a one-dimensional array of 1000 items.

```
Dim ScoreSum as Single
For i = 1 to 1000
    ScoreSum = ScoreSum + Scores(i)
Next i
```

When we declare the variable ScoreSum, its intial value is 0. The variable i is used as the index for the Scores array. The first time through the loop, it is set to 1, so the value of Scores(1) is added to ScoreSum. The next time the loop is executed, i is 2 and Scores(2) is added to the value already in ScoreSum. And so it goes until Scores(1000) is added to the value in ScoreSum. Then the loop is done and ScoreSum contains the sum of all 1000 elements in the Scores array.

You don't have to start the counter variable at 1, and you don't have to increment by 1. In fact, you can decrement instead of increment if that makes the most sense. The following For statement increments from 32 to 212:

```
For Degrees = 32 to 212
```

To increment by 2 (or some other number), we add Step to the end of the For statement, as in:

```
For Left = 1000 to 4500 Step 100
```

To count down from a high number to a low number, we use a negative increment:

```
For Top = 3800 to 100 Step -100
```

If the To number and the Step number don't make sense together, Visual Basic ignores the loop; this is what we meant when we said earlier that the loop could be executed zero times. For example, if you code For Top/ = 3800 to 100, without specifying a negative increment, the loop is ignored.

Nested For . . . Next Loops

You can nest a For . . . Next loop inside another For . . . Next loop. A two-dimensional array provides a perfect example. Let's go back to an array that we discussed in Chapter 10, comprising 100 students and 10 tests. The array was declared this way:

```
Dim Scores(100, 10) as Integer
```

The following routine sums all the scores in this array and caculates the average score:

```
Dim ScoreSum As Integer, AvgScore As Integer
For i = 1 to 100
    For j = 1 to 10
        ScoreSum = ScoreSum + Scores(i, j)
    Next j
Next i
AvgScore = ScoreSum / 1000
```

The outer loop starts off by setting i to 1. Then the inner loop starts off by setting j to 1. The first assignment statement adds Scores(1,1) to ScoreSum. Then the Next j statement is reached. Visual Basic increments j to 2 and returns to the top of the inner loop. Notice that i is still 1, so the next assignment statement adds Scores(1,2) to ScoreSum. The inner loop proceeds through j = 3, 4, . . . 10.

When the Next j statement increases j to 11, the inner loop is finished, and Visual Basic executes the Next i statement, increasing i to 2. Then, returning to the top of the loop, Visual Basic encounters For j = 1 to 10 and starts the inner loop all over again. This time, Scores(2,1) through Scores(2,10) are added to the sum. Then i is increased to 3 and Scores(3,1) through Scores(3,10) are added to the sum. In this manner, the routine eventually accesses every score in the array.

Do Loops

Not all loops can be based on a counter being incremented or decremented by even steps. Some loops should be executed *until* a certain condition becomes true, or, as an alternative, *while* a certain condition is true. Almost always, the condition is affected by the processing of the loop. The Do . . . Loop statement is used to create loops like this. The Do statement takes two forms: Do While *condition* and Do Until *condition*. In a Do While loop, the loop is repeated as long as the condition is true. In a Do Until loop, the loop is repeated until the condition becomes true. Here is an example:

```
Dim ScoreSum As Integer
x = 1
Do While x < 101
    ScoreSum = ScoreSum + Scores(x)
    x = x + 1
Loop
```

This routine sums the values in the Scores array of 100 elements. When x reaches 101, it's over. The same function can also be accomplished as a Do Until loop:

```
Dim ScoreSum As Integer
x = 1
Do Until x > 100
    ScoreSum = ScoreSum + Scores(x)
    x = x + 1
Loop
```

CALLS

A *call* provides another way to step out of the sequential flow of events. A call transfers control to another procedure temporarily. When the called procedure ends, control returns to the calling procedure, continuing with the line after the Call statement.

Calls to Other Procedures

The simplest form of a call simply mentions the name of another procedure in the same module, as in bold below:

```
Print #1, CustomerName
LineNumber = LineNumber + 1
If LineNumber >= 60 Then
     StartNewPage
End If
```

The statement StartNewPage refers to another procedure. (If this procedure doesn't exist, an error message occurs at run time.) This statement is actually a Call statement, with the word Call implied. You could spell it out, like this:

```
Call StartNewPage
```

There's no difference between the two statements, but the latter one might be clearer to an inexperienced person trying to read your program.

Passing Arguments to Called Procedures

Some procedures require *arguments* when they are called. An argument identifies the data the procedure works on. For example, suppose you have a procedure called PrintLine, which prints a line, increments the line number, and starts a new page if necessary. You can also request PrintLine to leave some blank lines before and after the printed line. Whenever you call PrintLine, you pass it the name of the data to be printed, the amount of spacing before, and the amount of spacing after. A typical call would look like this:

```
PrintLine CustomerName, 2, 1
```

When you don't use the word Call, the arguments simply follow the name of the procedure, separated from each other by commas. But if you code the word Call, you must place the passed arguments in parentheses like this:

```
Call PrintLine (CustomerName, 2, 1)
```

Creating Called Procedures

When you're designing a program, you may find certain routines that are performed several times. Rather than repeat the code each time, you can create a called procedure, then simply call it each time you need it.

The PrintLine routine described above is a perfect example. A program that prints a billing statement, for example, prints many different types of lines: customer name, address lines, previous balance, payments, new charges, new balance, and so on. Every time you print one of these lines, you must consider the space before and after the line. And you must keep track of the line count and start a new page when necessary. Perhaps 10 to 15 lines of code are involved. You can save yourself a great deal of time and hassle by making the line-printing routine into a called procedure.

There are a couple of important advantages to making a routine like this a called procedure:

▶ Your program will take up less space on disk and in memory because the statements appear only once in the program.

▶ If you need to revise the routine, you need to change it in only one place. Any changes to the called procedure automatically affect all the procedures that call it.

As usual, there is a small time penalty to pay for calling a procedure. It's faster to just execute a set of statements sequentially. But in most applications, the advantages of a called routine far outweigh this slight disadvantage. But don't create called procedures frivolously.

Where Do You Code Called Procedures?

A called procedure is often not tied to an event, so you code it in the (General) section at the beginning of your program. You can create a new procedure in (General) by choosing the Insert | Procedure command. Visual Basic asks for the name of the procedure, then places the appropriate Sub and End Sub statements in the (General) section for you.

NOTE

Once created, a called procedure shows up in the Proc drop-down list for the (General) section.

In your Guess a Number program, several branches execute the same statements: txtGuess.Text = "". Let's turn that statement into a called procedure.

1. Close your current project and open Guess a Number.

2. Edit the *cmdGo_Click* procedure to look like the following. Changed statements are shown in bold.

```
Select Case Val(txtGuess.Text)
    Case Is < 1
        Beep
        lblExplain.Caption = "Input error!"
        WrongAnswer
    Case Is > 100
        Beep
        lblExplain.Caption = "Input error!"
        WrongAnswer
    Case Is > x
        lblExplain.Caption = "Lower"
        WrongAnswer
    Case Is < x
        lblExplain.Caption = "Higher"
        WrongAnswer
    Case x
        MsgBox ("You got it!")
        End
End Select
```

3. Choose *Insert | Procedure*. Visual Basic displays a dialog box asking for the name of the procedure.

4. Type *WrongAnswer* in the dialog box. Visual Basic opens the WrongAnswer procedure in the (General) section.

5. Type the following statement in *WrongAnswer*:

```
txtGuess.Text = ""
```

6. Save your work.

7. Try out your revised program. It should work just like before.

8. If you want to see the interaction between the calling and the called procedures, step through the program using F8 or the Step Into icon.

If the called procedure receives no arguments, the Sub statement looks just like the ones you're used to:

```
Private Sub Sleeper
    [statements go here]
End Sub

Private Sub StartNewPage
    [statements go here]
End Sub
```

If the procedure will receive arguments, you must include an argument list at the end the Sub statement, enclosed in parentheses. In its simplest form, an argument list consists of a list of variable names:

```
Private Sub PrintLine (LineData, BeforeSpace, AfterSpace)
```

For each argument, you can also specify the type:

```
Private Sub PrintLine (LineData As String, BeforeSpace As Byte,
        AfterSpace As Byte)
```

The advantage of specifying the type in the declaration of the called procedure is that Visual Basic will type-check the variables you pass it when you call the routine. When you don't specify a type, the variables are of the Variant type and will take any value you pass. As you can imagine, declaring the data type of the arguments lets Visual Basic help you with your debugging—if you pass a procedure a type it isn't expecting, Visual Basic displays an error message.

As the preceding Sub statement example is now coded, all of its arguments are required. That is, any statement that calls this procedure must pass all three arguments. But you can make some of the arguments optional, as in the following example:

```
Private Sub PrintLine (LineData as String, Optional BeforeSpace as
        Byte, Optional AfterSpace as Byte)
```

All optional arguments must come at the end of the argument list. You cannot place a required argument after an optional one.

NOTE

The names in the Sub statement's argument list are the names of variables in the called procedure. It's up to you to write the code to handle them properly. And you must be sure to account for the possibility that an optional variable might not be passed, in which case its value is considered missing, and you'll get a run-time error message when you try to use it. (The actual text of the message depends on how you try to use it.). The PrintLine procedure, for example, might include these statements:

```
For x = 1 to BeforeSpace
    Print #1, ""
Next x
Print #1, LineData
For x = 1 to AfterSpace
    Print #1, ""
Next x
```

The first For . . . Next loop prints the number of blank lines indicated by BeforeSpace. Then the line indicated by LineData is printed. The second For . . . Next loop prints the number of blank lines indicated by AfterSpace. If either BeforeSpace or AfterSpace was not received as an argument, however, you'll get an error message.

The calling procedure does not necessarily use the same variable names for the passed data. It could use different variable names, or it could use constants. One calling procedure might want to print CustomerName with no BeforeSpace or AfterSpace:

```
Call PrintLine (CustomerName)
```

Another might print PrevBalance with one line before and two lines after:

```
Call PrintLine (PrevBalance, 1, 2)
```

Another might print ItemLine with spacing determined by the variables named Above and Below:

```
Call PrintLine (ItemLine, Above, Below)
```

How does Visual Basic match up the Call statement's arguments to the Sub statement's? By position, as indicated by the commas in the argument list. It matches ItemLine to LineData because they are each first in their argument lists. It matches Above to BeforeSpace because they are both second, and so on.

Even though BeforeSpace and AfterSpace are both optional, you couldn't omit BeforeSpace but include AfterSpace. If you code the following statement, Visual Basic matches up the 2 to BeforeSpace and assumes that AfterSpace has been omitted.

```
Call PrintLine (ItemLine, 2)
```

TIP You can use the IsMissing function to determine if a variable is missing. For example, to find out if AfterSpace is missing, you would code If IsMissing (AfterSpace) . . .

Let's convert more of the Guess a Number code into a called procedure. Each of the wrong answer branches includes a statement that begins lblExplain.Caption = followed by a string message. We can move that statement to the WrongAnswer procedure, passing it the message to be displayed as an argument.

1. Revise the code for *cmdGo_Click* as shown below. Changed statements are shown in bold.

```
Select Case Val(txtGuess.Text)
    Case Is < 1
        Beep
        WrongAnswer("Input error!")
    Case Is > 100
        Beep
        WrongAnswer("Input error!")
    Case Is > x
        WrongAnswer("Lower")
    Case Is < x
        WrongAnswer("Higher")
    Case x
        MsgBox ("You got it!")
        End
End Select
```

2. Revise WrongAnswer as shown in bold below. (Don't forget that you can find WrongAnswer in the (General) section.)

```
Private Sub WrongAnswer(Message)
    txtGuess.Text = ""
    lblExplain.Caption = Message
End Sub
```

3. Save your work.

4. Try out your revised program. It should work the same as before.

5. Try stepping through your program to see the interplay of procedures.

6. Try setting up an instant watch for the Message variable in WrongAnswer. Then step through the program and watch the result in the Debug window.

Function Procedures

You've already seen a number of the functions provided by Visual Basic, such as Sqr, Rnd, and Str. But did you know that you can create your own functions? All you have to do is create a procedure with the Function and End Function statements instead of Sub and End Sub.

When you choose Insert|Procedure, Visual Basic opens the dialog box shown in Figure 12-7. To create a Function procedure instead of a Sub procedure, you click the Function OptionButton in this dialog box. Visual Basic then creates the Function and End Function statements for you, although you probably need to edit the Function statement, as you'll see shortly.

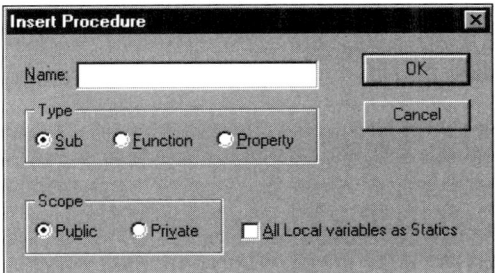

Figure 12-7: The Insert Procedure dialog box allows you to set the type and scope of a procedure.

What's the difference between a Function procedure and a Sub procedure? A Function procedure must behave like a function:

▶ It must return one value.

▶ You don't use a Call statement to call it; you use the function as a variable in a statement, as in:

```
y = RoundOff (x)
```

A Function procedure need not have any arguments, but most of them do. As with Sub procedures, arguments can be required or optional. For example, the RoundOff procedure would receive a value to be rounded off. In the above example, x is the numeric variable to be rounded off. The RoundOff Function statement would look like this, where InValue is the name that the procedure uses for the passed variable:

```
Function RoundOff (InValue)
```

With this definition, InValue is a Variant variable, which could cause trouble if a calling procedure passes it the wrong type of value, such as a string value. If you want to limit the data type of the argument, you can add a type declaration to it. To limit InValue to a Single variable, you would code:

```
Function RoundOff (InValue As Single)
```

Now if a procedure calls RoundOff using an incompatible type of variable, you'll get a run-time error message: *Type Mismatch*.

As with Sub procedures, Function procedures can have multiple arguments, some of which might be optional. For example, a more complex RoundOff procedure might be declared this way:

```
Function RoundOff (InValue As Single, Optional Places As Integer)
```

The Function procedure must return one value as output. It assigns this value to a variable with the same name as the procedure. For example, before it terminates, RoundOff should assign a value to a variable named RoundOff. The Function statement itself declares this variable, and by default its type is Variant. You can explicitly declare its type by adding As *type* to the end of the Function statement. For example, to declare that RoundOff returns a Single value, you would code:

```
Function RoundOff (InValue As Single, Optional Places As Integer)
As Single
```

Now the statements that call RoundOff must be careful to treat the returned value as a Single value or a run-time error could occur.

Let's create a function called Factorial. As its name implies, it calculates the factorial of a number. In case you don't quite remember your high school math, you calculate a factorial by multiplying together all the numbers from 1 to the number in question. For example, 5 factorial is 1 * 2 * 3 * 4 * 5 or 120.

Factorials can yield huge numbers. Recall that the highest value that Visual Basic can handle is approximately 1.8E308. A Double variable gets an overflow error if you try to calculate a factorial over 170. In this example, we'll limit our function to arguments between 1 and 170. To keep things simple, if the argument is out of this range, we'll simply report a factorial of 0.

1. Start a new project.

2. Create the form shown in Figure 12-8. Name the TextBox *txtInput* and the CommandButton *cmdGo*.

3. For *cmdGo_Click*, type the statement shown here. This statement converts the text in txtInput into a numeric value, finds the factorial of that value, converts the result back into a string variable, and displays the result in a message box.

```
Msgbox (Str (Factorial (Val (txtInput.Text))))
```

4. Choose *Insert | Procedure* to open the dialog box you saw in Figure 12-7.

5. Type the name *Factorial* and click the *Function* OptionButton. Then click *OK* to create the procedure.

6. Adapt the Function statement as shown in bold below.

```
Public Function Factorial (X As Integer) As Double
```

7. Insert this code in the procedure:

```
Dim y As Integer
If x > 0 And x < 171 Then
    Factorial = 1
    For y = 2 To x
        Factorial = Factorial * y
    Next y
Else
    Factorial = 0
End If
```

8. Save your work as *Factorial*.

9. Run the program.

10. Enter *5* in the TextBox and click *Go!* The result should be 120.

11. Try out other values including negative values and values above 170.

12. When you're convinced the program works, end the program.

Figure 12-8: We'll use this form to calculate factorials.

SCOPE

When you declare a variable at the module level, in the (General) section, outside of any procedure, that variable can be accessed by any procedure in the module. If a procedure changes the variable's value, the changed value is available to other procedures within the same module. But the variable is not available to other modules.

If you want a variable to be available to all modules in the program, declare it at the module level with a Public statement rather than the Dim statement. The Public statement looks just like the Dim statement except for the name of the statement itself. The following statement creates a variable named LineNumber that is available to all modules in the program:

```
Public LineNumber As Integer
```

You can also declare variables at the module level with the Private statement. Private makes variables available to the current module only. It is the same as using the Dim statement at the module level. Private and Public are available only at the module level; you can't use them to declare variables in a procedure.

However, variables can be declared in procedures with the Dim statement. When you declare a variable this way, that variable is local to the procedure only. It is not available to other procedures in the module. Not only that, but when the procedure ends, the variable is cleared by default. If you call the procedure again, the variable is redeclared, and its initial value is 0 (in the case of numerical variables), or the default value for other variable types (such as "" for string variables). These facts probably cause more grief to beginning Visual Basic programmers than any other feature of the language.

If you want the value of a variable to be retained when the procedure ends so that the next time the procedure is called the previous value is still available, declare the variable with a Static statement instead of the Dim statement. Static looks just like Dim, except for the name of the statement. The following statement declares a static variable named LineNumber:

```
Static LineNumber As Integer
```

Variables declared at the module level are automatically static. The Static statement can be used only within procedures.

If you want all the variables that are declared within a procedure to be static, you don't have to indicate Static for each one. You can include the word Static at the beginning of the Sub or Function statement to affect all the variables that the procedure declares. For example, all the variables declared in the following procedure will be static:

```
Static Sub SerialNumberGenerator
```

You can also use the keywords Private and Public on a Sub or Function statement, but they affect the entire procedure, not just its variables. When the word Private appears on a Sub or Function statement, the procedure can be called only by other procedures in the same module. When the word Public appears on a Sub or Function statement, the procedure can be called by all modules in the program. If neither Public or Private appears on the Sub or Function statement, Public is assumed. You can use the word Static together with the word Public or Private, as in:

```
Private Static Sub SerialNumberGenerator
```

SUMMARY

This chapter represents a major milestone in your Visual Basic training. Once you know how to write branches, loops, calls, procedures, and Function procedures, you're able create much more sophisticated and useful programs. Also, understanding the scope of your procedures and variables is a key factor in understanding how your programs work and, in many cases, why they don't work.

You're just about to "graduate" from the elementary level to the next part of the book, which deals with databases and add-ins. But first, we want to introduce you to a number of Visual Basic statements that we haven't covered so far, and some more debugging techniques. That's what the next couple of chapters are about.

CHAPTER OBJECTIVES

In this chapter we're going to take a look at the Basic language itself. Basic provides a lot more statements and functions than you have seen in the preceding chapters. You should be aware of what's available to you when you're creating applications on your own. In this chapter, you'll be introduced to:

▶ File management statements such as ChDrive, FileCopy, and Kill

▶ String management statements and functions such as Left, Right, Mid, and InStr

Basic Statements and Functions

So far, we've concentrated on creating objects, then writing the code to bring them to life. And that's appropriate for Visual Basic — such objects are what Windows applications are all about. You'll be learning more types of objects and related code in the remaining sections of this book, as we dig into databases, help libraries, OLE, and the like.

Before we do that, however, let's take a little excursion into the Basic language. We're going to use a standard module to try out various Basic statements and functions, rather than tie them to objects and events. In the following exercise, you'll create the module and tell Visual Basic that it should be executed first, instead of the form module.

---

1. Start a new project.

2. Choose *Insert I Module* to create a standard module. You'll see a code window for Module1, open to the (General) object, (declarations) procedure.

3. Enter this code:

```
Public Sub Main()
```

The editor adds the End Sub statement automatically when you press Enter.

4. Choose *Tools | Options* to open the Options dialog box.

5. Click the *Project* tab to display the Project page, as shown below.

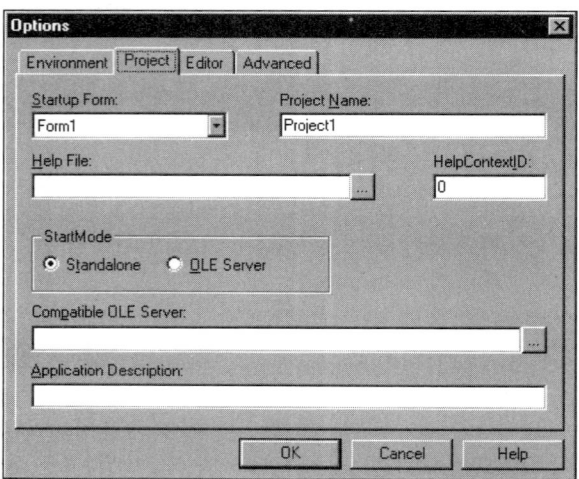

6. Drop down the *Startup Form* list and choose Sub Main.

7. Click *OK* to return to the module.

8. We'll add more statements to this procedure later. Just leave it as is for now.

FILE MANAGEMENT

We really should call this section "File, Folder, and Drive Management," because we're including statements that manipulate folders and drives, such as ChDir and ChDrive, along with file management statements. Most of the statements in this section closely resemble their old DOS counterparts, but there are differences, some of them subtle, so don't count on these statements to work exactly like their DOS kin.

Copying Files

The FileCopy statement is used to copy a file from a source location to a destination, which may or may not be in a different folder. Its syntax looks like this:

```
FileCopy source, destination
```

In the following example, we copy a file named readme.txt from a:\ to c:\counter\:

```
FileCopy "a:\readme.txt", "c:\counter\readme.txt"
```

If the destination file already exists, Visual Basic overwrites it without warning.

Did you notice that we included the file name in the destination parameter? Both the source and the destination must specify a file name, even if it's the same file name. If you omit either file name, you'll get a run-time error such as *File Not Found*, *Path Not Found*, *Access Denied*, and so on.

You can, however, specify a different file name for the destination file if you want to rename the copied file, as in:

```
FileCopy "a:\readme.txt", "c:\counter\document.txt"
```

To simply rename a file without copying it, you use the Name statement, discussed later in this chapter.

The *source* and *destination* parameters must have string values. You can include them as string constants, as we did in the preceding two examples, or you can use string variables, like this:

```
dim FromFile as String
dim ToFile as String
...
FromFile = "a:\readme.txt"
ToFile = "c:\counter\document.txt"
...
FileCopy FromFile, ToFile
```

Using string variables comes in handy when you're writing a general procedure that might be called from many different places using different file names.

So far, we've specified drives and absolute paths in both the source and the destination—that is, paths that start from the root folder. You can omit them if you want to access the current folder. Or you can use relative paths to access folders related to the current folder. For example, the following statement copies readme.txt from the current folder to its parent:

```
FileCopy "readme.txt", "..\readme.txt"
```

The following statement copies readme.txt from the parent folder to the current folder on drive C (no matter what that folder is):

```
FileCopy "..\readme.txt", "c:\readme.txt"
```

Let's try out a few FileCopy statements.

1. Insert a usable disk in drive A. It should have enough blank space to hold a few short files.

2. Add the following statement to the Main procedure:

```
FileCopy "c:\windows\readme.txt", "a:\practice.txt"
```

If your copy of Windows is not installed in c:\windows, please adapt the FileCopy statement accordingly.

3. Run your program. It should copy a file to your floppy disk. If you get an error message, make sure you typed the statement correctly. If it's correct, read the next section.

4. Display the contents of drive A. (Use Explorer, My Computer, File Manager, or whatever program you usually use for this purpose.) You should see the new *practice.txt* file on the drive.

5. Change the statement in Main to read as shown below:

```
FileCopy "a:\practice.txt", "a:\2ndcopy.txt"
```

6. Run the program and examine the results on drive A. You should see a new file called *2ndcopy.txt*.

You'll get a run-time error if Visual Basic can't make the copy for some reason. We can't possibly list all the situations that would result in a run-time error, but some common causes are:

The source file doesn't exist.

The destination folder doesn't exist. (Visual Basic won't create it automatically.)

The destination drive is full.

The destination drive is a floppy drive and doesn't contain a disk.

The source file is currently open. (Visual Basic won't copy or replace a file that is currently open.)

Sometimes the error message clearly identifies the problem, as in *File Not Found*, but at other times the message can be pretty cryptic. It's up to you to figure out what the problem is and fix it.

Renaming Files and Folders

The Name statement is used to rename files and folders. It has the following syntax:

```
Name oldpathname As newpathname
```

For example, if temp.dat is a file in the c:\liner folder, the following statement renames it as save.dat:

```
Name "c:\liner\temp.dat" As "c:\liner\save.dat"
```

> **NOTE**
>
> The word *pathname* indicates a file name which may be prefixed by a drive and/or path, as in temp.dat, a:temp.dat, and c:\windows\temp.dat.

The *oldpathname* parameter must refer to a single existing file or folder. *Newpathname* must identify a new name for the file or folder. If it duplicates an existing name, a run-time error occurs. You'll also get run-time errors if the file referred to by *oldpathname* doesn't exist or is currently open.

Let's try renaming the files you created previously.

1. Change the Main() procedure to look like this:

```
Public Sub Main()
    Name "a:\practice.txt" As "a:\newname.txt"
    Name "a:\2ndcopy.txt" As "a:\2ndname.txt"
End Sub
```

2. Run your program.

3. Examine the results on drive A.

You can use Name to move a file to a different folder on the same drive. All you have to do is specify the path where you want the file placed. (Note that you cannot move a *folder* with the Name statement.) For example, the following statement moves save.dat from c:\liner to c:\saved files:

```
Name "c:\liner\save.dat" As "c:\saved files\save.dat"
```

In the preceeding example, the file was not renamed, just moved. You could also rename the file when moving it, as in:

```
Name "c:\liner\save.dat" As "c:\saved files\newsave.dat"
```

Using Name to move a file is extremely efficient because the file's data is not moved; only the name entry is moved from one folder to another. By contrast, copying the file to the new location then deleting it from its former location takes much longer and is open to a multitude of errors. However, you must use the copy and delete method to move a file to another drive.

Setting File Attributes

You can set a file's attributes, such as hidden or system, with the SetAttr statement, which has this syntax:

```
SetAttr pathname, attributes
```

The *pathname* identifies a single file or folder that you want to set. *Attributes* identifies the attributes that you want to turn on; all others are turned off. For example, to set the ReadOnly attribute for c:\liner\save.dat, you might code the following statement:

```
SetAttr "c:\liner\save.dat", vbReadOnly
```

The expression vbReadOnly is a Visual Basic constant that has the attribute value 1. Table 13-1 shows the entire set of constants provided by Visual Basic to make it easier for you to set attributes. You can use either the numeric values or the constants in the statement.

You can set more than one attribute by adding them together. If you use the values, just add them up. For example, the following statement sets the ReadOnly and Hidden attributes:

```
SetAttr "c:\liner\save.dat", 3
```

You can add the attribute constants by using an arithmetic expression. The following statement has the same effect as the previous one:

```
SetAttr "c:\liner\save.dat", vbReadOnly + vbHidden
```

Let's set some attributes for one of the files we created earlier in the chapter.

Table 13-1: Visual Basic Attribute Constants

Constant	Value
vbNormal	0
vbReadOnly	1
vbHidden	2
vbSystem	4
vbVolume	8
vbDirectory	16
vbArchive	32

1. Check the attributes of a:\newname.txt. (Use whatever means you normally use to check attributes. For example, with Windows 95, you would choose the File | Properties command.)

2. Replace the Main procedure as shown below:

```
Public Sub Main()
    SetAttr "a:\newname.txt", vbReadOnly
End Sub
```

3. Run the program.

4. Check the attributes again. Notice that the read-only attribute is now set, but any former attributes (such as archive) have been cleared.

5. Now change the SetAttr statement as shown below:

```
SetAttr "a:\newname.txt", vbNormal
```

6. Run the program.

7. Check the attributes again. Notice that all attributes have been cleared by the vbNormal (0) setting.

You can set and clear the directory and volume attributes with this statement, but you should not do so unless you know exactly what you are doing. Working with these attributes takes advanced knowledge. In general, we recommend that you leave them alone.

Never set any attributes for a folder (or a directory) with the SetAttr statement unless you're careful to preserve its directory attribute.

Deleting Files

The Kill statement is used to delete files. Its syntax is:

```
Kill pathname
```

The pathname must be a string constant or variable, as in:

```
Kill "temp.dat"
...
dim TempFile as String
...
TempFile = "another.dat"
...
Kill TempFile
```

The pathname may be global; that is, it may contain wildcard characters to refer to multiple files. The following statement deletes all the files with extension .tmp in the folder named c:\fixer\workarea:

```
Kill c:\fixer\workarea\*.tmp
```

Let's delete the files that you created on drive A:

1. Replace the statement in Main with the statements shown below.

```
Kill "a:\newname.txt"
Kill "a:\2ndname.txt"
```

2. Run the program.

3. Examine the results on your drive A.

As you have just seen, Kill deletes files without seeking user confirmation first. Be sure to use it only on files that you're positive should be deleted, such as work files your program has created temporarily. Avoid using global pathnames unless you're sure exactly what files it will delete.

Kill can also result in a number of run-time errors such as *File Not Found, Path Not Found,* and various access errors (because a file is open or read-only).

> You can't use Kill on a directory. To delete a directory, use the RmDir statement, discussed later in this chapter.

Managing Drives and Folders

Visual Basic provides some very familiar-looking statements for managing drives and folders:

```
MkDir path
ChDir path
RmDir path
ChDrive drivename
```

Let's try out these statements.

1. Change the Main procedure as follows:

```
Public Sub Main()
    MkDir "a:\myfolder"      'To create a new folder on drive A
End Sub
```

2. Check the contents of drive A. You should see the new folder.

3. Replace the statement in Main with the following statements:

```
ChDrive "a"                'To switch to drive A
ChDir "myfolder"           'To switch to the new folder
FileCopy "c:\windows\readme.txt", "readme.txt"
```

4. Notice that the last statement does not specify a path for the destination. Therefore, the new copy was placed in the default folder. Check the contents of a:\myfolder to see it.

5. Now remove the new folder by replacing Main with these statements:

```
Kill "a:\myfolder\*.*"     'To delete all files in the folder
ChDir ".."                 'To change to the parent folder
RmDir "myfolder"           'To delete the folder
```

6. Run the program and check the contents of drive A again. The folder (and its files) should be gone.

Did you notice that we didn't include the colon after the drivename in the ChDrive statement? ChDrive ignores all but the first character of the string value, so it doesn't matter if you include a colon after the drivename or not.

Also, did you notice that we deleted all files from myfolder before attempting to delete it? If you try to remove a folder that still contains files, you'll get a run-time error.

STRING MANAGEMENT FUNCTIONS

Many programs require you to accept text data from your users, then manipulate it in some way. You might, for example, want to edit the punctuation out of a telephone number or a social security number that was entered by the user.

The Left, Mid, and Right functions return the indicated number of characters from the left end, middle, or right end of a string variable. For example, suppose you have a string variable called PhoneNumber in this format: *aaa-ccc-nnnn*, where *aaa* is the area code, *ccc* is the central office, and *nnnn* is the rest of the phone number. Now suppose that you want to copy the first three characters to another string variable called AreaCode. The following statement accomplishes the desired objective:

```
AreaCode = Left(PhoneNumber, 3)
```

Suppose you want to copy the final eight characters of PhoneNumber to LocalNumber:

```
LocalNumber = Right(PhoneNumber, 8)
```

To copy just the central office to a string variable called Exchange, you would use the following statement, which tells Visual Basic to start at the fourth character and access three characters.

```
Exchange = Mid(PhoneNumber, 4, 3)
```

The syntaxes of these three statements are shown below:

```
Left(string, length)
Right(string, length)
Mid(string, start[,length])
```

In the last syntax, the square brackets mean that the length is optional. If you omit it, Visual Basic returns all the characters from the start character to the end of the string.

If you're concerned about whether the user has entered the phone number in the correct format in the first place, you might use the Len function to check the number of characters in PhoneNumber. Len returns the number of characters in the referenced string variable. Its only parameter is the name of the variable (or a string constant, but that doesn't make a lot of sense since you would already know its length). The following statement checks to see if the length of PhoneNumber is eight or fewer digits, indicating that there is no area code:

```
If Len(PhoneNumber) <= 8 Then
    [handle missing area code]
EndIf
```

If you're concerned that the user left out the hyphens or included parentheses, you could use the InStr ("in string") function to look for these characters. InStr returns a zero value if a specified character or substring is not found; if it is found, it returns the starting position of the character or substring. InStr has the following syntax:

```
InStr(string, substring)
```

The following code eliminates a left parenthesis from a string, if one is present. It's explained in the paragraph after the code.

```
If InStr(PhoneNumber, "(") Then
    PhoneNumber = Left(PhoneNumber, InStr(PhoneNumber, "(") - 1) &
        Right(PhoneNumber, Len(PhoneNumber) - InStr(PhoneNumber,
            "("))
EndIf
```

We've created a monster! But if you examine it piece by piece, it makes perfect sense. (You'll often find yourself creating complex statements like this when you're working with functions.) Imagine that [before] represents the characters before the parenthesis and [after] represents the characters after the parenthesis. Then the following shows how the new phone number is arrived at:

```
PhoneNumber = [before] & [after]
```

We create the new phone number by concatenating [before] and [after], then replace PhoneNumber with the result.

Now, how do we create the [before] value? Imagine that [position] represents the location of the parenthesis. Then [position] - 1 represents the number of characters to the left of the parenthesis. So [before] consists of:

```
Left(PhoneNumber, [position] - 1)
```

If the parenthesis is in the fifth position, this expression evaluates as:

```
Left(PhoneNumber, 4)
```

If the parenthesis is in the first position, as is likely, it evaluates as:

```
Left(PhoneNumber, 0)
```

In other words, there are no characters to the left of the parenthesis, and none will be copied to the new phone number. Now all we have to do is substitute the InStr function in place of [position], because InStr returns the position of the indicated substring. So the left side of the concatenation becomes:

```
Left(PhoneNumber, InStr(PhoneNumber, "(") - 1)
```

We can also use [position] to examine the value of [after]. In addition, suppose that [length] represents the number of characters in the entire string. Then the number of characters after the parenthesis can be expressed as:

```
[length] - [position]
```

The Len function can be used to return the length of the string, as follows:

```
Len(PhoneNumber) - [position]
```

And of course, InStr can be used to return the position:

```
Len(PhoneNumber) - InStr(PhoneNumber, "(")
```

To create the [after] part of the equation, we use the Right function to access the desired number of characters:

```
Right(PhoneNumber, Len(PhoneNumber) - InStr(PhoneNumber, "("))
```

So now we have [before] and [after] and we can concatenate them like this:

```
PhoneNumber = Left(PhoneNumber, InStr(PhoneNumber, "(") - 1) &
Right(PhoneNumber, Length - InStr(PhoneNumber, "("))
```

And there you have the entire statement that creates the new phone number from the old one.

SUMMARY

We haven't covered all the statements and functions that Visual Basic offers — there are too many of them. But you now have a better idea what's available. If you need a statement or function that you're not familiar with, don't forget to search your online references. Visual Basic might provide exactly what you need.

In the next chapter, we take a more detailed look at Visual Basic's debugging features.

CHAPTER OBJECTIVES

This chapter digs into deeper detail on debugging techniques. You'll learn:

▶ How to test programs at full speed

▶ How to deal with run-time errors

▶ How to deal with erroneous results

▶ How to add new statements while your program is executing via the Debug window

▶ How to step through a program

▶ How to create and use a breakpoint

▶ How to create and use watches

▶ How to use the Calls window

We begin with an "it's good for you" lecture on good programming practices. Ignore us at your peril; someday we'll say we told you so!

CHAPTER

Debugging Techniques

14

▼ ▼ ▼

You've already created and tested quite a few programs in this book, and we hope you haven't encountered too many problems. When you get a run-time error with one of our exercises, you can go back and compare your version to ours, find the place where you typed something different, and fix it.

When you're writing your own programs, you won't have anything to compare them to. You'll have to use debugging techniques to isolate and fix problems. That's a lot harder, but it's also considerably more interesting — maybe even fun.

You can do yourself a great favor and avoid many bugs in the first place, as well as make it easier to diagnose and fix the ones that do get into your programs, by observing good programming practices. These include:

▶ *Develop only one feature or routine at a time.* Test and debug it thoroughly before adding the next feature or routine. About 20 statements should be your maximum before stopping to test. In most cases, don't add more than a dozen or so statements without testing and debugging. Why? The more untested code you add at once, the more likely you are to create multiple errors that interact with each other, hide behind each other, and generally muck things up. Trying to find a bug in 100 lines of code can be like trying to find the proverbial needle in the haystack.

▶   *Kid-test your procedures.* Treat them like a typical five-year-old would. Click in the wrong places, enter invalid values, reboot while they're processing, and otherwise try to confuse, trap, and break them. Too many programmers are gentle with their own code while testing. This does no good in the long run.

▶   *Know what results you're expecting.* Don't take the program's word for it—the program could be wrong. Plan a set of data with known answers. In keeping with the preceding practice, make sure the planned set includes invalid values, negative values, zero or null values, values that are too high or too low, and any other "difficult" values that you can think of.

FULL-SPEED TESTING

When you first test a new routine, you start by assuming that it's going to work, so you test it at "full speed." In other words, press F5 or click the Start icon to run it just as users will eventually run it. You have to play the role of the user, entering data and clicking CommandButtons as needed to make the various functions work.

But you're not really the user. While it's running, you'll see not only what the user sees—the forms—but also the Debug window, the code window, and the project window.

TIP You might want to arrange these windows on your screen so that you can see everything you need at once. You can arrange the forms, the code window, and the project window before you start the program. After you start the program, you can position the Debug window, and it will stay in that position for subsequent runs.

Dealing with Run-Time Errors

If you get a run-time error message, and you can figure out from the message what's wrong and needs to be fixed, you can fix it on the fly and continue the program. In the example in Figure 14-1, we accidentally used the Show method rather than Refresh with a Label control. The error message is clear, Visual

Basic has highlighted the error in the code window, and the fix is easy. After clicking OK to clear the message, we can replace "Show" with "Refresh" and click the Continue icon or press F5 to continue processing.

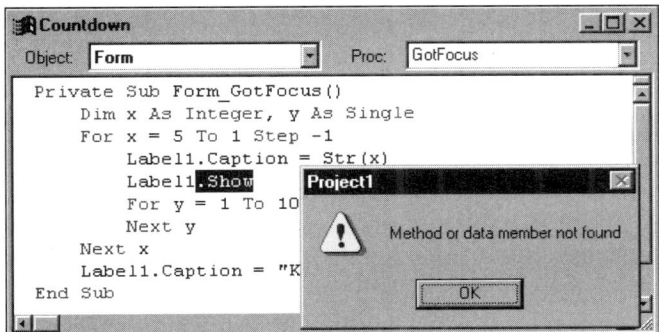

Figure 14-1: Visual Basic clearly identifies some run-time errors so that you know immediately what's wrong and how to fix it.

Sometimes Visual Basic does not highlight the error in the code window while the error message is displayed. Figure 14-2 shows an example of this kind of message. To find out which line Visual Basic could not process, click the Debug button. The error message closes and the current line is highlighted. You can fix the line and continue processing.

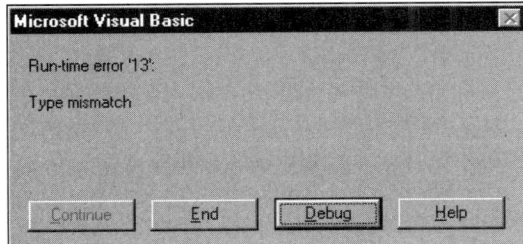

Figure 14-2: With this type of error message, Visual Basic does not highlight the problematic line until you click the Debug button.

If the real problem is in some other line, you may or may not be able to fix it on the fly. Visual Basic will tell you when you will have to restart the program in order for a change to work.

Let's try out some of these debugging techniques on the Guess a Number program.

1. Open *Guess.vbp.*

2. Open the code window and select *(General)* in the Object drop-down list.

3. Select *WrongAnswer* from the Proc drop-down list.

4. In the statement *txtGuess.Text* = *""*, erase the final *t* from *Text*. This introduces an error into the program that will cause a run-time error message.

5. Run the program.

6. The main Guess a Number window and the Debug window appear.

   Notice that the Debug window says "<running>," the Start icon is disabled, and the Break and End icons are enabled. (Many of the other icons are disabled.) This tells you that the program is running normally. It isn't doing anything at the moment because it's waiting for input from you.

7. Type a guess in the main window and click *Go!* Or press *Enter*. While trying to process your guess, Visual Basic runs into the error, highlights the phrase that it can't understand, and pops up a MsgBox saying "Method or data member not found."

8. Click *OK* to clear the MsgBox.

   Notice that the Debug window now says Project1.Form1.WrongAnswer, the Start icon is enabled (and its ToolTip says Continue instead of Start), the Break icon is disabled, the word [break] has been added to the title bar, and the End icon is enabled. (Several other icons that were disabled when the program was running normally are now enabled.) These clues tell you that the program is in break mode for some reason.

9. Add the missing *t* to *Text.*

   You can make changes to the program only when you are in break mode. If the program is running when you attempt to make a change, all you get is a beep.

10. Press *F5* or click the Run tool to continue running the program. Visual Basic picks up where it left off and finishes processing your guess.

11. End the program.

Now let's take a look at the other type of error message, where you have to click the Debug button to find out where the problem is.

1. Select *Form* in the code window's Object drop-down list. The Form_Load procedure is displayed.

2. In x = Int((100 * Rnd) + 1), add three zeros to *100* so that it says *100000*.

3. Close the code window.

4. Run the program. You'll get an immediate Overflow error message.

5. Click *Debug* in the message window. The code window opens with the assignment statement highlighted.

6. Change the *100000* back to *100*.

7. Click the Continue icon to continue the program. The main window appears.

8. End the program.

Dealing with Erroneous Results

Sometimes you don't get any run-time errors, but the results turn out to be wrong. You might be able to tell what went wrong from the results that you got. If not, you'll probably have to step through the program, perhaps using watches, to locate the source of the error. These techniques are discussed in the next sections.

ADDING NEW STATEMENTS ON THE FLY

Sometimes a statement fails and a run-time error occurs because you forgot to set something up earlier—for example, you forgot to initialize a variable. Whenever the program is in break mode, you can type statements in the Debug window and Visual Basic will execute them as soon as you press Enter. You can try out statements this way. And you can patch in a statement that should have been there but wasn't.

You type statements in the Immediate pane of the Debug window. This is the pane that is initially blank. To execute a statement immediately, type it and press Enter. The expression stays in your Immediate pane until you specifically remove it. You can copy and paste it from the Immediate pane into your code window during break mode or after you end the program.

TIP You can adjust the size of the Debug window to see more of its contents, and you can adjust the dividing line between the Watch pane and the Immediate pane by dragging it.

Let's try this out in Guess a Number.

1. Select *(General)* in the code window's Object drop-down list.

2. Select *WrongGuess* in the Proc drop-down list. The WrongGuess procedure appears in the code window.

3. Delete the statement *txtGuess.Text = ""*.

4. Run the program. Enter a few guesses and notice that your previous guess is not cleared from the TextBox.

5. Click the Break icon. The program pauses, and the Debug window says <break:Form1>.

6. Type *txtGuess.Text = ""* in the Debug window then press *Enter*. The value in the text box is cleared. Now you know the statement works, but it's not in your program.

7. Select the statement and copy it to the Clipboard.

8. Paste the statement from the Clipboard into the WrongAnswer procedure.

9. Click the Continue icon to test the result. The program should be working normally now.

10. End the program.

This technique is also good for playing "what if?". What if I initialized the index to 0 instead of 1? What if that condition used > instead of =? What if chkBold was False?

STEPPING

When you can't isolate a problem with a full-speed run, stepping through the program is your ultimate debugging resource. There are two ways to step:

▶ Stepping *into* every command of every procedure

▶ Stepping *over* called subprocedures

Which one you use depends on whether you have already debugged your called procedures. If you know they work, then step over them so you can concentrate on the routine you're trying to debug.

NOTE
When you step over called procedures, the called procedures are executed at full speed, as if they were one step in the current process.

In the following exercise, you'll try both types of stepping.

1. Press *F8* or click the Step Into icon (shown here). The program starts and the code window appears with the Private Sub Form_Load statement highlighted. This is the statement that will be executed when you execute the next step.

2. Press *F8* or click the Step Into icon again. The Randomize statement is highlighted.

3. Keep stepping until the main form is displayed on your screen and the stepping icons are dimmed.

4. Now you have to play the role of the user and enter a number in the TextBox and click *Go!* The cmdGo_Click procedure appears in your code window, with the Sub statement highlighted.

5. Keep on stepping until the stepping icons go dim again.

   Notice how Visual Basic examines the cases, looking for the one that matches your guess. Then notice how it switches to the called procedure (WrongAnswer), executes each line in that procedure, and returns to the calling procedure. It stops when it reaches the End Sub statement of the calling procedure because it has finished processing the cmdGo_Click event and has no further instructions. That's when the stepping icons go dim. Now Visual Basic is waiting for you to enter another guess.

6. Type another guess and click *Go!* again.

7. This time, use the Step Over icon (shown here) or press *Shift+F8* to execute the procedure. Keep stepping until the stepping icons go dim.

   Notice that you don't see the WrongAnswer procedure this time. That's because Step Over doesn't step into called procedures.

8. Continue stepping until you feel comfortable with the relationship between Step Into, Step Over, the procedures, and the user's role.

9. End the program whenever you're ready to continue with the next section.

Some programs appear to behave differently when you're stepping than when you run at full speed. This is usually because stepping gives the system time to complete each step before executing the next. Tasks such as displaying forms and playing sounds are very slow and often don't complete before the computer goes on to the next statements. If a routine changes the contents of a label several times within a short period of time, for example, the system might not have time to show each label before it gets the order to display the next one. It appears to be ignoring your orders. But when you step through the program, all is fine. The same can happen when you're playing sounds.

Let's try this out on a short program that counts down from 5 to 1, then goes Ka-Boom!

---

1. Start a new project.

2. Add a Label to the form.

3. Double-click the form to open the code window for Form_Load.

4. Select the *GotFocus* procedure from the Proc drop-down list.

5. Insert the following statements in Form_GotFocus. This routine displays the countdown from 5 to 1 in the Label, followed by "Ka-Boom!"

```
Dim x As Integer
For x = 5 To 1 Step -1
    Label1.Caption = Str(x)
    Label1.Refresh
Next x
Label1.Caption = "Ka-Boom!"
```

6. Run the program. Notice that you hardly see the countdown, just the "Ka-Boom!"

7. Step through the program. This way, you can see the countdown.

8. Add the code marked in bold below to the procedure. This adds a "sleeper" loop to the program that slows it down enough for the countdown to be displayed.

```
Dim x As Integer, y As Single
For x = 5 To 1 Step -1
    Label1.Caption = Str(x)
    Label1.Refresh
    For y = 1 To 100000
    Next y
Next x
Label1.Caption = "Ka-Boom!"
```

9. Run the program. You should see the countdown now. (If you have a really fast Pentium, you might have to use a number larger than 100000.)

10. End the program.

BREAKPOINTS

You often need something in between full speed and stepping. You want to execute full speed for several steps, then, when you reach a crucial point, break to examine the results. Visual Basic's *breakpoints* let you do just this.

A breakpoint is a statement where Visual Basic will halt execution and wait for instructions to proceed. You create a breakpoint by marking the desired statement. The following exercise lets you mark several breakpoints, then run the program.

If you tried to step through your countdown program now, it would take you forever, because you would have to step through all 100,000 iterations of the sleeper loop. Instead, let's walk through it using some breakpoints.

1. In the code window, click the line that says *Label1.Caption = Str(x)*.

2. Click the Toggle Breakpoint icon (shown here) or press *F9*. Visual Basic highlights the line to show that it is a breakpoint.

3. Click the line that says *Label1.Caption = "Ka-Boom!"* and click the Toggle Breakpoint icon or press *F9*. Visual Basic highlights the line to show that it is a breakpoint.

4. Run the program. Visual Basic stops before executing the first breakpoint. It highlights that line.

   Notice that the Debug window says Project1.Form_GotFocus to show you what procedure you are in. The Continue, Stop, and stepping icons are available (along with some other icons).

5. Click the Continue icon or press *F5* to execute the breakpoint and continue until the next breakpoint is reached. Visual Basic displays a 5 in the program's window, then stops on the same statement again (because it's in a loop).

6. Keep continuing until you complete the loop and reach the other breakpoint statement.

   Every time Visual Basic reaches a breakpoint statement, it pauses until you tell it to continue. This gives you a chance to examine the program in "slow motion."

7. Continue again to complete the procedure. Visual Basic stops automatically after displaying "Ka-Boom!" because there are no more events to process.

8. End the program.

WATCHES

When you're having trouble isolating a problem, sometimes it helps to see the values of variables that don't show up on any form. Rather than add them to the form, you can see them by adding watches to your Debug window. You've already used watches several times in previous chapters to see the effects of various statements on your variables, so you have a basic idea how they work. In this section, we'll discuss some of the variations on the basic concepts.

Adding Watches

You can add watches at design time or during break mode. The Add Watch dialog box, shown in Figure 14-3, provides many options in setting up a watch.

You open this dialog box by choosing Tools | Add Watch. If you select some text before opening the dialog box, that text is automatically displayed in the Expression box of the Add Watch dialog so that all you have to do is select the options you want and click OK.

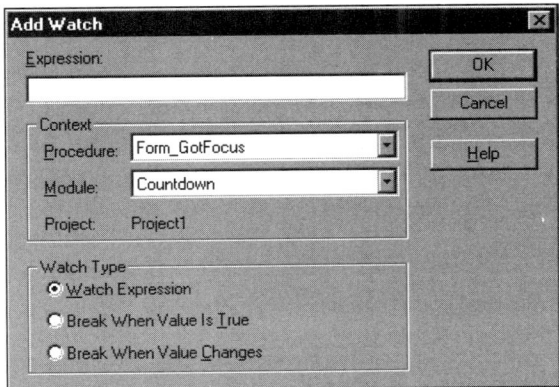

Figure 14-3: You create a new watch in the Add Watch dialog box.

You can watch any type of Visual Basic expression. You can watch a property of an object or a variable, for example. In some cases, rather than watch the variable directly, you might want to perform some math on it. For example, in addition to watching Radius, you might also want to watch Radius * 2 (the diameter), 3.1416 * Radius * 2 (the circumference), and 3.1416 * Radius ^ 2 (the area), even though those calculations are not in the current procedure.

In the Context group, you identify the module and procedure where you want to watch the expression. You can also select (All Modules) and (All Procedures). But be warned that Visual Basic evaluates every active watch after every line of code, so making all your watches apply to every procedure and every module could dramatically slow down your program.

In the Watch Type group, you set up the type of watch that you want for the current expression. If you choose to Watch Expression, the value of the expression is displayed in the Debug window only when you break for some other reason. Otherwise, you won't see the result of the watch.

If you choose to Break When Value Is True, the watch becomes another type of breakpoint. Suppose you are checking out a loop containing ten statements that is performed for x = 1 to 500000. You don't want to step all the way through this loop—it has five million steps—but you want to break when x = 499999. You could set up x = 499999 as the watch expression, then select Break When Value Is True. For Boolean variables or properties, you can just select the name of the item as the watch expression; when it takes on a True value, a breakpoint is generated.

If you choose to Break When Value Changes, a breakpoint is generated each time the expression changes values. For example, suppose the PicTracker variable is not working correctly. You could make it into a watch expression and choose Break When Value Changes. Then, each statement that affects PicTracker generates a breakpoint. This makes it much easier to evaluate what is happening to PicTracker as your program progresses.

When you're stepping through a program, you don't need to set breakpoints to see the results of your watches. They are updated after every step.

1. Choose *Run|Clear All Breakpoints* (*Ctrl+Shift+F9*) to eliminate the breakpoints that you created in the last exercise.

   You can clear an individual breakpoint by clicking the statement, then clicking Toggle Breakpoint or pressing F9.

2. Select the expression *Label1.Caption* in the code window. (You can select it any place that it appears.)

3. Choose *Tools|Add Watch* to open the Add Watch dialog box.

4. We'll use the Watch Expression feature for Label1.Caption, so click *OK* to set up the watch and close the dialog box.

5. Select *x* anywhere in the code window and choose *Tools|Add Watch*.

6. Select *Break When Value Changes* and click *OK*.

7. Select *y* anywhere in the code window and choose *Tools|Add Watch*.

8. Edit the Expression TextBox to read *y = 99999*.

9. Select *Break When Value Is True*.

10. Adjust the Debug window so you can see all three watches in the window.

Right now, the Value column says "Out of context" because you are not currently executing the procedure that you identified as the context for these watches, Form_GotFocus.

11. Arrange the form, the code window, and the Debug window so that you can see them all at once.

12. Run the program. It stops for the first time when the value of x changes, because that's one of the watches that you set up.

You can now see the values of all three watches in the Debug window. The x watch is highlighted because it is the watch that caused the break. The next statement to be executed (after the one that changed the value of x) is highlighted in the code window.

13. Click *Continue* or press *F5* to continue. The next break occurs when y = 99999 becomes True.

Did you notice how much longer it took to execute the sleeper loop than it did when you created the program? That's because Visual Basic is checking all your watches after every step in the loop!

14. Keep continuing and examining the results of the watches in the Debug window until the procedure finishes.

15. End the program.

Editing Watches

If you want to change a watch while the program is running, simply double-click it in the Debug window to open the Edit Watch window, which is nearly identical to the Create Watch window. Figure 14-4 shows the Edit Watch window. Notice that you can click the Delete button to remove the watch.

At design time, you also edit a watch by double-clicking it in the Debug window, but often you have to open the Debug window first. That's easy enough—just choose View | Debug Window.

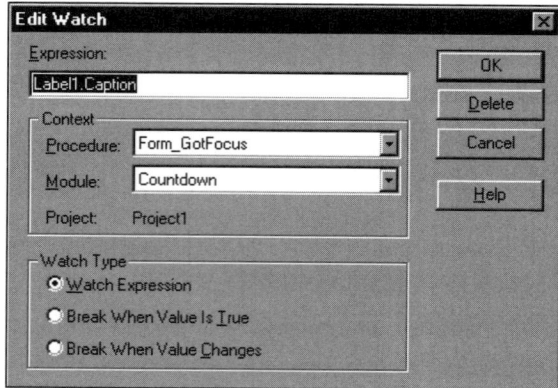

Figure 14-4: You use this window to edit an existing watch.

USING THE CALLS WINDOW

When you're working with a complex program, where procedures call subprocedures, which in turn call other subprocedures, which call yet even more subprocedures, you can get lost as to which procedures are currently active. The Calls window displays that information for you. Figure 14-5 shows an example. Reading up from the bottom of the list, you can see that the cmdGo_Click procedure called the Setup procedure, which in turn called the CheckItOut procedure. We are currently somewhere in all three of these procedures.

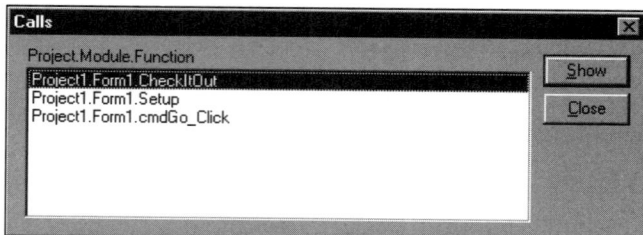

Figure 14-5: The Calls window displays all the procedures that are currently open, in the order of the Calls.

The Calls window is available only in break mode, and only when you're in a called procedure. You open the window with the Tools | Calls command or the Calls icon (shown here). You must close the window before you proceed. You can't leave it open while you run code.

Usually, the code window shows the procedure that's currently executing. If you want to see one of the other procedures that's open, double-click it in the Calls window.

SUMMARY

Debugging is never easy, but the challenge of making a program work correctly is what makes programming such an exciting job. As this chapter has shown you, Visual Basic gives you a number of debugging tools to make it as painless as possible:

▶ You can test programs at full speed.

▶ For run-time errors, Visual Basic displays error messages and highlights the statement where the problem occurred.

▶ You can step through a program one statement at a time, stepping into or over called procedures.

▶ You can execute at full speed but pause at specified breakpoints.

▶ You can try out statements "on the fly" by typing them in the Debug window; if they work, you can insert them into your program.

▶ You can set up watches on specific expressions.

▶ You can turn your watches into breakpoints.

▶ You can examine the nest of calls that got you to a particular point in the program.

Now that you can create and debug an elementary program, it's time to start working on some more advanced concepts. In the next chapter, you'll learn how to make your program interact with databases.

Databases and Add-Ins

One of the strengths of Visual Basic is its ability to access a wide variety of databases via the Windows ODBC features. In this part, you'll learn how to include database access in your Windows applications so that your users can create databases; add, read, update, and delete records; and extract database reports. Once you've learned that, we're going to show you an even easier way: The standard edition of Visual Basic includes an add-in called Data Manager that makes it relatively easy for you to create and access Microsoft Jet engine databases.

CHAPTER OBJECTIVES

There are a lot of database managers around—
Microsoft Access, Lotus Approach, dBASE, and
FoxPro, just to name a few—and Visual Basic tries
to give you the ability to access whichever ones
you have. In this chapter, you'll learn how to add
database capabilities to your Visual Basic
applications. You will learn:

▶ What database features are available to Visual
   Basic programmers

▶ How to use the Data control to access
   databases

▶ How to bind other controls to a Data control

▶ How to use Data Access Objects to enhance the
   capabilities of the Data control

▶ How to write a program that can display data
   from a database, add records, modify records,
   delete records, and seek out specific records

Database Access

Here's some good news for you. At the basic level, Visual Basic does almost all the database work for you. You'll see in this chapter that it's very easy to add database capabilities to your applications.

VISUAL BASIC'S DATABASE FEATURES

Before we go into the steps of adding database access to your programs, let's run down the basic database features provided by Visual Basic.

The Microsoft Jet Engine

You can interact with the most common types of databases via the *Microsoft Jet engine*, which is built into Visual Basic. For databases that the Jet engine can't work with, if they conform to the *Online Database Connectivity* (ODBC) protocol, you can still access them by installing special drivers, which are usually supplied by the database managers. You'll need custom controls for databases that don't fit in either of these categories.

NOTE Spreadsheets have similar structures to databases, and many spreadsheet managers, such as Microsoft Excel and Lotus 1-2-3, let you create and manage databases in tabular format. The Jet engine can also access and manage many common types of spreadsheet databases.

The Data Control

The Jet engine is by far the easiest way to interact with a database. It works with the standard *Data control* (see Figure 15-1), which provides most of the functions you'll want. The Data control lets you view and update a database without writing a single line of code. It also includes a few methods so that you can easily code additional functions. As you can see in Figure 15-1, you display and update database records in ordinary controls such as TextBoxes, which you *bind* to the Data control so that the Data control manages their contents.

Figure 15-1: The Data control provides most of the functions you need to access data via Microsoft's Jet engine.

Data Access Objects

The Jet engine also makes available a number of *Data Access Objects* (DAO) that let you code your own database functions beyond those provided by the Data control. These include objects such as Database, Field, and Index, which you use to define and manipulate data in databases. Each object has a related set of properties, methods, and events to provide the functions you need for working with the data. We'll use some of these objects at the end of this chapter when we expand the capabilities of the Data control.

USING THE DATA CONTROL

The Jet engine makes it easy to connect many types of databases to a form with
no code at all. The Jet engine performs this amazing feat through an object
called the Data control. The Data control provides the link between the records
in a database and the form that the user sees. It has properties that allow access
to databases of different types, the tables within each database, and the fields
within each table. Of course, the same can be done in code. However, the Data
control accomplishes it at design time. This is usually easier, faster, and more
accurate than writing code.

Data Control Properties

Figure 15-2 shows the properties of the Data control. The three properties
you'll need to set for every Data control are Connect, DatabaseName, and
RecordSource.

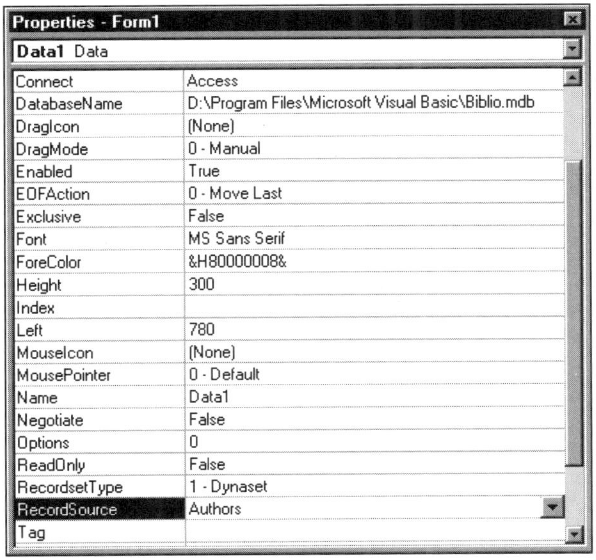

Figure 15-2: The Data control's properties identify the database and the table to be
connected to the form.

Connect Property

The Connect property allows you to specify the type of database, such as Microsoft Access, dBASE, or Lotus 1-2-3. We are using a Microsoft Access database in Figure 15-2.

DatabaseName Property

The DatabaseName property specifies the pathname of the file containing the desired database. Selecting this property opens a dialog box where you can locate and select the file you want to use.

RecordSource Property

A database is comprised of *tables* that extract content from the entire database. For example, an Employee database might include a Directory table consisting of name, address, and phone number; a Payroll table consisting of name, ID number, salary or wage rate, and deductions; and a Location table containing name, department, office number, phone extension, supervisor; and so on. The RecordSource property allows us to specify the table that we want to connect to the Data control.

Data Control Buttons

The Data control allows you to scroll through database records using VCR-style buttons. You can go forward or backward record by record, or you can jump directly to the beginning or end of your set of records.

Visual Basic's Sample Database

In this chapter, we'll develop an application to access a database that's provided by Microsoft in the Visual Basic package. It's called Biblio.mdb, and it's located in your Microsoft Visual Basic folder. It contains data about books, authors, and publishers in several tables. Our application will access the Authors table, which contains three fields: Author ID (a serial number), Author (the author's name), and Year Born. You have already seen the form for this application in Figure 15-1. Let's set up the Data control for this application now.

1. Start a new project.

2. Double-click the Data icon (shown here) to place a Data control on the form.

3. Resize the control so that it looks something like the one in Figure 15-1 and set the *Caption* to *Authors*.

4. Set the *Connect* property to *Access*.

   You don't have to have Microsoft Access to use this database. It was created by the Jet engine using its native format, which is the same as the Microsoft Access format. You can also create databases using this format via Data Access Objects, but such advanced techniques are beyond the scope of this book.

5. Set the *DatabaseName* property to *Biblio.mdb* in your Microsoft Visual Basic folder.

6. Set the *RecordSource* property to *Authors*.

7. Name the form *frmAuthor*.

8. Save your form as *Authors.frm* and your project as *Authors.vbp*.

USING BOUND CONTROLS

While the Data control specifies the database to be used and links it to a particular form, bound controls actually display and let you edit the data. Ten controls can be used as bound controls: DBCombo, DBList, DBGrid, Label, TextBox, CheckBox, ComboBox, ListBox, PictureBox, and Image.

How to Bind a Control

You *bind* a control by setting its DataSource and DataField properties. The DataSource property is set to the name of the Data control. The DataField property is set to the name of the field within the database that you want to display.

Bound controls display the data within the fields for the current record. When the Data control moves from one record to the next, all controls bound to that Data control change to display the fields from the next record.

Let's set up the bound controls for our Authors application.

1. Create the Labels and TextBoxes shown in Figure 15-1.

   You don't have to clear the default text from the TextBoxes. As soon as you start the application, the Data control displays the text from the first record, so the user never sees the default text.

2. Click the *Author ID* TextBox so that it is selected.

3. Set *DataSource* to *Data1*.

   Since there is only one Data control on the form, Data1 is the only name that's listed when you drop down the DataSource list. Setting this property binds the TextBox to the Data1 control.

4. Set the *DataField* to *Au_ID*.

   When you drop down the DataField list, all the fields in the table are listed. Setting this property binds the TextBox to the field.

5. Repeat Steps 2 through 4 to bind the Author TextBox to the Author field and the Year Born TextBox to the Year Born field.

6. Save your work.

Working with the Bound Controls

Would you believe that your application is ready to roll? It's true. The Jet engine and the Data control are going to do the rest of the work for you. Try it and see for yourself.

1. Start the application. Data from the first record appears in the TextBoxes.

2. Try out the four buttons on the Data control. They move forward or backward one record at a time, jump to the beginning, and jump to the end.

3. Select any record and change the Author's name and Year Born. (Don't change the Author ID.) Then switch to another record.

When you switch to another record, Visual Basic automatically records the changed data in the database in memory. But it doesn't actually save it on disk until you end the program or otherwise close the database file.

You can't change the Author ID because it's the key field for this table. If you try to change a key field, you get the message *Field cannot be updated*. This puts you in a loop that you can't get out of without ending the program.

4. Switch back to the record that you changed. You'll find that it still contains the changed data.

5. When you're done experimenting, end the program.

Adding New Records

You updated some records in the last exercise, but how do you add a new record? If you want to give users this facility, you must change the EOFAction property of the Data control. This property determines how the End-of-File (EOF) button responds. By default, it is set to *0 - Move Last*, meaning that it moves you to the last record in the file, as you saw in the last exercise. By setting it to *1 - Add New*, it jumps one record beyond the end of the file, adding a new record. Then all you have to do is fill in the blanks on the new record. Let's try it.

1. Change *EOFAction* to *1 - Add New*.

2. Run the program. The Jet engine displays the first record.

3. Click the EOF button. A new record appears with only the Author ID filled in.

   If instead you get the last record, click the Forward icon to move forward one more record.

   The Author ID is filled in because this database is programmed to generate an Author ID automatically for new records.

4. Move forward or backward to another record. As soon as you do this, the new record is saved in the database in memory.

5. Jump to the end of the database. If you get a new record, move backward one record to see the new record that you created.

6. When you're done experimenting with this feature, end the program.

USING DATA ACCESS OBJECTS

Okay, now we can change and add records, but how about deleting them? That is not a built-in function for the Data control. It isn't even a Data control method. If you want to include a delete function, you must code it yourself using a Data Access Object. Let's take a brief look at the Data Access Objects.

The Jet engine provides the DAO types shown in Table 15-1. Don't let the list scare you; you won't have to create or work with most of these objects until you're ready to write advanced database applications. We're including them all in the table just for future reference purposes, because your Visual Basic documentation doesn't define them all in one place. The one to pay atten-tion to for now is Recordset, which provides the Delete function that we need.

Table 15-1: Data Access Object Types

Type	Description
DBEngine*	The Jet engine itself; all other Data Access Objects are derived from this object.
Workspace*	The area where your databases are stored; the Jet engine automatically opens one default Workspace, called Workspaces(0). (The collection of Workspace objects in DBEngine is called Workspaces.)
Database	An object that contains an open database. Database properties and methods let you manipulate the contents of the database, such as the Updatable property, which indicates whether or not the database can be updated. (The collection of all Database objects in a Workspace is known as Databases.)
Recordset	An object containing all the records in a database table or all the records that result from a query. Recordset properties and methods let you manipulate the contents of the recordset, such as the Delete method, which deletes the current record. (The collection of all Recordset objects belonging to a Database is called Recordsets.)
QueryDef	A stored definition of a query in a database. QueryDef properties and methods give you the ability to define the selection parameters and manage the query. For example, the Execute method runs the query to create a new Recordset. (The collection of all QueryDef objects for a database is called QueryDefs.)

TableDef	The stored definition of a table within a database. TableDef properties and methods give you the ability to manipulate the table. For example, the Create Field method lets you add a new field to the table. (The collection of TableDef objects belonging to a Database is called TableDefs.)
Field	A column of data in a table, such as the First Name field or the Wage Rate field. Field properties and methods give you the ability to manipulate the data stored in that field. For example, the Size property defines the maximum size of the field. (The collection of Field objects belonging to a table is called Fields.)
Index	An index to the records in a table sorted according to one or more fields. The properties and methods of the Index object determine the order that the records in a table are accessed. (The collection of Index objects belonging to a table is called Indexes.)
Property	A built-in or user-defined characteristic of a Data Access Object. Property properties and methods give you the ability to control the nature of that property. (The collection of Property objects belonging to a Data Access Object is called Properties.)

*The DBEngine and Workspaces(0) objects can be assumed in expressions. For example, DBEngine. Workspace(0).AuDatabase is equivalent to AuDatabase.

Working with Database and Recordset Objects

When you use the Data control, the Jet engine automatically creates the necessary DBEngine, Workspace, Database, and Recordset objects. You can refer to the Database and Recordset objects by the names Data1 (or whatever Name property you assigned to the Data control) and Data1.Recordset. So to use the Recordset's Delete method, you simply code:

```
Data1.Recordset.Delete
```

Since Visual Basic continues to show the deleted record until you move to another record, which could be confusing to users, we'll also move to the previous record by using the MovePrevious method, like this:

```
Data1.Recordset.MovePrevious
```

But before we delete anything, we'll display a message to make sure that the user clicked the Delete button intentionally. Recall that MsgBox is a function that returns a value indicating which button the user clicked in the message box. We'll use the MsgBox function this way:

```
msgText = "Are you sure you want to delete this record?"
If MsgBox(msgText, vbYesNo + vbQuestion) = vbYes Then
    Data1.Recordset.Delete
    Data1.Recordset.MovePrevious
End If
```

You probably haven't memorized the constants for the MsgBox function, so let's review the ones we're using here. VbYesNo displays the Yes and No buttons in the message box. VbQuestion displays the question icon. VbYes indicates that the user clicked the Yes button.

Let's create the Delete function now.

1. Add a Delete CommandButton to the form.

2. Double-click the CommandButton to open the code window for Command1_Click.

3. Add the code shown above to the procedure.

4. Save your work.

5. Run the program. The first record appears.

6. Skip to the last record, which should be the record that you added earlier to the database.

   You won't be able to delete records that came with the database because they're linked to data in other tables.

7. Click the *Delete* button. The message box appears.

8. Click *Yes*. The record disappears from the screen.

9. Experiment with adding and deleting a few more records. When you're done experimenting, end the program.

Finding Specific Records

Another major function that most database applications provide is finding a specific record. This takes considerably more coding than the previous functions we've developed. Let's start by developing a second form where users can enter the name of the author they want to find.

1. Click the Form icon (shown here) or choose *Insert | Form* to add a second form to the project.

2. Design the form as shown below. Use the names *frmFind, txtName,* and *cmdFind.*

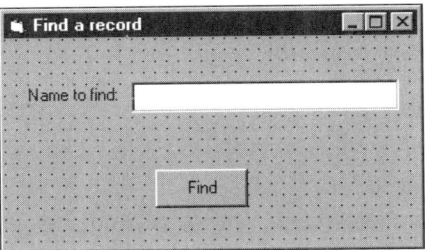

3. Save your work.

We also need to add a CommandButton to the main form that will display the new form. Let's do that now.

1. Add a Find CommandButton to frmAuthor. Name it *cmdFind.*

2. Double-click the *Find* CommandButton on frmAuthor (not frmFind) to open the dialog box for cmdFind_Click.

3. Add the code below to the procedure. This code displays frmAuthor when the user clicks the Find button on frmAuthor.

   ```
   frmFind.Show
   ```

4. Save your work.

5. Run the program and click the *Find* button. The second form should appear.

6. Close the second form and end the program.

Now we need to write the code that finds a record when someone types a name in the TextBox and clicks the Find button. To do this, we'll use some of the Recordset's Find methods. A Recordset object provides four Find methods for locating records:

FindFirst   Locates the first matching record in the record set

FindLast   Locates the last matching record in the record set

FindNext   Locates the next matching record

FindPrevious   Locates the previous matching record

The difficulty lies in specifying the criteria for a match. To do this, we code a string expression as a parameter for the Find method, like this:

```
frmAuthor.Data1.Recordset.FindNext "Author = 'Judi N. Fernandez'"
```

We have to qualify Data1 with frmAuthor in this example because we're writing code for frmFind, but the Data1 control is on frmAuthor.

Notice that the desired name must also be a string *inside* the expression's string, hence the single quotes around the name. That works fine if we always want to find the record for Judi N. Fernandez. But instead, we want to find the record for the name represented by txtName.Text. The following does *not* work:

```
frmAuthor.Data1.Recordset.FindNext "Author = 'txtName.Text'"
```

Because txtName.Text is in quotes, Visual Basic does not recognize it as a field name and looks for an author named txtName.Text. So we have to place txtName.Text outside the quotes. The following also does *not* work, although it's closer:

```
frmAuthor.Data1.Recordset.FindNext "Author = " & txtName.Text
```

Now Visual Basic will replace the txtName.Text with the name in the TextBox, but that name won't be inside the quotes, so it still doesn't work. We have to use string concatenation to place single quotes around the name, like this:

```
frmAuthor.Data1.Recordset.FindNext "Author = '" & txtName.Text & "'"
```

It's ugly, but it works. Try it and see:

1. Double-click the *Find* CommandButton on frmFind to open the code window for cmdFind_Click.

2. Enter the code shown below into the procedure.

```
frmAuthor.Data1.Recordset.FindNext "Author = '" & txtName.Text
    & "'"
frmFind.Hide
```

3. Save your work.

4. Run the program.

5. Click the *Find* button to open the Find a record dialog box.

6. Type *Simpson, Alan* in the TextBox and click *Find*. Alan Simpson's record should appear, and frmFind should close.

7. End the program.

What happens if you enter a name that isn't in the database? Or if the name you want precedes your current record? When Visual Basic reaches the end of the database without finding a match, it doesn't wrap around to the beginning. Instead, it sets the Recordset's NoMatch property to True and stops. In the next exercise, we'll test the NoMatch property. If it's true, we'll issue a FindFirst statement using the same match criterion. This creates the effect of wrapping around to the beginning and continuing the search. If this second Find statement also produces nothing, the name does not exist in the database and we'll display a message box that says, "No record matches that name."

Let's add this code to the cmdFind_Click procedure.

1. Double-click the *Find* button on frmFind to open the code window.

2. Adapt the procedure as shown in bold here.

```
frmAuthor.Data1.Recordset.FindNext "Author = '" & txtName.Text
    & "'"
If frmAuthor.Data1.Recordset.NoMatch Then
    frmAuthor.Data1.Recordset.FindFirst "Author = '" &
        txtName.Text & "'"
    If frmAuthor.Data1.Recordset.NoMatch Then
        MsgBox ("No record matches that name")
    End If
End If
frmFind.Hide
```

3. Run the program.

4. Click the Find button, type *Simpson, Alan* in the Find a record dialog box, and click *Find*. Alan Simpson's record appears in the main window.

   If someone has deleted Alan Simpson from your database, choose a name that does exist in your database and try again.

5. Now find the record for *Bard, Dick*. Visual Basic locates the desired record, even though it precedes Alan Simpson's in the database.

   If someone has deleted Dick Bard from your database, choose a name that does exist in your database and try again.

6. Try looking up the record for *Tabler, Donna*. You should get the message "No record matches that name."

7. Experiment with some more names if you wish. When you're satisfied that the procedure works, end the program by clicking the End icon in the Visual Basic toolbar.

   The next section explains why you need to click the End icon.

You're used to ending a program by clicking the Close icon in the main window. But that method doesn't work with our program now. Why? Because Visual Basic ends a program when the last form is unloaded. But the way our program is now written, we leave frmFind loaded; we just hide it when we're done with the Find function. This has two important advantages for the user. First, when the user wants to find another name, the form shows up faster since it doesn't have to be loaded. Second, since the form was not actually unloaded, the former name still appears in the TextBox, where the user can edit it or use it again.

The disadvantage, of course, is that the loaded form prevents the entire program from ending when we expect it to. How do we handle this? By unloading the form when the main form is unloaded. Let's add that code to our program now.

---

1. Double-click a blank area of frmAuthor to open the code window for frmAuthor_Load.

2. Drop down the Proc list and select *Unload*.

3. Insert to following statement to unload frmFind too.

```
Unload frmFind
```

4. Save your work.

5. Run the program, find a few records, then click the Close icon in the main window. The program should end normally.

We want to tweak one more little feature in this program. When the Find method doesn't locate a matching record, it loses its place in the Recordset, so it goes back to displaying the first record. But we can use the Bookmark property to keep track of the former position and restore that position if no match was found.

A Recordset's Bookmark property has a string value that identifies the current record. We can save that string value before doing the Find, then restore it to the Bookmark property if the Find doesn't succeed. Let's try that now.

---

1. Double-click the *cmdFind* button on frmFind to open the code window.

2. Add the statements shown in bold below to the procedure.

```
Dim DogEar As String
DogEar = frmAuthor.Data1.Recordset.Bookmark
frmAuthor.Data1.Recordset.FindNext "Author = '" & txtName.Text
     & "'"
If frmAuthor.Data1.Recordset.NoMatch Then
     frmAuthor.Data1.Recordset.FindFirst "Author = '" &
          txtName.Text & "'"
     If frmAuthor.Data1.Recordset.NoMatch Then
          MsgBox ("No record matches that name")
          frmAuthor.Data1.Recordset.Bookmark = DogEar
     End If
End If
frmFind.Hide
```

3. Save your work.

4. Run the program and check it out.

5. When you're done experimenting, end the program.

SUMMARY

Now you know how to add database capabilities to your applications. You've seen how to insert a Data control, set its Connect, DatabaseName, and RecordSource properties, and bind other controls to it. You know how to use the control to view and update the connected database, so you'll be able to write documentation for your users. And you've also learned how to use the Data Access Objects to expand on the built-in capabilities of the Data control.

You've learned the basics, but Visual Basic gives you a few more database features through its Add-Ins capability, which you'll learn about in the next chapter.

CHAPTER OBJECTIVES

Now that you've learned how to access a database, we're going to show you an even easier way. The standard edition of Visual Basic includes an add-in called Data Manager that makes it relatively easy for you to create and access Microsoft Jet engine databases. The Professional edition in addition provides a facility called Crystal Reports, which simplifies the process of drawing reports from your databases. In this chapter, you'll learn the basics of both Data Manager and Crystal Reports. You will learn how to:

▶ Create a new Jet engine database, including tables, fields, indexes, and relationships

▶ View and update the records in the tables

▶ Design a report drawn from the database

▶ Add a ScratchPad feature that displays the report while using ScratchPad

The Database Add-Ins 16

This chapter deals with database concepts such as index, key field, and relationship. Unfortunately, we can't define or explain such concepts here — they require a book of their own. We have to assume that, if you want to create database applications via Visual Basic, you already understand how today's databases work. If not, you'll need to get a good book on database concepts before trying to create and use your own.

ADD-INS

An *add-in* is a program that extends the features of Visual Basic's design environment. It is a program that you can run while you are creating and programming your applications. You might have several add-ins available on your Add-Ins menu. The two that are provided with Visual Basic are called Data Manager and Report Designer, which is Crystal Reports.

NOTE

Crystal Reports is not included in the Standard edition of Visual Basic.

DATA MANAGER

Data Manager gives you the ability to create new databases, connect them to other databases, view and update the data they contain, and query them for specific record sets, such as all your customers in the 90501 zip code area.

As you probably suspect, Data Manager works hand in hand with the Microsoft Jet engine. It creates databases in the Jet engine's native format, which is the same as Microsoft Access format. You can also access databases (but not create them) in several other formats: Paradox 3.X and 4.X, dBASE III and IV, FoxPro 2.0 and 2.5, Btrieve, and ODBC.

Creating a New Database

In this chapter, we'll create a database of name, address, and telephone information. We'll create three tables within the database: Home Address, Work Address, and Phone Numbers. Then we'll use Crystal Reports to draw reports from our new database.

Let's begin creating the database now.

1. Start a new project.

2. Choose *Add-Ins | Data Manager*. This opens the Data Manager window, shown here.

Notice that Data Manager is a separate application on your Taskbar. You could exit Visual Basic now, and Data Manager would stay open for you to use.

3. Choose *File | New Database* from the Data Manager's menu bar (not Visual Basic's). A common dialog box captioned New Database opens.

4. Name your new database *AddressBook* and save it in your Visual Basic folder. When the common dialog box closes, a Database form appears in the Data Manager window, as shown here.

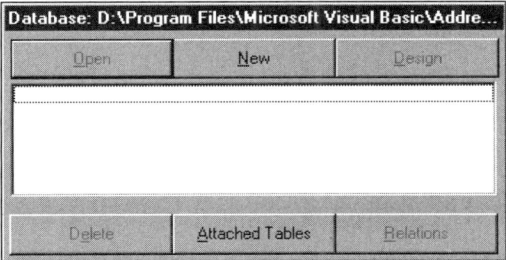

Defining Tables

Now our database exists, but it doesn't contain any data yet. Recall that you store database data in tables that are comprised of fields. Our next task, then, is to define some tables.

1. Click the *New* button in the Database window. This opens the Add Table dialog box, shown here.

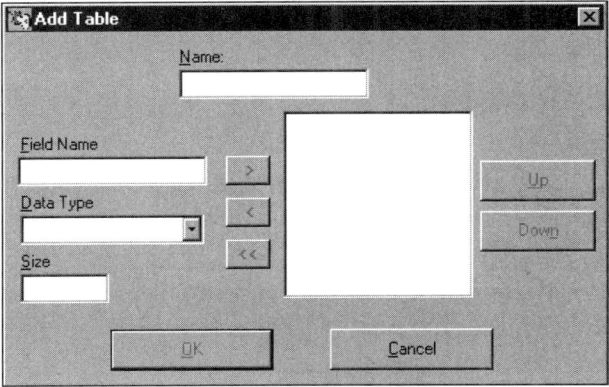

2. We'll create the HomeAddresses table first, so type *HomeAddresses* in the Name TextBox at the top.

3. The first field in this table is FirstName, so type *FirstName* in the Field Name TextBox.

4. The Data Type ComboBox (shown here) lists all the types of fields that you can use in a Jet engine database. Select *Text* for the FirstName field.

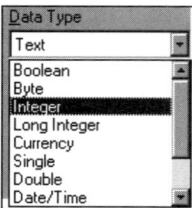

Data Type is a ComboBox, so you can select an item either by dropping down the list and clicking it or by starting to type its name in the box.

5. When you selected Text, Data Manager automatically popped a default size of 10 into the Size TextBox. Change the *Size* to *15*.

6. Now click the right arrow icon, shown here, to add the new field to the ListBox on the right. This records the definition of the field in the table.

7. Complete the table by defining the following fields, which are all text fields:

Name	Size
LastName	20
HomeAddressStreet	20
HomeAddressCity	15
HomeAddressState	2
HomeAddressZip	10

If you make a mistake, just keep going. You'll get a chance to correct it in the next exercise.

You can make some limited corrections in this dialog box, although many corrections are easier to make later on. But let's look at how you can make corrections here before we go on to the next topic.

1. In the list box, select the *HomeAddressCity* field. Then click the left arrow icon, shown here. This deletes the field from the table.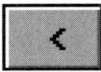

   Be careful not to click the left chevron icon, shown here, as it deletes *all* the fields!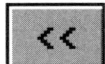

2. Type a new definition for *HomeAddressCity*, size *15*, and add it to the list. Notice that it appears at the bottom of the list.

3. Select *HomeAddressCity* in the ListBox and click the Up button several times to move it up in the list. Move it to appear after HomeAddressStreet.

   If you accidentally go too far, click the Down button to move it down again.

4. Use the above techniques to correct any mistakes that you made in the field definitions.

5. Click the *OK* button to close the Add Table dialog box and record the table in the database. Notice that the HomeAddresses table now appears in the Database window's ListBox. Data Manager also adds an SQL Statement form to its window.

Refining a Table Definition

Once you have created the basic table definition, you refine it in the Table Editor dialog box, shown in Figure 16-1, which opens when you click the Design button. Here you can edit the existing definitions, not only the values that you entered before, but also the default values that Data Manager supplied for properties such as DataUpdatable and Required. You can also create indexes and keys, which are explained shortly.

The properties listed in the editor are the properties of a field object in Visual Basic. Table 16-1 briefly summarizes them. If you're not familiar with these database concepts, your Visual Basic online documentation contains a separate topic for each property.

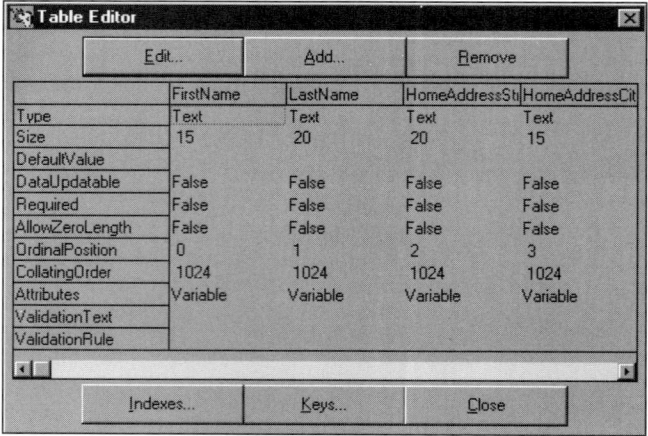

Figure 16-1: The Table Editor lets you modify a table definition.

Table 16-1: Field Properties

Property	Meaning
Type	The type of data to be stored in the field
Size	For text fields, the maximum number of characters the field can hold
DefaultValue	The value that Data Manager fills in automatically when you start a new record
DataUpdatable	A True/False value indicating whether you can update the field
Required	A True/False value indicating whether the field can be left blank
AllowZeroLength	A True/False value indicating whether the field can have no length
OrdinalPosition	A number indicating the order of this field in the table; the first field in the table has OrdinalPosition = 0
CollatingOrder	A number indicating how this field is sorted
Attributes	A number indicating several attributes of the field: fixed or variable length; automatic increments; descending sort order
ValidationText	The error message to be displayed if someone enters a value in the field that doesn't meet the ValidationRule
ValidationRule	An expression that defines the limit of permissible values for the field

In the following exercise, we'll add a default value for HomeAddressState and we'll add a new field, HomePhone.

1. Click *HomeAddresses* in the Database window and click *Design*. This opens the Table Editor.

2. Scroll to the right until you can see the *HomeState* field. Click anywhere in this field, then click *Edit*. This opens the Edit Field dialog box.

   You can also open the Table Editor by double-clicking anywhere in a field.

3. Type your state code for the *DefaultValue* property.

4. Click *OK* to close the dialog box. The Table Editor returns.

5. Click *Add* to open the Add Field dialog box, which is just like Edit Field except that the properties are all blank.

6. Enter these properties:

   Field Name: *HomePhone*

   Type: *Text*

   Size: *14*

   Attributes: *Fixed Length*

7. Click *OK* to add the field to the table and return to the Table Editor.

You can make other changes to the table while it's still in the design phase. For example, you could change the size of a field, change it from variable length to fixed length, even delete it. You can also make these changes after you have finished the design phase and started adding data to the table. But if you do, you lose all the data that you have entered in that particular field in all records. So try to complete your design before you start adding data to the table.

Defining Indexes and Keys

You can identify primary, secondary, and foreign indexes for your table, as well as primary and foreign keys. An index is a Visual Basic object, and Primary and Foreign are properties of an index object. If neither Primary nor Foreign are true, it is a secondary index. Primary indexes must also have the Unique property set to True.

In the following exercise, we create a primary index consisting of LastName and FirstName.

1. Click the *Indexes* CommandButton to open the Indexes dialog box, shown below.

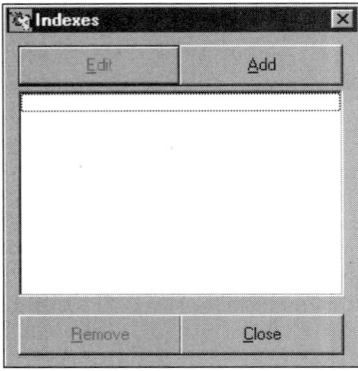

2. Click the **Add** button to open the Add Index dialog box, shown below. Notice that the fields are listed in the Fields in table ListBox in alphabetical order, not their order in the table.

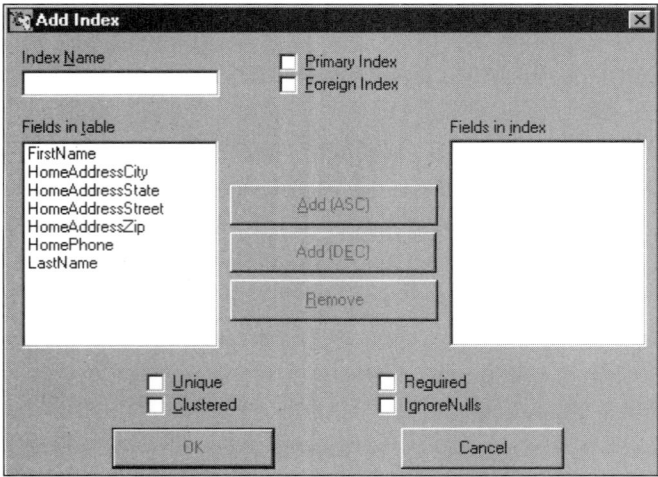

3. Type *NameIndex* in the *Index Name* TextBox.

4. Click the *Primary Index* CheckBox so that it contains a check mark.

5. Click *LastName* and click *Add(ASC)*. LastName disappears from the Fields in table ListBox and LastName(ASC) appears in the Fields in index ListBox.

(ASC) stands for *ascending*, meaning that this field will be sorted in ascending order. Use Add(DEC) for fields that you want to sort in descending order.

6. Click *FirstName* and click *Add(ASC)*. FirstName disappears from the Fields in table ListBox and FirstName(ASC) appears in the Fields in index ListBox.

7. Click the *Unique* and *Required* CheckBoxes so that they both contain check marks.

8. Click the *OK* CommandButton to record the index and close the dialog box.

Now let's create a secondary index based on HomeAddressZip. This will let us print address labels in zip code order for bulk mailings.

1. Click *Add* to open the Add Index dialog box.

2. Type *ZipIndex* in the *Name* TextBox.

3. Select *HomeAddressZip* from the Fields in table ListBox and click *Add(ASC)*.

4. Click *OK* to record the new index.

5. Close the Indexes dialog box and the Table Editor dialog box. You should be on the Data Manager main window.

You'll see the effect of these two indexes shortly, when we start adding data to the table.

Defining Relationships

You can also define relationships between tables in Data Manager. First, we need a second table, so let's create that now.

1. In the Database window, click the *New* button to open the Add Table dialog box.

2. Create the *WorkAddresses* table shown here (all fields are text fields):

FirstName	*15*
LastName	*20*
Position	*25*
Company	*25*
WorkAddressStreet	*20*
WorkAddressCity	*15*
WorkAddressState	*2*
WorkAddressZip	*10*
WorkAddressPhone	*14*
WorkAddressExtension	*4*

3. Make LastName and FirstName the Primary Index, called *NameIndex*.

4. Make WorkAddressExtension optional.

5. Close all dialog boxes and return to the Data Manager main window.

Now we're ready to establish the relationship between these two tables. We'll relate the LastName and FirstName fields so that we can draw reports containing data from both tables.

1. In the Database window, click the *Relations* button to open the Relationships dialog box, shown here.

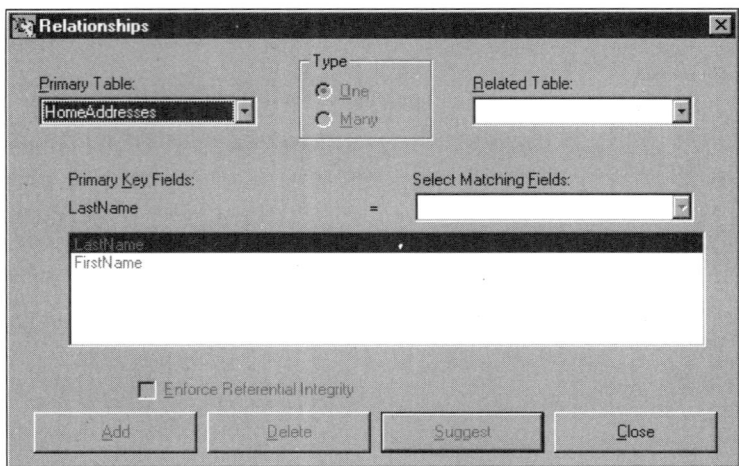

2. Drop down the *Primary Table* list and select *HomeAddresses*. (You can ignore this step if HomeAddresses is already selected.) Notice that Data Manager lists the key fields from the selected table in the ListBox.

3. Drop down the *Related Table* list and select *WorkAddresses*. Notice that Data Manager automatically selects a One relationship (one-to-one relationship) and relates the LastName fields from each table.

4. Click *Add* to create this Relation object.

5. In the ListBox, click *FirstName*. Data Manager automatically relates FirstName from each table.

6. Click *Add* to create this Relation object.

7. Click *Close* to close the dialog box.

In this particular example, we chose not to enforce referential integrity, because we want to be able to modify and delete entries from the primary table (HomeAddresses) without being forced to make the same changes in the related table (WorkAddresses). In other cases, it might be appropriate to enable the Enforce Referential Integrity option.

Adding Records to a Table

Now our tables are created and we're ready to start adding data. Let's do that now.

1. In the Database window, select *HomeAddresses* and click *Open*. Data Manager displays the first record in the table. Since the table is currently empty, the record is blank.

2. If necessary, expand the dialog box vertically so that you can see all the fields in the record.

3. Click *Add*. Data Manager opens a new, blank record. The Add button changes to Cancel.

   If you change your mind after you click the Add button, click Cancel to cancel the new record.

4. Type the following data:

   FirstName: *Jane*

   LastName: *Doe*

   HomeAddressStreet: *111 First Street*

   HomeAddressCity: *Madison*

HomeAddressState: *PA*

HomeAddressZip: *55501*

HomePhone: *(800) 555-1111*

5. Click *Update* to create the record.

6. Repeat Steps 3 through 5 to add the following records:

FirstName: *John*

LastName: *Doe*

HomeAddressStreet: *111 First Street*

HomeAddressCity: *Madison*

HomeAddressState: *PA*

HomeAddressZip: *55501*

HomePhone: *(800) 555-1111*

FirstName: *Mary*

LastName: *Smith*

HomeAddressStreet: *222 Second Ave.*

HomeAddressCity: *Monroe*

HomeAddressState: *CA*

HomeAddressZip: *55502*

HomePhone: *(800) 555-2222*

FirstName: *Frank*

LastName: *Smith*

HomeAddressStreet: *222 Second Ave.*

HomeAddressCity: *Monroe*

HomeAddressState: *CA*

HomeAddressZip: *55502*

HomePhone: *(800) 555-2222*

7. Add more records to the table if you'd like.

8. Scan through your records by clicking the arrow buttons at the bottom of the dialog box. Notice that the records appear in the same order that you entered them.

9. Click the *Refresh* button. This causes the indexes to be rebuilt.

10. Now scan through the records. Notice that they're in alphabetical order by LastName and FirstName (in other words, in the order of the Primary Index).

11. Click the *Close* button to close the table.

Now let's add some data to the WorkAddresses table.

1. Double-click the *WorkAddresses* table.

   You can open a table by selecting it and clicking Open or by double-clicking it.

2. Add the following records:

   FirstName: *Jane*

   LastName: *Doe*

   Position: *Executive Director*

   Company: *Jefferson Foundation*

   WorkAddressStreet: *333 Third Street*

   WorkAddressCity: *Jefferson*

   WorkAddressState: *PA*

   WorkAddressZip: *55503*

   WorkPhone: *(800) 555-3333*

   WorkExtension: (none)

   FirstName: *Mary*

   LastName: *Smith*

Position: *Physician*

Company: *Monroe Health Care*

WorkAddressStreet: *444 Fourth Ave.*

WorkAddressCity: *Monroe*

WorkAddressState: *CA*

WorkAddressZip: *55504*

WorkPhone: *(800) 555-4444*

WorkExtension: *44*

FirstName: *Frank*

LastName: *Smith*

Position: *Senior Analyst*

Company: *Longforth Corp.*

WorkAddressStreet: *555 Fifth Ave.*

WorkAddressCity: *Washington*

WorkAddressState: *CA*

WorkAddressZip: *55505-3000*

WorkPhone: *(800) 555-5555*

WorkExtension: *555*

3. Add any other records that you'd like.

4. Click *Refresh* to refresh the indexes.

5. Leave the table open while you read the next section.

Modifying the Database

Now we have two tables containing data in our AddressBook database. We can continue to use DataManager to view and work with this data.

Finding a Record

Now let's work on locating a specific record or set of records. In the following exercise, we'll locate all the records with LastName Smith.

1. Click the *Find* button to open the Find Record dialog box.

2. In *Fields*, click *LastName*.

3. Under *Operator*, click =.

4. For *Value*, type *Smith*.

5. Click *OK* to close the dialog box and select all records with LastName equal to Smith. Notice that four new arrow icons have appeared surrounding the Find button.

6. Use the new arrow icons to scroll through just the found recordset.

   The original arrow icons still scroll through the entire table.

Data Manager doesn't provide a means to find a record based on two fields, so you couldn't search for John Doe or Mary Smith directly. The Find feature is not limited to the key fields — you could locate all records where the state is CA, for example. Find operators include Like, which lets you search for a pattern instead of a specific value. For example, you could locate all zip codes starting with 555, all phone numbers in the (501) area, or all addresses on First Street. The Like operator is explained in Chapter 11.

Updating a Record

To update a record, you simply display it, overtype the current value with the new value, and click Update. Data Manager will display an error message if the changed field is not updatable.

Deleting a Record

To delete a record, you display it and click the Delete button. Data Manager will display an error message if you can't delete the record because of referential integrity considerations.

Adding New Records

To add a new record, you click the Add button, type the data in the blank record, then click Update.

Refreshing the Table

When you update, delete, and add new records, the indexes get out of sync. Be sure to click Refresh every so often to refresh the indexes. You should also choose File | Compact Database every so often to let Visual Basic reorganize the database, fill in holes left by deleted records, and so on. You must close the database before you compact it. If it's available on a network, everyone must close it, as it cannot be compacted if anyone has it open.

The compaction process creates a new copy of the database, which you must provide a name and path for, and the target drive must have enough room to store the new copy. After compaction, and after you check the new database to make sure that all is well, you can delete the old database and rename the new one with the old one's name.

CRYSTAL REPORTS

Crystal Reports is a great add-in for Visual Basic, masquerading as the Report Designer on the Add-Ins menu. The program gives report designers a wide range of custom reports for databases. It is extremely powerful, yet is simple to use.

Crystal Reports also has a custom control which you can use in your Visual Basic programs to print reports created in the Report Designer. Together, these two elements provide a great deal of power and flexibility in creating database reports.

Until you register Crystal Reports, you'll see a registration screen every time you start it up. We'll leave you to register Crystal Reports on your own and assume that the first screen you see is the main Crystal Reports window, shown in Figure 16-2.

The next exercise creates a report from the AddressBook database using the Report Designer.

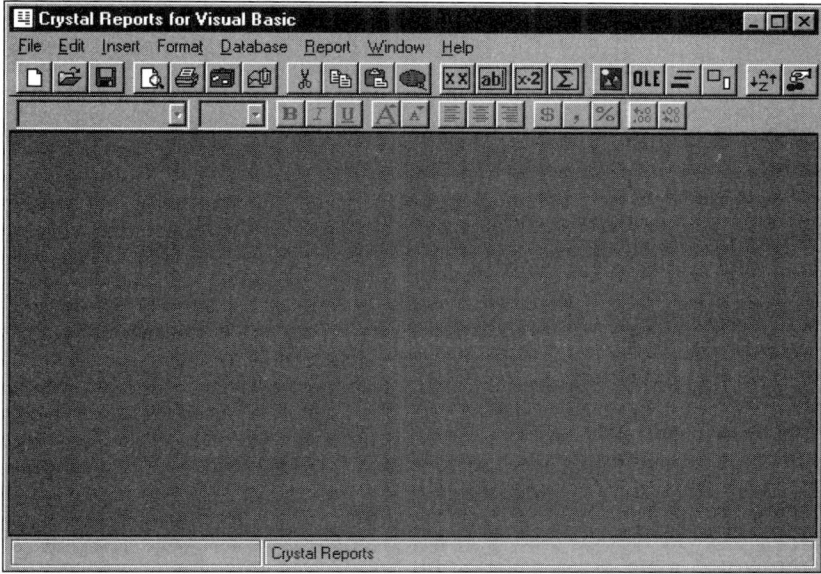

Figure 16-2: You design a report in the work area of this Crystal Reports window.

1. Choose *Add-Ins | Report Designer* to start the Crystal Reports program.

2. Create a new report by choosing *File | New | Report....* You will see the new report window, shown here.

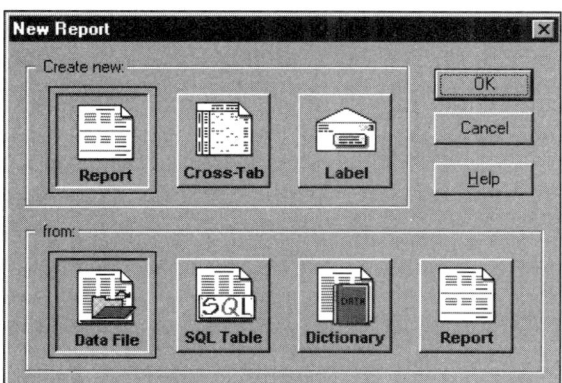

3. Click the *Report* icon in the *Create new* section.

4. Click the *Data File* icon in the *from* section.

5. Click *OK*. The Choose Database File window appears.

6. Select the *AddressBook.mdb* database file. Two windows should appear: the report window titled *Untitled Report #1* and the *Insert Database Field* window. Figure 16-3 shows both of these windows.

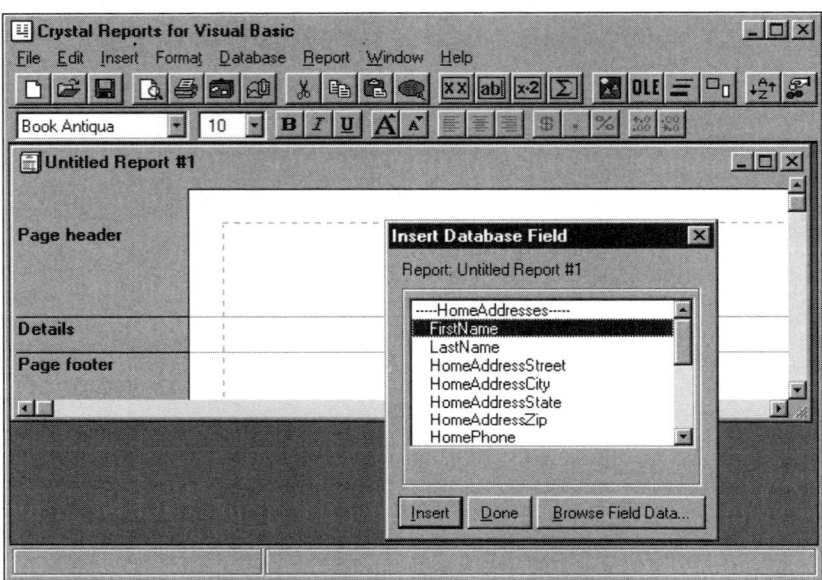

Figure 16-3: To add database fields to the report, you drag them from the Insert Database Field dialog box to the Report window.

The report window is where you can interactively insert, move, and size the various controls to design your database report. Notice that it is divided into three sections: Page Header, Details, and Page Footer. You can place text, pictures, or other objects in any of these sections. To keep things simple we'll place database field information only in the Details section of the report. Let's do that now.

1. In the Insert Database Field window, double-click *FirstName*. The mouse icon turns into a rectangular icon representing a database field.

2. Move this icon into the Details section of the report window. When the pointer enters the report window it changes back into an arrow shape, but a field outline shape moves along with the cursor.

3. Position the field outline shape at the left side of the Details section and click the mouse to position it.

When you place fields in the Details section, Report Designer automatically places header text containing the name of the field above the field.

4. Using the same method, place the *LastName* field into the report window next to the FirstName field.

5. You can also drag a field into the report. Try dragging the *HomePhone,* *WorkPhone,* and *WorkExtension* fields, placing them next to LastName.

   Hint: Crystal Reports assigns a default size to each field. You can adjust the size by selecting a field and dragging its handles.

6. Click *Done* in the Insert Database Field window to close the window.

7. Now you're ready to take a look at your handiwork! Choose *File|Print Preview* to preview the report. It should look like Figure 16-4.

8. Save your file as *PhoneList.rpt.*

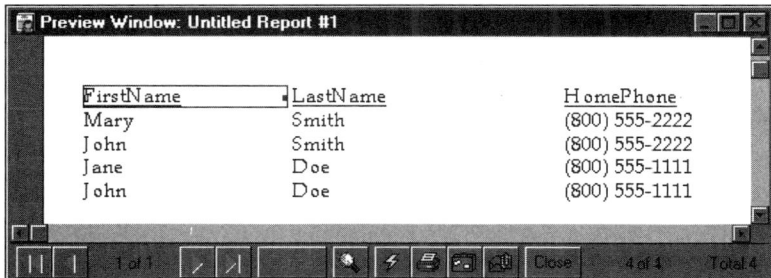

Figure 16-4: You've completed a simple database report.

Now that you've created a report, the real fun can begin! The next exercises will show how easy it is to modify the ScratchPad application so it can automatically print out the reports you create.

Crystal Reports provides a control that lets you access the report features from your applications. The Crystal Reports control properties give you a wide range of control over the look and feel of your reports. The properties we will focus on are the ReportSource and Destination properties. Let's try using the Crystal Reports control.

1. Open the ScratchPad application in Visual Basic and add the Crystal Reports control to your toolbox by clicking *Tools | Custom Controls* and selecting *Crystal Report Control*.

2. Add the control to the mdiform by selecting it from the toolbox window.

3. In the *Properties* window for the Crystal Report control, select *0 - Report File* for the *ReportSource*.

5. Select *0 - To Window* for the *Destination* property.

6. Click the ellipsis button in the *ReportFileName* property. Select the *PhoneList.rpt* report file from the dialog box that appears.

7. Enter *Phone List* as the *WindowTitle* property.

8. On the mdiform, use the menu editor to create a menu called *Database* and an item called *Print to Window*. Name them *mnuDatabase* and *mnuDatabasePrintToWindow*.

9. Display the code window for *mnuDatabasePrintToWindow_Click*, and enter the code shown below. Setting the Crystal Report control's Action property to 1 displays the report. Its other properties determine where and how it is displayed.

```
Private Sub mnuDatabasePrintToWindow_Click()
    'Setting this property to 1 displays the report window
    CrystalReport1.Action = 1
End Sub
```

10. Now run the ScratchPad application and select *Client Database | Print to Window*. Your report of the client database should appear!

11. Save your work.

Now you can call up a quick list of the phone numbers you use most often at any time from ScratchPad. You might want to go back to Data Manager and add real names and phone numbers to the AddressBook database, so that you have your personal phone numbers at your fingertips while you're working at your computer.

Can you see how easy it would be to add other reports, such as an address list, to the application? All you have to do is set up the report in Report Designer, then set the ReportFileName and WindowTitle properties before displaying the report.

SUMMARY

Data Manager and Crystal Reports don't really extend Visual Basic's database facilities — all these features are available via normal Visual Basic statements. But these two add-ins make it much easier to create and work with databases and reports.

These are not the only two add-ins in the world. You can get others, which you access through the Add-In Manager command on your Add-Ins menu. And you can create your own add-ins when you're ready to learn more advanced Visual Basic techniques.

In the meantime, however, we're done with databases in this book. In the next chapter, you'll start learning how to build a help library for your applications.

PART

V

Adding Help to Your Program

You probably know from your own experience how important good online help is, in even the simplest of Windows applications, and how irritating an insufficient help system is. In this part, you'll learn how to add help facilities to your applications — from a help menu to context-sensitive help via the F1 key.

Once you know the basics of creating a help library, we'll move ahead and add some familiar Windows Help features (hypertext jumps and pop-ups, and a help contents page), as well as some features that may be new to you, like adding graphics and graphic links to your help screens.

CHAPTER OBJECTIVES

In this chapter, we'll get your started on your first help library — for ScratchPad, of course. You will learn how to:

 Write help topics

► Create a help project file

► Insert help information into the application

► Compile the help library

We'll expand on your skills in Chapter 18, where you'll learn how to add such things as graphics and jumps to your help topics.

Help Library Basics

17

As a user of Visual Basic and Windows, you're familiar with online help systems. In Chapter 4, "Getting Help," you learned your way around Visual Basic's online help. That chapter described Help from the user's standpoint; in this chapter we'll start looking at how Help works from the Visual Basic programmer's point of view.

If you are the only user of your applications, a Help library is probably not necessary. However, if you are developing an application to be used by others, your program is incomplete without well-written help topics. Badly planned and badly written help files, plus a bad index, are a source of intense frustration for clients. Developing a good help library to go with your program warrants the time spent.

A PROGRAMMER'S VIEW OF HELP

Most Windows applications use WinHelp.exe to display their Help topics. This WinHelp engine, which is included in Windows, provides the interface that makes the help system work — the Help window with its menus and button bar, the contents and index features, and in Windows 95, the Find feature. The application provides one or more help library files (extension .hlp) that contain its help topics. WinHelp accesses the .hlp files for the material that it displays in the contents, indexes, and topic windows.

The Text File and the Help Project File

The programmer creates a help library file by creating a text or rich text file using any word processor. The file contains one topic per page, as delimited by hard page breaks. We also create a *help project file* (extension .hpj) that contains code linking each topic in the help library file to the application itself. It is the help project file that tells WinHelp to display a topic named "Opening an Existing File," for example, when a user highlights the File | Open command and presses F1.

Compiling the Help Library File

Once the text file and the help project file are ready, we run a program called Hc.exe to *compile* the help library. (Hc stands for *help compiler*.) Hc gathers the information from the help project file and the text file to create the .hlp file. Of course, if it finds syntax or logic errors, it displays the appropriate messages so that you can fix them.

Hypertext Links

A typical Windows Help topic screen contains several *hypertext links* and *hypergraphic links* to related information — commonly known as *hotspots*. Hotspots can be jumps or pop-ups, textual or graphical. Clicking a jump displays an entirely new window; clicking a pop-up displays a box that gives additional information about the highlighted text.

A graphical image may have more than one hotspot. Such images are referred to as *segmented hypergraphics* — a bitmap image with multiple links invoked by clicking various parts of the image. You might, for example, include an image of your application's main screen, permitting users to click its various objects to see additional information.

CREATING HELP TOPICS

There are lots of places you could start working on your Help system, but it seems logical to us to start by writing the topics themselves. Then we'll link them to the various menus, dialog boxes, ToolTips, and so on.

A help library is a text or rich text file, with each topic a separate page in the file. We prefer rich text, of course, because you can add formatting and graphics to the text, giving it a lot more impact. Some special footnote symbols are used to identify the topic's title, the entries for the help index, and other administrative information.

To create help topics for ScratchPad, you'll have to use whatever word processor or editor you have on your PC. Be sure to select one that lets you create rich text files and insert footnotes. The examples in this chapter were created with Microsoft Word for Windows 95, version 7.0.

Creating a Topic File

Let's start by writing a general topic that describes ScratchPad.

---

1. Start up your word processor.

2. Start a new document.

3. Save the new document as *SP.rtf.* Be sure to save it in rich text format.

   Note: As of this writing, the Hc compiler does not recognize long file names. We could use the DOS short names that Windows 95 assigns to each file and folder, such as Scratc~1.rtf, but it's easier to just give the .rtf and .hpj files short names to start with.

4. At the beginning of the file, type the following text, which briefly explains ScratchPad. (Feel free to edit this text as desired or write your own explanation.)

   Note that although the text you're typing appears in italic in this book, you should format it however you want it to look (see Step 5, below).

   ScratchPad Introduction

   ScratchPad gives you a handy way to jot down notes to yourself as you work at your computer throughout the day. You can create numerous windows, or "ScratchPads," in which you can enter, modify, and format any text you'd like. You can also copy graphics into a ScratchPad. You can print your ScratchPads and save them to a disk.

The ScratchPad program also allows you to display a list of phone numbers from the AddressBook database, putting the numbers you need most at your fingertips.

5. Format the topic to look attractive. For example, you might want to set the title in 16-point Arial font and the body text in 12-point Arial. You might even want to display the title in a different color. (Don't choose green, as that color indicates a hypertext link in Windows.)

6. Save your work.

7. Leave the document open while you read the next section.

Now that we have our first topic, we want to assign it a title, some keywords for the Help Index, and a context string. The *context string* is a special identifier that tells WinHelp when to display this topic. For example, you might want it displayed if someone presses F1 on the main ScratchPad window. Later on, we'll link our context strings to ScratchPad.

We have to insert footnotes in our topic to create the title, keywords, and context string. We insert all three footnotes at the beginning of the topic, before the text that we have already typed. We have to use special symbols for the footnote references instead of the usual numbers, as shown in Table 17-1.

Table 17-1: Footnote Symbols for Help Topics

Item	Symbol
Context string	#
Topic Title	$
Keywords	K

Let's add these footnotes to our first topic now.

1. Position your cursor at the beginning of the topic.

2. Insert a footnote using the symbol # as the footnote reference.

   How you do this depends on your word processor. In Microsoft Word for Windows 95, you choose *Insert|Footnote*, type # in the *Custom Mark* TextBox, and click *OK*.

3. In the footnote itself, type the following text:

   scratchpad_general

4. Insert another footnote using the symbol *$* as the reference mark.

5. In the footnote itself, type the following text:

   ScratchPad Introduction

6. Insert another footnote using the capital letter *K* as the reference mark.

7. In the footnote itself, type the following text:

   Introduction to ScratchPad; ScratchPad, introduction; Overview of ScratchPad; ScratchPad, overview; ScratchPad features; Features of ScratchPad

8. Save your work.

9. Leave the document open while you read the next section.

The footnote you inserted in Step 7 will eventually yield several entries in the Help Index. In the Index itself, they'll be sorted in alphabetical order and look like this:

Features of ScratchPad
Introduction to ScratchPad
Overview of ScratchPad
ScratchPad
    features
    introduction
    overview

Of course, these entries will be mixed in with all the other keywords that you'll create for the Help index.

The ScratchPad Document Topic

You use hard page breaks to separate topics, so let's insert a hard page break and start a second topic now.

1. Position your cursor at the end of the current topic.

2. Insert a hard page break.

   How you do this depends on your word processor. In Microsoft Word for Windows 95, you press *Ctrl+Enter.*

3. Enter the following text (feel free to edit it or write your own):

   Document Window

   This is a ScratchPad document. You can enter, modify, and format text in this window. You can have multiple ScratchPad documents open simultaneously.

4. Format the text to be consistent with your other topic.

5. Position the cursor at the beginning of the text.

6. Insert a footnote using the *#* symbol and enter the following text into the footnote:

   scratchpad_document

7. Insert a footnote using the *$* symbol and enter the following text:

   ScratchPad Document

8. Insert a footnote using the letter *K* and enter the following text into the footnote. (Feel free to add any other keywords you think a user might want to look up for this topic.)

   ScratchPad window; Document window; ScratchPad; ScratchPad document; Child window

9. Save your work.

10. Leave your document open while you read the next section.

You're probably starting to get the hang of things by now. You can come back later and add a lot more topics to this file, but for now, let's go on to the project file.

CREATING THE PROJECT FILE

WinHelp uses numbers, not names, to relate help topics to particular elements in an application. The help project file relates the names that you have already assigned in the text file to the numbers that you assign in the application. It also provides other administrative information.

The project file must be an ASCII text file, also known as a DOS text file. Like a DOS batch file or a Windows .ini file, it cannot have any formatting. Also like an .ini file, it is divided into sections by headers that look like this:

[HEADER_NAME]

The headers that we will use are:

[OPTIONS]   Includes information such as the caption for the Help window's title bar

[FILES]   Indicates which text files contain the help topics

[MAP]   Links the help context strings in the topics to ID numbers in the application

Let's create the project file now.

1. Start a new text document in your word processor.

2. Save it as an ASCII (or DOS) text document with the name *SP.hpj*.

3. Enter the following text to create the [OPTIONS] section:

```
[OPTIONS]
      title=ScratchPad Help     ;sets the caption for the Help
         window
      errorlog=SPlog.err        ;tells hc.exe where to write
         error messages during the compilation
```

4. You can also enter copyright information in the [OPTIONS] section if you'd like. Include a statement such as the following, substituting your name for Your Name and the current year for 1996:

```
copyright=Your Name, 1996
```

5. Add the following text to create the [FILES] section:

```
[FILES]
    SP.rtf   ;identifies the text file containing the
ScratchPad topic
```

6. Add the following text to create the [MAP] section:

```
[MAP]
    scratchpad_general 100
    scratchpad_document 110
```

7. Save and close the file.

ADDING CONTEXT IDs TO SCRATCHPAD

Now we have set up the project file, but we still haven't inserted any help information into ScratchPad. We need to insert the help context IDs along with some other information.

First, we need to insert context ID numbers for the main window and the document window. From the project file, you can see that we'll use 100 for the main window, to bring up the general topic, and 110 for the document window. Let's insert those numbers now.

1. Open your ScratchPad project.

2. View the main form, *frmScratchPad*.

3. Display the Properties window.

4. Locate the *HelpContextID* property and enter *100*.

5. View the child form, *frmDocument*.

6. Locate the *HelpContextID* property for the child form and enter *110*.

7. Save your work.

Another thing we must do is to tell the ScratchPad program which .hlp file to use when someone requests help. We do this by using a global variable named App, short for application, which is available to every application. App has a property called Helpfile. We simply set this property to our ScratchPad help library file name. Let's do that now.

1. Open your ScratchPad project.

2. Display the code window for *frmScratchPad*.

3. Display the *Form_Load* procedure.

4. Enter the following code:

```
App.HelpFile = "SP.hlp"
```

We can't include a pathname here because we don't know the correct path on users' systems. We'll assume that the .hlp file will be installed in the same folder as the application itself, or in a folder in the search path, so that no pathname is needed.

COMPILING THE HELP FILE

Now everything is all set up for the compilation step. The compiler, Hc.exe, runs under DOS, not Windows. To run it, you must enter a DOS command in this format:

```
hc project-file
```

For example, if you want to compile the project file named SP.hpj to produce the library file named SP.hlp, you would enter this command if they were both in the same folder:

```
hc SP
```

But since Hc and SP.hpj are in different folders, we'll have to use a pathname with one or both of the parts of this command. And as we mentioned before, Hc has a problem with long names such as Program Files or Microsoft Visual Basic — two folders in the path of these files. To avoid that problem, we didn't use any pathnames in the [FILES] section of SP.hpj, which means that Microsoft Visual Basic must be the default folder when we run the compilation because that's where SP.hpj is located. Since Hc.exe is located in the Microsoft Visual Basic\hc folder, when Microsoft Visual Basic is the current folder, you can access Hc.exe this way:

```
hc\hc SP
```

This is not the only solution to this problem, but it's the easiest in our opinion. Let's compile the help file now.

1. Open a DOS prompt window. In Windows 95, you can do this easily by choosing *Start | Programs | MS-DOS Prompt*.

2. Switch to your Microsoft Visual Basic folder.

3. Enter the following command:

```
hc\hc sp
```

The Hc compiler displays some copyright messages, then begins compiling the .hlp file. It displays a series of dots as it works, much like a ProgressBar, just to let you know that it is still working. The SP.hpj file is so small that only one dot is displayed.

When the file compiles perfectly, no messages are displayed. You just see the next command prompt, as shown below.

```
D:\Program Files\Microsoft Visual Basic>hc\hc sp
Microsoft (R) Help Compiler Version 3.10.505
Copyright (c) Microsoft Corp 1990 - 1992. All rights
reserved.
sp.HPJ

.

D:\Program Files\Microsoft Visual Basic>
```

4. If you get any error messages, go back to the earlier exercises and reexamine all your work. Try to find and correct your error, then run the compiler again.

You should now have a help file called SP.hlp in the Microsoft Visual Basic folder. Let's try it out and see if it works.

1. Run ScratchPad.

2. Unmaximize the document window so that you can select the parent window.

3. Click anywhere in the client area of the parent window and press *F1*. WinHelp should start up and show the ScratchPad Features topic.

4. Click anywhere in the document window and press *F1*. WinHelp should switch to the ScratchPad Document topic.

5. Click the *Search* button in the Scratchpad Help window. The Index should open. Notice the list of items that you created in the .rtf file.

Your help index is rather short right now, so all the repetition is obvious, but when you flesh out the help library with other topics, the index will provide a valuable resource for users.

HELP FOR MENU COMMANDS

Now you know how to link a help topic to an object such as a form, a TextBox, or a CheckBox — just set the object's HelpContextID property. But how do you set the HelpContextID for a menu item? You do it in Menu Editor. Let's create a couple of help topics for ScratchPad.

1. Open *SP.rtf* in your word processor and add these two topics. Rather than walk you through the footnotes separately, we'll show them at the beginning of the topic from now on. Also, we'll assume that you'll format each topic to be consistent with the rest of your library.

   #   *scratchpad_filenew*

   $ *File|New Command*

   K   *Menu Commands, File|New; File|New command; New document; Starting a new document*

   New Command (File Menu)

   This command opens a new, blank ScratchPad document. The document will be untitled until you save it for the first time by using the File|Save or File|Save As command.

   ------------(add page break)---------------

   #   *scratchpad_filesave*

   $ *File|Save command*

K   *Menu Commands, File | Save; File | Save command; Saving a document; Naming a document*

Save Command (File Menu)

This command saves the current document on disk. If the document has been saved before and has a name, it saves the document to the same name. If the document has not yet been saved, it behaves exactly like the File | Save As command.

2. Add these lines to the [MAP] section in SP.hpj:

```
scratchpad_filenew 120
scratchpad_filesave 130
```

3. In your ScratchPad project, select the mdiform and choose *Tools | Menu Editor.*

4. In the list box, select the *&New* item, as shown below.

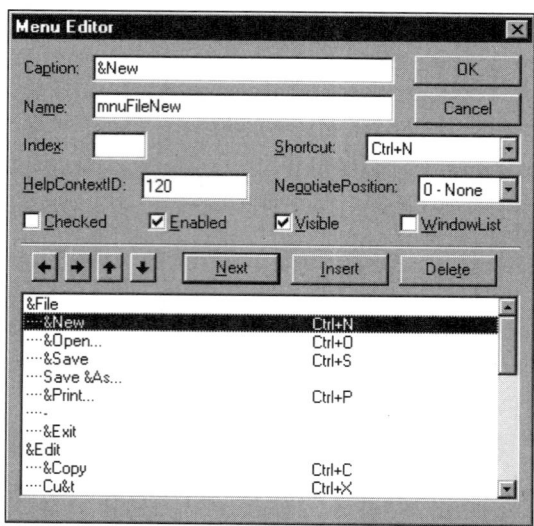

5. In *HelpContextID,* enter *120.*

6. Select the *&Save* item and enter *130* for *HelpContextID.*

7. Close Menu Editor and save your project.

8. Open a DOS prompt and enter the following command to compile the changed library:

```
hc\hc sp
```

9. Start ScratchPad if it isn't already running. If it is running, close the Help window (if open) so that WinHelp is forced to access the Help library file all over again. Otherwise, you'll get an error message when you try to access help.

10. Pull down the *File* menu and highlight *New* without selecting it. Press *F1* to see your new help topic.

11. Move the highlight to the *Save* topic and press *F1* again to see the File | Save help topic.

12. Take a look at the index. You'll see a lot more items than before.

Before you go on, if you plan to actually use and share ScratchPad, now is the time to define help topics for the remaining menu commands, using the preceding exercise as a guide.

TOOLTIPS

You can't link help topics to the toolbar per se, but you can do two things to provide help for the toolbar:

▶ Define ToolTips that pop up when someone pauses the mouse pointer over an icon on the toolbar.

▶ Create help topics for the toolbar that can be accessed from the Index and the Contents page.

You'll begin creating toolbar help in the following exercise.

1. In your ScratchPad project, select the ToolBar and view the Properties window.

2. Set the *ShowTips* property to *True.* This enables the ToolTips.

3. Click *(Custom)* and open the *Toolbar Control Properties* dialog box. Click the *Buttons* tab, as shown below.

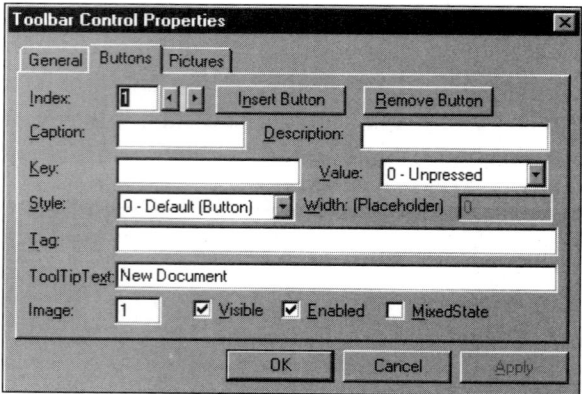

4. The first icon is for the File | New command. Enter **New Document** in the ToolTip Text box.

5. Next to Index (at the top of the page), click the right arrow icon to go to the next tool.

6. Enter *Open Document* in ToolTip Text.

7. Continue defining ToolTip Text for the remaining icons in the toolbar.

8. Close the dialog box and save your project.

9. Start ScratchPad if it isn't already running. If it is running, close the Help window.

10. Try out your ToolTips.

We won't create any toolbar help topics at this time, because we'll want to use graphics with them, and that's the subject of the next chapter.

MAKING THE HELP MENU WORK

One more task remains — we have to make the Help | ScratchPad Help Topics command work. And unfortunately, it's not as easy as what we've done so far. That's why we left it until last.

We want to display the Index when someone chooses Help|ScratchPad Help Topics. But we need to do it from the procedure for mnuHelpTopics_Click, which means we need to write code to do it. So far, we've been depending on the automatic procedures that are invoked by the F1 key. But now we need to write our own procedure.

To do that, we have to invoke the WinHelp API function. API stands for *application program interface*, and refers to a set of functions provided by Windows for you to use in your programs.

The first thing we need to do is *declare* the function so that Windows sets aside some room for its variables. It requires four variables:

▶ *hWnd* — This Long variable is the handle of the form requesting help. Every form or window has its own 32-bit number or *handle* associated with it. Windows uses this number to manage and keep track of all the information associated with your window.

▶ *lpHelpFile* — This String variable is the pathname of your help file.

▶ *wCommand* — This Long variable tells the WinHelp engine which function you want.

▶ *dwData* — This Long variable provides any additional data needed by the function specified in wCommand.

We'll deal with values for these variables in a minute. Right now, we're just concerned with declaring space for them.

The 32-bit WinHelp function is located in the user32 API library, with an alias of WinHelpA. So the framework of the declaration looks like this:

```
Declare Function WinHelp Lib "user32" Alias "WinHelpA" (variables)
    As Long
```

Why does it say As Long at the end? Because we're declaring a function, and like all functions, it returns a value — in this case, a Long value. We don't much care about the value that it returns, but we still have to declare it correctly.

When you insert the variables in the parentheses, the entire statement looks like this:

```
Declare Function WinHelp Lib "user32" Alias "WinHelpA" (ByVal hWnd
    As Long, ByVal lpHelpFile As String, ByVal wCommand As Long,
    ByVal dwData As Long) As Long
```

You're not allowed to declare API functions in a form or class module, so we'll have to add a standard module to our program. Let's do that now.

1. In your ScratchPad project, choose *Insert|Module* to insert a standard module. The code window for the new module opens.

2. Enter the Declare statement shown above into the code window. (It does not go into a procedure.)

3. Save your project. Name the new module *stdHelpDeclaration*.

Now we need to write the statement that calls the WinHelp function. First, let's decide what values we're going to use for the four parameters. The first parameter is the handle of the current window, which is always contained in the object called Screen.ActiveForm.hWnd. The second parameter is the name of the help file, which, as you know, is contained in App.HelpFile. The third parameter is a Long number that identifies the desired function. WinHelp provides a lot of functions; Table 17-2 shows a few of the handier ones.

Table 17-2: Some WinHelp wCommand Values

wCommand	Function
1	Display a particular topic, identified by context ID
2	Close the Help window
3	Display the Help contents
4	Display the Help on Help (WinHelp.hlp) index
&H105&	Display the Help index

We don't have a Help contents page yet (that's coming in the next chapter), so we'll use function &H105&.

The final variable provides specific data for the selected function. Function &H105& doesn't require any specific data, so we'll just enter a 0 for this variable.

Given these four variables, the entire statement for calling WinHelp looks like this:

```
x = WinHelp(Screen.ActiveForm.hWnd, App.HelpFile, &H105&, 0)
```

We'll code this statement in the procedure for mnuHelpTopics_Click. Let's do it now.

1. In frmScratchPad, click *Help|ScratchPad Help Topics* to open the code window for *mnuHelpTopics_Click*.

2. Insert the WinHelp statement shown above.

3. Save your project.

4. Run ScratchPad.

5. Choose *Help|ScratchPad Help Topics*. You should see the ScratchPad Help index.

6. Close the Help index and end ScratchPad.

SUMMARY

Now you have a working help library. You've learned how to create the text file containing the topics and the necessary footnote references, how to create the project file that relates the context strings to context ID numbers, how to insert the context ID numbers into your application, and how to compile the help library. You've also learned how to create ToolTips and how to invoke the WinHelp API function to display the Help index.

Your help library isn't very fancy, but it's a start. In the next chapter, we're going to add a lot of the bells and whistles everyone has grown to expect in Windows: graphics, jumps, pop-ups, and Contents topics.

CHAPTER OBJECTIVES

Now you have a Help library, but it isn't very sophisticated. In this chapter, you'll learn how to add some bells and whistles to it:

- ▶ Hypertext jumps and pop-ups
- ▶ Bitmap graphics
- ▶ Hypergraphic jumps and pop-ups
- ▶ A contents page consisting of jumps

You'll practice on ScratchPad, of course. We'll walk you through adding a few jumps and pop-ups. If you're planning on using ScratchPad and sharing it with others, be sure to take the time to add more jumps and pop-ups to create a complete library system.

Adding Pizzazz to Help

18

Now that you know the basics of creating a help library, it's time to add some Windows help features that are probably very familiar to you (hypertext jumps and pop-ups, and a help contents page), as well as some features that may be new to you: adding graphics and graphic links to your help screens.

HYPERTEXT LINKS

To create jumps and pop-ups you need to create hypertext links. You've seen many of them in your work: they are green and underlined. A single underline indicates a jump and a dashed underline indicates a pop-up. Now it's time to create your own jumps and pop-ups.

Here are the basic steps for creating jumps or pop-ups in your word processor help file:

1. Select the text that you want to turn into hypertext.

2. Underline it once for a pop-up or twice for a jump.

3. Immediately after the text, insert the context string of the topic to jump to.

4. Turn the context string into hidden text.

We'll go through all of these steps in our exercises.

A jump in your .rtf file looks like this (where italics indicate hidden text):

```
The File|Newscratchpad_filenew command
```

When WinHelp displays the topic in a help window, it appears like this (where bold indicates green):

The **File | New** command

When you click the hypertext, you jump to the topic identified as scratchpad_filenew.

Similarly, a pop-up in your .rtf file looks like this (where italics indicate hidden text):

```
...you can dragglossary_drag the selection...
```

When WinHelp displays the topic in a help window, it looks like this (where bold indicates green):

...you can **drag** the selection...

When you click this hypertext, a box pops up containing the topic identified as glossary_drag.

Your topic for File | New refers to File | Save. Let's turn that reference into a pop-up.

---

1. Open *SP.rtf* and locate the page containing the Save command.

2. Position the cursor at the end of File | Save and insert *scratchpad_filesave*.

   Warning: Make sure that there is no space between File | Save and scratchpad_filesave, or you will get an error when you run the help compiler.

3. Select *File | Save* and choose the command to underline it.

   How you do this depends on your word processor. In Microsoft Word for Windows, you choose *Format | Font* and select *Single* from the Underline drop-down list.

4. Select *scratchpad_filesave* and choose the command to mark it as hidden text.

   How you do this depends on your word processor. In Word for Windows 95, you choose *Format|Font* and click *Hidden*.

5. If you have a File|Save As topic, repeat Steps 2 through 4 to turn it into a hyptertext pop-up.

6. Save the file. (You don't have to close it.)

7. Compile the help library.

8. Start ScratchPad if it isn't already running. If it's already running, close the Help window so that WinHelp has to access the Help library file from the start.

9. Pull down the *File* menu and highlight *New* without selecting it.

10. Press *F1*. The New Command (File Menu) topic should appear, with File|Save marked as a pop-up.

11. Click *File|Save*. The Save Command (File Menu) topic should appear in a pop-up box.

12. Click the pop-up box to clear it.

CREATING A CONTENTS PAGE

Now that you've got the basic idea of creating hypertext, let's create a Contents page for our Help library. Each of the items on this page will be a jump to the appropriate topic.

1. Open *SP.rtf*, start a new page by inserting a hard page break, and enter the following topic:

   # *scratchpad_help_contents*

   $ *ScratchPad Help Contents*

   K *Help Contents; Help Topics; Contents; Topics*

   ScratchPad Introductionscratchpad_general

Document Windowscratchpad_document

Menu Commands

File | Newscratchpad_filenew

File | Savescratchpad_filesave

2. Underline *ScratchPad Introduction* with a double underline.

This is not the same as underlining it twice. A double-underline is a specific type of underline. How you do this depends on your word processor. In Word for Windows 95, you choose *Format | Font,* then select *Double* from the Underline drop-down list.

3. Select *scratchpad_general* and mark it as hidden text.

4. Repeat Steps 2 and 3 for *Document Window* and *scratchpad_document.*

5. Repeat Steps 2 and 3 for *File | New* and *scratchpad_filenew.*

6. Repeat Steps 2 and 3 for *File | Save* and *scratchpad_filesave.*

7. Add any other items that you have created topics for.

8. Save your document.

Now that we have a Contents page, we have to tell Hc about it so that WinHelp will treat it like a Contents page. In other words, WinHelp will display it when users request the contents. To do this, we must add a *contents=* line to the SP.hpj [OPTIONS] section. Also, of course, we need to set up the context ID for this new topic. Let's do that now.

---

1. Open *SP.hpj* for editing in your word processor.

2. Add the following line to the [OPTIONS] section:

```
contents=scratchpad_help_contents
```

3. Add the following line to the [MAP] section:

```
scratchpad_help_contents 0
```

4. Save the file.

5. Compile the help library.

6. Start ScratchPad if it isn't already running. If it is running, close the Help window.

7. Press *F1* to open a help topic.

8. Click the **Contents** button. Your new contents page should appear, complete with hypertext jumps.

9. Try out the jumps.

10. When you're satisfied that your hypertext jumps work, exit ScratchPad.

11. Take a look at your help topics in SP.rtf and add any other jumps you would like. Don't forget to recompile the library and try them out.

INSERTING GRAPHICS IN A HELP TOPIC

Would you like to incorporate a nifty icon or graphic in your help file? Graphics are an important part of many applications, and the help compiler recognizes several graphical formats, shown in Table 18-1.

Table 18-1: Graphical Formats Recognized by Hc.exe

Format	Description
.BMP	Windows Bitmap
.DIB	Device Independent Bitmap
.MRB	Multi-Resolution Bitmap
.SHG	Hypergraphic Bitmap
.WMF	Windows Metafile

In this chapter, we'll insert some bitmaps into our help topics. To do this, you insert a command like the following into the topic:

{bml *pathname*}

The code *bml* stands for *bitmap left* and causes the graphic to be aligned on the left. You could also use *bmc* to center the bitmap or *bmr* to align it on the right.

Let's add a topic to our Help library that explains the toolbar. We'll include each icon from the toolbar, with a brief explanation.

1. Open *SP.rtf* in your word processor and add the following topic at the end. (*Tip*: After you type the first bml command, copy and paste it to create the others.)

   # scratchpad_toolbar

   $ Toolbar

   K Toolbar; Icon bar

   Toolbar

   The toolbar provides several icons as a shortcut for menu commands. When you pause your mouse pointer over an icon, a short explanation of its function pops up. Shown below is each icon and a brief explanation of what it does.

   {bml bitmaps\tlbr_w95\new.bmp}File | New command

   {bml bitmaps\tlbr_w95\open.bmp}File | Open command

   {bml bitmaps\tlbr_w95\save.bmp}File | Save command

   {bml bitmaps\tlbr_w95\print.bmp}File | Print command

   {bml bitmaps\tlbr_w95\cut.bmp}Edit | Cut command

   {bml bitmaps\tlbr_w95\copy.bmp}Edit | Copy command

   {bml bitmaps\tlbr_w95\paste.bmp}Edit | Paste command

   {bml bitmaps\tlbr_w95\bld.bmp}Bold text

   {bml bitmaps\tlbr_w95\itl.bmp}Italic text

   {bml bitmaps\tlbr_w95\undrln.bmp}Underline Text

   {bml bitmaps\tlbr_w95\lft.bmp}Paragraph | Left command

   {bml bitmaps\tlbr_w95\cnt.bmp}Paragraph | Center command

   {bml bitmaps\tlbr_w95\rt.bmp}Paragraph | Right command

2. Add any hypertext you would like to the topic. For example, you might want to turn all the menu items into hypertext jumps or pop-ups.

3. Save your file.

4. Compile your revised Help library. Notice that it takes longer to compile now.

5. Start ScratchPad if it isn't already running. If it is already running, close the Help window.

6. Choose *Help|Scratchpad Help Topics* to open the index.

7. Select *Toolbar* from the index. You should see your new topic, complete with graphics.

8. Try out any jumps and pop-ups you have included in this topic.

Now that the graphics are in place, it's a simple matter to turn them into hypergraphic links! The process is just the same as creating a hypertext link. Let's do it now.

1. Locate the *Toolbar* topic in *SP.rtf*.

2. Select *{bml bitmaps\tlbr_w95\new.bmp}* and underline it with a double underline.

3. Position the cursor after {bml bitmaps\tlbr_w95\new.bmp} with no intervening space. Insert *scratchpad_filenew*.

4. Repeat Steps 2 and 3 for the other graphics that you have topics for.

5. Save the file.

6. Compile the revised Help library.

7. Start ScratchPad if it isn't already running. If it is running, close the Help window.

8. Choose *Help|ScratchPad Help Topics*.

9. Select *Toolbar*.

10. Position your mouse pointer over the New icon. Notice that it turns into a pointing hand, indicating that this graphic is a hotspot.

11. Click the icon. You jump to the New topic.

12. Click *Back* to return to the Toolbar topic.

13. Try out any other hotspots that you created.

SUMMARY

Now you know how to create a basic Help library, complete with hypertext and hypergraphic links. You know how to create a contents page, jumps, and pop-ups. And you can insert bitmap graphics into your topics and turn them into hotspots.

Congratulations! You've covered all the basic elements of programming in Visual Basic. In Part VI we'll move on to Advanced Topics.

PART

VI

Advanced Topics

You've learned enough now to create some very exciting Visual Basic applications. We could stop here, but there are a few more Visual Basic 4 features to explore before saying good-bye: how to use OLE in your applications, and how to use SetupWizard to create a Setup program for distributing applications.

CHAPTER OBJECTIVES

OLE can be an extremely complex subject, requiring an entire book or more. This chapter introduces the basics:

► Some fundamental concepts (linking, embedding, servers, clients)

► The Visual Basic OLE control

► Using the OLE control to add OLE capabilities to an application

In this chapter, you'll revise ScratchPad so that it can link or embed OLE objects from other applications into a document window.

Introduction to OLE

19

Object linking and embedding (OLE) gives you the ability to include objects from other Windows applications in a current application. For example, we could copy a graphic created by Paint, a range from a Lotus 1-2-3 spreadsheet, or a portion of an Access database into a word processing document.

First we'll describe some of the basics of OLE, so you'll have an understanding of what we're going to do in the step-by-step exercises. If you've already used OLE in your applications and are already familiar with terms such as *linking*, *embedding*, *client*, *server*, and *OLE container*, you can skip right to "Adding OLE Capabilities to ScratchPad."

NOTE
Dynamic Data Exchange (DDE) was an earlier method of exchanging data between applications. Although it is still available and you can access it with Visual Basic, OLE provides much more advanced features. When you're creating a new application, you'll want to use OLE.

WHAT IS OLE?

Object linking and embedding is a powerful capability of the Windows environment that allows two applications, or even objects, to communicate and dynamically share objects, which can be text, sound, graphics, video, or other data. For example, you might include a spreadsheet range created by Microsoft Excel in an e-mail that you're creating in Lotus WordPro. You could also include a sound clip that you created using EasyWave (remember that application from Chapter 8?) in which you explain the spreadsheet data. The spreadsheet data would appear as is, but the sound clip would be represented by an icon. Recipients would double-click the icon to listen to the recording.

You already know that you can copy data from one application to another via the Windows Clipboard, so what's all the fuss about OLE? The difference lies in the way that data is communicated from its original source to the object. When you copy or move data, it simply becomes a part of the destination application's document, just like data that you created originally in that application. It no longer has any relationship to the source application. But when you use OLE, a relationship still exists with the source. The nature of that relationship depends on whether you link or embed the object, which we'll discuss a little later.

The other advantage, of course, is that you can insert data that is foreign to an application, such as inserting part of a spreadsheet in a graphic, a video clip in a spreadsheet cell, or a sound clip in a text document. As an example of OLE, let's try out this last example and add a sound clip to a Cardfile card. (This will work only if you have installed the Windows 95 version of Cardfile, a sound board, and Windows Media Player. Otherwise, you might as well skip this exercise.)

1. Start Windows Cardfile. A blank card appears in the Cardfile window.

2. Choose *Edit|Picture*. This tells Cardfile that you want to insert something other than text on the card, not necessarily a picture. It also makes the Insert Object command available.

3. Choose *Edit|Insert Object*. The Insert New Object dialog box appears with a list of all the types of objects you can insert.

   The contents of this list depend on what software you have installed on your system. Your list will be different from ours. More about that shortly.

4. Select *Media Clip* and click *OK*. A window captioned Media Clip in (Untitled) appears, as shown on the next page.

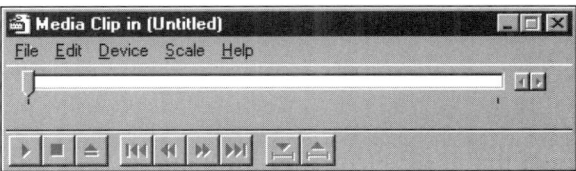

5. Choose *File|Open* in the Media Clip window. A common Open dialog appears.

6. Locate and open any .wav or .mid (wave or midi) file. (There are lots of them in your Media folder, which is a child of your Windows 95 folder.)

7. In the Media Clip window, choose *File|Exit and Return to (Untitled)*.

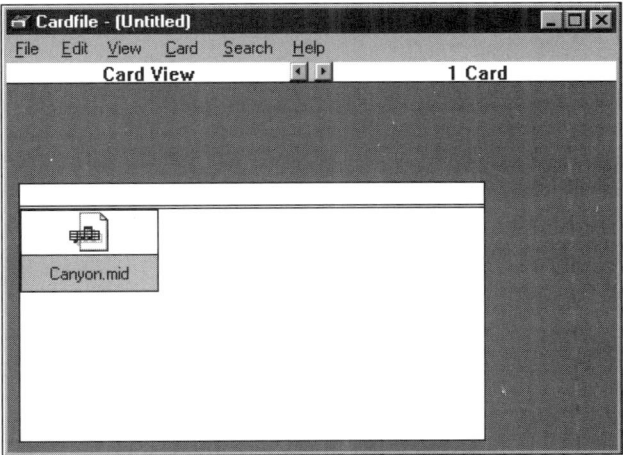

8. A dialog box asks if you want to update (Untitled). Choose **Yes**. When the Cardfile window returns, you'll see an icon representing the sound file in the card, as shown here.

9. Double-click the icon to hear the sound file via Windows 95's Media Player.

   Even if you created the sound using another application, such as EasyWave, this object was inserted via Media Player and so Media Player is called upon to play it.

10. Try moving and sizing the icon in Cardfile. Notice that you can move it but not size it, as it has no border.

The Windows Clipboard feature is enhanced by OLE. When an application is OLE-aware, you can copy OLE objects to it via the Clipboard. Let's try this out in Cardfile.

1. Open Windows 95's Paint program. An untitled drawing appears in the Paint window.

2. Choose *File|Open* and open any Bitmap (.bmp) file. (There are lots of them in your Windows directory.) This inserts the graphic into your untitled drawing.

3. Choose *Edit|Select All* to select the entire drawing.

4. Choose *Edit|Copy*. This copies the graphic to the Clipboard, replacing any bitmap graphic that was previously there.

   The Clipboard can hold several types of objects at once. A new object replaces the former object of the same type but does not disturb any other objects on the Clipboard.

5. Return to Cardfile.

6. Choose *Card|Add* to add a new card to your stack. A dialog box asks for the index line of the card.

7. Type *Bitmap graphic* and click *OK*. The card appears on the top of your stack.

8. Choose *Edit|Paste Special.* The Paste Special dialog box appears, as shown here, listing the various objects you can paste.

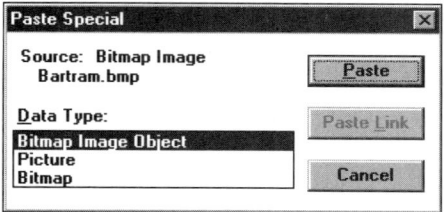

9. Select the *Bitmap Image Object* and click *OK*. The graphic is pasted onto the card.

10. Close Paint but leave Cardfile open.

Servers and Clients

An application can be an OLE server, client, or both. An OLE *server* is an application that can be the source of an OLE object. An *OLE client* receives the object. For example, when you include Excel spreadsheet data in a Word document, Excel is the server and Word is the client. Clients are also known as *containers*, because they contain the OLE object.

 In Visual Basic 3.0, the server was referred to as the *source* and the client was referred to as the *destination*. You might still find these terms used by older applications.

Many contemporary Windows applications are programmed to act as servers and/or clients. You can tell if an application has been programmed to act as a client by looking for a Paste Special or Paste Link command on its Edit menu. It might also have an Insert Object command somewhere. Your server applications show up on the dialog box that opens when you choose the Insert Object command, as you saw in the previous exercises.

Linking and Embedding

OLE objects can be either linked or embedded. Data is said to be *embedded* if a fully independent, editable copy of the source data is stored inside the container application; in this case there are two separate copies of the data, the original data and the embedded copy. Embedding is useful when you want to add functionality to your application, not just access it to a specific set of data.

With *linked* data, the container holds not a copy of the data but a set of references to the source data in the server application. There is only one copy of the data, the original. Therefore, all changes to the original are reflected in all its links, and this is the main advantage of a link. Linking is useful if you need to have one, updatable version of an object.

An embedded object, on the other hand, is self-contained. It does not point to the server application for its information; all of the information it requires is included in the container application. The object includes not only the desired data, but also a portion of the server application, so that you can edit the object from within the client application. When you edit it, you edit only the client copy; the original data is unaffected.

Exploring Embedded Objects

The two objects you have created so far are embedded, not linked. Let's take a couple of minutes to explore the editing features of an embedded object.

1. Double-click the graphic that you inserted on the Cardfile card. This tells OLE that you want to edit the object, and it obliges by opening the embedded version of Paint.

   The embedded version looks a lot like the original version. The major differences are on the File menu, which now contains several different commands.

2. Pull down the *File* menu to see the new commands: Update (Untitled), Save Copy As, and Exit and Return to (Untitled). These commands help you manage the graphic when it's embedded in another document. Notice also that there is no Open command.

3. Make any change to the graphic. Draw a circle on it, write text on it, change the colors — anything at all.

4. Choose *File | Update (Untitled)*. Notice that the change you just made now appears on the Cardfile card.

5. Make a couple of more changes, then choose *File | Exit & Return to (Untitled)*.

6. Click *No* when OLE asks if you want to update (Untitled). The Paint window disappears and your latest changes are dropped.

7. Now open Paint as an independent program and open the same bitmap graphic that you opened before. Notice that the graphic has not changed, even though you made changes to the copy that is embedded in Cardfile.

8. Close Paint but leave Cardfile open while you read the next section.

Exploring Linked Objects

Now let's try linking an object instead of embedding it.

1. In Windows 95 or NT Explorer or My Computer, open the *Microsoft Visual Basic\Bitmaps\Assorted* folder.

2. Highlight but do not open any .bmp file.

3. Choose *Edit|Copy* to copy the entire file to the Clipboard.

4. Return to Cardfile.

5. Press *F7* to add a new card.

6. Type *Linked graphic* for the index line and click *OK*.

7. Pull down the *Edit* menu. Notice that the Paste Link and Paste Special commands are both available. This means that linking is available for this object.

   You could create the link by choosing Paste Link, but we'll use Paste Special instead. Both methods have the same effect.

8. Choose *Paste Special* to open the Paste Special dialog box, shown here. Notice that the Paste Link CommandButton is enabled.

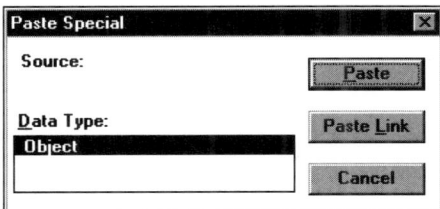

9. Click *Paste Link*. The graphic appears on your Cardfile card.

What's the difference between the linked and embedded graphic? When you change a linked graphic, you change the original file. The change affects not only the file itself and the current document, but any other linked documents. When you change an embedded graphic, you change only the current document; the original graphic and any other documents are not affected.

A linked object requires very little space in the container application, while an embedded object takes up a lot of space. A linked object is nothing more than a set of references, but an embedded object is the data plus a great deal of programming information.

Drag and Drop

Drag and drop has been available in Windows for a long time, but before OLE you couldn't drag data from one application and drop it on another. With OLE you can, but only if both applications are programmed for it. Let's try dragging a graphic to Cardfile.

1. Start a new card captioned *Dropped graphic*.

2. Move and size Cardfile and Explorer (or My Computer) so that you can see them both at once.

3. Drag any .bmp file from the *Assorted* folder to Cardfile.

   Notice that the mouse pointer changes into a file copy symbol when it moves over Cardfile. This tells you that Cardfile is capable of receiving the dropped file.

4. Drop the file on your new card. The graphic appears in the card.

5. Is the new graphic linked or embedded? Double-click it to find out. The Windows Paint program starts up.

6. Examine Paint's File menu, shown here. You'll see that this is not an embedded version of Paint. Therefore, the graphic is linked, not embedded.

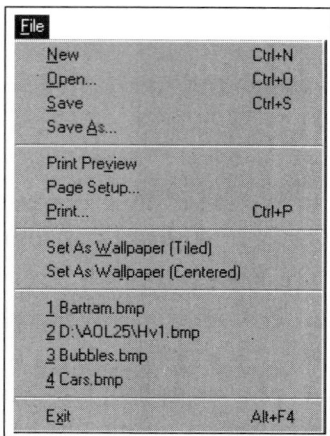

7. Close Paint, Explorer (or My Computer), and Cardfile. You don't need to save your card file unless you've grown attached to it.

ADDING OLE CAPABILITIES TO SCRATCHPAD

You can add OLE capabilities to any of the applications you develop with Visual Basic. The easiest way is to add an OLE Container control to a form. Depending on which properties you set, an OLE Container control can contain an embedded or linked object.

For ScratchPad, we'll add an OLE Container control to the document form, but make it invisible until the user indicates that he or she wants to insert an OLE object. Then we'll hide the Rich TextBox and show the OLE Container control.

Let's start by adding the control to the form and setting its properties.

1. Open your ScratchPad project if it isn't already open.

2. View the *frmDocument* form.

3. In the toolbox, double-click the OLE control, shown here. This adds an OLE control to the form and immediately displays the Insert Object dialog box.

    The dialog box opens so that you can insert an OLE object at design time, making the object an initial part of the form.

4. Close the dialog box. Now you can see the OLE control on the form. It's just a large, empty box.

    Don't worry about its size or location. We'll set those properties in code later on.

5. Set these properties:

    Appearance: 0 - Flat

    AutoActivate: 2 - DoubleClick

    AutoVerbMenu: True

    OLEDropAllowed: True

    OLETypeAllowed: 2 - Either

    SizeMode: 1 - Stretch

    UpdateOptions: 0 - Automatic

    Visible: False

So what do these properties we've just set do? The AutoActivate property sets or returns a value that allows the user to determine how to activate an OLE object. The object can be activated manually, or by single- or double-clicking. We just set this OLE property so that it is activated with a double-click, just as the Cardfile object was activated.

The AutoVerbMenu property controls whether or not a menu of commands is displayed when a user right-clicks the object. The contents of the menu (the *verbs*) are determined by the type of object. We've set this option to True, meaning that the menu will be displayed in response to a right-click.

The OLEDropAllowed property means that you can drag an object from somewhere else and drop it on this container. Dropping an object on this container will have the same effect as the Paste command from the Edit menu.

The OleTypeAllowed property allows an OLE object to be a linked object, an embedded object, or either. If you set the property to Linked, when you display the Insert Object dialog you will only see information allowing you to link the OLE object to other applications. If you set the property to Embedded, when you display the Insert Object dialog you will only see information allowing you to embed the OLE object in other applications. We set this property to Either for ScratchPad, so that users can choose either type of connection.

The SizeMode property determines how the OLE object is sized within the container:

▶ *0 - Clip* The object is displayed as-is in the OLE container. If the OLE container is smaller than the OLE object, the object is clipped to fit. If the OLE container is larger, the object appears in the upper left corner of the container.

▶ *1 - Stretch* The image of the object is stretched to fit the OLE container. The image may not retain its original proportions when this setting is used.

▶ *2 - Autosize* Resizes the OLE container so that it displays the entire OLE object.

▶ *3 - Zoom* Stretches the object as much as possible within the control while retaining its correct proportions.

Now that we've set the properties for the OLE control and you understand what they do, let's add an Insert Object command to the Edit menu, add the code to make it work, and try out the result.

1. Select the *frmScratchPad* mdiform and open Menu Editor.

2. Insert a command at the bottom of the Edit menu with these properties:

   Caption: Insert Object

   Name: mnuEditInsertObject

3. Click *Edit | Insert Object* to open the code window for mnuEditInsertObject_Click.

4. Add the following code to the procedure:

```
'Allows user to insert an OLE object.
mnuFileNew_Click        'Adds a new document window
Screen.ActiveForm.rtbPage.Visible = False
With Screen.ActiveForm.OLE1
    .Visible = True     'Makes the OLE control visible
    .InsertObjDlg       'Displays the Insert Object dialog
End With
```

5. Save the project.

6. Run ScratchPad.

7. Choose *Edit | Insert Object.* The Insert Object dialog appears.

8. Select the *Create from File* OptionButton. The rest of the dialog changes to reflect this option.

   Notice that linking options appear in the dialog.

9. Click the *Browse* button. A common Open dialog appears.

10. Locate and open any .bmp file (your choice). (There are lots of them in Microsoft Visual Basic\Bitmaps\Assorted.) The Insert Object dialog returns with the selected file's pathname displayed in the File TextBox.

    Notice also that the file's type, Bitmap Image, is displayed above the TextBox.

11. Click *OK* to close the dialog and embed the object in the document.

12. Right-click the object to pop up its menu of verbs. The menu should contain Edit and Open.

13. Choose *Open* to open Windows Paint, where you could edit the object if you wished.

14. Exit Paint and ScratchPad.

The inserted graphic probably looked pretty awful, because we stretched it to fit the OLE container control. We'll fix the sizing in a minute, but first let's talk about how we referenced the Rich TextBox control and the OLE control in our code.

As you may recall, when you're working with MDIChild forms, you don't know how many forms are on the screen or which one is active. But you can access the currently active form via Screen.ActiveForm followed by the name of the object and the property or method. So to access the Visible property of the rtbPage on the active form, you code

```
Screen.ActiveForm.rtbPage.Visible
```

Similarly, to access the Visible property of OLE1 on the active form, you code

```
Screen.ActiveForm.OLE1.Visible
```

And to invoke the InsertObjDlg method, which displays the Insert Object dialog, you code

```
Screen.ActiveForm.OLE1.InsertObjDlg
```

Rather than typing out the two statements:

```
Screen.ActiveForm.OLE1.Visible = True
Screen.ActiveForm.OLE1.InsertObjDlg
```

we saved some time with this shorthand:

```
With Screen.ActiveForm.OLE1
    .Visible = True
    .InsertObjDlg
End With
```

Now let's work on sizing the OLE object. We want to let users size the OLE object as they would any document window, but this turns out to be a little more complicated than you might expect. The complication arises because OLE container controls are not sizable; the only two BorderStyle settings are

0 - None and *1 - Fixed Single*. So to let users size the object, we have to make the control the same size as the document window, which is sizable. Here are the changes we'll make:

1. When we first insert the document window, change its size from maximized to the cascaded size that occurs when you choose the Window | Cascade command. This keeps the object from being ridiculously large when it first appears.

2. Stretch the OLE control to fit the document window. The easiest way to do this is the Move method, which takes four parameters:

   Top: We'll set this to 0 to position the control at the top of the form.

   Left: We'll set this to 0 to position the control at the left edge of the form.

   Width: We'll set this to the same width as the active form, as indicated by Screen.ActiveForm.Width, minus 30 twips to allow for the form's 3D border.

   Height: We'll set this to the same height as the active form, as indicated by Screen.ActiveForm.Height, minus 20 twips to allow for the form's 3D border.

3. If the user changes the size of the document window, as indicated by the Form_Resize event, we'll use the same Move method to match the control to the form's size.

The overall effect of these techniques is to allow users to control the size of the object by adjusting the size of the document window. Let's insert the code for these steps now.

1. Open the code window for *mnuEditInsertObject_Click*.

2. Add the code shown in bold below to the procedure:

```
'Allows user to insert an OLE object.
mnuFileNew_Click            'Adds a new document window
mnuWindowCascade_Click      'Unmaximizes the document windows
Screen.ActiveForm.rtbPage.Visible = False
With Screen.ActiveForm.OLE1
    .Visible = True    'Makes the OLE control visible
    .Move 0, 0, Screen.ActiveForm.Width - 30,
        Screen.ActiveForm.Height - 20
    .InsertObjDlg    'Displays the Insert Object dialog
End With
```

3. Open the code window for *frmDocument Form_Resize*.

4. Insert the following statements:

```
If Screen.ActiveForm.OLE1.Visible = True Then
    .Move 0, 0, Screen.ActiveForm.Width - 30,
        Screen.ActiveForm.Height - 20
End If
```

5. Save your work.

6. Run ScratchPad.

7. Choose *Edit|Insert Object* and insert the .bmp file of your choice, as you did before.

   Notice the difference in the initial size of the object.

8. Resize the document window and observe how the size of the embedded object changes.

9. Leave ScratchPad running while you read the next section.

LINKING

Because we set our OLE container control's OLETypeAllowed property to *2 - Either*, we can either embed or link an object in the control. So far, we've tried out embedding. Now, let's try linking an object.

1. Run File Manager to make a copy of any bitmap file. Use the name *Practice.bmp* for the name of the new file.

2. Choose *Edit|Insert Object* to open the Insert Object dialog.

3. Select the *Create From File* OptionButton.

4. Click the *Link* CheckBox to enable this option.

5. Open *Practice.bmp* and click *OK* to link it to your ScratchPad document.

6. Right-click the linked object to pop up its verb menu. Notice that the menu hasn't changed. It still offers the Edit and Open verbs.

7. Choose *Edit*. A copy of Paint opens.

   Tip: You could also open Paint by clicking the object and pressing Enter.

8. Pull down Paint's *File* menu and notice that this is the complete Paint, not an embedded copy.

9. Make any change to the graphic.

10. Save the graphic and exit Paint. Notice that the changes appear in the linked version.

SUMMARY

Now you know how to add OLE capabilities to a file by adding the OLE control to a form and setting its properties. You've seen that you can link or embed an object at design time or run time. And you've seen some of the sizing complications that arise and how to handle them.

We're getting near the end of our story. It's time to learn how to prepare your completed application for distribution to others — the subject of the next chapter.

CHAPTER OBJECTIVES

Your programs have been tested and debugged. They work on your system, but will they work on someone else's? When you distribute your programs — whether you make floppies to hand to friends, place a program on a network server, upload it to a BBS, or package it in a fancy package and sell it in software stores — what do you need to do to make sure the distributed version works? You'll learn how to do that in this chapter.

In this chapter we will:

▶ Explore the SetupWizard

▶ Learn how to distribute Data Access Engines

▶ Include OLE servers

▶ Create distribution media

▶ Make Setup templates

Distributing Your Applications

20

Visual Basic's SetupWizard is designed to make it as easy as possible to prepare your software for distribution. SetupWizard creates a Setup program for your software, identifying and including all the files necessary to make the software run on someone else's system. We'll show you how to use SetupWizard to prepare your program for distribution.

Instead of the usual step-by-step exercises, the sections in this chapter show the succession of steps a programmer takes to distribute a program.

USING SETUPWIZARD

SetupWizard completely prepares your application for distribution via floppy disk, network server, or CD-ROM. If you're going to use floppy disks to distribute the program, it even creates the first set of floppies.

Here's what SetupWizard does:

▶ Creates a setup program for your application, called Setup1.exe

▶ Builds the executable version (.exe file) of your program

▶ Identifies and includes in the distribution version all the support files needed by the program — custom control files, .dlls, OLE servers, and so on

▶ Compresses all the files to be distributed

▶ Creates the first set of distribution floppies, or

▶ Places the distribution files on your hard disk so that you can copy them to a network server, a BBS, or a CD-ROM generation system

Here's what the setup file Setup1.exe (created by SetUpWizard) does:

▶ Registers the program in the user's System Registry

▶ Creates the necessary Windows program group (16-bit version) or Start menu items (32-bit version) so that users can start up your program

▶ Sets up the installed application for later removal via Windows 95's Add/Remove Programs feature (32-bit version of Setup1.exe only)

NOTE

There are some things that SetupWizard can't do. It can't create a setup program that lets users choose among features to be installed, for example. For the Enterprise Edition, it can't install Remote OLE Automation servers (32-bit version) or client OLE Automation servers (16-bit version). If you need capabilities beyond what SetupWizard provides, you must create your own setup files using the Setup Toolkit. See the Visual Basic online books for information on using it.

Starting SetupWizard

Before you start SetupWizard, make sure that all the files belonging to the application that you want to set up have been saved in their latest versions and are closed: the project file, and all form and other modules. You can't set up an application if any of its files are currently open.

When you installed Visual Basic, the Setup program created an Application Setup Wizard icon for you. If you're using Windows 3.1 or later, it's in your Visual Basic 4.0 group. If you're using Windows 95, it's on your Visual Basic 4.0 menu in your Start menu system. The most likely path is Start | Programs | Visual Basic 4.0 | Application Setup Wizard, as shown in Figure 20-1.

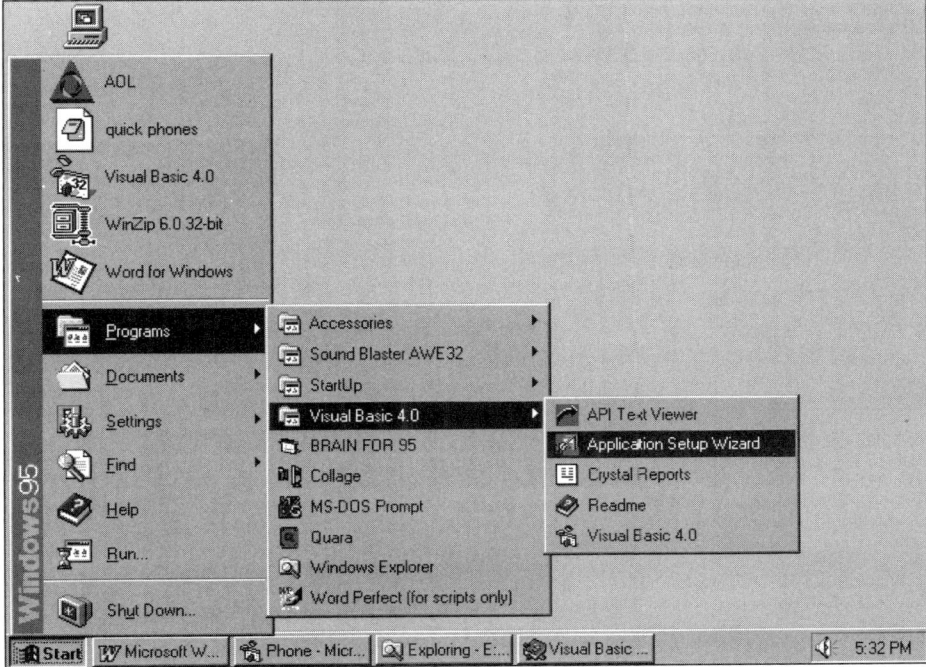

Figure 20-1: In Windows 95, you'll find the Application Setup Wizard on your Visual Basic 4.0 menu.

If someone has modified your Start menu since Setup installed Visual Basic 4.0, your Setup Wizard might be in a different location, or it might not be there at all. But you can always start it from the actual .exe file on your hard drive, as shown in Figure 20-2. Look for the file called Setupwiz.exe in Microsoft Visual Basic\Setupkit\Kitfil32. Double-click the file name to start up SetupWizard.

The first time you start up SetupWizard after installing Visual Basic, it must establish the location of several important files that it needs in order to set up applications. It may be able to find them on its own, in which case it takes just a few moments to complete the task. If not, it will ask you to locate any files that it can't find, as you can see in Figure 20-3. SetupWizard stores file location information in a file named Swdepend.ini in your Windows folder so that it needs to go through this process only once.

Figure 20-2: If the Application SetupWizard isn't on your Start menu, you can always start up the SetupWizard by double-clicking the Setupwiz.exe file on your hard drive.

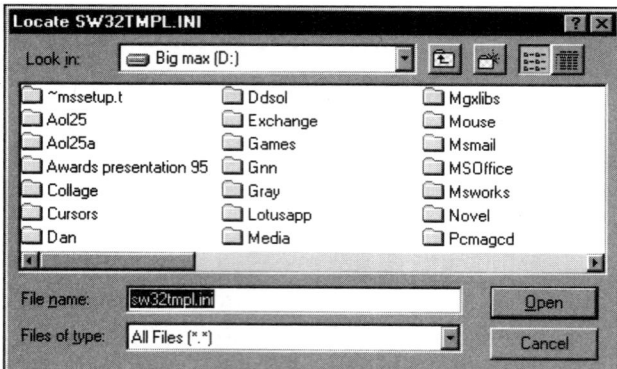

Figure 20-3: During SetupWizard initialization, you will be asked to locate any necessary files the wizard can't find on its own.

When you start up SetupWizard with the Swdepend.ini file present, you'll see a brief initialization screen while SetupWizard loads the file.

Identifying the Project File (Step 1)

In Step 1 of the SetupWizard, as shown in Figure 20-4, you're asked to identify the project that you want to create a Setup program for. If you know the exact path and name of the project, you can type it in the TextBox. Otherwise, click the button next to the TextBox so that you can browse for the desired .vbp file.

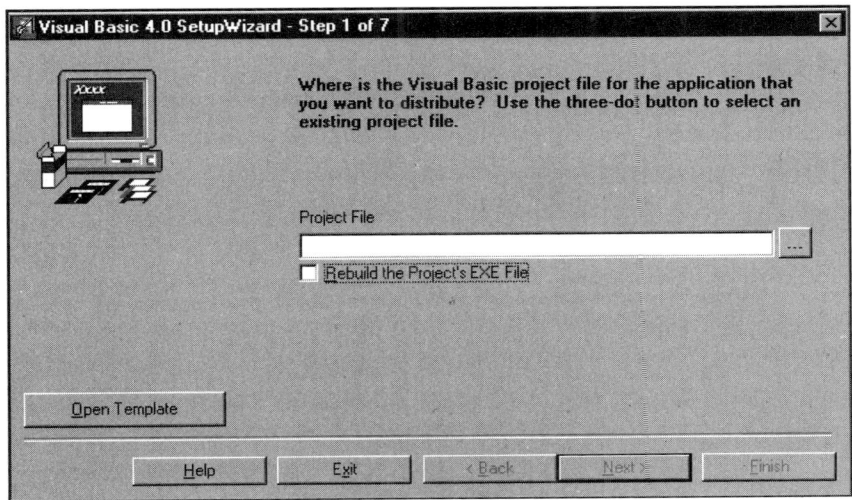

Figure 20-4: In Step 1 of the SetupWizard, you identify the project to be set up.

The Next button doesn't become available until you have identified an existing .vbp file. If you type an invalid path or name and press Enter, the wizard simply beeps and waits for a correct file identifier.

TIP

Each step of SetupWizard includes a Help button that accesses the help topic directly related to the current step. You can also exit the wizard from any page by clicking the Exit button.

When you click the Next button, SetupWizard compiles the program to create an .exe file. However, if the .exe file already exists — because you have compiled the program separately using Visual Basic's File | Create EXE File command, or because you have set this program up before — the wizard simply uses the .exe file without recompiling it. But suppose you have changed the program since the last time you compiled it. To force the wizard to recompile it, check the box captioned Rebuild the Project's EXE File.

SetupWizard does not include its own copy of the Visual Basic compiler. If it must compile the program, you'll see it start up Visual Basic and run the compiler from there. All this happens automatically, so just sit back and watch.

NOTE

If SetupWizard discovers references to OLE servers that do not contain the needed dependency information, it displays a dialog box to warn you that you will need to add the servers manually in Step 4. Be sure to write down the names of any files that it warns you about, so that you can insert them in Step 4.

If the compiler encounters a syntax error and displays an error message, don't try to fix the error and continue running the wizard. You should go back to Visual Basic, fix the problem, and completely retest the program before trying to make a distribution copy. But first, you need to get out of SetupWizard. The steps below are not an exercise; we're including them to help you extract yourself from SetupWizard if you encounter a compiler error.

1. Click OK to clear the error message.

2. Exit Visual Basic.

3. If the wizard doesn't return to your screen automatically, click its button in your taskbar. The wizard displays a message that the .exe file could not be found, which certainly is true since it never got created.

4. Click OK to clear the message.

5. The wizard's Step 1 returns to your screen (refer back to Figure 20-4).

6. Click Exit to exit SetupWizard. (You'll have to confirm your choice.)

Now you can debug your program, then begin the setup process again.

Distributing Data Access Engines (Step 2)

If your application includes database access, you might want to distribute some of Visual Basic's ODBC data access engines along with your product. (Data access is discussed in Chapter 15.)

TIP
Starting with Step 2, you can click the Back button to return to the previous step(s) and change your selections. You can back all the way up to Step 1 and choose a different project, if you wish.

If the application doesn't include database access, SetupWizard may skip this step and go directly to Step 3. If not, you can click Next immediately to go on to the next step.

Identifying the Target Drive/Path (Step 3)

You identify where you want to place the setup files in Step 3 (see Figure 20-5). If you want to create setup floppies, select Disk Drive and choose which floppy drive you want to use. Only your floppy drives are listed in this drop-down list.

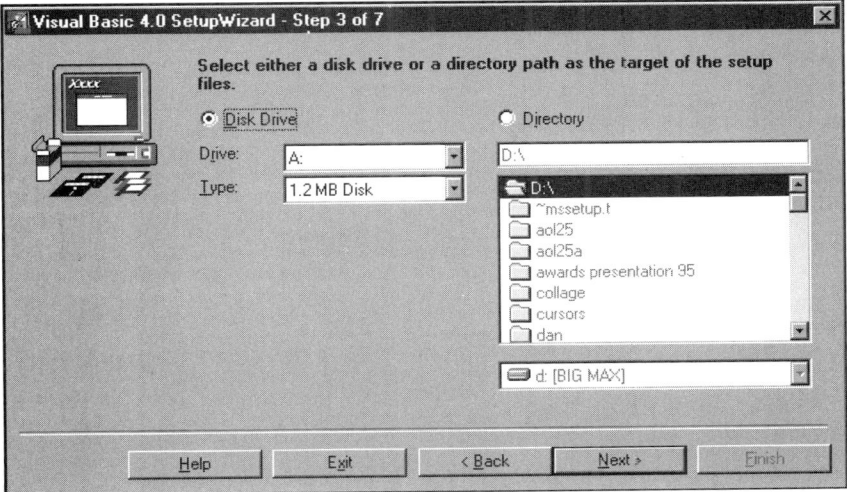

Figure 20-5: In Step 3, you indicate where you want to place the distribution files.

If you plan to distribute the program by some means other than floppy, such as network or CD-ROM, click the Directory option and select the drive and directory where you want the distribution files to be placed.

Including OLE Servers (Step 4)

If your project references an OLE server, you of course need to include that server along with the project. In between Step 3 and Step 4, SetupWizard searches your project to find any references to OLE servers.

OLE is discussed in Chapter 19.

If none are found, you'll see the step shown in Figure 20-6. If you don't need to add any files manually, you can click Next to continue. If you do need to add files manually, click Add OLE Servers to open a browse box where you can select a server to be added to the project.

If your project does include references to OLE servers, you'll see a list of the servers that should be included in the distribution media. If you want to include all these files in the distribution media, just click Next to continue. (Also see the sidebar entitled, "Enterprise Edition Remote Server Details," later in this chapter.)

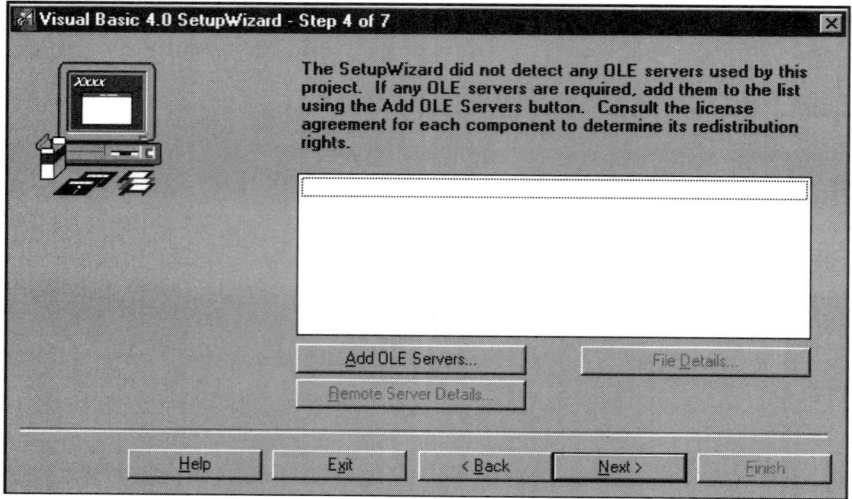

Figure 20-6: If your project doesn't include any references to OLE servers, you'll see this dialog box for Step 4.

If you know that the user already has some of the indicated files — for example, if you're distributing via a local area network — then you can uncheck the files that shouldn't be included in this new setup program. You must also uncheck any files that you don't have the rights to distribute. Then click Next to continue.

 If your program depends on OLE servers that you can't distribute, be sure to include that information in your release notes so that users can make sure they have (or can get) the necessary files before deciding to install your program.

Additional Dependent Files (Step 5)

In Step 5, SetupWizard lists any additional file dependencies it has discovered (see Figure 20-7). Here again, you should uncheck any files that you do not have the right to distribute or that end users already have. Then click Next to continue.

 Notice in Figure 20-7 that the last file's path is so long that you can't read the name of the file. You can see the full name, along with other information about the file, by selecting the file in the list box and clicking the File Details button.

Enterprise Edition Remote Server Details

If you select a remote OLE Automation server registration file (.vbr), the Remote Server Details dialog box will appear, prompting you for the proper information.

This dialog is reached by choosing the Remote OLE Server Details button at Step 5 of the SetupWizard. Enter the network address, network protocol, and any required authentication information for the registry to be correctly modified in order for the OLE Automation component to work correctly.

The Network Address refers to the server name upon which the OLE Automation Server resides. The Network Protocol refers to the type of network through

which the OLE Client and OLE Server will be communicating; SetupWizard generates this list from those listed in the swdepend.ini file. If at the time of the disk build the Network Protocol field is left at its default setting, *[End user must specify]*, then the installing end user will have to choose the network protocol at run time. The Authentication field allows six valid options, listed in the drop-down box. For further details, refer to the Remote Automation documentation (in the Enterprise Edition only).

Once you are done filling in the server information. choose the OK button to continue.

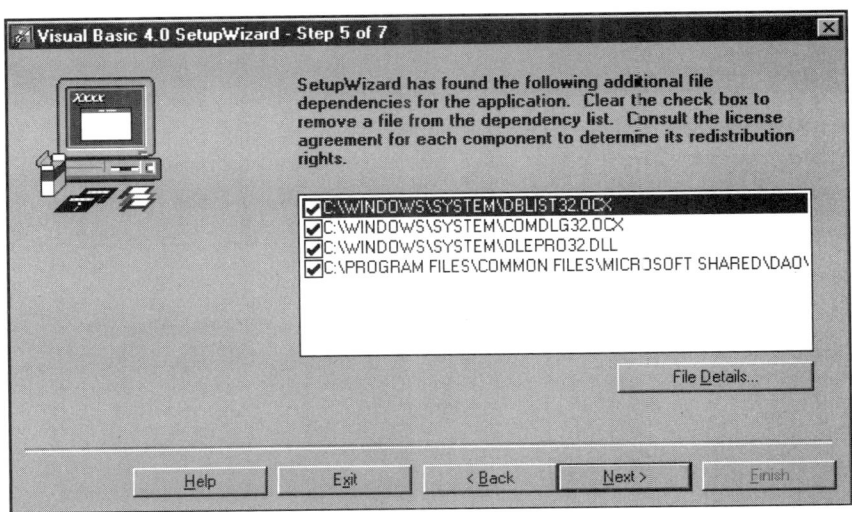

Figure 20-7: In Step 5, SetupWizard lists any other file dependencies so that you can uncheck any files that you don't want to distribute.

Selecting the Deployment Model (Step 6)

You're getting very close to the end of the process. All the difficult decisions have been made! When you get to Step 6, SetupWizard asks you to select one of two possible deployment models (see Figure 20-8).

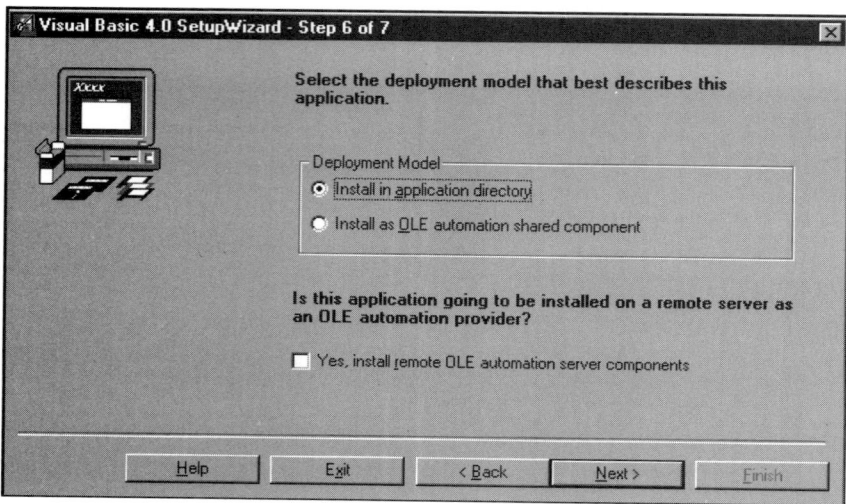

Figure 20-8: In Step 6, you choose a deployment model for your program.

If you have designed your program as a stand-alone application, you choose Install in Application Directory. But if your application is intended to be a shared OLE component, choose Install as OLE Automation Component. When you make the second choice, your software will be installed in the Olesvr folder on the user's hard disk.

The OLE Automation Server CheckBox appears only with the 32-bit Enterprise Edition of SetupWizard. If you check this box, the Automation Manager support files are added to the list of files to be distributed. The final list is displayed in Step 7.

Finalizing the File List (Step 7)

When you click Next after Step 6, quite a bit of processing takes place as SetupWizard locates all the files needed for the distribution version. You might be asked to locate one or more files that the wizard can't find.

TIP

Don't forget that you can use Windows 95's Find feature or Windows 3.x's File Manager to locate a missing file. You don't really have to search through all your folders manually.

Eventually, SetupWizard displays a list of all the files that will be distributed with your program. Figure 20-9 shows a typical Step 7. This is your last chance to add and remove files from the distribution list.

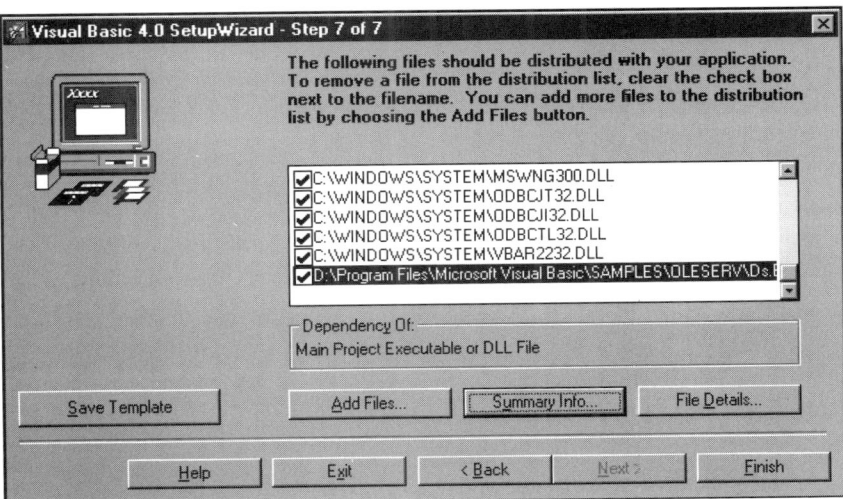

Figure 20-9: Step 7 gives you one more chance to add and remove files from the distribution list.

To find out how each file is used in the program, select the file and look at the Dependency Of box. If Dependency Of becomes a drop-down list, the file is used in more than one way in the project.

The Summary Info button opens a dialog box where you can see how much space your distribution files will take. Figure 20-10 shows a typical example.

Creating the Distribution Media

Notice in Figure 20-9 that the Next button is dimmed, but a Finish button has appeared. When you click Finish, the distribution files will be created.

You'll see a list develop as SetupWizard compresses all the selected files. Then it copies the files to the distribution directory. If you are creating distribution floppies, SetupWizard instructs you when to insert blank floppies in the drive.

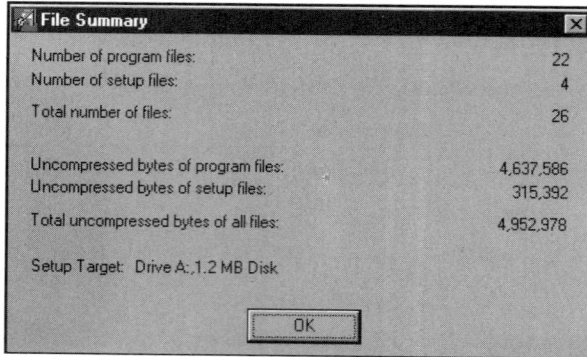

Figure 20-10: Summary Info shows you how much space your distribution files will take, compressed for distribution as well as uncompressed on the user's hard drive.

When you see the dialog box shown in Figure 20-11, your program is ready to for testing. But before we talk about testing, let's talk about that Save Template button, which appears on both Step 7 and in this final dialog box.

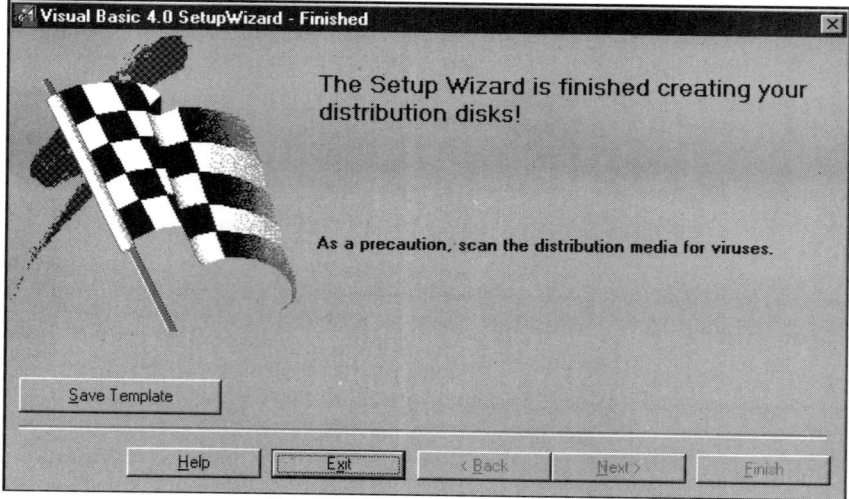

Figure 20-11: This final SetupWizard dialog box tells you that your distribution media have been successfully created.

Setup Templates

You can save all your choices from this SetupWizard session by clicking the Save Template button. A Save As dialog box lets you select a folder and give the template file a name; the extension is automatically .vbz.

The next time you want to create a setup file for the same project, or for a similar project, you can click the Open Template button in Step 1. (You can see the button in Figure 20-4.) An Open dialog lets you select the .vbz file that you want to open. Then all your choices are filled in for you as you proceed through the steps of the wizard, and all you have to do is make changes as appropriate.

TESTING THE SETUP

After the new setup file is created, it's not really ready for distribution. You should test it first to make sure it works. Don't just test it on your own system — you know the program works there. Test it on several systems that represent various end-user configurations. Try installing and running the program.

As you can see in Figure 20-11, Microsoft also suggests that you test your new distribution floppies for viruses. Since you'll use them as masters to create distribution disks, you don't want to be responsible for spreading a virus that you didn't know was in your system. So be sure to take the time to do this before making copies and distributing your new program.

SUMMARY

In this chapter you learned to use the SetupWizard to prepare your Visual Basic program for distribution. And now we've come to the end of the road! You now know all that you need to begin creating your own Visual Basic applications. Congratulations and good luck!

IDG BOOKS WORLDWIDE LICENSE AGREEMENT

Important — read carefully before opening the software packet. This is a legal agreement between you (either an individual or an entity) and IDG Books Worldwide, Inc. (IDG). By opening the accompanying sealed packet containing the software disc, you acknowledge that you have read and accept the following IDG License Agreement. If you do not agree and do not want to be bound by the terms of this Agreement, promptly return the book and the unopened software packet(s) to the place you obtained them for a full refund.

1. License. This License Agreement (Agreement) permits you to use one copy of the enclosed Software program(s) on a single computer. The Software is in "use" on a computer when it is loaded into temporary memory (i.e., RAM) or installed into permanent memory (e.g., hard disk, CD-ROM, or other storage device) of that computer.

2. Copyright. The entire contents of this CD-ROM and the compilation of the Software are copyrighted and protected by both United States copyright laws and international treaty provisions. You may only (a) make one copy of the Software for backup or archival purposes, or (b) transfer the Software to a single hard disk, provided that you keep the original for backup or archival purposes. The individual programs on the disc are copyrighted by the authors of each program respectively. Each program has its own use permissions and limitations. To use each program, you must follow the individual requirements and restrictions detailed for each in the "Contents of the CD-ROM" appendix of this book. Do not use a program if you do not want to follow its Licensing Agreement. None of the material on this disc or listed in this Book may ever be distributed, in original or modified form, for commercial purposes.

3. Other Restrictions. You may not rent or lease the Software. You may transfer the Software and user documentation on a permanent basis provided you retain no copies and the recipient agrees to the terms of this Agreement. You may not reverse engineer, decompile, or disassemble the Software except to the extent that the foregoing restriction is expressly prohibited by applicable law. If the Software is an update or has been updated, any transfer must include the most recent update and all prior versions. Each shareware program has its own use permissions and limitations. These limitations are contained in the individual license agreements that are on the software discs. The restrictions include a requirement that after using the program for a period of time specified in its

457

text, the user must pay a registration fee or discontinue use. By opening the package which contains the software disc, you will be agreeing to abide by the licenses and restrictions for these programs. Do not open the software package unless you agree to be bound by the license agreements.

4. Limited Warranty. IDG Warrants that the Software and disc are free from defects in materials and workmanship for a period of sixty (60) days from the date of purchase of this Book. If IDG receives notification within the warranty period of defects in material or workmanship, IDG will replace the defective disc. IDG's entire liability and your exclusive remedy shall be limited to replacement of the Software, which is returned to IDG with a copy of your receipt. This Limited Warranty is void if failure of the Software has resulted from accident, abuse, or misapplication. Any replacement Software will be warranted for the remainder of the original warranty period or thirty (30) days, whichever is longer.

5. No Other Warranties. To the maximum extent permitted by applicable law, IDG and the author disclaim all other warranties, express or implied, including but not limited to implied warranties of merchantability and fitness for a particular purpose, with respect to the Software, the programs, the source code contained therein and/or the techniques described in this Book. This limited warranty gives you specific legal rights. You may have others which vary from state/jurisdiction to state/jurisdiction.

6. No Liability For Consequential Damages. To the extent permitted by applicable law, in no event shall IDG or the author be liable for any damages whatsoever (including without limitation, damages for loss of business profits, business interruption, loss of business information, or any other pecuniary loss) arising out of the use of or inability to use the Book or the Software, even if IDG has been advised of the possibility of such damages. Because some states/jurisdictions do not allow the exclusion or limitation of liability for consequential or incidental damages, the above limitation may not apply to you.

7. U.S.Government Restricted Rights. Use, duplication, or disclosure of the Software by the U.S. Government is subject to restrictions stated in paragraph (c) (1) (ii) of the Rights in Technical Data and Computer Software clause of DFARS 252.227-7013, and in subparagraphs (a) through (d) of the Commercial Computer —Restricted Rights clause at FAR 52.227-19, and in similar clauses in the NASA FAR supplement, when applicable.

Index

(continued)

E

F

M

▼▼▼▼▼▼▼▼▼▼▼▼▼

(continued)

Q

▼▼▼▼▼▼▼▼▼▼▼▼▼

R

▼▼▼▼▼▼▼▼▼▼▼▼▼

T

U

V

W

X

Z

IDG BOOKS WORLDWIDE REGISTRATION CARD

RETURN THIS REGISTRATION CARD FOR FREE CATALOG

Title of this book: **Learn Visual Basic® 4 Today!**

My overall rating of this book: ❑ Very good [1] ❑ Good [2] ❑ Satisfactory [3] ❑ Fair [4] ❑ Poor [5]

How I first heard about this book:

❑ Found in bookstore; name: [6]

❑ Advertisement: [8]

❑ Word of mouth; heard about book from friend, co-worker, etc.: [10]

❑ Book review: [7]

❑ Catalog: [9]

❑ Other: [11]

What I liked most about this book:

What I would change, add, delete, etc., in future editions of this book:

Other comments:

Number of computer books I purchase in a year: ❑ 1 [12] ❑ 2-5 [13] ❑ 6-10 [14] ❑ More than 10 [15]

I would characterize my computer skills as: ❑ Beginner [16] ❑ Intermediate [17] ❑ Advanced [18] ❑ Professional [19]

I use ❑ DOS [20] ❑ Windows [21] ❑ OS/2 [22] ❑ Unix [23] ❑ Macintosh [24] ❑ Other: [25]_____
(please specify)

I would be interested in new books on the following subjects:
(please check all that apply, and use the spaces provided to identify specific software)

❑ Word processing: [26]

❑ Data bases: [28]

❑ File Utilities: [30]

❑ Networking: [32]

❑ Other: [34]

❑ Spreadsheets: [27]

❑ Desktop publishing: [29]

❑ Money management: [31]

❑ Programming languages: [33]

I use a PC at (please check all that apply): ❑ home [35] ❑ work [36] ❑ school [37] ❑ other: [38] _____

The disks I prefer to use are ❑ 5.25 [39] ❑ 3.5 [40] ❑ other: [41]_____

I have a CD ROM: ❑ yes [42] ❑ no [43]

I plan to buy or upgrade computer hardware this year: ❑ yes [44] ❑ no [45]

I plan to buy or upgrade computer software this year: ❑ yes [46] ❑ no [47]

Name: _____ Business title: [48] _____ Type of Business: [49] _____

Address (❑ home [50] ❑ work [51]/Company name: _____)

Street/Suite# _____

City [52]/State [53]/Zipcode [54]: _____ Country [55] _____

❑ **I liked this book!** You may quote me by name in future
IDG Books Worldwide promotional materials.

My daytime phone number is _____

IDG BOOKS

THE WORLD OF
COMPUTER
KNOWLEDGE

❏ **YES!**
Please keep me informed about IDG's World of Computer Knowledge.
Send me the latest IDG Books catalog.

BUSINESS REPLY MAIL
FIRST CLASS MAIL   PERMIT NO. 2605   FOSTER CITY, CALIFORNIA

IDG Books Worldwide
919 E Hillsdale Blvd, STE 400
Foster City, CA 94404-9691

IDG BOOKS WORLDWIDE REGISTRATION CARD

RETURN THIS REGISTRATION CARD FOR FREE CATALOG

Title of this book: **Learn Visual Basic® 4 Today!**

My overall rating of this book: ❏ Very good [1] ❏ Good [2] ❏ Satisfactory [3] ❏ Fair [4] ❏ Poor [5]

How I first heard about this book:

❏ Found in bookstore; name: [6]   ❏ Book review: [7]

❏ Advertisement: [8]   ❏ Catalog: [9]

❏ Word of mouth; heard about book from friend, co-worker, etc.: [10]   ❏ Other: [11]

What I liked most about this book:

What I would change, add, delete, etc., in future editions of this book:

Other comments:

Number of computer books I purchase in a year: ❏ 1 [12]   ❏ 2-5 [13]   ❏ 6-10 [14]   ❏ More than 10 [15]

I would characterize my computer skills as: ❏ Beginner [16] ❏ Intermediate [17] ❏ Advanced [18] ❏ Professional [19]

I use ❏ DOS [20] ❏ Windows [21] ❏ OS/2 [22] ❏ Unix [23] ❏ Macintosh [24] ❏ Other: [25]_____
(please specify)

I would be interested in new books on the following subjects:
(please check all that apply, and use the spaces provided to identify specific software)

❏ Word processing: [26]   ❏ Spreadsheets: [27]

❏ Data bases: [28]   ❏ Desktop publishing: [29]

❏ File Utilities: [30]   ❏ Money management: [31]

❏ Networking: [32]   ❏ Programming languages: [33]

❏ Other: [34]

I use a PC at (please check all that apply): ❏ home [35] ❏ work [36] ❏ school [37] ❏ other: [38] _____

The disks I prefer to use are ❏ 5.25 [39] ❏ 3.5 [40] ❏ other: [41]_____

I have a CD ROM: ❏ yes [42]   ❏ no [43]

I plan to buy or upgrade computer hardware this year: ❏ yes [44]   ❏ no [45]

I plan to buy or upgrade computer software this year: ❏ yes [46]   ❏ no [47]

Name: Business title: [48]   Type of Business: [49]

Address (❏ home [50] ❏ work [51]/Company name:)

Street/Suite#

City [52]/State [53]/Zipcode [54]:   Country [55]

❏ **I liked this book!** You may quote me by name in future
IDG Books Worldwide promotional materials.

My daytime phone number is _____

IDG BOOKS

THE WORLD OF COMPUTER KNOWLEDGE

 # YES!

Please keep me informed about IDG's World of Computer Knowledge.
Send me the latest IDG Books catalog.

BUSINESS REPLY MAIL

FIRST CLASS MAIL   PERMIT NO. 2605   FOSTER CITY, CALIFORNIA

IDG Books Worldwide
919 E Hillsdale Blvd, STE 400
Foster City, CA 94404-9691